Colonel Josiah Wedgwood's Questionnaire: Members of Parliament, 1885–1918

Colonel Josiah Clement Wedgwood, 1st Baron Wedgwood, DSO, PC, DL (1872–1943).
Reproduced with the kind permission of Newcastle-under-Lyme Borough Museum and
Art Gallery.

Colonel Josiah Wedgwood's Questionnaire: Members of Parliament, 1885–1918

By

Priscilla Baines

Wiley-Blackwell

for

The Parliamentary History Yearbook Trust

and

The History of Parliament Trust

© 2012 The Parliamentary History Yearbook Trust and The History of Parliament Trust

Wiley-Blackwell is now part of John Wiley & Sons

Registered Office
John Wiley & Sons Ltd, The Atrium, Southern Gate, Chichester, West Sussex, PO19 8SQ, United Kingdom

Editorial Offices
350 Main Street, Malden, MA 02148–5020, USA
9600 Garsington Road, Oxford, OX4 2DQ, UK
The Atrium, Southern Gate, Chichester, West Sussex, PO19 8SQ, UK

For details of our global editorial offices, for customer services, and for information about how to apply for permission to reuse the copyright material in this book please see our website at www.wiley.com/wiley-blackwell.

The right of Priscilla Baines to be identified as the author of the editorial material in this work has been asserted in accordance with the Copyright, Designs and Patents Act 1988.

Wiley also publishes its books in a variety of electronic formats. Some content that appears in print may not be available in electronic books.

Library of Congress Cataloging-in-Publication Data
Library of Congress Cataloging-in-Publication data is available for this book

A catalogue record for this title is available from the British Library
Set in 10/12pt Bembo
by Toppan Best-set Premedia Limited
Printed and bound in Singapore
by Hó Printing Pte Ltd

1   2012

CONTENTS

Parliamentary History: Texts & Studies

ACKNOWLEDGMENTS

I am very grateful to the History of Parliament Trustees under Lord Cormack's chairmanship for allowing me to work for well over six years on the Wedgwood questionnaire and its associated material in the History's archives. Dr Paul Seaward, Director of the History of Parliament, first suggested early in 2005 that I should sort out the material. The trustees then agreed that I should write it up for publication. He and they have shown infinite patience during the ensuing years when family commitments and other activities got in the way of my progress.

The final result has benefited immeasurably from Dr Seaward's unstinting encouragement, support and advice as well as his editorial skills. I owe particular thanks to Dr Kathryn Rix, of the History of Parliament staff, who commented in detail on a late draft and much improved the contents, as did Professor Miles Taylor, Director of the Institute of Historical Research, on behalf of the Editorial Board of the History of Parliament. Professor Gavin Drewry and John Wakefield also read and commented constructively on a late draft. Dr Ross Young, a former colleague in the House of Commons Library and now of the United Kingdom Statistics Authority, gave valuable help in making sense of some unwieldy data and analysing the answers to the questionnaires. I have relied heavily on Professor Michael Rush's database of members of parliament from 1832 to 2001 and on his other work on the personal and professional backgrounds of members of parliament; Dr Stephen Lees supplemented the information in the database. I am very grateful to them both, and to the many other colleagues and former colleagues from the house of commons and the Study of Parliament Group, too numerous to name, who have provided insights and inspiration at different times. Responsibility for the errors is of course mine.

NOTE ON SOURCES

This study is based almost entirely on the replies to the questionnaire sent in July 1936 by Colonel Josiah Wedgwood, the founder of the History of Parliament project, to surviving members and former members of parliament who had served up to 1918. The original questionnaires and replies, plus the associated correspondence, are preserved in the History of Parliament's archives in an alphabetical sequence. Their contents have also been transcribed and will in due course be made available online via the History of Parliament website.

The members of parliament who completed the questionnaire are generally referred to throughout by the name they used when first elected; their parties and sometimes their constituencies have been identified where relevant. The replies and correspondence have mostly been allowed to speak for themselves, with only minimal editorial intervention. The majority of the quotations are from the questionnaires and are identified simply by the name of the member concerned; references to the correspondence with Colonel Wedgwood include a date.

The first appendix contains a table listing the members of parliament, or former members or their families, who completed questionnaires or provided biographical information in response to the questionnaire. The second appendix contains a transcription of the original version of the questionnaire, annotated to show the changes that were made in the second version. The third appendix contains a copy of a printed version of Wedgwood's own questionnaire which he circulated with a chasing letter in late 1936. The fourth contains a reproduction of a completed questionnaire by one member, Sir Henry Bowles, plus the associated correspondence and Wedgwood's biography. The last appendix contains the biographies that Wedgwood compiled from the questionnaires, as well as the small number in the sequence prepared by History of Parliament staff.

Chapter 1. Colonel Wedgwood and the History of Parliament

1. Introduction

The survey of members of parliament on which this book is based was almost entirely the work of Colonel Josiah Wedgwood DSO (1872–1943), member of parliament for Newcastle-under-Lyme from 1906 until 1942, when he was raised to the peerage as Lord Wedgwood of Barlaston. It was initiated in the mid 1930s as part of the *History of Parliament* project which owes its existence largely to Wedgwood's efforts during the late 1920s and 1930s. The *History of Parliament* was intended to be a comprehensive biographical dictionary originally covering the house of commons and its members in the period from 1264 to 1832 but later extended to 1918 and to include the house of lords.[1] It has been described as one of those 'iconic' British undertakings that, along with such ventures as the *Dictionary of National Biography*, the *Survey of London*, the *Victoria County Histories* and the *Buildings of England* series, comprise the 'great engines of national historical endeavour and collective historical memory'.[2] It has also been described as Wedgwood's most enduring personal achievement and 'greatest legacy', 'the one public act that would not have happened without him'.[3]

The questionnaire was designed to elicit contributions to two planned volumes on the house of commons in the late 19th and early 20th centuries. For about 18 months in 1936–7, Wedgwood devoted a great deal of time and effort to it. It then appears to have become a casualty of a combination of the vicissitudes of the main *History of Parliament* project, external events in the late 1930s and, perhaps most of all, its dependence on Wedgwood's own input as editor and in compiling biographies which largely ceased in mid 1937. The whole *History of Parliament* project went into cold storage in the early 1940s. When it was revived in 1951, it was decided to revert to the original cut-off date of 1832 and almost all the raw material related to the questionnaires remained unpublished in the *History*'s archives.

---

[1] There are several accounts of the genesis of the *History of Parliament* and its progress before the Second World War. The main ones are: David Cannadine, *In Churchill's Shadow* (2003), ch. 6: 'Piety: Josiah Wedgwood and the History of Parliament'; David Cannadine, 'The History of Parliament: Past, Present – and Future', *Parliamentary History*, xxvi (2007), 366–6; D.W. Hayton, 'Colonel Wedgwood and the Historians', *Historical Research*, lxxxiv (2011), 348–55; Edith Mary Johnston, 'Managing an Inheritance: Colonel J.C. Wedgwood, the History of Parliament and the Lost History of the Irish Parliament', *Proceedings of the Royal Irish Academy*, lxxxix (1989), 167–86; Paul Mulvey, *The Political Life of Josiah C. Wedgwood* (2010), esp. ch. 13; Alan Sandall, 'The History of Parliament', *The Table* (1986), 80–91; and C.V. Wedgwood (Wedgwood's niece, the historian Dame Veronica Wedgwood), *The Last of the Radicals: Josiah Wedgwood MP* (1951), esp. ch. VII, 'History and Literature'. See also ch. XII of Wedgwood's own memoir, *Memories of a Fighting Life* (1941).

[2] Cannadine, 'History of Parliament', 367.

[3] Mulvey, *Political Life of Josiah C. Wedgwood*, 177.

The replies to the questionnaires, their associated correspondence and Wedgwood's draft biographies provide a rich source of information about members of parliament during the late 19th and early 20th centuries. Much of that richness derives from Wedgwood's personality, his very characteristic approach to parliament, more particularly to the house of commons and its history, and the nature of his relationships with his colleagues. For the purposes of this analysis, the questions and replies have been grouped into a series of themes, each covered in a separate chapter: motivation; personal and political careers; personal and political finances; and speeches, speech making and voting behaviour. The last chapter deals with the biographies that Wedgwood compiled on the basis of the replies to the questionnaire.

2. Wedgwood's Political Career

Wedgwood was the great-great-grandson of an earlier Josiah, the potter and founder of the eponymous family firm. He came from a well-established tradition of independent-minded freethinkers with a strong puritan streak and was 'at least as much the product of his dynasty as a child of his time'.[4] The family was well connected and Wedgwood was 'at the heart of England's entrepreneurial and intellectual aristocracy',[5] his family part of an extensive, closely knit social network. They were comfortably off with an estate and other resources derived mainly from the family business. Wedgwood had read widely, thanks mainly to the influence of his mother, was a good linguist and much travelled, particularly in Germany. He went to a public school (Clifton, near Bristol), where he did well academically and formed some lasting friendships before leaving at 16.

Wedgwood never worked in the family business; in his own generation that fell to one of his brothers, then to one of his sons. Having failed the medical tests for the army, by his own choice he did not go to university but trained as a naval engineer and architect. He married for the first time in 1893 and worked for three years for Armstrong's shipbuilders at Elswick in Newcastle-upon-Tyne. He abandoned that occupation in 1899 to fight in the South African War,[6] after which he served for 18 months in South Africa on the fringes of Lord Milner's kindergarten.[7] Although gregarious and sociable, he shared many of the Boers' puritan values; his memoir shows how he relished his time as a resident magistrate at Ermelo in the Transvaal, forming a lifelong attachment to South Africa. In 1904 he was forced to return to England with his family because of his first wife's ill health, 'tail between legs'[8] and with his personal finances somewhat depleted. 'For the second time his chosen path had come to an abrupt end.'[9] He never again

---

[4] Cannadine, *In Churchill's Shadow*, 136.

[5] Cannadine, 'History of Parliament', 367.

[6] Wedgwood claimed that he and his fellow countrymen mostly went 'from motives of exasperated patriotism'. *Memoirs of a Fighting Life*, 43.

[7] Lord Milner was British high commissioner in South Africa 1902–10 and gathered round him a group of about 20 young men who became known as his 'kindergarten'; many went on to have distinguished careers in business and public life. For more details see Alex May, *Oxford Dictionary of National Biography (ODNB)*, http://www.oxforddnb.com/public/themes/93/93711.html 14 Mar. 2012; and Mulvey, *Political Life of Josiah C. Wedgwood*, 7–12.

[8] J.C. Wedgwood, *Memoirs of a Fighting Life*, 59.

[9] J.C. Wedgwood, *Memoirs of a Fighting Life*, 67.

undertook paid work, thanks to the Wedgwood family resources and an inheritance from an uncle on his mother's side, although his large family (he had seven children by his first marriage) meant that at times his means were 'somewhat straitened'.[10]

Wedgwood's parliamentary career began in 1906, when he was first elected for Newcastle-under-Lyme. When he returned late in 1904 to live in Staffordshire at Barlaston Hall, close to the Etruria Works where the family pottery was based, he immediately became involved in local affairs. Despite the Wedgwood family's radical history, by then the 'dominating members' – his mother and the uncle and cousin who, with his eldest brother Frank, were running the family business – had become staunchly Conservative and were uneasy when he threw himself with characteristic vigour into the activities of the local Liberal Party. He required a good deal of support from, among others, his brother Ralph to counter strong family disapproval when he was adopted as Liberal candidate for what was, in effect, the family seat.[11] The sitting Unionist member had only a relatively small majority and the seat was regarded as 'among the best chances of a [Liberal] win that the whole country had to offer'.[12] Wedgwood himself said 30 years later in reply to his own questionnaire that 'The Liberal candidate at Newcastle-under-Lyme struck a bad patch of trade & withdrew; as there was a Wedgwood available prepared to spend £400 a year, he got it (Jan 1905)'.

Wedgwood won the seat in the Liberal landslide of January 1906 with a majority of over 2,000. He remained in parliament as member for the same seat until he was raised to the peerage in 1942, a year before his death in 1943. His only break from parliamentary activity occurred during the First World War when, at the age of 42, he volunteered for military service in the navy although he retained his seat in the house of commons. Despite his earlier hankerings for a military career, before the First World War he, like some other Liberals, had become an avowed isolationist and strongly opposed to the idea of war. His motives for changing his mind and accepting Winston Churchill's offer of a commission were complex but in his memoir he claimed in support of his decision to volunteer that the French could not be left in the lurch and, furthermore, that 'I do not think it right to *compel* people to go and face it by Act of Parliament unless I go myself'.[13] After service in Belgium and France, he fought in the Gallipoli campaign where he was seriously wounded, subsequently being awarded the DSO. He returned briefly to South Africa in 1916 and then served under General Smuts in East Africa, but his active military service ended late in 1916, when he resumed his parliamentary and political activities. As a consequence of a government-sponsored visit in 1917 to Russia, travelling there via the United States, he also acquired the honorary military rank of 'colonel' which, despite his naval service, he used for the rest of his life.[14]

---

[10] J.C. Wedgwood, *Memoirs of a Fighting Life*, 58; Wedgwood's niece and biographer, Dame Veronica Wedgwood, recorded in her memoir of her uncle that after his return to England his finances no longer allowed him to keep a horse so he adapted himself, 'with typically romantic enthusiasm', to the bicycle. C.V. Wedgwood, *Last of the Radicals*, 73–4.

[11] C.V. Wedgwood, *Last of the Radicals*, 75–7; J.C. Wedgwood, *Memoirs of a Fighting Life*, 59.

[12] J.C. Wedgwood, *Memoirs of a Fighting Life*, 59.

[13] Mulvey, *Political Life of Josiah C. Wedgwood,* 55–7; C.V. Wedgwood, *Last of the Radicals*, 99.

[14] Wedgwood described his wartime career in ch. VII of *Memoirs of a Fighting Life*; there is a more summary account in his niece's biography of him in the *Oxford Dictionary of National Biography*.

Wedgwood was always an exceptionally active member of parliament, asking questions and making speeches on a prodigious scale even when increasing age and ill health ought to have slowed him down. His memoir recorded how at an early stage he mastered different aspects of parliamentary procedure, especially the art of asking questions. According to his niece and biographer, the historian C.V. (later Dame Veronica) Wedgwood, he always gave the impression of confidence and, after a hesitant start, became a practised, fluent and sometimes witty speaker. The independence of mind that was to characterise his whole parliamentary career was soon demonstrated in the number and variety of causes, national and international, that he was to espouse. These causes followed three main themes: the land tax campaign (a long-term near obsession), personal freedom and the future of the British empire,[15] but they also included among many other minor issues the protection of children, the docking of horses' tails, agricultural wages, support for conscientious objectors in the First World War and support for refugees, as well as Zionism and Indian independence. 'Causes, old or new . . . were to be the speciality of the member for Newcastle-under-Lyme', although 'in the end there [was] only one cause, an old one, that of justice'.[16] His complete inability to be a team player emerged very early. Soon after he was first elected, he was made parliamentary private secretary to Walter Runciman, an old family friend who was then financial secretary to the treasury. It did not last long. As Wedgwood said, 'a time came when Chief Whip Whiteley really had to put his foot down . . . So I became a rogue elephant sitting as near as might be to the corner on the third bench below the gangway'.[17]

His personal circumstances did not help his career. His first wife left him in 1913, to his immense distress, and he was subsequently 'to navigate the muddy rapids of a much publicized divorce, [and] to figure in the newspapers repeatedly in the guise of troublemaker and irresponsible [*sic*]'.[18] More importantly, throughout his time in parliament he found it impossible consistently to toe any party line or 'to work within formally organised structures'.[19] He believed very strongly that parliament was a place 'where independent voices could be heard and where contrary opinions could be expressed'.[20] As his niece observed, 'Although a staunch member of the Liberal party, nothing was further from Josiah's conception of his duty to his constituents and his conscience than the idea of a slavish obedience on all questions'.[21] Before the First World War, he became increasingly disaffected with the Liberals, whom he came to regard as insufficiently radical, and the direction of the party during the war under Lloyd George's leadership reinforced his disaffection. He repudiated the Lloyd George 'coupon' which he was offered in 1918, standing instead as an independent radical. He was nevertheless re-elected unopposed, unlike many of his erstwhile Liberal colleagues.

Wedgwood joined the Independent Labour Party in April 1919 and the Labour Party a few months later, serving as vice-chairman of the parliamentary party from 1921 to

---

[15] Mulvey, *Political Life of Josiah C. Wedgwood*, chs 2–4.

[16] C.V. Wedgwood, *Last of the Radicals*, 78.

[17] J.C. Wedgwood, *Memoirs of a Fighting Life*, 64.

[18] C.V. Wedgwood, *Last of the Radicals*, 78.

[19] Mulvey, *Political Life of Josiah C. Wedgwood*, 14.

[20] Cannadine, *In Churchill's Shadow*, 140.

[21] C.V. Wedgwood, *Last of the Radicals*, 81.

1924, although still irked by party discipline. In the early 1920s he was a Labour front-bench spokesman, mainly on colonial affairs, and afterwards saw that period as the happiest of his parliamentary career. With some justification, in view of his position in the parliamentary party, he hoped for ministerial office should Labour get into power. However, his brief service in the cabinet as chancellor of the duchy of Lancaster during the minority Labour government of 1924 was not happy, partly because of his dislike of the prime minister, Ramsay MacDonald. He was also frustrated because his official position gave him little to do. He became disillusioned by the whole process of government.[22] 'A Cabinet from inside is not awe-inspiring', he wrote;[23] he was particularly frustrated by not being able to speak whenever he wanted in the house of commons.[24] 'In so far as his hopes had been fixed on playing a part in the government of his country, his career was virtually over in 1924.'[25]

From then on, although among the best-known back-bench members of parliament, he became increasingly detached from the mainstream of the Labour Party. '[F]or the last nineteen years of this life he made the best of his position as a free agent, untrammelled by party ties, political caution or hope of office.'[26] 'He relished being a one-man opposition and on the side of the underdog' and became content to be a political gadfly, able to be 'simultaneously patriot and dissenter, conformist and rebel, critic and clubman, local representative and national personality. It was where his generosity, his integrity and his wit were much admired, and where his lack of judgment, his wild knight-errantry and his incorrigible bloody-mindedness were gently tolerated'.[27] He was able to campaign, sometimes successfully, on whatever issues he chose, although often the battles 'showed him at his worst: short-tempered, bureaucratically inept and with a Manichean view of the world that was simplistic at best and bigoted at worst, and which frequently undermined the essentially sound arguments he was making'.[28]

3. Wedgwood and the History of Parliament

Some of Wedgwood's most strongly held convictions were about the nature and purpose of the institution of parliament. His family was politically aware and like most of his parliamentary contemporaries he had first become interested in politics as a young man. Much later he was to describe himself as having been 'soaked in politics' for almost all his life[29] but his memoir does not suggest that before election to the house of commons he knew much about the institution that was to dominate the rest of his life. His description of the House when he was first elected implies, however, that he soon

---

[22] His duties included acting as chief civil commissioner should the Emergency Powers Act be invoked in the event of a general strike, an appointment that A.J.P. Taylor saw as 'particularly ironical' since 'Wedgwood was generally considered to be more of an anarchist than a socialist'. *English History 1914–1945* (1965), 213.

[23] J.C. Wedgwood, *Memoirs of a Fighting Life*, 186.

[24] Mulvey, *Political Life of Josiah C. Wedgwood*, 139.

[25] C.V. Wedgwood, *Last of the Radicals*, 153.

[26] C.V. Wedgwood, *Last of the Radicals*, 160.

[27] Cannadine, *In Churchill's Shadow*, 140–1.

[28] Mulvey, *The Political Life of Josiah C. Wedgwood*, 149.

[29] J.C. Wedgwood, *Testament to Democracy* (1942), vii.

developed the romantic attachment that was to be a powerful element in his attitudes towards parliament. It became the driving force behind his extensive historical studies of parliament and its members as well as the *History of Parliament* project. *Testament to Democracy*, written shortly before his death, is imbued with the conviction expressed in the opening sentence that 'British parliamentary government is better than any other method of government'[30] and that parliament had a magnetic quality which meant that 'to write the letters M.P. after your name has become a decoration and a title valued beyond all others'.[31]

Wedgwood saw parliament as the connection between locality and the nation: 'the history of Parliament – as revealed through the biographies of the men who were sent there, a knowledge of their constituencies, and a study of the way in which the Commons evolved and functioned – was synonymous with all that was best in the history of the nation'.[32] In his introduction to the first of the two medieval volumes of his *History of Parliament* he argued that 'Knowledge of the personnel is essential to knowledge of the working of the institution. The institution illustrated is not merely the Commons, nor Parliament, nor democracy, but the whole government of a people'.[33] In the preface to one of his earliest works of parliamentary history he set out more colourfully what amounted to a personal credo, subsequently reworked and reused many times, in which he explained why he thought it so important to record the contribution of individuals to parliament and its history:

> To me, personally, Parliament is everything; the members are the staunchest friends man ever had; the life combines the mental gymnastics of college with the fresh wind of the outer world; only the recesses are intervals of stagnation. There is no other Parliament like the English. . . . [T]he man who steps into the English Parliament takes his place in a pageant that has been filing by since the birth of English history . . . These men who have gone by, who have had the glimmer of the torch on them for a little time, are those whose memories I want to rescue, and in doing so reincarnate a small section of the Parliaments which made us.[34]

Wedgwood's interest in parliamentary history was originally inspired by a combination of his close and lasting attachment to his Staffordshire roots,[35] family pride and a long-standing interest in family and local history. After he entered the house of commons, his life acquired a metropolitan focus but he always retained strong local connections; he even managed to serve as a Staffordshire county councillor from 1910 to 1919 and as mayor of Newcastle-under-Lyme in 1930 and 1931. His niece remarked that history 'had always been his favourite spare-time reading and local history his

---

[30] J.C. Wedgwood, *Testament to Democracy*, 9.

[31] J.C. Wedgwood, *Testament to Democracy*, 16.

[32] Cannadine, *In Churchill's Shadow*, 141.

[33] J.C. Wedgwood, *History of Parliament 1439–1509 The House of Commons: Biographies* (1936), iv.

[34] J.C. Wedgwood, *Staffordshire Parliamentary History from the Earliest Times to the Present Day: Collections for a History of Staffordshire*, ed. The William Salt Archaeological Society 1917 (1919), I, 1213 to 1603, xxi–xxii; see also J.C. Wedgwood, *History of Parliament 1439–1509: Biographies*, lii; and Cannadine, *In Churchill's Shadow*, 141.

[35] Cannadine, *In Churchill's Shadow*, 137–8.

favourite hobby'[36] and he claimed that 'Probably the Public Record Office has occupied more hours of my life than the Commons Chamber'.[37]

Wedgwood started work on his *Staffordshire Parliamentary History*, 'which took twenty years to seek out and record',[38] as soon as he was first elected to the house of commons. It was eventually published in four volumes between 1917 and 1933 and was to be 'his most sustained and influential piece of research',[39] forming the prototype for his later historical work on parliament. He acknowledged in the preface to the first volume that he had some help from local and other historians but did most of the work himself 'in the stolen hours of fourteen years'.[40] It was a natural consequence of his research on Staffordshire and his views about parliament that he 'should conceive a much more ambitious project: a national dictionary of parliamentary biography, recording and identifying the 75,000 Members who had sat in Parliament down to 1918'.[41] The idea of such a collective biography developed during the 1920s as he became increasingly aware that the social composition of the house of commons was changing and that the democracy he cherished so strongly was under a growing threat elsewhere in Europe.[42]

The case for a large-scale project to compile biographies of all members of parliament for all parliaments to 1832 was first formally set out in a letter to *The Times* of 24 May 1928, accompanied by a petition signed by 200 members of parliament to the prime minister, Stanley Baldwin, 'asking for the appointment of a committee to consider the possibility and method of production of such a work'.[43] The prime minister approved the request for a departmental committee which was appointed in March 1929 under Wedgwood's chairmanship and made what was intended to be an interim report in July 1932. The members consisted of equal numbers of members of parliament and academic historians and it was, by Wedgwood's own account, a distinctly unsuccessful mixture.

[T]he M.P.s rarely attended, the historians did not care for any non-professional element; and Dr Pollard ought to have been in the chair. It was a terrible business. We had got an agreed Report at last (7 October 1931); but I had to whip up and rush in my M.P. cohorts to vote against the professionals, a very bad start for a cooperative enterprise.[44]

Much of the report consisted of accounts of the work that had so far been done on the subject and suggestions for source material on which a more comprehensive study could be based. The main recommendation was that 'the task of preparing and publishing a record of the Commons House was possible' and should be undertaken:

[36] C.V. Wedgwood, *Last of the Radicals*, 163.

[37] J.C. Wedgwood, *Memoirs of a Fighting Life*, 213.

[38] J.C. Wedgwood, *Memoirs of a Fighting Life*, 213.

[39] Cannadine, *In Churchill's Shadow*, 138.

[40] J.C. Wedgwood, *Staffordshire Parliamentary History*, preface, xx–xxi.

[41] Sandall, 'The History of Parliament', 82–3.

[42] Cannadine, *In Churchill's Shadow*, 142; C.V. Wedgwood, *Last of the Radicals*, 167.

[43] Report by the Trustees of the History of Parliament (chairman Lord Macmillan), 30 July 1942 (Macmillan Report), para.1.

[44] J.C. Wedgwood, *Memoirs of a Fighting Life*, 215.

the preparation of a record of the personnel of the House of Commons and of the politics of its Members should include, first, the compilation of a list as complete as possible of the Members, and second, the collection of political and biographical details covering them, particular regard being paid to facts bearing on their standing, their election or selection, their political and economic affiliations and activities, their service in the House of Commons, and their official positions.[45]

The justification for this undertaking was expressed in 'unmistakeably Wedgwoodian' language,[46] stating unequivocally Wedgwood's belief that parliament was not:

> a cold and remote abstraction. It must always be to us a long series of assemblies and of men who were our ancestors. . . . of the men who gave the institution life, who shaped it and in so doing shaped our history and even our minds, no record has ever been attempted. . . . An institution has its foundations in the past, and at any moment in its history can only be understood through a knowledge of the past.[47]

The committee recognised that a potentially unlimited amount of research might be undertaken but estimated that 'a valuable piece of work' could be prepared within five to ten years at a cost of around £30,000.

The timing of the report was unfortunate. It had originally been hoped, not least by Wedgwood, that it would be the first of a series but, 'in consequence of the financial stringency of the times', the committee was dissolved and the interim report became its final one.[48] Although the prime minister had approved the project in principle, the treasury could not find the money. In March 1933 Wedgwood, 'whose zeal and enthusiasm had in no way abated', convened an informal committee of members of the Lords and Commons 'to consider ways and means of continuing the work, and particularly of raising funds to provide for the expense of research'.[49] The committee recognised that an appeal would have to be made to the public and, in order to make it more attractive to potential benefactors, one of its first decisions, at Wedgwood's urging, was to extend the project's scope to include the house of lords and to cover the period up to 1918. Wedgwood thereby hoped to attract more subscribers among living members, past and present, of both houses. It was also decided that each historical 'section' was to include a volume of conclusions dealing with the history of both houses and their relationships with each other. That decision was ultimately to undermine the whole project, mainly because it led to the loss of the co-operation of the professional historians who had served on the original departmental committee and on whose support Wedgwood had hitherto assumed he could depend. As a result, he was forced more or less to go it alone with at best intermittent support from his fellow politicians and a series of increasingly bitter and time-consuming disputes with the historians.[50]

[45] Macmillan Report, 1.

[46] Sandall, 'The History of Parliament', 82.

[47] *Interim Report of the Committee on House of Commons Personnel and Politics 1264–1832* (July 1932), Cmd. 4130, 52–3.

[48] Macmillan Report, 2.

[49] Macmillan Report, 2.

[50] There is a detailed account of the project's vicissitudes immediately before the Second World War in Mulvey, *Political Life of Josiah C. Wedgwood*, 171–7; Wedgwood's quarrel with the historians is described in detail in Hayton, 'Colonel Wedgwood and the Historians'.

Wedgwood started raising money in the second half of 1933, initially with only moderate success. In 1934 he persuaded the chancellor of the exchequer that, provided a minimum of £15,000, or half the expected total cost, could be raised privately, the Stationery Office should bear the remaining cost of publication, in anticipation of ultimately recovering the money from sales of the *History*. Wedgwood's subsequent efforts at fund-raising showed that he had acquired an understanding of one of the realities of political life. 'For the next six months all my time was devoted to writing personal begging letters to all M.P.s and ex-M.P.s. Circulars have no effect upon hard-boiled M.P.s; typewritten letters often fail to be read. Only the personal touch, in the old friend's bad hand, could produce results.'[51] That personal touch succeeded to the extent that he managed by May 1935 to raise the necessary £15,000, afterwards remarking: 'is it to be wondered at if I now hold in affection all men and women in all parties in that house of 1931–35?'[52]

Sadly for Wedgwood, that success coincided with the first stages of his battles with the historians over his 'conclusions' to the two medieval volumes that he had overseen and edited. The first volume was published in January 1936 and the second in 1938; each generated ever more rancorous exchanges, mainly in the *Times Literary Supplement*. Wedgwood responded to his critics 'with unabated fighting skill' but war was approaching and it was becoming clear that the project would have to be suspended. In 1940 the quarrel was settled by the formation of a History of Parliament Trust[53] and Wedgwood himself said he hoped that the trustees would appoint a salaried editor-in-chief to take his place. By 1942 that was possibly not the admission of defeat that it would have been earlier. He nevertheless recorded in his memoir his feelings of 'surrender' and his continuing defiance towards his critics about the nature of his achievement.[54]

Wedgwood's stubbornness and insistence on doing things his own way undoubtedly fuelled his quarrel with the historians who did not share his whiggishness or his perceptions of the role of parliament. In addition, he could not readily accept challenges to his approach to a subject where he felt, possibly justifiably, that he had an expertise at least equivalent to that of the professional historians. He resented any suggestion that he was one of the despised amateurs, arguing that he had:

> spent thirty years writing biographies of M.P.s, – have written 4,000 from the 13th to the 20th century. I may be permitted to think that I too am something of a specialist in that subject, in form, in sources, in what is called scholarship. Do not hold me to be just the tiresome amateur. You cannot have faced all the special problems that I have been meeting for thirty years.[55]

His arguments with the historians probably encouraged Wedgwood to divert his attention to the post 1832 period and, more particularly, to the biographies of his parliamentary contemporaries with whom he felt far more comfortable. The decision in 1933

---

[51] J.C. Wedgwood, *Memoirs of a Fighting Life*, 217.

[52] J.C. Wedgwood, *Memoirs of a Fighting Life*, 218.

[53] C.V. Wedgwood, *Last of the Radicals*, 171–2.

[54] J.C. Wedgwood, *Memoirs of a Fighting Life*, 222–3.

[55] Note prepared by Wedgwood for meeting of joint committee, 26 Feb. 1936. Wedgwood Papers in possession of the History of Parliament Trust, hereafter HoP MSS.

to extend the *History* to 1918 was based primarily on the need to raise money but Wedgwood also wanted to 'capture' members of parliament who had served in that period and were still alive. He was especially anxious to ensure that parliament's wartime achievements received the recognition he felt was their due.[56] He made strenuous efforts to persuade Winston Churchill, a long-standing parliamentary friend, to supervise those volumes, stressing in a letter of 30 September 1934 the urgency of recording the war record of the House before it grew dim. 'Those 26 who died [and to whose memory Wedgwood's first medieval volume was to be dedicated] were your friends and mine, and the chapter on the war record of that great House can only be done by you.' He was 'not in the least blind to the fact that if you did that period it would be the making of the whole series; but I think and you think how well Parliament shone beside Generals, Admirals and all other Parliaments – yes & all other ages – during those 5 bright years'.[57]

Churchill resisted Wedgwood's pleas on the grounds that he already had too much to do. In May 1935 Wedgwood approached the historian H.A.L. Fisher, a former member of parliament and by then warden of New College, Oxford, to act as editor for the two periods of 1865–85 and 1885–1918.[58] Fisher also refused, although he agreed 'to give all the advice necessary to start work on these later periods' and acknowledged the urgency of getting the last period under way.[59] At a meeting in February 1936 of the informal joint committee of members of the two Houses, Wedgwood strongly urged the importance of getting on with the modern periods (1832–1918) and the committee agreed to the immediate appointment of three assistants to start the work.

At the same meeting, he announced a plan for inviting 'the present generation' to write their own biographies, a suggestion that 'caused much amusement to the meeting'.[60] The minutes do not record any suggestion that he intended to use a questionnaire, but it was the first public hint of how he proposed to tackle those particular biographies. The proposal was not formally approved but it was not rejected. Wedgwood had already started to draft a questionnaire as the basis for the 'autobiographies' and seems to have assumed that he had received agreement to go ahead. He did not believe in wasting time.

---

[56] Wedgwood's preoccupation with parliament's wartime achievements was part of a wider concern in some quarters during the 1930s about the importance of ensuring that the First World War, particularly those who had died, continued to be appropriately commemorated. Although by then there was a well-established 'Peace Movement', supported mainly by those on the left, the 'Moment of Silence' on Armistice Day was still almost universally observed and great significance attached to the annual ceremony at the Cenotaph in Whitehall. Adrian Gregory, *The Silence of Memory: Armistice Day 1919–1946* (1994), chs 4 and 5.

[57] MS letter, copy in HoP MSS.

[58] Cannadine, 'History of Parliament', 381.

[59] PA, History of Parliament files, minutes of Historians Sub-committee, 23 July 1935.

[60] PA, HoP File 3.191, draft minutes of meeting, 26 Feb. 1936.

Chapter 2. The Questionnaire

1. *Introduction*

Wedgwood's 'biographical dictionary' approach to recording the lives and careers of parliamentarians was in a well-established tradition of 'group biography'[1] which he had followed in both his *Staffordshire Parliamentary History* and his two medieval volumes of the *History of Parliament*. He seems always to have intended that his 19th- and early 20th-century volumes would follow that model, providing short factual accounts of the subjects (personal information, family, education, pre-parliamentary occupation and so on), plus summary accounts of their parliamentary careers written, where possible, from a personal perspective. He may have been inspired in his idea of asking the surviving subjects to write their own biographies by the series of short autobiographies by 26 of the 29 new intake of Labour MPs in 1906, published in the periodical *Pearson's Weekly*.[2]

In the 1930s, surveys of the background and opinions of members of parliament were unusual and in that respect Wedgwood was something of a pioneer. The only published contemporary study of that kind was by the academic J.A. Thomas, who sought to identify 'the changing and functional character' of the House's membership and how the House reflected the structure of the economic system, and had changed as it had changed. Thomas concluded that:

> With the growth of the 'Great Industry', and as the social structure in Great Britain came to rest more and more upon a basis which was at once urban and industrial rather than rural and 'landed' in character, industrial and commercial interests began to supplant the landholding interest in the Commons.[3]

That conclusion would certainly have resonated with Wedgwood, who was very conscious of what he saw as the 'representative' nature of the members of the house of commons. There is no evidence that he knew of Thomas' work (which was not published until 1939) but he nevertheless recognised how the composition of the house of commons had changed in the late 19th and early 20th centuries and that it was still changing rapidly. However, his project was in no sense a systematic or statistical attempt to map those changes, as Thomas' had been and as Namier would later advocate.

---

[1] See Keith Thomas, *Changing Conceptions of National Biography: The Oxford DNB in Historical Perspective* (2005), 2–4. Reference works that listed members of parliament and gave basic information about them had existed since at least the early 19th century; *Dod's Parliamentary Companion* was first published in 1834 but was not the first of its kind.

[2] Jonathan Rose, *The Intellectual life of the British Working Classes* (2001), 189.

[3] J.A. Thomas, *The House of Commons 1832–1901: A Study of Its Economic and Functional Character* (1939), 157. See also Thomas' *The House of Commons, 1906–11: An Analysis of Its Economic and Social Character* (Cardiff, 1958).

The idea of using a questionnaire as the basis for the planned 'autobiographies' appears to have been Wedgwood's own, although by the early 20th century questionnaires had become a common means of gathering data to inform public policy; by the 1930s they were also widely used as tools for sociological and psychological research.[4] Wedgwood would have been familiar with their use and must have recognised that a questionnaire could provide an appropriate vehicle for ensuring that his subjects supplied a consistent range of information for their biographies. As he explained in 1942, his real desire was to gain an insight into the minds of his subjects: 'I wanted their minds rather than their deeds; and in the case of those surviving in 1934 [*sic*], I made a bold attempt at political psycho-analysis, by questionnaire'.[5]

There are drafts of Wedgwood's questionnaire in the *History of Parliament* archives which probably date from late in 1935. Wedgwood gave an early description of what he sought in the biographies in a letter of 3 February 1936 (i.e. before the meeting of 26 February 1936 with the informal committee at which he first suggested that he planned to ask his subjects to write their own biographies) to Colonel Arthur Murray:

> We are now starting on the period 1885 to 1918, and I wish you would send me your own biography to be enshrined in that great work. I want it not necessarily true but really intimate. I want to know why you came to the House of Commons, how your views changed, and what you thought about the whole thing. Of course I can improve on it, but you are just the sort of person who might do your own and get away with it.[6]

The desire for insight into his subjects' 'political minds' was similarly expressed to the novelist and playwright A.E.W. Mason, who was Wedgwood's parliamentary contemporary and served as Liberal MP for Coventry from 1906 to 1910. Wedgwood observed that Mason's willingness to do his own biography was widely shared (he did not say by whom) but 'It is obvious that many of these biographies will be unduly long [and] . . . they will have to be cut to something averaging 500 words each. I am proposing therefore to preserve for further record biographies as long as they care to write, cutting down where essential for publication'. He sought Mason's views on a draft questionnaire but admitted that 'Of course the peculiar value of the biographies done in this way will not be an accuracy of fact, though there too we shall probably be better off than by relying on who's Who [*sic*]'.[7] He also told Sir Algernon Law that he was 'very anxious to avoid Biographies resembling Obituary Notices, and . . . to get beyond the bald facts of "who's Who [*sic*]". Etc.'.[8]

Wedgwood seems always to have planned to edit the biographies himself and explained to his cousin, Leonard Darwin, how he would use a questionnaire to provide

---

[4] Beatrice Webb, for example, had used questionnaires extensively from the 1880s onwards in her work in the East End of London as had Charles Booth in his *Inquiry into the Life and Labour of the People in London*, undertaken between 1886 and 1903. Mass Observation, was, as David Cannadine has noted, founded in 1937 and was based on questionnaires – see sources listed in 'History of Parliament', 381.

[5] J.C. Wedgwood, *Testament to Democracy*, 18.

[6] HoP MSS: J.C. Wedgwood to Col. Arthur Murray, 3 Feb. 1936.

[7] HoP MSS: J.C. Wedgwood to A.E.W. Mason, 10 Mar. 1936.

[8] HoP MSS: J.C. Wedgwood to Sir Algernon Law, 23 Sept. 1936. Law, a former diplomat and senior official in the foreign office, had offered to check the biographies of four members of his family who had been members of parliament in the 19th and early 20th centuries.

a structure for the autobiographies and to determine their content. Surviving MPs from 1885 to 1918 would be asked to write their own biographies but:

> We do not want such biographies to consist of a series of dates, facts, achievements etc . . . but rather to embody the reactions to and reflections on public life such as can be known only to those who have lived through the Parliaments of their time. . . . [The] Questionnaire has been devised, not with a view to specific answers, but to indicate what we hope to have dealt with in each biography.

However, since 'few men' could deal with their personal biographies in the less than five hundred words that they could be allowed, 'we propose to print only censored summaries, as coherent as we can make them, and subject to the approval of the writer. The biographies as first written will be sealed up, only to be open to research after 100 years'.[9]

Darwin was an engineer, statistician and well-known eugenicist who had served from 1892 to 1895 as Liberal Unionist member for Lichfield. He replied with suggestions about the text of specific questions, adding that 'it would be worth saying that any part of the written statement not to be immediately published should be included between [ ]. For example, I do not want to be troubled with any questions about my religious opinions'.[10] He also suggested that 'you would get a more coherent reply if you stated that it is not intended that the questionnaire should be answered as such, but are [sic] only given as indicating the kind of topics you suggest should be dealt with', adding that 'If you limit the biographies to 500 words, I suspect they must be written in your office. You will always get more than that'. A member of the *History of Parliament* staff replied on Wedgwood's behalf on 6 May 1936, explaining that Wedgwood was ill but that 'It will probably not be necessary to state that the questionnaire is just a suggestive guide to topics, as a large number of M.P.s will probably write as the spirit moves them' and that there would always have to be some editing to control the length of the biographies.

There was no scientific method in Wedgwood's approach and he did not attempt to ensure that the questionnaire was sent to a representative sample of members and former members. He concentrated simply on getting the maximum possible number of responses. The questions directly reflected his avowed concern with getting inside his colleagues' minds and finding out about their reactions to their experiences of parliament. That approach was entirely consistent with his views about the institution of parliament and its members. He never expressed any intention of undertaking a quantitative analysis of the answers and the questions were not devised with that in mind. Some were blunt and 'characteristically trenchant'[11] while many were completely open-ended and gave little if any indication of the nature of the information sought. There were gaps, such as the absence of questions about education and its impact and about the background to party affiliations, despite the number of Wedgwood's contemporaries who had, like him, changed party during their parliamentary careers. Some questions lent themselves to discursive answers if the subjects chose, which quite a few of them did.

---

[9] HoP MSS: J.C. Wedgwood to Leonard Darwin, 21 Apr. 1936.

[10] HoP MSS: Leonard Darwin to J.C. Wedgwood, 23 Apr. 1936.

[11] Cannadine, 'History of Parliament', 382.

Wedgwood was seriously ill for much of May and June 1936 but the preparation of the questionnaire was still completed in time for the first batch to be printed and sent to surviving members around 10 July 1936. Those to families were sent later that year (the exact date is not recorded in the files). The initial response was slow and only about a hundred questionnaires had been returned by September. A first round of chasing letters was sent in November/December 1936 and at least two further, more limited, efforts were made in 1937 and 1938 to chase those who had not replied. A few replies were still appearing in mid 1938. In the original version of the questionnaire, the printed questions were listed on the front page which was attached to three blank pages for the answers. The preamble did not explain exactly what was expected of the recipients since Wedgwood only partially followed Darwin's advice about the need to explain that the questions were intended as an indication of the topics to be covered. All it said was:

> It has been suggested that it would be desirable for living Members or ex-Members of Parliament to assist in the compilation of their own biographies. Below are questions which ought to be dealt with. It would be useful to have answers to these from our predecessors and contemporaries; they will inform and guide our contemporaries and successors on this and other lands. No biographer, only the man himself, can answer such questions.

Following complaints that the original layout made the questionnaire difficult to complete as it was not explained that the blank pages were to be used for that purpose, the chasing letters were accompanied by a revised version with the same questions but an amended preamble and layout, plus a specimen questionnaire completed with Wedgwood's own answers to show what sort of information he wanted. There was also an additional question about books written by the subjects.[12] The new preamble included the statement, previously in a note at the end of the list of questions, that answers to all the questions were optional and 'if it is desired that answers be treated as confidential, they should be enclosed in brackets; these will remain unpublished for 100 years'. The commitment mentioned to Darwin that the completed questionnaires were to be sealed for a hundred years was never made, possibly because Wedgwood had realised that it might be unnecessarily restrictive. Recipients were also asked to supply 'the usual bald facts' from *Who's Who* or another reference work 'to save the compilers trouble'.

2. Responses to the Questionnaire

History of Parliament staff made considerable efforts to keep track of the replies to the questionnaire, although the state of the records suggests that they struggled to control the paperwork and record the replies. A worn and heavily annotated typed 'List of Members 1885–1918' contains an undated manuscript note which records that the total number of names was 2,363, of whom 425 'overlapped', presumably with the pre 1885 period. That left 1,939, of whom 550 were alive in mid 1936. The note claimed that 1,100

---

[12] Wedgwood later claimed that sometimes in accompanying letters 'to old friends' he asked additional questions, such as 'Why did you fail?', but there are no such letters, or replies to them, in the surviving correspondence. J.C. Wedgwood, *Testament to Democracy*, 19.

questionnaires were sent out, 550 to the surviving members and former members, and the same number to families of deceased former members. The note also recorded that replies were received from 400 surviving members and 332 relations, although there is no indication of what form those replies had taken. There is a second annotated manuscript list of 419 'Surviving Members of War Parliament' to whom 'circulars have been sent'. That list was probably compiled by one of the *History of Parliament* staff after the first round of chasing letters had been sent in late 1936. The note records that 84 replies had been received and 34 promises. By 21st-century standards, the overall response was relatively high for such an exercise, but it required a very substantial effort to achieve it.

The *History of Parliament*'s archives now contain a single sequence of replies to 352 questionnaires, of which 292 were answered by their subjects and 60 by the families of subjects, filed in the same sequence. The replies are by no means all complete or consistent: many of the subjects did not answer all the questions, or did so very briefly, while some replies consist of notes or letters containing responses to some of the questions.[13] There is correspondence connected with the questionnaire, some of it very brief, relating to 525 members, including 78 apparently unfulfilled promises of a proper response to the questionnaire and 94 refusals. There are several references in the correspondence to completed questionnaires that are no longer in the files but no indications of what might have happened to the missing ones.

Most of the surviving questionnaires completed by their subjects came, as might be expected, from members who had served in the later part of the period from 1885 to 1918, mainly from those first elected between 1900 and 1918. The respondents nevertheless covered a very long period ranging from several, including Charles Cochrane-Baillie, Henry Hobhouse, Weston Jarvis, Harry Lawson (Lord Burnham), Hastings Lees-Smith, George Leveson-Gower and Sir George Sitwell, who were first elected in the 1880s to those who, like Wedgwood, were still serving in the mid 1930s and a handful who served until 1945 (J.R. Clynes, Will Thorne, both Labour, Lloyd George and his fellow Liberal George Lambert and the Conservative George Courthope). There was also a questionnaire from the son of the banker Thomas Salt, first elected in 1859 and who retired from the house of commons in 1892.

The party breakdown of the respondents corresponded fairly closely with overall party representation in the house of commons in the early 20th century and included several of the growing number of Labour and Lib–Lab members. The outcome of individual elections varied greatly between the Conservatives and Liberals but between them those two parties held over 80% of the seats in the house of commons at each election between 1900 and December 1910 (the last before the First World War). Labour's seats rose from 29 in 1906 to 42 (6%) in December 1910 while the Irish nationalist parties held an average of 82 seats (12%) at each election during the period. Of the 354 replies to the questionnaire, including those completed by families, 140 (39%) were from Conservatives, 144 (41%) from Liberals, 15 (4%) from Labour including several from the 1906 intake and one or two from earlier elections, 17 (5%) from Liberal Unionists,

[13] In some cases, answers to the questions were given in letters or in draft biographies. For the purposes of counting the total responses, and in the analyses in the following chapters, if at least one question was answered, whether as part of a reply to the questionnaire or in the associated correspondence, the subject has been treated as having supplied a response.

11 (3%) from Unionists and 22 (6%) from Irish nationalists. Replies from other parties such as Independent Labour and Lib–Labs were in single figures.

There were numerous replies from those who had held senior government or party positions, although lack of complete information about the original recipients of the questionnaire makes it impossible to judge the significance of that. Lloyd George (or possibly Frances Stevenson on his behalf) completed a questionnaire as did four former leaders of the Parliamentary Labour Party, or their families (George Barnes, Keir Hardie's brother on his behalf, George Lansbury and J.R. Clynes). Leo Amery, William Bridgeman (Lord Bridgeman), Lord Robert Cecil (Lord Chelwood), Austen Chamberlain, Eric Geddes (Lord Geddes), John Hodge, Alfred Lyttelton (completed by his widow), Reginald McKenna, Edwin Montagu (completed by his sister), John (Jack) Seely (Lord Mottistone) and Edward Wood (Lord Halifax) were among the respondents who were nationally well-known political figures and had achieved senior government positions. There were several former whips and parliamentary private secretaries, including two Liberal chief whips (Alexander Murray, master of Elibank and chief whip from 1910 to 1912, completed by his brother, and Frederick Guest, chief whip 1917–21), and one deputy (George Leveson-Gower, deputy chief whip 1892–5), while the names of families traditionally associated with British politics (Bathurst, Cavendish, Cecil, Hamilton, Lane-Fox, Lowther, Pease and Verney, to list the most obvious) appeared frequently.

Despite Darwin's efforts, the ambiguity of the preamble to the first version of the questionnaire led to misunderstandings about how it was to be used. Few respondents (around 25) took Wedgwood at his word and provided their own autobiographies in a usable form, or biographies of their immediate family members; most assumed that only replies to the questions were wanted. Several questions overlapped, so the replies were often confused. The businessman Eric Geddes (Lord Geddes, who served in the house of commons briefly during the First World War) was the only respondent to invoke for the whole questionnaire the escape clause that any answers to questions that were put in brackets would not be reproduced. Several others did, however, invoke it occasionally, especially in the case of the question (Q9) about their incomes when first elected. Many availed themselves of the get-out that they did not have to answer all the questions if they did not want, while some of the replies were very brief. Most seemed to have assumed that they were expected to give honest replies to the questions they did answer, no doubt encouraged by Wedgwood's candour in his own questionnaire about his personal circumstances and career. Despite the obvious temptations, there was a notice-able absence of self-promotion in most of the replies.

3. Reactions to the Questionnaire

Initial reactions from the recipients were very mixed. There were a few more or less immediate replies accompanied by completed questionnaires and little or no comment but some strong reactions, both for and against the whole enterprise. Wedgwood almost certainly anticipated that kind of reaction and may even have sought it: by then he seems to have enjoyed his reputation as a maverick and his niece described him as having 'a little private fun' by sending the questionnaire to his fellow members. 'The great quiz fashion had not then set in, and a number of the stuffier members were incensed at being suddenly presented by the outrageous Colonel Wedgwood with a request to fill in answers to such questions as: "What were your religious convictions at 21?" "What was your annual income, earned or unearned, when you first stood for Parliament?"[14]

Receipt of the questionnaire often provoked vigorous correspondence between Wedgwood and his current and former colleagues. The general tone of the letters to him was almost uniformly warm and affectionate, even when tinged with exasperation or irritation. His former colleagues often said how pleased they were to hear from him; there was frequent praise for his enterprise and energy and widespread support for the *History of Parliament* project as a whole. Sir George Sitwell remarked that 'Your power of getting things done amazes me! You ought to be dictator',[15] while Archibald Weigall wrote of his feelings of 'amazement and gratitude to you for compiling this extraordinary and interesting work'.[16]

Many of the questionnaire's recipients heartily disliked it, even those who expressed warm personal feelings towards Wedgwood and approved of the project. The questions were often seen as far too intrusive and difficult or impossible to answer. There were many references to the 'catechism', 'inquisition', 'Star Chamber document', 'third degree', 'soul searching' and 'searching cross-examination', while Joseph King quoted back at Wedgwood his own description of 'corkscrew questions' and Edward Wood referred to 'your awful questionnaire' and 'searching conundrums'. George Lambert remarked: 'What an acquisition you would have been in Spain 400 years ago', while Wedgwood was described several times as 'importunate' and by Thomas Shaw as 'a perfect Pest & I don't know how to do that "self" job – an odious affair'. Leslie Scott was among many who saw the questionnaire as impertinent: 'It would indeed produce confidences worthy of the most relentless psycho-analyst if only you had the powers and the apparatus of Torquemada to extract answers'.

There was a widespread and often apparently genuine reluctance to reveal publicly what were seen as personal feelings; many also questioned the value to posterity of doing so. H.A.L. Fisher, the professional historian whom Wedgwood had had in mind to edit the late 19th- and early 20th-century volumes, felt that 'it seems almost indecent to expose so much of myself to the public eye'. Percy Harris disliked 'making these "Confessionals" even to such a broadminded High Priest as yourself'. Walter Perkins 'could not face such an appalling confession of my lurid past . . . You have set us all a brave example, however, in disclosing your own case'. Rowland Prothero (Lord Ernle) 'hated the job he had been asked to do' and disliked 'self-advertisement' while Charles Roberts asked to be let off the catechism:

> I dare say revelations as to our motives, and our favourite film star, are of interest in the case of the big names but I cannot imagine any human being having the faintest interest in or curiosity about my doings. And though I admire your historical zeal, I never had the faintest wish for any posthumus [*sic*] recollection; and as for my political career, I think we can very well forget it.

Alexander Shaw did not see himself as being 'in the running for any form of celebrity' and Arthur Ponsonby found 'something repulsive in auto-biography . . . Let posterity

[14] C.V. Wedgwood, *Last of the Radicals*, 170.

[15] HoP MSS: Sir George Sitwell to J.C. Wedgwood, 3 Oct. 1936.

[16] HoP MSS: Archibald Weigall to J.C. Wedgwood, 5 Aug. 1936.

ferret out what they can find though probably they will get it all wrong'. Arthur Crosfield, who had had a long and active career in his family business of soap and candle manufacturers as well as being a member of parliament, asked 'who in the future will ever care one brass farthing about the likes of me?' George Tryon 'found it very difficult to reply to some of the questions because one does not like to attribute good motives or merit to oneself'.

Some apparently successful public figures felt that their parliamentary careers had not been distinguished enough to merit recording. Neither Freeman Freeman-Thomas (the marquess of Willingdon, who served only briefly in the house of commons as a Liberal but became in succession governor-general of Canada and viceroy of India) nor Francis Mildmay (Lord Mildmay of Flete, a prominent member of the great and good of his day) could possibly have seen his own career as unsuccessful but both clearly felt that their parliamentary careers had been insufficiently distinguished to bear undue public exposure. Freeman-Thomas told Wedgwood that he was 'a real nuisance to want to rake up my miserable Parliamentary past', while Mildmay saw himself as 'a very ordinary person, on whose behalf no very striking performances call for record, and I feel most strongly that to set out very interesting details about my life would be far from justifiable'. Samuel Hoare had 'the greatest disinclination for circulating details and impressions about myself', and Arthur Lee (Lord Lee of Fareham) could not bring himself 'to believe that the answers to most of the questions which you have drafted – at any rate in my own case – could be of the faintest interest to posterity . . . Indeed, I am not sure looking back that the least said about my parliamentary career the better'.

Some were clearly genuinely modest and self-effacing about their own achievements but overcame their reticence because they recognised the importance of Wedgwood's project and the wider value of the information sought. Arthur Marshall 'hated doing it because it is against my grain to talk or write about myself – but your work is so important and self-sacrificing my conscience has driven me on'. Arthur Wills saw the survey as 'most intriguing and, if I may say so, not less characteristic of your customary daring. . . . But I'm not sure that even the details asked for, even of such political nonentities as myself, may not be, in a sense, a vital fact. After all, we did represent, for a time, a great and sane if uninstructed people'. Many were prepared to do what they could, if reluctantly, to help Wedgwood personally. As Basil Peto put it, 'Of course I hate you for giving me all this bother when I no longer have a secretary but as I have a soft corner in my heart for you, I yield to some extent to your blandishments'. George Lane-Fox (Lord Bingley) replied that 'If this request had not come from you, I should have put it in the waste-paper basket' and Philip Snowden would 'not go so far in my abomination of your questions as to refuse to answer them. So here is the Questionaire [*sic*] returned'.

Most of the 94 refusals were relatively polite but some were snubbing. Lord Stanley thanked Wedgwood for his letter and enclosure but added: 'The first must be answered at once, the second perhaps never as it would entail too great a strain on my powers of imagination & intention'. Lord Astor was 'completely bowled out by your questionnaire and would have neither the knowledge, nor the desire, nor the nerve to answer 95% of your queries!' Winston Churchill simply claimed (again) that he was too busy – 'It is all that I can do to get through my present work' – while Bolton Eyres-Monsell (Lord Monsell) claimed that he had managed to retain his seat in parliament 'in spite of refusing to fill up every questionnaire that was put before me, and I do not propose to start now'. Bernard Coleridge's son (Lord Coleridge) disliked the 'modern mania for publicity & advertisement'; the questions were 'inquisitive & might almost be described as impertinent'; he had 'far too great a respect & affection for my father's memory to satisfy a morbid & inquisitive curiosity'; the questionnaire had been 'framed entirely to meet the conditions for the members of the House of Commons in the present day'. Charles Hobhouse replied in response to a chasing letter in December 1936: 'Neither rage — despair, stupidity misdescription [*sic*] nor misdirection led me to neglect an answer to your previous circular. But I am not persuaded that my sending an answer to your questionnaire will interest or improve any human being'.

Others argued that posterity would not (or should not) necessarily be interested in them. Lord Balfour wrote distinctly frostily in response to a request for a questionnaire about his father, the former prime minister, A.J. Balfour:

> I find a difficulty in believing that posterity, merely because one has been a Member of Parliament, will care to know more about one than can be gathered from the ordinary sources of information. . . . It would be distasteful to me to attempt anything in the nature of an autobiography covering questions that 'only the man himself can answer'.

Reginald McKenna wrote in similar terms while Ramsay MacDonald (who supported the *History of Parliament* project despite Wedgwood's well-known dislike of him) sent an oft-quoted letter of refusal:

> I am glad to see that you are about again, but am sorry that the first request you make to me is quite an impossible one. Some of the questions I cannot answer because I have forgotten; others I never could answer because they imply that thoroughly false view of life that a man never does anything without consulting his own freewill; others I could only answer by saying I do not know; others because they are of no importance except in showing how that sensible man Josiah Wedgwood has at last become infected by an interest in the vulgar trivialities of a personal character which are being scattered abroad by a debased and debasing popular press![17]

MacDonald identified an important issue over the use of the questionnaires: Wedgwood's expectation that his colleagues, or their families, could recall accurately influences and events from at least 30 years earlier and sometimes much more. Many of the gaps or uncertainties in the answers to some of his 'corkscrew questions' can be explained by his subjects' inability to remember accurately, or at all, such details as the books that had impressed them in youth or their financial circumstances 30 or 40 years before. Wedgwood may well not have been particularly worried about that, in view of his declared desire for good stories and to get inside the minds of his subjects.

The responses to the questionnaire from 22 members of Irish nationalist parties stood out as a group apart. The 18 members of the Irish Nationalist Party in particular had been a tightly knit and politically cohesive group at Westminster, outwardly bound by their party pledge to speak, act and vote together, despite their many and often bitter

---

[17] HoP MSS: Ramsay MacDonald to J.C. Wedgwood, 29 Jul. 1936.

internal party disputes, one recorded at length in D.D. Sheehan's questionnaire. They all sank from Westminster politics more or less without trace in 1918 (some of their unionist counterparts from Ulster were another matter). The correspondence showed that at least some, particularly those whose political careers had ended when they left Westminster, were pleased to be approached by Wedgwood and to have an opportunity for their Westminster careers to be revisited and publicly recognised. There were offers to contact former colleagues and several, like D.D. Sheehan, took advantage of the opportunity to describe their careers and personal histories in detail. William Cosgrave, one of four Sinn Fein members elected at by-elections between 1914 and 1918 who never took their seats, also explained that although he was 'elected to the British Parliament in 1917 . . . I was never a member of it. . . . I was elected . . . for the purpose of staying away and of taking Ireland entirely from under the authority of that Parliament'. He nevertheless wanted to be helpful to Wedgwood, saying that he had no desire to cause offence by stating publicly the position about his membership of the house of commons.[18]

The processes of drafting and distributing the questionnaires, chasing responses, corresponding with the subjects and then preparing and checking biographies proved far more time-consuming than Wedgwood had envisaged. From early in 1936 until the middle of 1937 he must have devoted a great deal of time to the questionnaire, including corresponding with many of his subjects, analysing replies and preparing biographies. After that he became less actively involved and wrote no more biographies but was still engaged in correspondence until at least mid 1938. He was punctilious and an indefatigable correspondent and at first wrote personally to thank virtually all those who completed questionnaires, as well as adding handwritten pleas to many of the routine chasing letters. This direct involvement probably contributed significantly to the level of response that was eventually achieved, but at the expense of Wedgwood's own work on preparing biographies.

4. *War Service of Members of Parliament*

Wedgwood also pursued, separately, his long-held desire to record the wartime achievements of his parliamentary colleagues.[19] He approached the war office some time in 1936 to ask for details of the service of members of the house of commons in the First World War. The initial response must have been favourable but on 30 November 1936 Duff Cooper, the secretary of state for war, wrote, apparently in response to a chasing letter from Wedgwood, to tell him why progress with the work was much slower than had originally been expected. The task could not be given the priority Wedgwood wanted because of the demands of the rearmament programme; although around 60 'statements of service' had already been prepared and could be provided immediately, 'the work on your history will take much longer than was originally estimated'. Wedgwood

---

[18] HoP MSS: W.T. Cosgrave to J.C. Wedgwood, 19 Sept. 1936.

[19] See Chapter 1, p. 10 for his efforts to persuade Winston Churchill to edit the late 19th- and early 20th-century volumes, partly because of the urgency of recording the war record of members of the house of commons before it 'grew dim'.

replied on 3 December 1936, asking for the 60 statements to be supplied immediately and adding: 'Please ask your people to make what haste they can now because I ought to be getting the thing out by next June'.

Duff Cooper wrote again on 17 December 1936, sending the first batch of 61 statements and saying that he would see that every effort was made to expedite the completion of the remaining 160 statements. He reiterated, however, that his department was under very great pressure and it was unlikely that the statements would be completed before the end of June. By then even Wedgwood must have realised that his demands were possibly unreasonable. He replied on 19 December 1936 that he would be 'glad to have the rest whenever you can send them'. In a further letter on 19 January 1937, Duff Cooper supplied a promised list of those members of the 1911–18 parliament who were recorded as having served in forces other than the British army, plus a further 22 statements of army service. The remaining statements, which totalled 168 plus a further 43 on those who had served before the First World War, were not supplied until June 1938. A letter of 23 June 1938 from Duff Cooper's private secretary described the exhaustive (and, given the circumstances, astonishing) efforts that had been made to trace and record the military service of all the members of the 1911–18 parliament. The statements were accompanied by lists of the members for whom statements had been provided. In total, *History of Parliament* staff calculated that there were statements of service of 251 members.

Despite his stated desire to record the wartime achievements of his colleagues, there are no indications of how Wedgwood intended to use the statements of service, although they must have been intended for publication in some form. Twenty-one of those initially supplied in December 1936 were filed with the questionnaires, as were a further eight of those supplied in January 1937. Eight of the biographies that Wedgwood compiled were of members for whom the war service records were available by January 1937 but he appears to have made little, if any, use of the information provided. Had he used that material, it would have added to the information in some of the questionnaires and thus enhanced the biographies. By June 1938, however, when the majority of them were supplied, he had not written any biographies for at least a year and was no longer making any significant input to the work on the late 19th and early 20th centuries.

Chapter 3. 'Getting Inside Their Minds': Formative Influences and Personal Backgrounds

1. *Introduction*

Wedgwood was well aware of the many changes in the house of commons that had taken place in the late 19th and early 20th centuries. He knew that he and his contemporaries had been part of those changes and that they had lived through 'interesting times'. The house of commons service of his subjects covered a period of well over 50 years which straddled the First World War, from those first elected in the 1880s (one or two even earlier), who remembered hearing Gladstone speak at the peak of his career, to those still serving in the mid 1930s when they completed the questionnaire. Their personal backgrounds and careers reflected the effects on the composition of the house of commons of the Corrupt and Illegal Practices Act of 1883 and the 1884 Reform Act. They had seen the growth of government activity in the late 19th and early 20th centuries and the gradual emergence both of more disciplined parties and of a new style of politics. They had taken part in the debates about the beginning of the welfare state and Lloyd George's 1909 Budget as well as the reform of the house of lords. They had also been involved in the later stages of the long-running and deeply divisive debates over Ireland and the build-up to the First World War. Like several of his contemporaries, Wedgwood himself had been personally involved in the decline of the Liberal Party and the emergence of the Labour Party.

The responses showed how, to a considerable but diminishing extent, British politics in the period still 'depended on the existence of an independent leisured class, willing and able to devote the greater part of their days, or at least of their ample spare time, to the business of government'.[1] The answers to the questions about how their interest in politics first arose illustrated how both main parties still contained many hereditary politicians whose involvement in politics arose from family tradition, accompanied by a strong sense of public duty and sufficient private means to afford the financial sacrifices that a political career usually entailed. Politics was seldom seen as a 'career' and they did not see themselves as what have come to be termed 'professional' politicians. They were, however, a disappearing breed, gradually being replaced by new generations from rather different backgrounds. Apart from the Labour or Lib–Lab members who were almost all of working-class origins, the respondents included numerous examples of the 'new middle class', mainly drawn from business or the professions and largely dependent on their own earnings but whose politics were often inspired by idealism and the need for social reforms, particularly among the Liberals.

---

[1] W.L. Guttsman, *The British Political Elite* (3rd (revised) impression, 1965), 195.

2. Early Influences

The first two questions (Q1: 'When did you first become interested in politics? Why?'; and Q2: 'What influenced you in this line of thought?') overlapped with each other and with Q6 ('Why did you want to be an M.P.?') and Q7 ('What or who first led you to think of it as a career?'). Many found it difficult to distinguish between them so the answers were often combined (and sometimes confused), repeated or used to amplify or embellish each other. The open-ended nature of the questions encouraged discursiveness in the answers, possibly helped by the position of the first two at the start of the questionnaire; that may also explain the relatively high level of response to them. Qs 6 and 7 also sometimes encouraged self-promotion, although that did not necessarily mean that the answers were untruthful. A few used them as a vehicle for rehearsing details of their political careers while others, particularly among the Irish, saw them as an opportunity for rehearsing old grievances.

Of the 310 respondents to Q1, 56 (18%) provided a combined answer with Q2. The 310 included 129 Liberals, 119 Conservatives (including two Unionists), 16 Irish Nationalists and 15 Labour or Lib–Lab. There were 208 separate respondents to the second question, nearly all of whom had also answered the first. Seventy were Conservatives, 93 Liberals, 15 Irish Nationalist, 12 Labour and four Lib–Lab. Two-thirds of the respondents to the first part of the first question claimed, regardless of party, to have been interested in politics since childhood or early youth while the interest of a further 6% dated from their student days. Nearly a quarter claimed that their interest started at a specific date or was triggered by a specific event, or both, usually when they were relatively young and only rarely later than in their 20s. Many of those who did not become actively engaged in politics until later in their careers claimed to have been interested from early in their lives.

For members of all parties, family background was the single most important factor in creating a lasting interest in politics or public affairs. Forty-five per cent of the respondents to the second part of Q1 cited family influence of some kind: their father or another close family member had been a member of parliament or parliamentary candidate or was actively involved in national or local politics. Forty-two per cent of the rather fewer respondents to the second question cited their family as the main influence. Since the respondents included numerous hereditary politicians from both the Conservative and Liberal Parties, that was to be expected. The Conservatives included four Salisbury Cecils (Lord Cranborne, Lord Hugh (Lord Quickswood), Lord Robert (Lord Chelwood) and Evelyn (Lord Rockley)) whose childhood interest in politics arose because they were brought up in a political atmosphere; the father of Lord Cranborne and Lords Robert and Hugh was the 3rd marquess of Salisbury and prime minister, while Lord Salisbury's younger brother, Lord Eustace, father of Evelyn, was an active member of the house of commons. For Ben Bathurst, 'Each of the five generations before me had sat in the House for Cirencester, since the beginning of the 18th century' while John Ryder (Lord Sandon) cited 'Family tradition, 6 generations of M.P. without any break'.

The Liberals and Liberal Unionists included even more hereditary politicians. Samuel Whitbread's family 'had sat in the House of Commons almost continuously from 1765 to 1910'. The mother of Freeman Freeman-Thomas (the marquess of Willingdon) 'had strong Liberal views'; his grandfather, Viscount Hampden, had been speaker of the house of commons. Frederick Guest's interest dated from the Boer War and 'an urge which I presume I inherited from the Churchill blood' (Winston Churchill was his first cousin). For Francis Mildmay, 'Active concern for National politics has long been a characteristic of my family'; Lord Grey, of the Great Reform Bill, was his maternal great-grandfather. Harry Verney was four when his father was elected as a Liberal member of parliament and took him to the house of commons where he shook hands with Gladstone. Lionel de Rothschild (a Liberal Unionist) was 'by religion a Jew' and proud 'that one of my ancestors was the first Jew ever to sit in the British House of Commons. . . . I felt it was my duty to continue the tradition which enabled a Rothschild to sit in the first legislature of the world'.

Even where there were no family members directly engaged in national politics, interest in politics was often inspired by families. From the early youth of the Conservative George Courthope, 'my Father, to whom I was devoted, taught me that it was the duty of everyone to take an interest in national politics'. William du Pre's mother 'took an active part in Primrose League and other political work'. Alfred Hopkinson was born in 1851 and first became interested when he was about five years old, 'when my Father told me all about the Russian War & the Chartists of the forties & took active part for John Bright when he was defeated for Manchester in 1857'. Anderson Montague-Barlow's father was an anglican clergyman whose 'conversation first turned my thoughts to public affairs'. Allan Bright recalled how, at the age of three, his father showed him a flag flying at half mast for the death of Palmerston, then prime minister. 'I did not know who Lord Palmerston was, or what the word Prime Minister meant, but the incident made a great impression on me.' Joseph King's father was 'an active worker for Wm. E. Gladstone. . . . My home was a political home where I heard & learned much'.

Labour and Lib–Lab respondents were sometimes brought up in a 'political' environment although their interest was more often originally influenced by external events. The teacher and trade union official Frank Goldstone was influenced 'by early religious associations & friendships formed with progressive young assistant masters on leaving college'. The family of the former miner and miners' agent, John Hancock, was always interested in politics and Fred Maddison's interest arose in his early teens 'Largely due to my father's keen interest'. Philip Snowden was 'a child from a Radical father' and John Hodge's father 'held Chartist opinions, my mother was an extreme radical, thus was laid my outlook on life politically'.

For many of those who experienced them, the strong feelings that underlay both Welsh and Irish politics exerted a powerful influence from early in their lives. For Lloyd George, every Welshman was a politician while his fellow Welsh Liberal Edgar Jones described how living 'in the intense atmosphere of Welsh Nonconformity in a mining village I was keenly interested in national politics from 12 years of age and at 15 was actively engaged in public platforms dealing with political issues'. Ellis Davies was equally typical of a strand in his party: he was 'brought up hearing repeatedly of my grandfather's denunciation of the land laws, whilst my father . . . was interested in the question of Welsh Disestablishment. At that time, Welsh politics consisted almost entirely of the land and the Church. Social questions were never discussed, financial reform never'.

Both Unionists and Nationalists in Ireland experienced strong influences at an early age. For William Allen, a Unionist from Armagh North, 'In Ulster we take in our politics with our mothers' milk' and John Newman was a 'South Irish Loyalist as soon as I could talk'.

His fellow Unionist James Craig (Lord Craigavon) claimed that for his community, 'daily conversation turned to the vital issues at stake, especially to us Protestants, who feared interference with our religion, education and social ideals and felt instinctively that Home Rule meant the eventual severance of our connection with Great Britain'. The Nationalist John Campbell was interested in politics '[from] the cradle. Every Irish child begins a political career there'. For John Boland, 'The whole course of Irish history . . . was a sufficient influence to make any Irishman worthy of the name endeavour to win back that Parliament by constitutional means'. William Duffy wrote of his 'intense hatred of England' and the 'scenes of military terrorism which were brutally in evidence' around 1880 with the country 'seething with discontent'. 'It was only natural that young men should throw themselves heartily into the movement of revolt & I did.' Active dislike of English attitudes to Ireland was engendered in both John Boland and Stephen Gwynn by their experiences among their fellow students at Oxford University. Hugh Law was exposed to a range of Irish influences, his father having served under Gladstone as Irish attorney-general and as lord chancellor of Ireland at the time of the Phoenix Park murders in 1882.[2] Law could not recall any time 'when I was not interested in National Politics, chiefly of course from an Irish angle'. However, 'Holidays spent with . . . relations in Co: Antrim . . . bred in me, an abiding dislike of the Orange Order and all its works and ways . . . in reaction against the Unionist atmosphere in which I was then plunged'.

The politics of Ireland, particularly Gladstone's home rule policy, was the trigger for a wider interest in politics for members of all parties. At the Liberal Cecil Cochrane's school, 'Home rule for Ireland was a burning question at the time and the senior boys were keenly interested & sharply divided over it'. The experiences of John Sinclair, while serving in Ireland with his regiment, of 'Bitterness and violence, usually so friendly [*sic*], inevitably aroused doubts on English management of Irish politics'. Charles Buxton became interested in the controversy on Irish home rule as early as 1885 at the age of ten: 'I was then a Unionist', but he subsequently became a Liberal, then Labour. For Alexander Boulton, 'the Irish Home rule question led me to support the Liberal Party', his upbringing in Canada having made him a 'firm believer in Home Rule for all parts of the Empire'. Robert Wallace was 'a great admirer of Mr Gladstone & his Irish Policy & that largely shaped my political career'.

Leonard Darwin, by contrast, became a Liberal Unionist because events in Ireland 'led me to believe that in many cases the conversions to Home Rule taking place . . . were surrenders to crime'. Both Ernest Jardine and Lancelot Sanderson became Liberal Unionists because they opposed home rule. James Clyde, a Conservative, 'was shocked by the aims and methods of the Irish agitation, & by Gladstone's attitude towards it'. John Randles had been 'brought up in the Liberal tradition, but the Home Rule question made me into a Unionist and Conservative'. For J.A.R. Marriott,

living in Cheshire I was alarmed by the Fenian attack on Chester; and was glad when the 'Manchester Martyrs' were hanged. Then our Vicar, an ardent Orangeman was to

[2] The 'Phoenix Park Murders' were the fatal stabbings on 6 May 1882 in Phoenix Park in Dublin of Lord Frederick Cavendish, newly appointed chief secretary of Ireland and married to Gladstone's niece by marriage, and Thomas Burke, permanent undersecretary and most senior Irish civil servant. The assassination was carried out by members of the 'Irish National Invincibles' and was strongly condemned by Parnell.

preach against the disestablishment of the Irish church; and, at the age of seven I signed a petition against the (as I then thought) iniquitous act passed by Gladstone who was in my home always regarded as a 'Jesuit'.

Respondents from all parties claimed to be at least partly motivated by a sense of public duty or the desire to be of public service, also often cited as the reason for wanting to become a member of parliament. The Liberal Freeman Freeman-Thomas succeeded 'at the age of 2 years old' to his father's estate, growing up 'in the possession of a certain income whc. made it unnecessary to earn my living & led me to look forward to political life in Parliament as the natural purpose of one in my position if he wanted to engage in public service'. Similarly, the Conservative earl of Dalkeith (duke of Buccleuch) 'stood from a sense of duty and because he considered the policy of his party to be the correct one for the welfare of the State'. Thomas Hare 'took no interest in politics (qua politics)' but when asked to stand for the house of commons by his friends, did so 'from a sense of duty'. Thomas Ashton was 'Brought up in political atmosphere of Manchester School and duty of public service' and Thomas Bethell felt 'it was the duty of every person to take an interest in National Affairs'. Theodore Taylor cited 'The influence of my father and the study of history. My sympathy early excited for the "bottom dog" of the community'. Herbert Samuel's experiences of the 'abominable conditions in East London . . . convinced me that Social Reform was by far the most important of all questions'. The Irish Nationalist Robert Ambrose, a medical practitioner, 'always had a feeling that it was my duty – as that of everybody else – to help my fellow beings in any way I could'.

   Most of the Labour and Lib–Lab intakes of 1906 and 1910 came from very different social backgrounds from their parliamentary contemporaries but were similarly inspired by a desire to improve the welfare of their fellows, often as a result of their own experiences of social conditions. George Barnes, a trade union official of the 1906 intake, was influenced early in his working life by 'Seeing poverty & plenty in my native place – Dundee'. J.R. Clynes, another trade union official of the 1906 intake, was influenced 'in early manhood' by 'industrial conditions and factory life to regard politics as a means for improvement'. The teacher Frank Goldstone became interested in 'The hope of securing better educational & social conditions for the less fortunate members of the community'. According to his brother, Keir Hardie:

> recognised that the Parliamentary machinery as manipulated by Tories & Liberals gave little or no practical results so far as the wellbeing of the working people was concerned. . . . the Social & Industrial injustice which condemned the toiling masses to perpetual anxiety – often to privation & suffering – while giving lavishly to those who perform no useful service for the common wellbeing – directed his thoughts.

John Hodge, a metal worker of the 1910 vintage, had seen the 'dominating & unfair treatment of workmen by their employers' and Ben Tillett, the dockers' champion, had seen 'bad accomodation [*sic*] & bad payment of seamen, lack of safety measures & sailing ship equipment'.

   Religion, especially nonconformism, and temperance both exercised strong political influences, often in tandem and particularly among Liberals. Although the answers to Q4 about religious convictions suggested that the impact of religion was declining, it could still have a strong effect at an impressionable stage in people's lives. Evan Hayward experienced 'the daily conversations of a liberal nonconformist – temperance family – reinforced by associations at the little congregational church; and accentuated by conflict with the "church and tory" lads in a very small country town where the dividing lines between "liberal and tory" and "church and chapel" are very sharply defined'. Edgar Jones was driven by 'the intense feeling amongst Welsh people against a privileged Church, Schools, and against the devastation of Intemperance in the homes of the mining population'. Arthur Marshall's father was 'a strong Liberal non-conformist – a Liberal Methodist Church Minister – living always in West Riding industrial towns – constantly discussing housing & wage problems – and temperance questions'. Sidney Robinson's interest grew out of the temperance movement while Nathaniel Micklem and John Lloyd Morgan had both attended nonconformist schools. The Lib–Lab Arthur Richardson's 'political interest and activity naturally grew out of my strong non-conformist convictions'.

Experiences at school or university, particularly debating societies but also individual teachers, influenced some. When Allan Bright was at Harrow, he became 'a strong Radical . . . intensely disliking the Imperialism of Lord Beaconsfield'. Percy Harris was inspired first by masters 'with Liberal sympathies', also at Harrow, and afterwards at university. Hubert Carr-Gomm 'First became interested by taking part in House Debating Society debates at Eton'. Anderson Montague-Barlow was initially influenced in childhood through his father's involvement in local government but then became involved in debates at both school and university. Raymond Greene's father was a member of parliament but his interest was first stimulated by a lecturer on political economy at Oxford, L.R. Phelps. Percy Alden's views were formed by his 'knowledge of Thomas Hill Green', professor of moral philosophy at Oxford. The historian George Gooch became interested in politics 'during the Salisbury Parliament, 1886–92. My parents were strong Unionists & Imperialists. I had no party feelings or affiliations till I went to Trinity College Cambridge in 1891, when I realised that I was Liberal'.

Those whose interest in politics was first aroused in adult life tended to have been influenced by external events or specific policies or politicians, particularly Gladstone. Charles Mallet's interest 'began in admiration for Mr Gladstone, in the days of the first Midlothian campaign & that feeling – that no British statesman can compare with him – remains unaltered now'. Similarly, Arthur Wills met Gladstone in the house of commons and 'some words he said to me (and others) then had a powerful effect on me'. Joseph Chamberlain and his tariff reform campaign also had a significant impact and attracted both Lord Duncannon (later earl of Bessborough) and Henry Croft to politics. The Conservative George Terrell was in his 40s in 1908 when he heard Chamberlain make his 'Big Loaf and Little Loaf' speech in favour of tariff reform and 'became enthused in the subject'. Max Aitken (Lord Beaverbrook) 'became interested in national politics on account of the Chamberlain policy' and the 'Contemplation of Imperial relationships'. William Mitchell-Thomson's consciousness was first aroused by the Jameson Raid in South Africa in 1895–6 but later (in 1903), after a business career, 'Mr Chamberlain's crusade stirred my imagination' and he became 'a strong crusader for Tariff Reform'.

The interest of the Liberal Norman Lamont was first aroused in his mid 20s when he heard A.J. Balfour (then newly reappointed as Conservative leader of the house of commons) speak in Glasgow in November 1895: 'as he proceeded, I felt myself more & more strongly in disagreement with him'. The Conservative John Norton-Griffiths' interest was aroused in 1908–9 in his late 30s on his return from 'many years' travels in Africa and Canada' when he was 'so impressed with the vast possibilities awaiting a closer Imperial Federation and disgusted with the then prevalent "little England" policy'. Carlyon Bellairs, first elected as a Liberal but who later joined the Conservatives, found that living overseas brought an early interest in politics and at the age of nine wrote to his father to tell him that he would 'join the artillery from there I will try and become a member of Parliament'. The Liberal Percy Molteno had been brought up in South Africa where his father was prime minister of the Cape of Good Hope. 'The Home Government was interfering unwisely in South Africa, causing wars and ferment among the Native Populations. Thus I heard much of these great questions.' The Conservative Richard Cooper 'was engaged . . . in manufacturing steel goods in America and importing them into Britain at lower prices than the cost of production in Britain', despite paying much higher wages in America. 'I realised that the outlook for British Industry and the British Working man over a period was a bad one.'

3. Why did you Want to be an MP?

Whatever the nature and origins of their interest in politics, a surprisingly high proportion of the 247 respondents to Q6 ('Why did you want to be an M.P.?') claimed that they had not initially planned to become a member of parliament and often said that there was an element of chance in their doing so. Forty-two (17%) from all parties said that they had not wanted or actively sought it although their replies often suggested a significant prior interest in politics or public affairs and some were party activists. They were often persuaded by others (or so they said) to stand, sometimes in the interests of their party or in an attempt to keep others out. The Irish Nationalists seem to have been particularly open to such persuasion, although that may have been a result of the faction-ridden nature of nationalist politics at the time. Robert Ambrose (a medical practitioner) said he never wanted to be an MP but 'was persuaded by my late colleagues to join them in Parliament'. The barrister John Campbell's friends suggested it while William Duffy was selected in his absence as candidate for South Galway. He 'occupied a humble position – a shopkeeper in my native town. I felt I was unworthy & unequal to the great responsibility . . . & the delegates must have felt that I would fill the position & perform the duties of an MP to their satisfaction'. Denis Cogan 'never looked forward to it, but when my friends and admirers called upon me to stand as a representative of the principles which I and they had always held and worked for I responded with some reluctance to their wishes'.

Both Conservatives and Liberals sometimes claimed to be motivated by a desire to keep the other side out. The Irish Conservative Edward Archdale 'Stood in consequence of repeated requests to keep out undesirables' while Thomas Calley stood 'From a strong sense of duty, to save the local constituency from the Liberals'. Viscount Dalrymple (later earl of Stair) stood 'because I was asked to do so, & thought correctly that I could prevent somebody I considered most undesirable & a stranger representing my home county'. Daniel Dixon 'only stood to save a most important seat which was in grave danger'. The Liberal Julius Bertram 'wanted to divert the Tories from retaining a nearby constituency (E Herts) where they had only a majority of 40'.

Both Liberals and Conservatives had their share of (allegedly) reluctant members. The Liberal William Barton 'Never specially wanted, as a party official I was put in the way and just went on'. Francis Neilson's 'friends connected with the movement for the taxation of land values urged me to fight a constituency'. The Conservative Sir Aylmer Hunter-Weston, a long-serving professional soldier, 'never desired to be a Member of Parliament' but while serving in France during the First World War was eventually persuaded 'to represent my ain folk in Parliament' although 'during the War my whole thoughts and energy must be devoted to beating the Boche'. George Courthope had 'wanted to be a soldier, but yielded to family tradition that, as an eldest son, I must qualify to become a useful country squire'. Thomas Nussey was another thwarted soldier who 'thought as a second best I would go into the House'.

Their financial circumstances understandably meant that some Labour and Lib–Lab members initially lacked any ambition to enter parliament. J.R. Clynes 'attached great importance to the Trade Union work which then I was doing in the Lancashire District. I was pressed to stand for Parliament by friends in Manchester Division'. George Lansbury admitted characteristically that:

> I <u>never</u> had more than a passing thought about becoming anything – M.P. Guardian Councillor, I just fell into it. . . . I try to do any job that comes my way but have never consciously schemed or intrigued to get a position but I have always liked to try & leave there is no merit in this. . . . Service called me to politics as a child & has kept me there ever since.

John Hancock and James Parker both claimed that they had never wanted to be MPs.

Those with explicit parliamentary ambitions had a variety of motives but expressed relatively little of the ambition often held to drive politicians. When an active interest in politics often ran so strongly in families, it is not surprising that 25 (10%), both Conservatives and Liberals, said they were influenced wholly or mainly by family tradition. They included two Peases (Alfred and Joseph) from north-east England as well as members of the landed aristocracy such as Ben Bathurst, George Stanley and Richard Cavendish who 'thought anyone who was in a position to go into Parliament should do so'. For Lord Ronaldshay (the marquess of Zetland), 'It had always been understood in my family that as the heir to large landed estates a period of public service, preferably in the House of Commons, was the proper training to pursue'. For Lord Duncannon, 'Public life was still at that time accepted as the normal career for the eldest son of a peer' and for Frederick Guest, 'After ten years of soldiering, travelling and racing I thought it time to become a serious citizen – all my family had been politicians'. Edward Wood 'supposed I had to do something – & my father had always assumed that I shd. go into Parliament'.

The answers to Q7 ('What or who first led you to think of it as a career?') likewise confirmed the importance of family tradition in determining parliamentary careers. Just over a fifth (22%) of the 182 respondents were from political dynasties and/or had members of parliament in their immediate families, while 13% had friends or colleagues who were present or former members of parliament. Lord Cranborne 'knew as I was an eldest son that I must ultimately be in Parliament, so I might as well begin at once' while Ben Bathurst cited 'Family tradition and the desire to render some service to the party and neighbours . . . I had no aspirations to parliamentary fame, but as a regular attender at the House and reliable supporter of the party, I hope I did my duty'. Sir George Sitwell referred to 'Traditions of class and family' and Harry Verney 'knew that every male owner of my home, since the time of Queen Elizabeth, had been in the House of Commons, and always on the progressive side'.

Others followed in their fathers' footsteps or were encouraged by their parents. William Rees Davies expressed 'A desire to perpetuate the family tradition' but as a barrister 'was probably tinged with professional ambition!' When Herbert Jessel's father died in 1896, 'the question [was] which member of the family should succeed him. My eldest brother declined as he said he preferred spending his money on shooting pheasants and so the Executive of South St Pancras selected me'. George Lane-Fox attributed his ambition to 'Family tradition – & a desire to live usefully'. Francis Mildmay said simply: 'A traditional ambition in my family'. Ernest Morrison-Bell did not think of becoming an MP 'but my father (who payed [sic] expenses) was very keen that all his sons, who could be persuaded to, should fight on the T.R. [tariff reform] platform'. For Robert Williams, 'The fact that my father, grandfather and great-grandfather were all in Parliament made me willing to accept the offer of the constituency when it came to me'.

Parental influence could also be reinforced by the desire, particularly among those of independent means, to be of public service. Philip Sassoon wanted to be an MP 'Partly to fill my father's place, partly to provide myself with an occupation which I hoped might be of public service, and partly because I was genuinely interested in politics'. Herbert Samuel had 'inherited an independent income, a life spent in public affairs appealed to me as best, and one for which I might be able to adapt myself. It would also furnish some justification for the receipt of an unearned income'. Charles Trevelyan 'was more interested in politics than anything. I was not forced to earn my living unfortunately. It was easy for my father's son to get a good constituency'. James Hope (Lord Rankeillour) 'thought sharing in the government of the country was the best earthly career for a man not obliged to work'. Plunket Barton was 'impelled by family tradition and atmosphere, by the example of certain ancestors and relatives, and by a desire to be and to do something worthy of them'. Hugh Law's background was unusual for his party in that he was an affluent Irish Nationalist and originally a protestant but he was also the son of a member of parliament and had developed a strong desire to further the nationalist cause. He added:

> having no profession or occupation at that time, I was bored; because, having then an independent income of some £1,500 a year . . . and some interest in public affairs, I thought it my duty to do what I could for my country & people, the more so since few Irishmen of my class and religious affiliation were willing to throw themselves into the National movement; . . . and finally and chiefly, <u>because I was a very ignorant and foolish young man.</u>

Sixty-seven respondents to the question (27%) from all parties declared that they wanted to go into parliament because they were driven by what Arthur Marshall called a 'General disposition to assist in social reform'. Some, like Thomas Agar-Robartes and Sir Aylmer Hunter-Weston, sought primarily to further the interests of their constituents, but there was a more general desire, particularly but not exclusively among those on the left, to help the cause of the poor or to promote the welfare of the people. As the Liberal George Marks put it, 'I wanted to be an M.P. as my home life had led me to feel that was the highest position where interest in and for others could be developed through Parliament that would uplift and improve the conditions of the people'. Edgar Jones sought 'To reform the social conditions and particularly the horrors of intemperance in those days'.

The Conservative William Adam wanted 'To have greater and better opportunities to help others' and Edward Moon 'hoped to make myself useful'. Sir George Sitwell thought 'It seemed the best chance of public usefulness'. Arthur Black, Robert Brassey, Henry George Chancellor and Charles Carew all saw it as a duty and 'as a way of being of some use' while Edward Strauss saw it as 'an opportunity of agreeable public service'. Archibald Weigall mitigated 'The usual selfish motive of exercising some power and patronage' with 'the mild hope that one might be able to put something back into the public pot'. The Liberal Alfred Hutton wanted 'To put the world right' and Wilfred Lawson 'To try to be useful congenially'. For Labour, George Barnes wanted 'To help the cause of the poor', John Hodge 'To help my fellow workmen' and Keir Hardie 'felt that Parliament provided a platform from which the needs & wishes of the Common people could be most widely made known'.

Many, particularly Liberals, sought to further a range of causes, often summarised as 'reforms'. Edward Hemmerde wanted to 'give practical assistance in securing the reforms in which I believed' while C.P. Scott thought that 'Parliament was the best place for people who wanted to influence the public mind and push reforms'. Percy Molteno sought:

> To extend liberty, remove abuses, provide for progress. Re-people English and Scottish land with men who lead a wholesome life on the land. Extend Self-Government to the Dominions and stop rash and ignorant interference in their affairs from afar. Preserve their liberties by the automatic safeguard of Self-Government. Above all secure the reign of peace.

Thomas Shaw 'thought it wd. be first rate to fight publicly for what was right, & to show up all kinds of humbug & insincerity' but added: 'My mother (a widow & my only adviser) had deep sympathies with the ordinary well-doing working people, & the state of the miners in the nearby coal pits'. Richard Winfrey sought to carry out 'those reforms I believed so necessary and, specially, to give the Agricultural Labourer access to the land'.

Not surprisingly at the end of a prolonged period of agricultural depression, the Conservatives Harry Hope, John Starkey, Harry Verney and George Ormsby-Gore, who represented rural seats, wanted to 'revivify agriculture' as well as improve village life and rural conditions. Labour's William Brace, as a miner, wanted 'to serve the miners cause' and Ben Tillett had 'found no legislative protection for the lives of dockworkers'. Max

Aitken said simply 'Protection', an interest shared by others who supported Joseph Chamberlain's tariff reform campaign. On the other side of that particular argument, George Gooch described his 'increasing dislike of . . . Imperialism, embodied in Chamberlain, Rhodes, Milner, Kipling' although he 'never thought of Parliament till the South African War, which stirred me to the depths'. Arnold Herbert found that 'The attack on Free Trade made me wish to become an M.P.'. The politics of Ireland also encouraged some to go into parliament, including both supporters of Gladstone's home rule policy such as Charles Mallet and opponents such as Thomas Barclay and J.A.R. Marriott. Those of the Irish Nationalists who did not share Patrick Kennedy's desire 'to see more of the big world' were primarily concerned, like Daniel O'Leary, 'to take an active and prominent part in the Home Rule movement for Ireland' and, like Michael Flavin, 'To fight for & free Ireland on the floor of the House of Commons' as well as to 'improve the political and material conditions of my countrymen' (John Hackett).

A handful of respondents such as the Liberal Eliot Crawshay-Williams (whose 'heart was in politics') saw parliament as a natural extension of their interest in politics. For the Lib–Lab Arthur Richardson, 'Accepting an invitation to contest a Parliamentary Division seemed to rise naturally out of my political activities'. Some shared Wedgwood's romantic attachment to parliament. Christopher Addison 'loved it from afar; and wanted to be in it' as well as being interested in 'the great things that could be done for the health of the people and were not being touched at all at that time'. Carlyon Bellairs 'had a superstitious reverence for Parliament & great orators', although by the time he was 60 years old, 'I had lost it all for the moral cowardice of elected representatives appalled me'. Hastings Lees-Smith 'thought it was the finest & most interesting life' and for Robert Munro, 'the adventure of it appealed to one's imagination'.

Going into parliament often followed involvement in local government or other public activities. The Liberal Percy Alden became involved in local authorities 'to reshape the environment of the working classes' which led to his standing for parliament although 'there is for the average man perhaps a more useful part to play on the local authority but . . . any sincere politician who is in Parliament has a real chance, if he takes the trouble, to influence the life of the community'. Arthur Black and Frederick Chance had both served on their local county councils while Willoughby Dickinson moved from involvement in local politics in Wandsworth in south London to membership of the London County Council and then 'became anxious to become a member of the House of Commons myself'.

Some admitted to simple ambition. Harry Brodie 'had the sort of ambitious vanity of some young people . . . I wanted to make a name for myself – and I did not realize the difficulties or my own limitations'. For Felix Cassel, 'it was largely because I was foolish enough then to hope that I might acquire distinction in the House'. Lord Robert Cecil attributed his desire to go into parliament to 'Ambition, I suppose & interest in public affairs' as did James Fortescue-Flannery and Walford Green. Reginald McKenna 'had many enthusiasms, and in my younger days no little ambition'. Several lawyers, particularly Scots, saw the possibility of professional advancement. For James Clyde, 'Parliament is a possible door to the attainment of the highest professional ambition' and for Graham Murray 'It provided the way to the highest posts in my profession'. William Rees Davies' desire to perpetuate his family tradition 'was probably also tinged with professional ambition!' while the Unionist William Moore stated baldly: 'To help me to promotion at the Irish Bar'.

Forty respondents (22%) did not think of the house of commons as a career, although 'career' was often seen primarily in terms of holding ministerial office. The majority had not served in government and some had no such ambitions but gave no opinions about colleagues who aspired to or had held ministerial office. There was a distinction between those who entered the house of commons relatively young, probably with independent means and possibly with ministerial ambitions, and those who were first elected later in life. Thomas Barclay served only between the two elections in 1910 and said that in 1886 he would have been 'young enough to think of Parliament as a career: In 1910 I was too old to be anything but a backbencher'. For Harry Hope, 'To serve the interests of agriculture and advance the welfare of our rural population was my only object in entering Parliament – there was never any ambition for office'. Cecil Cochrane 'never regarded membership of the House as a career to the exclusion of my other interests'. For Clarence Smith, 'It was not my career. I was obliged to earn my living, and could not, probably, have done so in politics'. George Lansbury 'never thought of it as a career except for the short periods I was in office. . . . There is no place in a true democracy for careerists', although he did not say what he meant by 'careerists'.

The dislike of 'careerists' was shared by Carlyon Bellairs who looked upon them 'with suspicion': 'Parliament should be a great opportunity for service & not careers'. Allan Bright always had 'the greatest distaste for professional politics and professional politicians' and Henry Bowles 'never regarded being a Member of Parliament as a career, now M.P's are paid Civil Servants it may be different'. For lawyers such as Graham Murray it was never more than 'a subsidiary career' and for trade unionists such as David Shackleton it was 'an addition to my Trade Union work'. Arthur Wills 'did not think so much of having a political "career", as serving a particular cause. My financial circumstances did not warrant my standing for Parliament, and I should have had to content myself with other forms of service, had not my father suggested this, and promised to find the money'. Percy Alden 'never thought of it as a career but only as part of my life as a social reformer'. For Will Thorne, 'having to start work at six years of age . . . I wanted future generations of the working class to enjoy a fuller & happy life'.

Personal influences could initiate parliamentary careers. Thirty-six respondents (20%) mentioned individuals who had encouraged them to stand for parliament, often senior party figures including W.E. Gladstone and his son Herbert (Liberal chief whip from 1899 to 1906), Winston Churchill, Bonar Law, Sir Henry Fowler, Sir Henry Campbell-Bannerman and Keir Hardie as well as friends already in parliament. Such influences could arise directly from political or professional connections: Wilfrid Ashley, for example, was Sir Henry Campbell-Bannerman's private secretary and Percy Harris 'was approached by Mr Herbert Gladstone in 1904 particularly because of my association with New Zealand'. John Norton-Griffiths was persuaded by Mr Dudley Docker, a well-known Birmingham industrialist, 'who was anxious to have Wednesbury represented by someone who could further its material interests, both in the House of Commons and elsewhere'.

There were several claims to have been approached by sitting members or constituency associations. Henry Montgomery mentioned a former member, W.S. Caine, and Robert Munro referred to John Gulland, although in neither case was there a direct constituency link. The Irish Nationalist Michael Joyce was proposed to John Redmond after Michael Davitt heard him speak at a public meeting, and Vincent Kennedy was told by his predecessor, Tom McGovern, that 'he would like me to succeed him about 1900'. Other connections were social: for Archibald Weigall, 'The late Lord Chaplin, who was a great friend in social and sporting life, imbued me', while Wedgwood attributed his parliamentary career to a suggestion by Hilda Runciman, wife of Walter and a close family friend, when he and his wife were on their way back from South Africa in 1904. Occasionally, straightforward nepotism openly played a part and may well have contributed to other careers without being specifically acknowledged. Henry Wyndham-Quin said that 'The late Earl of Dunraven, whose heir I was, desired me to stand for South Glamorgan and paid all the expenses of my election'. Lord Ninian Crichton-Stuart's widow said that 'The idea came largely from his guardian Lord Fitzalan of Derwent then a Whip in the House of Commons as Lord Edmund Talbot'.

4. *Other Influences: Books*

Whatever the initial sources of their interest in politics and in a parliamentary career, other influences could affect individuals' views. A few respondents to the first two questions, mainly Labour members, specifically attributed their interest in politics to their reading. In 1880, the Irish Nationalist William Duffy 'purchased a book "Speeches from the dock" . . . [which] fired my young mind with intense hatred of England'. Other books 'fed my young mind with Historical feeling which forced me into Political life'. In his early 20s, Labour's James Parker discovered Fabian Society pamphlets that were being read 'by numbers of studious working men' and for ten years he 'read two serious works weekly'. Albert Smith's interest was aroused in 1896 'after reading Blatchford's Merrie England' while Will Thorne was first inspired by 'Hyndman's "Historical Basis of Socialism"' as well as by works by Marx and Engels. George Wardle's attention 'was called to "The Clarion" edited by Robert Blatchford' and he then joined the Independent Labour Party.

Books did not otherwise have as significant an effect as Wedgwood's third question ('What books formed your political views?') implied that he expected. His apparent assumption that his colleagues' political views had, like his own, been influenced by their reading may have owed something to a 1906 survey which asked newly elected Labour members to name the books and authors that had most deeply affected them.[3] The responses from members of all parties provided mixed evidence of the impact of books. Only just over half the respondents (189) answered the question. Of those, 15 answered 'Nil' or 'None' and one-third, mainly Conservatives, explained the lack of influence of books. The Liberal Walter Runciman thought that 'Books written by politicians are rubbish' and the Conservative Henry Bowles claimed that he inherited his political views 'and I have tried to keep my party on the Main Line and not side tract [sic]'. Algernon Borthwick, among others, 'thought things out for himself' while Henry Gooch's political views 'resulted somewhat naturally from my general outlook'. William du Pre 'was born "a little Conservative", & I cannot remember any book of Political Economy etc which

---

[3] Published in *Review of Reviews*, xxxiii (1906).

modified or seriously affected my views'. Felix Cassel's political views 'were not formed from books but from conversation, speeches, newspapers and observation' and Wilfrid Ashley said 'Not books but daily papers'. The Liberal Colin Coote found it 'difficult to attribute influence to books, when in fact the main influence was personal conversations' although he also claimed to have been influenced by 'J.S. Mill, Bagehot and John Morley'. John Lloyd Morgan formed his views 'from what Liberalism had done for the people in the course of its history'.

Many respondents were widely read but, like Harry Brodie who had been 'an avid reader from the age of 8', could not identify specific books that had influenced them. The Liberal Arnold Herbert's views were formed 'by my general education & reading which of course included Bentham, Mill, Adam Smith & the like'. George Leveson-Gower 'read widely both before, during and after my time at Oxford, in History, Philosophy and Economics; all this confirmed me in the breadth of view which, I take it, is the essence of Liberalism'. George Lansbury, although clearly a voracious reader, could identify 'No particular book but general reading of simple history & experience of life plus a dose of political economy'. The Scottish Conservative James Clyde 'read a great deal of orthodox political economy' but 'Books only helped me by making me critical' and Jack Seely found that 'the books I read cancelled each other. I always disagreed with the political views advocated'.

Of those who said they were influenced by their reading, many mentioned authors rather than specific works. The books often fell into the general category of what was then termed 'political economy'; some acknowledged that their choices probably reflected their innate prejudices as well as cultural influences and the books available to them. The Conservative Robert Sanders found that when he studied the standard political economists in any depth he found that 'they were very often wrong'. The Liberal Arthur Wills found, by contrast, that 'all great books, especially histories, seemed to me where they touched politics, to support Liberal theory and practice. At Trinity college, writers such as Adam Smith, J.S. Mill, and John Morley added philosophical grounds for these views'.

The more intellectually inclined tended to have been influenced by a wider range of authors or books. Lloyd George listed 'Carlyle, Victor Hugo, Ruskin, Fabian Essays, Kidd's Social Evolution, Macaulay' but without attempting to choose between them. Daniel Turner Holmes similarly listed Burns, Ruskin, Carlyle, Mill and Macaulay. The historian J.A.R. Marriott was the only person to mention de Fonblanque's *How We are Governed*; he was one of two who mentioned Dicey (in his case the *Law of the Constitution*) and one of three to include Bagehot's *English Constitution*. Others to whom there were occasional references included William Lecky, Sir Henry Maine and John Seeley. Leo Amery specifically attributed his interest in 'the closer union of the British Empire' to Seeley's *Expansion of England*.

John Stuart Mill was the single most frequent choice of author, mentioned by 24 respondents, mainly Liberal supporters of free trade or Labour but also four Conservatives. Carlyle, particularly his *French Revolution*, was cited by 15 respondents, all Liberals, and Ruskin by 11, all from the left, while Adam Smith attracted ten supporters, including two Conservatives. There were only six references to Edmund Burke and eight to John Morley, including two to his life of Gladstone, but biographies and memoirs of politicians were often mentioned in general terms. Daniel Dixon read 'Books dealing with the lives of great men, such as Napoleon, Bismarck etc.' while John Gilmour included Moneypenny and Buckle's *Life of Disraeli* and Percy Molteno cited John Morley's *Lives of Cobden and Gladstone*. Novels, novelists and poetry were mentioned by a surprisingly large number of respondents from all parties, usually in conjunction with other writers. The choices included Victor Hugo, Charles Dickens, Benjamin Disraeli, Mrs Gaskell, Walter Scott and Tolstoy among novelists and Burns and Yeats among poets.

Wedgwood's choices of 'Macaulay: "Looking Backwards" till 1905; Henry George thenceforward' were shared by others. Henry George inspired Wedgwood in his passionate advocacy of a land tax and he, or one of his works, was mentioned by 18 respondents, all Liberals, Labour or Lib–Lab, with four specific references to *Progress and Poverty* and one (by Albert Spicer) to *Our Land and Land Policy*. Macaulay was identified by 13 respondents from all parties, although the Conservative Arthur Brookfield was impressed by Macaulay's style but found that 'if he informed my views in any way it was certainly not in the direction he would have desired'. Lord Hugh and Lord Robert Cecil both admired Macaulay and Anderson Montague-Barlow found his essays '(at school) a great stimulus'. Alfred Hopkinson and the Liberal Christopher Addison mentioned Macaulay's *History* while for George Gooch 'The Whig presentation of English history by Hallam & Macaulay left a much deeper mark' (than Carlyle's *Gospel of the Superman*) and he had also been influenced as a boy by 'Burke's Reflections on the French Revolution & Mill on Liberty'. Carlyon Bellairs, first elected as a Liberal but who later became a Conservative, remarked that Macaulay's '"Looking Backwards" made me a Socialist, Seeley's "Expansion of England" made me a Conservative and Walter Bagehot's books made me a Liberal. Experiences of the book of life made me a Fascist'.[4]

Some Irish Nationalists were strongly influenced by their reading, particularly of Irish history. John Campbell's list of Irish authors included 'Banini, Carleton, A.M.M. Sullivan, Kirkham etc' while Denis Cogan mentioned the writings of Isaac Butt, Michael Davitt and Henry Grattan. Of the 14 who answered the question, however, one (the medical practitioner Robert Ambrose) said that no particular book influenced his views, while John Boland and D.D. Sheehan dismissed books as 'unnecessary' and John Cullinan's 'political views were in the nature of an article of faith' although the writings of the group known as the 'Young Irelanders' had some impact. He had nevertheless learned 'the tragic story of my country' through 'Mitchel's "History of Ireland"', also cited by Denis Cogan. Mitchel's *Jail Journal* was cited by Michael Flavin and John Hayden; Hayden also mentioned A.M. Sullivan's *Young Ireland* as did John Hackett and Hugh Law. Despite his English education, Law said he was much influenced by Irish literature, including poetry, as well as Irish history.

5. *Other Influences: Religion*

A few respondents specifically mentioned the influence of religious works. Labour's John Hancock's 'Parents were very poor, family was large, had very few books and they were

---

[4] Taken together, the responses were a distinct contrast to the findings of the 1906 survey of Labour members where the most commonly cited authors were Ruskin (17), Dickens (16), the Bible (14), Carlyle (13), Henry George (12), Walter Scott (11), John Stuart Mill (10) and Shakespeare (9). See Jonathan Rose, *The Intellectual Life of the British Working Classes* (2001), 41–2.

all of a religious character'. Keir Hardie mentioned the New Testament while Samuel Montagu's 'Hebrew Bible and Rabbinical Studies quickened the spiritual sense and the emotional sympathy which characterised him'. Thomas Shaw as a boy read mainly religious books '& owed much to the concentrated thought and imagery of Bunyan'. The 268 answers to the fourth question ('What were your religious convictions?') also showed that the overwhelming majority (over 90%) outwardly adhered to some form of religious belief, mainly christian, although one or two were reluctant to reveal what they considered to be an essentially personal matter. George Leveson-Gower said: 'This is immaterial and, I think, an improper question to ask. Shall I answer "The religion of all sensible men"?', and Hilton Young (Lord Kennet) asked: 'At 7? – does it matter now?' Some equivocated, Raymond Greene claiming 'The simple faith of an ignorant child' and Alfred Hopkinson 'The religion of all sensible men & "sensible men never say" but in political life people circulated reports that I was a Roman Catholic or an Atheist or Agnostic. Both untrue but I would not contradict'.

Of the respondents, 22 (8%) claimed to have no religious views or to be agnostics or, more rarely, atheists. Austin Hopkinson and Alfred Scott's religious beliefs were 'Nil' and 'None', Robert Brassey's convictions 'My own conscience', Wilfred Lawson's 'very unformed' and William Barton's 'Outwardly evangelical, inwardly agnostic'. Wedgwood described himself as 'Agnostic and puritanical, mixed'[5] and Charles Trevelyan was an unqualified agnostic. Athelstan Rendall was 'Agnostic from my teens on – earlier Unitarian upbringing' and Eliot Crawshay-Williams 'was brought up more or less conventionally Church of England; but agnosticism set in early (at Eton, or even before)'. Some retained general, if vague, christian beliefs and attached some importance to christian ethics and religious tolerance but expressed doubts that had often emerged in their teens or earlier about the strength and nature of their religious convictions. Labour's David Shackleton's beliefs were 'Not particularly orthodox' but he 'always preferred a good ethical standard', while Jack Seely declared himself to be 'Christian, [and] antidogmatic, except when organ and choir at an evening service swept me off my feet. This often happened, and prevented me from being even more wicked than I have been'.

Leo Amery was brought up 'a strict Protestant' and remained 'religious in outlook' but from the age of 11 or 12 he never regarded 'the supernatural part of Christianity as otherwise than mythology'. George Gooch was similarly 'Brought up as a church-going Anglican' but 'About the age of 17 I ceased to be orthodox' while Leonard Darwin had 'a great admiration for Christian Ethics, but I cannot believe in Christian dogma'. Both Richard Winfrey and Arthur Wills accepted christian doctrine but had no belief in 'established creeds'. Colin Coote's beliefs changed as he grew up, having been 'Originally strongly Nonconformist, but it was the fashion when I was at Rugby & Oxford to treat lightly all religious convictions . . . But I remain deeply grateful to those who insisted on study of the Bible'. Percy Harris claimed 'Broadminded Deism', while Sigismund Mendl was 'Theistic in the widest sense. I am a Jew by birth'. The Irish Conservative Plunket Barton acknowledged the element of chance in his beliefs: he was born and brought

---

[5] His niece declared in her memoir of her uncle that 'He cared deeply about the English Church' with 'a powerful, if rather undefined, faith'. C.V. Wedgwood, *Last of the Radicals*, 241. He was also drawn by temperament to elements of nonconformity, and had a lifelong and increasing aversion to Roman catholicism. Mulvey, *Political Life of Josiah C. Wedgwood*, 179.

up in the (anglican) church of Ireland but recognised 'that a man's religious sect is an accident of birth. If I had been born next door I must have been a Roman Catholic' and he and his family were traditionally strong advocates of catholic emancipation and equality.

Surprisingly few answers made direct or explicit connections between religious belief and politics or party. They revealed the importance for some of the distinctions between shades of protestantism, from the high church (anglo-catholic or tractarian) end of the church of England through its evangelical wing to those like Arthur Richardson who was, according to his children, 'a very strongly confirmed Non-conformist of the Primitive Methodist Church'. Some defined the church to which they belonged in a detail that implied its significance to them. The Liberal Richard Holt was a 'Protestant Dissenter from Church of England commonly called Unitarian' and the Conservative Arthur Marshall a 'Nonconformist Liberal (Methodist) – not Wesleyan but Methodist New Conversion'. Two of the founding fathers of the Labour Party, Keir Hardie and George Lansbury, were influenced by strongly held, if generalised, christian beliefs. Keir Hardie's religious convictions were said by his brother to be 'the simple teachings of Christ apart from latter day dogma on theological pronouncements. These gave him the inspiration which carried him on all his activities'. George Lansbury hoped he was 'a Christian with a big "C" broad tolerant & at the same time firm & clear in my belief in God as upholder of the universe & Father of us all & Jesus as his son in a special & redemptive sense who came to teach us how to live'.

The largest religious category comprised the 95 members of the church of England (34% of respondents). Thirty-eight (14%) were unspecified christians or protestants including Ughtred Kay-Shuttleworth who described himself as 'Broad-unsectarian-Christian' and John Whitehouse who was 'Broadly Christian but anti-dogma'. There were 19 (7%) unspecified 'non-conformists' and 18% from specific types of nonconformity (presbyterian, methodist, unitarian, etc.). The 24 Roman catholics (9%) included all the 16 Irish Nationalists who answered the question, among them the convert Hugh Law who described his transition from his upbringing in 'the straitest tenets of Irish Protestantism' to becoming a Roman catholic in adult life. There were five quakers and five Jews. Some of the Jews, such as Benjamin Cohen and Samuel Montagu, were clearly more observant than others. Edwin Montagu's sister said that her brother, although not observant, was 'thoroughly Jewish in his keen sense of justice and desire to work for a better time' and 'very loyal to Judaism'.

The beliefs of the majority were relatively uncomplicated. Most members of the church of England did not qualify their beliefs, other than sometimes to state how strongly they were held or that they were low church, evangelical or high church. Lord Hugh Cecil described himself as a 'Tractarian' and Edward Wood as 'Anglo-Catholic – C of E' while Guy Wilson was 'Church of England, intensely anti-High Church & Ritualism'. Two-thirds of the 97 Conservatives who answered the question claimed to belong to the church of England or its Irish and Scottish equivalents. As Henry Bowles put it, 'I was baptised into the faith of the Church of England, which has always been good enough for me'. The Conservative nonconformists included Austen Chamberlain (unitarian), Max Aitken (presbyterian) and John Randles (methodist/wesleyan).

The 121 Liberals and Liberal Unionists who answered the question included just fewer than 30 members of the church of England, among them two converts. The

remainder confirmed the links between Liberals and nonconformism, but often emphasised their religious tolerance. Percy Alden was a 'Free Churchman' who believed in 'the
separation of the Church from the State' and in his latter years 'gradually separated myself
from all dogmas and ecclesiasticism'. Evan Hayward was 'Congregational – first by
compulsion or acquiescence and later by conviction – this being the only sect which
allows its adherents unlimited latitude of interpretation of Christian doctrine'. Francis
Channing was a 'broadminded Churchman, who advocated undenominational teaching
in schools'. By contrast, some retained strongly held beliefs: Arthur Black became a local
preacher at the age of 17 and remained one, Robert Munro 'was & am a Presbyterian'
and Theodore Taylor described himself as 'broadly but intensely evangelical in my views'.
The 15 Lib–Lab or Labour respondents demonstrated similar links between the Labour
Party and nonconformism. Only two (John Baker and John Sutton) were members of
the church of England and one (Ben Tillett) described his beliefs as 'nebulous with
Catholic tendencies'.

6. *Other Influences: Newspapers*

Like religious affiliations, to some extent the choice of newspaper followed party lines.
The 238 answers to Q5 ('What was then your favourite newspaper?') included altogether
around 20 titles, some weeklies, as well as local, Scottish and Irish titles. Lloyd George
and Arthur Marshall claimed to have read several papers, although how thoroughly or
consistently is not clear, while others explicitly sought to keep in touch with a range of
political views. The Conservative Alfred Pease 'never had favourite newspapers but
read the Daily News, Times Pall Mall Gazette, Spectator regularly'. George Lansbury had
from boyhood:

> always read Tory Liberal Radical & Socialist Press. . . . the more I think I know the
> more there is to know so I read all sides & find all newspapers one-sided unfair &
> partisan with no idea of giving the public any other view except what they are
> established to propagate & I say this of myself as an Editor.

Sir Aylmer Hunter-Weston 'liked any newspaper which gave clearly the position of
Foreign Affairs, and good information as to the state of the Country' and Leo Money
'always surveyed all shades of opinion'. Henry Gooch 'was not interested in the political
side of any newspaper . . . but the correspondence in the "Times", and the Cartoons in
"Punch" were helpful'.

The clear favourite among the papers listed was *The Times*, mentioned by 90 respondents (38%), of whom 48 were Conservatives, and the first choice of 72 (30%), well
ahead of any other paper. Some, such as the Liberal George Gooch, valued it primarily
for its news coverage while its Conservative supporters included William du Pre, who
described it as 'first, last & in the middle. Always has been', and Samuel Montagu who
'considered the Times the only really reliable newspaper, but read some popular papers
from a sense of duty rather than inclination'. Similarly, Philip Sassoon 'read many and
relied on the Times' and Alan Sykes 'Read the "Times" as a sort of daily duty'. Otherwise
Conservatives favoured the *Standard*, the *Morning Post* and *Daily Telegraph* but none in

large numbers compared with those who read *The Times*. *The Times'* readership included some detractors such as Leonard Darwin who 'felt at times that it has sinned greatly by "cooking" its news in order to affect public opinion, especially during the Great War', and William Rees Davies who mentioned 'when the Times was guilty of the faux pas over Parnell and the Pigott letter'.[6]

Liberals and others of the left often favoured the *Daily News*, precursor of the *News Chronicle* and the choice of 44 (18%) respondents, or the *Manchester Guardian* (the choice of 22 or 9%), particularly popular among those from the north of England, as was the *Leeds Mercury* among those from Yorkshire. Liberals were also strong supporters of the *Pall Mall Gazette* and later the *Westminster Gazette*, especially when edited by J.A. Spender. One or the other was mentioned by 37 respondents (15%) and for Joseph Pease, the *Westminster Gazette* under Spender's editorship 'expressed my own thoughts on current political events more accurately than in any other newspaper before or since'. Arthur Wills also thought it came 'near perfection in spirit and sense, but it lasted all too short a time'.[7]

The Scots tended, regardless of party, to choose the *Scotsman*, possibly because of lack of choice other than strictly local papers in many parts of the country. The Liberal Daniel Turner Holmes remarked on the absence of an 'influential Liberal newspaper with a wide circulation in the Lowlands of Scotland' and read the *Glasgow Herald* which he commended for 'its eminently fair reporting of public meetings'. Thomas Shaw, Robert Munro and Arthur Murray (all Liberals) read the *Scotsman*, as did the Conservative Viscount Dalrymple, and Thomas Barclay read *The Times* when in London and the *Scotsman* when in Scotland. Of the 15 Irish Nationalists who answered the question, only two did not mention the Dublin *Freeman's Journal*, sometimes in conjunction with other, more local, papers. Otherwise local papers figured relatively little, possibly because the respondents took it for granted that they would have had to read them, if only for their local news.

7. *Other Influences: Political Heroes*

Q15 about political heroes – 'Who, at that time, was your ideal living British statesman, or dead statesman of any land?' – was among the most confusingly worded; the answers were correspondingly confused. Only about half the respondents (181 or 51%) answered it; both their choices and comments showed that they mostly saw the questions as being primarily about their views of their party leaders. Many found it difficult to distinguish between living and dead heroes because the two often overlapped, particularly Gladstone. Even the historian George Gooch equated 'ideal living' with party leaders and 'dead' with heroes: 'My two chief leaders were Campbell-Bannerman, 1906–8, then Lloyd George. My chief heroes of earlier times were Gladstone and Lincoln'. Richard Winfrey

---

[6] Richard Pigott, an Irish journalist, was the forger of a series of letters purporting to be written by Charles Stewart Parnell condoning the Phoenix Park murders of May 1882. *The Times* bought Pigott's forgeries for £1,780 and published the most damning letter on 18 Apr. 1887. Parnell immediately denounced it as a forgery and was subsequently vindicated by an investigating commission. Pigott later committed suicide.

[7] The *Westminster Gazette*, a liberal paper, lasted from 1893 to 1928 when it merged with the *Liberal News*. J.A. Spender was its editor from 1896 to 1921 but the paper was at its most influential before its ownership changed in 1908.

likewise ran through most of his party leaders of his early career: 'Mr Gladstone up to 1894; then Sir Henry Campbell-Bannerman; afterwards Mr Asquith and Mr Lloyd George'.

Some could not choose because, like Willoughby Dickinson, they 'never knew any statesman, living or dead, whom I should consider to be ideal'. Alfred Pease had not been 'a worshipper of political leaders' and Leo Money 'entered Parliament in the hope of changing ideals'. Rowland Whitehead 'had read too much history to have any illusions about an "ideal" statesman' but 'regarded Mr Asquith as the soundest leader to follow'. Of those with heroes, the choices among 'living' statesmen reflected mostly, but not exclusively, party allegiances in the early stages of the respondents' political careers, but a handful chose a real hotchpotch. The Conservative Robert Brassey reeled off 'Joseph Chamberlain. Arthur Balfour. Lord Salisbury. Lord Cromer. John Redmond. Edward Carson. Cecil Rhodes'. Walter Runciman's selection included 'Sir Henry Campbell-Bannerman, Rosebery, Palmerston, Cromwell, Chamberlain, Napoleon top of the lot; excellent Mussolini, Hitler, Baldwin. I loved Arthur Balfour. He was a great man'. For George Lansbury, 'when I was young Gladstone, Mazzini, Randolph Churchill for his cheek & courage. Arthur Balfour Bonar Law & lots of others especially the old Radicals whose names I forget & the crowd of Irish Patriots & English writers like Tom Paine'.

Gladstone was the 'living' choice of 15% and mentioned in one capacity or another by a total of 81 respondents, or 45%, particularly among the older generation and mainly those from the left. Others high on the list were Joseph Chamberlain (not a party leader but the choice of 14%, mainly Conservatives) and Asquith (12.7%, almost all Liberals), with Balfour (11.6%) and Campbell-Bannerman (11%) not far behind. Lord Salisbury and Lloyd George were each the choice of 6% and Sir Edward Grey of 4%, including Wedgwood. Gladstone's position reflected both his prominence and his service in the house of commons until the mid 1890s; he would have been personally known to many of the older respondents and well known by repute to all of them. The replies showed what a heroic figure he was for both his contemporaries and subsequent generations. Alfred Pease, despite not being a worshipper of political leaders, 'had a great admiration for Gladstone & was fond of him'. For Edmund Harvey, 'Gladstone still had (& has) something of a halo about him'. Charles Mallet said simply 'Gladstone!!!' and Thomas Shaw, 'Mr Gladstone above all others'. Henry George Chancellor saw him as the 'champion of freedom' and he was admired by Irish Nationalists for his support for home rule. His Irish policies had, however, caused some to change their minds about him. Lord Wolmer (later earl of Selborne), for example, 'started with Mr Gladstone as my ideal but I lost the ideal over the Irish question' while Richard Winfrey cited 'Mr Gladstone up to 1894'.

Lloyd George likewise had both admirers and detractors among his own party. Christopher Addison admired him 'far more than anybody else because he was keen to get the sort of things done that I loved'. Edmund Bartley-Denniss was 'a strong supporter of Lloyd George during his term as Prime Minister during the war though he did not approve of him before or after'. Joseph King 'much admired D. Lloyd George' in the years 1906 to 1914 'but not after 1914'. Lloyd George himself chose Gladstone and also had 'a great admiration for Joseph Chamberlain', a choice shared by some of his fellow Liberals as well as Labour's Will Thorne, who bracketed him with Keir Hardie 'as the two greatest Democrats of that period'. Chamberlain's other admirers included his son Austen and other Conservatives, as well as Liberal Unionists, particularly for his views on protectionism. Few reasons were given for the choice of Lord Salisbury (the third marquess) by nearly 7% of Conservatives, including two of his sons. Sir Edward Carson had a handful of fervent admirers among Unionists. Sir Henry Campbell-Bannerman's admirers were mainly Liberals; he was seen by Theodore Taylor as 'the more reliable and capable leader' than Rosebery but the Irish Nationalist Hugh Law 'had a great affection & regard' for him.

Asquith attracted cross-party support as well as admirers in his own party. Among Liberals, Arthur Wills thought Asquith 'added to his more brilliant qualities, a sober judgment, a steadfastness, and a generosity which I do not think have been excelled in political history'. Like most Irish Nationalists, John Nugent's greatest admiration was for the leaders of his own party, but 'outstanding' among the others 'would have been Mr Asquith'. For D.D. Sheehan, 'in intellectual stature, deportment and fineness of character [Asquith] approached more nearly to my ideal of statesmanship than any other politician of my time' and 'towered above all others', although 'As a man of action . . . he definitely lacked strength, his handling of the Irish question being essentially weak'. For William du Pre in 1914 it was 'oddly enough Asquith, but he wasn't wholly ideal, & I happened to be opposed to his politics' and Ernest Morrison-Bell 'was opposed to [Asquith's] policy. But I admired his manner, & his way of speaking'.

The choices of 'dead' statesmen were more varied; some probably reflected the respondents' historical knowledge but few clues emerged about what were seen as 'heroic' qualities. The selection was remarkable primarily for its emphasis on 19th- and early 20th-century British politicians. Gladstone was the first choice of 48, or 31%, of respondents, followed a long way behind by Disraeli (Lord Beaconsfield), the first choice of 25 respondents, or 16%. Few chose 'foreign' statesmen and of those the most prominent was Abraham Lincoln, seen by Theodore Taylor as a 'great man' and admired by Keir Hardie for his 'broad humanitarianism [which] took shape in the emancipation of American slaves'. The Irish Nationalist Michael Joyce bracketed Lincoln with Napoleon; Lincoln was also the choice of D.D. Sheehan: 'for bigness of mind, felicity of expression, sound democratic principles, and absolute human-ness of character always had and still holds my admiration. He was of the people, possessing all their rugged strength and remaining ever faithful to them in thought and act'. Wedgwood and Charles Trevelyan both bracketed Lincoln with Cromwell while Herbert Samuel bracketed him with George Washington.

8. Other Influences: Occupations

The answers to the question (Q8) about the respondents' 'trade, profession or occupation' before entering parliament are hard to compare with later more rigorous and systematic studies of the occupational backgrounds of members of parliament of the time.[8] They covered members who sat over the whole period from 1885 to 1918, and beyond it, and the responses were impressionistic and subjective. They show the persistence of personal and aristocratic connections in politics but also the growing

[8] See, again, Guttsman, *British Political Elite*; and Michael Rush, *The Role of the Member of Parliament since 1868* (2001), especially ch. 4.

importance of those from a professional background, as Wedgwood implied in the wording of the question. The answers also convey in anecdotal form, and as statistics never could, a picture of a social world that was gradually disappearing and was to be largely wiped out by the First World War.

Some of the answers from the 277 respondents to the question (77% of the total) were imprecise or difficult to classify. The Liberal Hilton Young described himself as 'Chemist. Barrister. Journalist. Author. Businessman. Soldier Sailor tinker & Tailor', without saying which, if any, of those was his principal occupation. He was not alone in having had a varied career. Labour's James Parker 'had no trade unskilled labourer of many different occupations from riding to hounds to serving Beer from digging to journalistic work etc.'. Other answers showed that, despite the changes in the socio-economic composition of the house of commons in the late 19th and early 20th centuries, particularly in the Liberal Party, there were still a significant number of members who had not been actively engaged in an identifiable 'trade, profession or occupation' before entering parliament because they had independent means and did not need to earn.

Thirty-seven of the respondents to the question (13%, almost all Conservatives) came into that category. As Lord Ronaldshay put it, he had 'No trade or profession; occupation chiefly travelling'. Some were too young when first a candidate to have had an occupation. William Allen, Austen Chamberlain and Ughtred Kay-Shuttleworth were all still undergraduates when their political careers started. Austen Chamberlain's father offered him at the end of his student career 'the choice of law, business or politics', Ben Bathurst was only 21 when invited to stand for the 'family' seat, Francis Mildmay was 23 when first adopted as a candidate and Philip Sassoon had only just left Oxford when he entered politics. Colin Coote went straight from university to serve in the army in the First World War before being elected in 1917. Others like Lord Hugh Cecil, Viscount Lewisham (later earl of Dartmouth), William Ormsby-Gore, Sir George Sitwell and Edward Wood answered simply 'None' or 'Nil', and Wilfred Lawson had done 'Nothing definite. I had read for the Bar'.

A small group of aspiring politicians had no formal occupation but filled positions designed to prepare them for their future careers. They included the Conservatives James Hope who 'made politics my profession' and William Bridgeman who 'had no real profession apart from politics. In his very early days he was a master at Eton, and later Private Secretary to Lord Knutsford and Sir Michael Hicks Beach, the latter as a preparation for politics'. The younger Michael Hicks-Beach 'served his apprenticeship to politics as assistant private secretary to his father ... In 1904 he became private secretary to Sir Alexander Acland Hood (Chief Conservative Whip)'. Two Cecil brothers, Lord Cranborne and Lord Robert Cecil, had both acted at different times as private secretary to their father, the 3rd marquess of Salisbury. Plunket Barton's political involvement started as 'Private Secretary to the Lord Lieutenant of Ireland (Duke of Marlborough)' and to the lord chancellor of Ireland. The Liberal Hubert Carr-Gomm acted for about two years as private secretary to Winston Churchill when he was member for Oldham in 1900–6. 'After that for some time I devilled for Geake who edited the Liberal Magazine and managed the Liberal Publication Dept.'. George Leveson-Gower was Gladstone's private secretary for five years before standing for parliament. Others explicitly devoted themselves to public life: unlike his Liberal brother George, a historian with a long-standing interest in social reform, the Conservative

Henry Gooch did not follow any profession since his father had left him 'the means to devote my whole time to public life'.

George Gooch was one of a group who could loosely be described as social reformers who engaged in various forms of social or voluntary work, mostly unpaid. Gooch described his occupation as 'Historical writing, social work etc. Teaching in University Settlements, member of Executive of the Church Army etc.'. After leaving Balliol College, Oxford, the Liberal Percy Alden 'went down to East London and started a Settlement and since then I have always been engaged in social, education and philanthropic work'. Edmund Harvey was 'From 1906 Warden of Toynbee Hall, but did not draw any salary'. Edward Noel Buxton was a director of Truman's Brewery but 'was also occupied with Toynbee Hall, Evangelism, London Hospital and Territorials'. Clive Morrison-Bell was a professional soldier but when first elected 'was engaged in a very interesting job with the late Earl Roberts. I was organizing his Miniature Rifle Clubs all over England, having been lent (by arrangement with Lord Haldane) from my regiment, the Scots Guards, for this purpose'.

About 10% of respondents could be described as 'country gentlemen', including those who described themselves as landowners or farmers. Greville Verney was 'an eldest son of a landowner, who lived at home, on the ordinary elder son's allowances'. Charles Carew and Walter Carlile were typical of the 'squirearchy' in that they were both justices of the peace and involved in 'county work'. Gilbert Willoughby (Lord Willoughby de Eresby) 'had no occupation except a County Councillor and a Yeomanry Officer' while Lord Cranborne 'was an eldest son and, of course, interested in the land'. Savile Crossley admitted to 'hunting & shooting' as well as 'county work' while Rowland Hunt described himself as 'Landowner & M.F.H.' and George Lane-Fox, although called to the bar, 'never practised – was busy in County work . . . and helped my father with the Bramham Moor hounds'. Raymond Heath had likewise been called to the bar, 'but was then leading a more or less idle life as a country gentlemen of those times, hunting & shooting & J.P.'. William du Pre had been a soldier but became a 'Landowner, Squire & Magistrate' and George Lambert was a 'Yeoman'. The Liberal Norman Lamont was a 'Landlord, & West Indian Planter' and another Liberal, Leslie Renton, was a 'Retired soldier. Country gentleman'.

Of those who did admit to a 'trade, profession or occupation', 58 (21%) were lawyers. Fifty were barristers and eight solicitors, the latter including Lloyd George. Raymond Heath and George Lane-Fox were not alone, particularly among the Conservatives, in having read for the bar but never practised or only briefly. The 17 Conservative barristers included George Courthope, who was 'studying agriculture & estate management', and Granville Wheler, a 'Barrister, landowner and farmer'. Anderson Montague-Barlow, who became chairman of Sotheby's auctioneers, and the shipowner Percy Molteno, qualified for the bar before going into other occupations. When he was elected in 1915, Edmund Turton had retired from the bar and was living in the family home, 'farming 500 acres, & the director of many companies, including the Midland Bank and the Yorkshire Insurance Company, & North Eastern Railway'. The Liberal barristers were more likely to be in regular practice; they included Reginald McKenna and Scots such as Robert Munro. There were practitioners among the Conservatives including Plunket Barton, Felix Cassel, Evelyn Cecil, Lord Robert Cecil, Bertram Falle (Lord Portsea) and Charles Tyrrell Giles, the Unionist William Moore who practised at the Irish bar and Irish

Nationalists such as John Boland and John Campbell, both of whom practised at the English bar.

There were 32 respondents (12%) who gave the armed forces as their profession (all but one, Carlyon Bellairs who had served in the royal navy, were in the army), of whom 20 were Conservatives. Colin Coote, Austin Hopkinson and Sir Aylmer Hunter-Weston (a career soldier) were on active service during the First World War when first elected, and continued to serve until the end of the war. Most of the others had left the army before they became candidates, although members of the armed forces were not then disqualified from sitting in the house of commons. Their answers to the question about incomes suggests that they had mostly followed the common pattern among army officers of having private means and did not depend on their army pay. Some, such as Robert Brassey, Arthur Brookfield, William du Pre and Gilbert McMicking, retained their army connections by subsequently becoming territorials or serving in their local yeomanry.

Other professions were much more sparsely represented but included two teachers (Labour's Frank Goldstone and the Liberal Daniel Turner Holmes, for whom it was 'The least lucrative & most enjoyable of all professions' and a good preparation for public speaking), five medical practitioners (including the Irish Nationalist Robert Ambrose, Christopher Addison, first elected as a Liberal, and three Williams – William Chapple and William Collins (Liberals) and Sir William Cheyne (Conservative)), 12 journalists and/or writers, among them the Conservatives Leo Amery and Algernon Borthwick (subsequently Lord Glenesk and owner of the *Daily Telegraph*), and the Liberals Cecil Harmsworth (Lord Harmsworth) and C.P. Scott (editor of the *Manchester Guardian*) plus five academics. The academics included the historians George Gooch and J.A.R. Marriott, Joseph Larmor, Lucasian professor of mathematics at Cambridge, and Hastings Lees-Smith, vice-principal of Ruskin College, Oxford. There were also two chartered surveyors, an architect, three publishers, two accountants, four engineers and two former members of the Diplomatic Service, both Conservatives. Perhaps the most exotic was Francis Neilson who described himself as a 'Reporter, journalist, actor, playwright and producer of plays'. Before entering parliament, he had been a stage director in both New York and London as well as director of the national opera in Covent Garden.

Both major parties but more particularly the Liberals included their share of those engaged in manufacturing of some kind (24 respondents or 9%). By the end of the 19th century businessmen tended to find seats away from where their businesses were located and two of Wedgwood's respondents illustrated this trend: the shipowner Richard Holt, whose business was in Liverpool but who sat for Hexham in Northumberland; and Walter Runciman, whose shipbuilding business was in Tyneside but who sat for Dewsbury in Yorkshire.[9] The Liberal respondents also included some, particularly from the north of England, who sat for the seats where their businesses were located. The textile industries were well represented by, among others, Thomas Ashton, member first for Hyde where he was a mill owner, William Barton, a cotton textile manufacturer and shipper who sat for Oldham, Frederick Chance who sat for Carlisle and was chairman and managing director of a local firm of cotton manufacturers (as well as a director of

[9] Martin Pugh, *The Making of Modern British Politics* (3rd edn, 2002), 14.

Martin's Bank in Liverpool) and Frederick Whitley-Thomson, who sat for Skipton and was a clothing manufacturer in Halifax. Theodore Taylor also did not represent the constituency where his business (woollen cloth manufacturing) was located but 'went into my father's business at 16 and have been the head of the profit sharing business of JT & J Taylor Ld Batley for 45 years past'. Henry George Chancellor was first a 'Manufacturer's Agent, afterwards . . . Paint Manufacturer' and John Brunner was a director of the family firm of Brunner Mond, 'Alkali Manufacturers'. Thomas Howell Idris was an 'Aerated Water Manufacturer' who changed his surname to Idris in order to name himself after his product.[10] Samuel Whitbread had inherited his share of the family brewery. The three members of the quaker Pease family from Darlington who answered the question (Alfred (2nd baronet), Herbert Pike (Lord Daryngton) and Joseph (Lord Gainford)) were all engaged in one or other of the family businesses of railways, banking, coal mining and limestone quarrying. Cecil Cochrane, who sat for South Shields, was in 'The Coal and Iron Trades'.

The few Conservatives who were directly involved in manufacturing included Stuart Coats who worked for his family business of cotton manufacturers and Henry Croft who went into the family business of maltsters. Alan Sykes was a director of the family business of 'Sykes & Co., Ltd, Bleachers, established 1793'. The Conservatives were otherwise more involved than the Liberals in the financial sector, particularly banking. Thomas Salt worked for a bank in his constituency and later became chairman of Lloyds Bank, Weston Jarvis worked in his father's bank, later merged with Barclay's, and Robert Williams was a partner of Williams Deacon's Bank. George Touche had started as an accountant but also managed investment trusts. Max Aitken described his occupation as 'Banking and finance' and only later became involved in the newspaper industry. Lionel de Rothschild (a Liberal Unionist) was 'a salaried partner in N.M. Rothschild' and the Liberal Joseph Bliss was a 'Merchant Banker'.

Both Conservatives and Liberals were involved in commercial activities of various kinds including shipping, the import/export trade and retailing. The Liberal Walter Runciman had inherited his father's shipping business, while Charles Barrie had been a shipowner but later became a civil servant. Allan Bright was a 'Merchant and shipowner'. Harry Brodie went into the family business in the 'colonial trade', as an admitted second choice heavily influenced by his father. The Conservative William Mitchell-Thomson had been called to the bar but became 'Assistant Manager of a company engaged in trading, shipping and the sugar industry' in the West Indies while John Norton-Griffiths was a 'Public Works Contractor', working mainly overseas. Edward Strauss was a hop merchant and Thomas Wiles a grain merchant. The Welsh Liberal Edward Pryce Jones had inherited his father's textile business which was also 'the pioneer of shopping by post' in Wales.

Twelve of the Labour and Lib–Lab respondents to the question had originally been in manual occupations. William Brace, Keir Hardie and John Sutton had been coal miners, John Hodge a steel worker, Fred Maddison a compositor, J.H. Thomas an engine cleaner and Ben Tillett a 'sailor or docker'. George Nicholls had been a 'Farm Labourer and Navvy' and James Parker and Will Thorne general labourers. They had, however, mostly moved into trade union and sometimes other work before starting their political careers.

---

[10] Information supplied by Stephen Lees.

Keir Hardie became a miners' secretary '& later journalist & lecturer on social and economic affairs'. George Barnes was a 'Mechanical Engineer' and trade union official. George Lansbury 'started as an office boy about 10 or 11 years of age' and later went into business as well as becoming an editor and newspaper proprietor but, unlike many of his Labour contemporaries, was never a trade unionist. Arthur Richardson had started as a shop assistant but ended as a wholesale grocer. Of those who did not come from working-class backgrounds, Frank Goldstone had been a teacher, Philip Snowden a civil servant and Edward Noel Buxton a writer/journalist. Like Wedgwood (and others), Noel Buxton had originally been elected as a Liberal but lost his seat in 1918 and was re-elected for Labour in 1922.

The backgrounds of the 16 Irish Nationalist respondents were varied. John Boland, John Campbell, Stephen Gwynn and Hugh Law were all largely English-educated and attended Oxford University. Gwynn became a London-based journalist while Boland, Campbell and Law were at the London bar. D.D. Sheehan had started as a teacher, then became a journalist and studied at the English bar, although after qualifying he mainly practised at the Irish bar. John Hayden was another journalist. John Newman and Sir Walter Nugent were both landowners and Nugent had also worked in the United States in 'Banking & general Business'. Robert Ambrose was a medical practitioner, William Duffy a small shopkeeper and Michael Joyce a Shannon river pilot.

9. Other Influences: Public Work

In response to Wedgwood's Q10 – 'Had you experience of public work – if so, what?' – the majority of respondents seem to have assumed that he meant elected office of some kind. Of the 258 respondents, 84 (33%) said no, or none. Altogether, about two-thirds of the respondents had had previous experience of 'public work' of some kind, however defined, and could therefore be regarded to some extent as being prepared for life in the house of commons. That did not include those who had pursued non-elected positions which were deliberately intended to prepare them for a political career.

There were 110 respondents (43%) from all parties who had had experience of local government at levels ranging from parish councils to district and county councils and the London County Council. That experience had often started at an early age and lasted for a considerable time, sometimes continuing, as in Wedgwood's case, after entry to the house of commons. It was often preceded by, or overlapped with, involvement in various local good causes. Some mentioned party work or work in other public organisations: Christopher Addison 'had had a fair amount of administrative experience in professional and university matters'. With two exceptions (Keir Hardie and George Lansbury), those first elected as Labour or Lib–Lab members had all been involved in trade union work of some kind. Some professional soldiers, such as Sir Aylmer Hunter-Weston and William Adam, counted their military careers as 'public work'. Eighteen (7%) had been justices of the peace or magistrates while others claimed to have undertaken unspecified 'county work'.

Some of those who had no experience of 'public work' regretted it: Godfrey Dalrymple-White found that his lack of experience 'made my candidature extremely harassing and difficult'. Some were 'non-joiners' like the Irish Nationalist and barrister,

John Campbell, who declared: 'I'm afraid not unless in courts, I have always hated associations & gangs T.U.C. or other'. Sir George Sitwell 'had prepared myself for political life by a long study of history and political economy, etc.' but had no other experience of public life and did not appear to have found it a disadvantage. Those whose parliamentary careers started very early had usually had no opportunity to seek other elected office. They were, however, often hereditary politicians whose family circumstances had prepared them for what being a member of parliament might involve. Most of the remainder, including the later entrants to politics, also came from back-grounds which meant that they too knew what being a member of parliament involved. As their answers to some of the other questions showed, that did not invariably mean that they liked what they found in the house of commons or that they were satisfied with their political careers.

Chapter 4. Political and Parliamentary Careers

1. *Introduction*

Wedgwood's second major group of questions was about his colleagues' political and parliamentary careers, especially their reactions to their parliamentary experiences. Like the first group, the questions reflected his desire to gain a fully rounded picture of his subjects as individuals. The bare bones of their parliamentary careers were a matter of record with which he would have already been familiar; the questions were designed to put flesh on those bones. The answers brought together much scattered information, such as that about parliamentary likes and dislikes, which can otherwise be gleaned only incidentally from such sources as diaries, biographies and memoirs. Other questions, such as those about how the subjects were first selected for a parliamentary seat and their election expenses, elicited details that amplified the relatively sparse information available from other sources.

Like the questions about motivation, those about careers were not all well drafted. A high proportion of respondents (79%) answered Q11 ('How did you first get a seat?') but showed understandable confusion between the processes of selection and election. Of the 285 who answered the question 44% gave no specific information about how they were selected; some answers included long accounts of the respondents' electoral history while others simply said for which seat they were first elected, or when, and gave no further background. Q23 ('What was your best piece of work?') was answered by 60% of respondents but sometimes inspired accounts of non-parliamentary rather than parliamentary achievements. Q12 ('What was your chief political interest?'), Q13 ('On what did you, in fact, concentrate most in Parliament?'), the three questions on reactions to their parliamentary experiences (Q16: 'How did Parliament modify your views?'; Q18: 'What did you enjoy most in Parliamentary life?'; and Q19: 'What did you dislike most, apart from getting re-elected?') and the final one (Q24: 'If you are no longer in Parliament, why did you leave?') were more directly worded and therefore more straightforward to answer.

2. *Selection and Election*

Candidates' recollections of their initial experiences of getting selected and elected were often vague. The confusion between selection and election was well illustrated by the Liberal, Percy Harris, who had stood for Ashford in 1906 and for Harrow in 1910, but who said only that in 1916, following a by-election, 'I sat for the Harborough Division of Leicestershire' and nothing about how he became a candidate on any of those occasions. The replies gave little information about the details of the selection process at local level or about the interaction, if any, between local and national parties. They showed the importance of parties at both levels but suggested that selection processes were often relatively informal, with no consistent pattern, and that local parties had considerable autonomy in selecting candidates, however nominated. Most of those nominated, whether locally or nationally, must already have been known as party activists, even if they were not actually seeking a parliamentary seat. It is unlikely, for example, that the Liberal Thomas Barclay, who served only between the two elections of 1910, was unknown to his local party when he claimed that he 'did not seek an election at any time' but it was 'on the urgent request of a radical committee' that he stood in Blackburn.

Getting selected for a seat depended on such factors as local, family and party connections, chance friendships and professional or business acquaintances. An invitation to stand from a constituency party was said to be the single most common method of getting selected (35% of the total), regardless of party; a further 10% were nominated by national parties but did not say how that led to selection at constituency level. Sometimes the process seems to have been ridiculously easy. The Liberal Charles McCurdy contested Winchester in 1906 'In response to a casual suggestion made by a friend'. 'Defeated by 50 votes I sought no other constituency. Received a surprise invitation to contest Northampton in 1910, accepted and three weeks after found myself a Member of Parliament. Attended no party meetings and only two party social functions until ten years later.' He then served in a series of government posts, among them chief whip for the Coalition Liberals in 1921–2. The Liberal Austin Hopkinson, son of the Conservative Alfred Hopkinson, was first elected for Prestwich at a by-election in October 1918 and claimed that he simply 'Told my lawyer to put down my name'. Otherwise, getting selected and then elected could be a long and complicated process and changing seats, especially following electoral defeat, was common.

Personal contacts and, occasionally, straightforward patronage helped to start parliamentary careers, particularly for Conservatives. The Conservative John Cator's friend A.E. Fellowes (later Lord Ailwyn) sat for Huntingdon North and 'was instrumental in getting me adopted as Unionist Candidate for South Hunts in 1908'; he was duly elected in 1910. For Alfred Tobin, 'The Earl of Derby (then Lord Stanley) suggested that I should stand with him for the Borough of Preston in Lancashire'. Arthur Brookfield was first elected for Rye in Sussex at a by-election in 1885 when 'Lord Abergavenny [a local landowner] nominally supported me as member for the new County Division' although he had 'reason to think [he] would have preferred some much more important person'. Wilfrid Ashley got his seat (Blackpool) for which he was first elected in 1906, despite the Liberal landslide, 'By being a friend of the son of the local Conservative Assn. Chairman' and Ian Malcolm 'Through the influence of Lord Cadogan in N.W. Suffolk'.

Constituency parties could initiate the selection of candidates known to them. John Hancock was elected for Labour at a by-election in mid Derby in 1909: 'Liberal Party Leaders and Officials of the Miners' Federation had considered this vacancy and agreed that I should be their candidate . . . I stood as Labour candidate but was supported also by the Liberal Party'. The Liberal Evan Hayward described how 'The old S.E. Durham division was held by the Hon. F.W. Lambton, a liberal unionist free trader unopposed in 1906. The liberal organisation was practically nonexistent and it was regarded as a forlorn hope, but Headquarters wanted it fought in January 1910. Having gained a little local reputation as a speaker . . . I was asked to contest it' (he did not say who asked him). The

Conservative Clive Morrison-Bell was selected in 1908 for Honiton, the adjoining seat to that of his twin brother Ernest, elected at a by-election earlier that year: 'with a plethora of <u>local</u> candidates, the Selection Committee, in their embarrassment turned to me, as brother of the "Victor of Mid-Devon", and offered me the seat or rather the nomination'.

Those with parliamentary ambitions sometimes offered their services to local constituency associations or national parties. The Jewish Liberal Samuel Montagu 'chose Whitechapel as his constituency, as so many of his co-religionists lived there, and as a leader of the Community he had a considerable influence in the East End of London'. Athelstan Rendall asked 'friends in Whips office & Sir R Hudson to find me [a seat]' and James Fortescue-Flannery 'placed myself at the disposal of the Liberal Unionist Party Organisation at Westminster'. Julius Bertram claimed that he 'created the organizn. & obtd. support by saying I wd contest the seat if no one else would do so'. In 1905, Leo Money noticed a report of the death of the Liberal candidate for North Paddington and 'got in touch with the Liberal Association and was unanimously chosen'. In 1909, Anderson Montague-Barlow 'got in touch with 3 constituencies & eventually selected South Salford . . . where I was elected in 1910'. For the Conservative Max Aitken, Ashton under Lyne in December 1910 'was a fighting chance and nobody else wanted it' while James Majendie:

> Called on Central Cons Off & said I wished to stand & was promptly offered a hopeless seat, after that I was adopted. I was offered a practically safe seat in my own county, but refused as I wished to have a sporting shot at Portsmouth as all said Cons Assoc then always sent young ambitious men to hopeless seats!!

Labour's Frank Goldstone 'Got in touch with old friends in my native town of Sunderland shortly after the death of the late Mr Tom Summerbell in 1910, & was adopted as Labour candidate at a local conference of the Party in May 1910. Was elected in the December following'.

Wedgwood's selection in Newcastle-under-Lyme in 1904 was an example of how local and family connections could influence selection, sometimes, as in his case, leading to long parliamentary careers in safe seats despite his politics being rather different from that of his immediate family. There were numerous examples of candidates who were selected for the constituency in which their families lived and of sons succeeding their fathers. The Conservative Philip Sassoon was adopted for Hythe 'in succession to my father, and was duly elected in 1912', serving until 1939. The Liberal John Lloyd Morgan 'got the seat because I had the good fortune of being the son of a very good & highly respected father. . . . I had the great advantage of his good name & high reputation'. For Nathaniel Micklem, 'At the 1906 Election, it was obvious that my home constituency (West Herts) had to be contested & we could find no other suitable candidate'. The Liberal Unionist Lionel de Rothschild succeeded his cousin in the Aylesbury division of Buckinghamshire which 'had been represented by a member of my family since 1865 and when my cousin proposed to retire I felt I ought to offer myself as a candidate in his place'. Hubert Carr-Gomm succeeded his mother as 'Lord of the Manor of Rother-hithe' on her death. Then, 'In 1905 was adopted prospective Liberal Candidate, held the seat for 12 years and am the only Liberal who has sat for it'. Lord Cranborne's house of commons career showed that aristocratic connections could still kick-start parliamentary careers at an early age although that did not necessarily guarantee a safe seat. He was first elected for Darwen in 1885 at the age of 24 but defeated in 1892; he was re-elected for Rochester in 1893 and sat until he succeeded his father as marquess of Salisbury in 1903.

Getting elected could require careful nursing of a constituency, sometimes for several years, and considerable persistence and expense. The Liberal Harry Brodie 'worked very hard' at nursing Reigate, a Conservative seat, for three years before being elected in 1906. For Arnold Herbert, it was 'rather a hopeless task to attack a Tory stronghold like S. Bucks. It took years of hard work to nurse & educate the constituency'. The Conservative Charles Cochrane-Baillie got elected by 'Electioneering, canvassing & meetings' and Walter Essex 'By working, and abundantly speaking throughout one of the largest county constituencies (e. [*sic*] Glos.)'. Many stood unsuccessfully three or four times, sometimes more, often in hopeless seats, before getting elected. Richard Winfrey recounted how, 'As a result of my public work in the Spalding & Wisbech Divisions, I was invited and adopted as the Liberal Candidate for S.W. Norfolk in 1892 – a seat that had never been won for Liberalism'. He was finally elected at the third attempt in 1906. Labour's George Lansbury stood altogether five times before getting elected in December 1910 and finally got a seat by 'Keeping on keeping on'.

By-elections could provide a short cut for those who had been trying to get elected for some time. They were relatively frequent and not only because of deaths or resignations for personal reasons. By the early 20th century the number of by-elections following ministerial appointments was falling, but they still sometimes occurred, although the majority of those immediately following general elections were unopposed.[1] By-elections also occurred when seats were vacated for such reasons as appointments to the judiciary (a fairly common career progression among barrister members) or to official positions overseas. By-elections were not invariably contested, particularly during the First World War. The Liberal Herbert Samuel had stood unsuccessfully twice (in 1895 and 1900) for Henley, having 'addressed 250 meetings there in a period of seven years', and was eventually elected for Cleveland at a by-election in 1902, his name having been one of three put forward by the Liberal whips' office. The Unionist (later Conservative) Leo Amery made four unsuccessful attempts before he was elected unopposed at a by-election in Birmingham South in 1911 while the Liberal Allan Bright stood three times before getting elected for Oswestry at a by-election in 1904.

The nature of Irish politics meant that for nationalists the contests were often at the selection stage and seats were uncontested at general elections. John Boland had to fight off two other candidates in order to be selected for South Kerry but was elected unopposed in 1900. John Cullinan was both selected unanimously and returned unopposed for South Tipperary in 1900, as was John Hayden for Roscommon South in 1897. John Hackett, member for mid Tipperary from 1910 to 1918, was unusual in that a local opponent both contested his selection and then forced him to fight a general election. He was first elected in January 1910:

> when I was selected as Candidate by a large Convention of delegates of Mid-Tipperary United Irish League by a majority over my opponent Martin O'Dwyer

---

[1] See Martin Pugh, 'Queen Anne is Dead: The Abolition of Ministerial By-elections, 1867–1926', *Parliamentary History*, xxi (2002), 351–66.

Esq. . . . When Parliament was dissolved in November 1910, the Standing Committee of U.I. [United Irish] League decided that all sitting members of the late parliament be adopted as the nationalist candidates at forthcoming elections. Mr. O'Dwyer challenged this decision and had himself nominated for Mid-Tipp. I was returned at the election by a majority of over 400 votes.

By contrast, Hugh Law thought he had been selected 'because those who then ordered the conduct of electoral affairs in Ireland imagined that I might be of some use in the House of Commons & in the British constituencies West Donegal was a safe Nationalist seat, which was never contested in my time'.

3. *Political Interests*

The answers to Q12 ('What was your chief political interest?') showed that the large majority (90% of the 268 respondents) had interests in specific policy areas before entering parliament. Those interests tended to be packages that followed party allegiances. A few, mostly Conservatives, saw themselves as primarily creatures of their party whose main interest was to support that party and its policies, more or less regardless, and/or oppose the others. James Hope sought 'To keep the right people in and the others out'. After being elected, Viscount Dalrymple continued his desire 'to prevent radical party ruining the country & breaking up the Empire'. The interests of the Liberal Austin Hopkinson were 'Exposure of socialist quackery', for Sigismund Mendl they were 'General Liberal politics' and Edward Noel Buxton's were 'Gladstonian, especially re liberation of victims of Turkish tyranny' but he added 'Temperance, Poor law, and "Social Reform" in general'.

Most of the pre-parliamentary interests inevitably reflected the political concerns of the time. Social or welfare reform was the primary interest of 10% of respondents to Q12 and mentioned by nearly half, embracing a wide-ranging series of causes which could touch numerous policy areas. Herbert Samuel listed a typical Liberal package: 'Social Reform in all its branches – Labour conditions, housing, education, child welfare, land questions, etc.'. William Clough's interests were equally wide: 'Free Trade, Temperance, Education, Abolition of the vote of the House of Lords, Irish Home rule, Retrenchment and economy, Franchise reform, Civil and religious equality, "Peace on earth, good will to men"'. Lloyd George's interest both before and after entering parliament was 'Fair play for the underdog', Allan Bright's was 'Personal Freedom and sound finance', while that of Walter Essex was 'Freedom – in persons and politics'.

Some deliberately pursued a range of interests. Willoughby Dickinson 'was keenly interested in the whole Liberal platform between 1880 and 1914' and Eliot Crawshay-Williams 'deeply interested all round'. The Conservative Austen Chamberlain's interests were 'General' while the Lib–Lab Fred Maddison 'had no one dominating political interest – I was not a single plank politician'. However, 'For a time . . . my activities were mainly in opposition to what I regarded as reactionary proposals. Such questions as Free Trade, a creedless National System of Education, Disestablishment and Disendowment of State Churches, and Social Reform especially old age pensions attracted me. I was always non-Socialist in my views'. Labour's James Parker 'never did concentrate, I just carried on with no ambition doing the job that seemed to be mine as best I could'.

Social reform and welfare issues were most often cited by Liberals and Labour Party members, and by a high proportion of both, but also by significant numbers of Conservatives. George Bartley's pre-parliamentary interests were in 'Education, Poor Law, Thrift and Finance', those of Herbert Pease in 'many social questions' and of William Ormsby-Gore in 'social reform generally'. Walter Carlile had an enduring interest in old age pensions, describing with pride his part in the introduction of the Old Age Pension Act, while Godfrey Dalrymple-White included 'Old Age pensions and other Social Reforms'. The Liberal Unionist James Fortescue-Flannery's only interest was 'The advancement of the workers' and Rowland Hunt's 'The protection of British Industries; the protection of British Working people from cheap labour & from unfair & subsidised foreign competition'. More specific interests such as education, listed by 10% of the respondents to Q12 and 7% of those to Q13, also crossed party lines. Agriculture and related topics such as agricultural wages, land reform and rural affairs were listed by 11% of respondents to Q12 and 7% to Q13, mainly by those such as John Starkey from Nottinghamshire who represented rural constituencies, including several in Scotland and Ireland.

Irish affairs, particularly the issues surrounding home rule, were the most common pre-parliamentary interest, often the only one, cited by respondents from all parties. Fifty-eight (22%) respondents to Q12 mentioned some aspect of Irish affairs among their interests and of those 38 specifically cited home rule. Because the issue of home rule was not finally resolved until the end of the First World War, it was an interest that tended to continue once the respondents had entered parliament: Irish matters were a specific interest of 15% of those who replied separately to Q13. The main interest of the Irish Nationalists was support for home rule and any others (for example in land reform or housing) were generally confined to Ireland. Stephen Gwynn remarked that 'conditions for an Irish member were very special. We had really only one interest' although some 'incidentally touched much of interest. I was e.g. on the Dardanelles Commission' but he was in a minority among his party in that respect. William Duffy was more typical: his 'only political interest in Parliament was to give an ungrudging support to Mr John Redmond in his heroic & extraordinary struggle to give to Ireland a native Parliament'.

The effect on the Liberal Party of Gladstone's home rule policy remained divisive. Apart from Liberal Unionists such as Leonard Darwin, Liberals almost invariably supported home rule, usually combined with other topics. Alexander Boulton listed a package of 'Home Rule, disestablishment of the Church of England, monopoly of the drink trade' and Charles Corbett was 'chiefly interested in matters appealing to nonconformists, such as education and school questions, and Home Rule for Ireland'. Home rule was Charles Trevelyan's 'first enthusiasm, but I soon began to care for social reform'. The only declared Conservative supporter of home rule was Mark Sykes. For other Conservatives such as Raymond Greene, George Hamilton, Daniel Dixon and Roger Newman, maintenance of the Union was their major political concern. The chief interest of Charles Craig, member for Antrim South, 'at all times was opposition to Home Rule, and safeguarding the interests of Ulster'. Plunket Barton, member for mid Armagh, opposed 'Gladstonian Home Rule Proposals' but, 'on the basis of a United Parliament, [promoted] a rapprochement between Britain and Ireland'. Clive Morrison-Bell's interest in 'the Union' led him 'to an attack on the Irish over-representation in the House' which led him 'to questions like the Reform of the House of Lords, and electoral matters in general'.

After Ireland, the most commonly cited pre-parliamentary interests (by 15% of respondents, taken together, to Q12) were tariff reform and free trade. Tariff reform was specifically cited by 10%, almost all Conservatives like William Bridgeman, 'an ardent Tariff Reformer of the original school [who] remained consistently so'. The chief interest of the Unionist/Conservative Leo Amery was in 'Imperial affairs, and more particularly . . . the campaign for Imperial Preference and Tariff Reform', and Herbert Pease 'was convenor of the Tariff Reform Party acting for Mr Joseph Chamberlain'. Conservatives were not invariably tariff reformers: Lord Robert Cecil was 'on the whole opposed' and Benjamin Cohen 'Believed fully in Free Trade. Gave only qualified assent to protection when brought forward by Joseph Chamberlain'. Otherwise free trade was listed by 24 Liberals while Henry Hobhouse, although a Liberal Unionist because of his opposition to home rule, was otherwise a 'moderate Liberal' and 'Always a Free Trader'.

Foreign affairs, including 'the Empire', were a primary interest of 9% of respondents to Q12, mainly Conservatives, often from the more patrician strand of the party. Richard Cavendish sought 'The maintenance of the Unity of the Empire' and Evelyn Cecil headed his list with 'Imperial problems'. Sir George Sitwell's interests were 'Foreign policy and finance' and Lord Duncannon and Viscount Lewisham shared an interest in tariff reform and imperial policy. William Ormsby-Gore combined his interest in 'Foreign and imperial affairs' with social reform. Defence, listed by 6% of respondents, tended to be another Conservative preoccupation, particularly among former soldiers such as William Adam, Wilfrid Ashley, Arthur Brookfield and Sir Samuel Scott, while another former soldier, James Majendie, and Bertram Falle (Lord Portsea) represented Portsmouth seats which led to a shared interest in the royal navy. Leo Amery coupled his interest in 'Imperial affairs' with 'defence questions' on which he 'concentrated a great deal'. The Liberal Unionist and former soldier Herbert Jessel was interested in the army but 'soon found that neither my constituents or the House of Commons cared much about military decisions'.

Only a handful of Liberals were interested in defence. The only interest of Edward Smallwood was in 'the fighting men at the Great War' while Rowland Whitehead was 'keen on maintaining the Navy at overwhelming strength'. A few Liberals such as George Gooch, Malcolm Kincaid-Smith, Arthur Murray and George Leveson-Gower were interested in foreign affairs while Labour's George Lansbury listed it along with 'The condition of the People . . . and Peace'. Alfred Emmott was 'a sane Imperialist & at all times deeply interested in the development of the Dominions & Colonies' and Norman Lamont's only pre-parliamentary interest was 'Hatred of the South African War, & of the policy which led up to it'.

Most of the interests listed in answer to Q12 were in broad policy areas and the big issues of the day; more specific interests were often dictated by constituency or personal or business concerns. The Conservative Sir Aylmer Hunter-Weston's 'chief political interest was the welfare of my constituency and especially of my constituents' while Granville Wheler, although of Yorkshire origins and with property there, sat for Faversham in Kent and farmed extensively in the area, which gave him a strong personal interest in agriculture. Lord Ninian Crichton-Stuart's interests in 'Coal & Shipping' reflected both his own Cardiff constituency and his family's extensive business and property interests in the area. Edmund Bartley-Denniss, Conservative member for Oldham, 'devoted himself principally to the interests of his constituency, Cotton Spinning & Production'. Archibald Corbett's interest in temperance was shared by many of his fellow Liberals including Henry George Chancellor, Wilfred Lawson and George Marks. The Conservative brothers Lord Hugh and Lord Robert Cecil were both interested in 'Church questions', while Arthur Murray 'concentrated very largely on Scottish questions, Foreign Affairs, and measures against cruelty to animals'. Wedgwood's obsession with a land tax was shared by several colleagues, including Labour's George Barnes and Liberals such as Edward Hemmerde, Francis Neilson and Albert Spicer.

The 50 who combined the answers to Qs 12 and 13 – 'On what did you, in fact, concentrate most in Parliament?'– all pursued the same interests once in parliament, as did just over half the 213 separate respondents to Q13. Willoughby Dickinson 'took up different questions at different times; at first the reform of London and other Local Government; then the Franchise, especially women's suffrage'. George Touche and Godfrey Dalrymple-White added women's suffrage to their existing interests. Christopher Addison's professional interest in health matters led to involvement in national health insurance and welfare reform. Apart from Wedgwood himself, there were members like Henry George Chancellor who 'took up unpopular questions especially Humanitarian, and man's right to his own person, e.g. Vaccination, Inoculation, Vivisection, particular soldiers' rights during the war'. Michael Hicks-Beach and William Young's interests included 'the all embracing subject of public finance'. Jack Seely added army reform, 'in concert with Winston Churchill and Hugh Cecil', and free trade to his interest in South Africa. Lord Robert Cecil and Alfred Lyttelton both exploited being in opposition after 1906, Lord Robert taking 'a very active part speaking almost every night' while, according to his widow, Lyttelton 'threw himself into such questions as Housing, Town Planning, Education, the fight against the Disestablishment of the Welsh church, the Trades Board Bill, minimum wages and sweated industries'.

A few concentrated on parliamentary matters – Wilfrid Ashley on 'Question Time – 3 to 3.45 pm', Wilfred Lawson on 'Attending Divisions' and Godfrey Dalrymple-White on, among other things, 'Railway Fares for M.P.s, although opposed to Salaries'. The Conservative Sir George Sitwell 'was generally interested in parliamentary work' while as a new member Philip Sassoon concentrated on 'learning my duties as a Member of Parliament' as well as on tariff reform. The Liberal Percy Alden was not alone in finding 'all parliamentary work most interesting but especially the work in Committees'. William Barton was 'more interested in the Public Accounts Committee than any other' and Reginald Blair in 'Public Accounts and Estimates'. Ben Bathurst and Henry Bowles both became involved in private bill committees, Bathurst remarking that it was 'perhaps for the reason that one felt one was doing real work' while Bowles served for many years as chairman of the committee on railway bills. Two respondents made careers out of their interest in parliamentary procedure. James Hope 'developed an aptitude for the uses and abuses of procedure' and, after serving as a whip, became a deputy Speaker in 1921. Frederick Whitley-Thomson served first as Winston Churchill's parliamentary private secretary but also concentrated 'on studying the operation of the parliamentary machine which led Mr Speaker Lowther to appoint me to the Court of

Referees, and later led to my appointment as First President of the Indian Legislative Assembly'.

Those who spent much of their parliamentary careers in government positions had little scope for pursuing their own interests. They included lawyers such as Robert Munro (Lord Alness), who served as lord advocate and then secretary of state for Scotland, Graham Murray (Lord Dunedin), who 'entered Parliament as a Member of the Government in 1891 & until I left it in 1905 sat always on the Front Bench', and Plunket Barton, who became solicitor-general for Ireland. The whips included Austen Chamberlain (who subsequently had a long ministerial career), George Leveson-Gower and Robert Sanders. As Sanders remarked, 'Whips do not concentrate'; Leveson-Gower saw his role as a whip in government as 'keeping the Government in; as Opposition Whip on turning the Government out'. Parliamentary private secretaries had to follow their masters: both Eliot Crawshay-Williams and Henry McLaren served as PPS to Lloyd George when chancellor of the exchequer, so had 'to concentrate on Treasury work'; Rowland Whitehead served as PPS first at the home office, then to the attorney-general 'on whom fell much of the burden of Mr Lloyd George's Budget. I devoted my time to helping the A.G. in a very uphill fight'; as unpaid PPS to James Bryce, chief secretary for Ireland, George Gooch had to concentrate on Ireland.

4. *Parliamentary Experiences*

Most of Wedgwood's subjects must have hoped or expected that membership of the house of commons would enable them to pursue their interests or further the causes in which they believed. For some, however, the experience did not live up to those expectations. Q16 ('How did Parliament modify your views?') was answered by just over half (199 or 55%) of all respondents. Of those, 16% from all parties said that the main effect was disappointment or disillusionment with parliament, often because of the strength of vested interests and consequent difficulty of achieving anything concrete. Even Lloyd George remarked on 'the very unpleasant impression of the difficulties of getting things done and of the tremendous power of vested interests in every direction'. Wedgwood found that 'vested interests are too strong for abstract justice; . . . one can only hope to modify injustice & protect liberty'. Frank Goldstone 'was soon disillusioned as to the possibility of realising quickly my political ideals & often disgusted at the prodigal waste of time'. Some came to terms with the frustrations: Leo Amery found that 'Parliament has taught me patience and made me realise how long it takes to get things through' and Clive Morrison-Bell 'came to realise that things could not be done quickly, and that any big change might take years to bring about'. Edward Smallwood learned that 'matters can only progress at the rate electors permit' while Richard Cooper initially 'disliked the wide exercise of compromise and tardy action; but in later life I see that these features appear to serve well the British public, and is [*sic*] to be preferred to the hasty ill-digested and ungrammatical legislation which too often reaches the Statute Book'.

Some disliked feeling powerless, particularly as backbenchers. The Liberal Unionist James Fortescue-Flannery was disappointed 'that any individual can do so little', as was William Adam, 'except in individual cases where he could render assistance'. James

Majendie and Thomas Barclay both disliked being what Barclay called 'a mere voting unit for the government, whatever my ideas were'. For Percy Alden, an idealistic social reformer if ever there was one, 'Parliament modified my views as to the possibility of rapid reform. In 1908 all of us younger men thought that the millenium [*sic*] was not so far distant, but evolution is a slow process and towards the end of the war I was greatly disillusioned as I am afraid many other people have been'. Alfred Gelder remarked how 'The ordinary M.P. has very little chance to make any impression for good when he starts his career at 55. To be of real effective service a man should enter Parliament at an early period of life and also be prepared to devote the whole of his time to the very necessary work in connection with the Nation's affairs'.

Others were disappointed at how the house of commons conducted its business. John Sutton 'found the work very slow after being a City Councillor for many years'. As a 'keen businessman', Charles Shaw was 'forced to the conclusion that it was the most unbusiness-like assembly imaginable'. Labour's Ben Tillett found that 'Parliament its inefficiency & serious lack of organisation or arrangement of business & utilisation of personnel alarmed me'. Robert Ambrose complained about the amount of time wasted and John Whitehouse 'realized the insincerity of much of political life'. Evan Hayward saw the 'great disadvantage' that 'the "other side" and all its works must be denounced, and much of the criticism and attack is unreal and spurious as a consequence'. He also discovered that 'party labels did not accurately reflect party principles – many real conservatives being in the ranks of the liberal party and vice versa'.

The need to conform to party discipline and the operation of party machines could both cause disappointment. George Lansbury was convinced that 'If we were all free we would find unity of purpose to work for the common good'. John Lloyd Morgan 'at times felt uneasy after having to support my party. I should have liked a free hand'. Alfred Scott was always 'vexed that under the influence of [the party machine] members broke their pledges'. The Irish Nationalist Vincent Kennedy 'felt wrong was often done by Members voting on the merits of important questions when they did not even know the subject under Debate much less listen to any portion of it'. William Clough and Viscount Dalrymple both became disillusioned about their colleagues. Clough found that 'Parliament modified my views of M.P's as men considerably, insomuch that their votes when in opposition and when in office were so inconsistent' while Dalrymple found that it 'Cured me entirely of any delusions I had previously had of the honesty of Liberal politicians'. Sir George Sitwell 'found that Conservative policy never looked beyond the next election. Our leaders had no foresight or under-standing of what was coming'.

Developments in Ireland often contributed to the disappointment, although usually in ways for which parliament itself could not (or should not) have been blamed, other than for existing as a forum where minds did not meet. William Allen, first elected in 1917 as a Unionist for Armagh North, was 'bitterly disappointed with the so-called Conser-vatives who bartered away the lives, liberties and properties of a people whose only fault was their loyalty to the British Crown and constitution'. From the other side of that divide, the Nationalist John Boland found that the 'surrender to Carsonism by the British Government was the greatest shock I received. It modified my views thus to see apparently fair-minded Englishmen acting when a privileged minority in Ireland could use the appeal of "Protestantism in danger", threaten to give up their traditional "loyalty" and resort to civil war if the Home Rule Bill were passed'. However, Irish Nationalists sometimes found unexpected attitudes towards their cause among their parliamentary colleagues. Hugh Law 'soon came to realise how much goodwill there was towards Ireland among men of all British parties' and was impressed by 'the high level of courtesy and tolerance exhibited towards holders of unpopular opinions or by the patient hearing given to those who voiced sentiments little in accord with those entertained by the great majority of members'. William Duffy 'was satisfied the Minister for Ireland was friendly & inclined to meet reasonable demands'.

Both Irish and Scottish members felt that the house of commons did not pay enough attention to their interests. The experiences of the Irish Nationalist Daniel O'Leary confirmed 'that the Government of Ireland should be through a native Parliament' and Stephen Gwynn thought that 'Parlt had not <u>time</u> to deal with Irish affairs'. Will Thorne wanted more power to be given to Scotland and Wales 'so as to prevent congestion of business in the House' and Robert Munro discovered at an early stage not only 'that a private member did not posses the powers which I anticipated' but also that 'it was difficult to interest the House of Commons in Scottish questions'.

The majority of respondents to Q16 were not disappointed by their parliamentary experiences and 40% from all parties said that parliament did not modify their basic political views. A further 10% from all parties claimed that it strengthened them. For the Conservative Henry Croft 'it merely proved them right' and for Robert Sanders 'It increased my dislike of Liberalism and all its works. This was 1910–1914'. The Lib–Lab William Brace became 'more pro-Labour' and for Labour's George Nicholls 'It did not modify my views it strengthened them'. Sigismund Mendl, by contrast, moved to the right, his views mellowing 'from rather advanced to moderate Liberal', while John Bethell's (Lord Bethell) views 'became more advanced, especially on social reform'. Harry Brodie claimed that 'When I started was only really a Liberal because I believed (& still believe) very earnestly in Free Trade & Free Imports. . . . in Parliament I became much more Liberal I may say Radical . . . [and] to believe in Home Rule for Ireland which I did not when I was elected'. Athelstan Rendall found that 'Starting as party man became broader, whilst going left & joining Labour Party lost all fervour whilst retaining & increasing my Left views'. Lord Robert Cecil remained a Conservative but 'Parliament did not modify my views except that I moved gradually to the Left. I always found myself in close agreement with Sir E Grey & more than once contemplated joining the Liberal party on the Free Trade issue. But for Welsh Disestablishment & to a lesser degree Home Rule I should probably have done so'.

The remaining 30% of respondents from all parties found that being in parliament made them more tolerant, especially about their colleagues and their motivation, and often more open-minded. Labour's George Barnes found that parliament 'did modify my views of personalities. I found MPs just like other folk – better if anything, but not so clever as I expected to find them'. The Liberal George Lambert learnt 'To be tolerant of stupidity' while for William Rees Davies 'Experience of Parliament . . . encourages deference for the opinions of one's opponents'. Evan Hayward may have been disillusioned but developed 'more respect for Parliament as a whole than for the members who composed it' and 'generally there was something to be said for the other's point of view'. For the Conservative Richard Cooper, 'An M.P's education only begins when he gets into the House. . . . he soon learns that there are two sides to most problems. I learned

very much about human nature and the "milk of human kindness"'. For Arthur
Griffith-Boscawen, 'The House of Commons inevitably broadens one's views.
. . . Though remaining a strong Tory, church and State man & Imperialist, I became more
& more interested in "social reform" – & I learned to respect my opponents, among
whom I had many personal friends'.

Being in parliament may have brought its share of disappointments but the replies
to Q18 ('What did you enjoy most in Parliamentary life?') showed the compensations.
Few went as far as Willoughby Dickinson, for whom 'The whole of it interested me
continually and when one is interested one is happy', but nearly half the 232 respondents
(64% of the total) said that they most enjoyed the social side of parliamentary life and
the comradeship. They were not invariably as enthusiastic about their fellow parliamentarians as the Liberal Austin Hopkinson, who referred to 'The companionship of a
number of the very best fellows of the world', but there were many in all parties who,
like Savile Crossley, greatly enjoyed 'The House of Commons as a Club', the Smoking
Room, tea on the terrace and the 'feeling of camaraderie'. Cross-party friendships were
often highly valued. Freeman Freeman-Thomas enjoyed 'The many advantages gained
from constant association with fellow-members of all types, classes & conditions' and the
Conservative Leonard Brassey appreciated 'the companionship of men of experience
in many different walks of life'. Henry George Chancellor noted 'the absence of snobbishness (with exceptions) and especially friendships with members of interparty groups'.
The Irish Nationalist D.D. Sheehan, despite observing that 'The Irish Nationalists were
not in Parliament to enjoy life', liked 'the Camaraderie of Parliament. . . . within the
precincts of Westminster, there was a fine friendliness into which rank or wealth did not
enter'. The Liberal Archibald Corbett, a long-term supporter of the temperance movement, most appreciated 'the fact that many of his [parliamentary] friends were among the
brewers and distillers against whom he had worked all his life'.

A significant source of enjoyment was the opportunity, as George Gooch described it,
to 'get to know the leading actors' and of 'Being in the swim' (Eliot Crawshay-Williams).
Cecil Harmsworth enjoyed 'Being at the centre of things & rubbing shoulders with all
sorts of interesting men'. The Conservative Weston Jarvis cited 'getting to know everybody worth knowing at the time'. The Irish Nationalist Patrick Kennedy enjoyed 'the
mixing with eminent men' and Charles Shaw 'The smoke room listening to Labouchere,
Dilke & chess matches'. The power to influence events, if only occasionally, also
appealed. The Liberal Charles Buxton liked the feeling, which he shared with Labour's
Fred Maddison, the Lib–Lab Arthur Richardson and the Conservative Wilfrid Ashley, of
being 'at the centre of Government'. Richardson also enjoyed 'being able to assist in
some small way, both through legislation and by personal touch with the Ministers and
important permanent officials, in the direction and government of the people'.

What Colin Coote called 'The fun of modest importance' was valued because it
helped backbenchers such as Richard Holt to get things 'better done', even if only in a
small way. Arthur Murray found that 'To a hardworking Member, Parliament is a real
labour but there is a sense of power and of "doing one's bit" that is a constant source of
elation', a counter to the frustration of Robert Munro and Theodore Taylor (in answer
to Q19) caused by the difficulty they found as backbenchers of getting things done. The
Liberal Edmund Harvey was glad 'of being able sometimes to help in exposing injustice
or getting some improvement in the lot of some less fortunate people'. Being someone

in the constituency and the ability to help constituents were also valued. Henry Montgomery most enjoyed 'Visiting my constituents' while for Arthur Brookfield it was 'the Annual Dinners of the Tunbridge Wells Tradesmen's Association . . . [where] I used to find the members particularly appreciative'.

A surprisingly large number of respondents to Q14 (14%) most enjoyed debates, but as spectators rather than participants. They liked the excitement of big occasions, particularly when feelings ran high, accompanied by what the Conservative James Hope called 'The atmosphere of strife' and Godfrey Dalrymple-White 'The thrilling experience of a heated debate, with cheers and counter cheers, on any subject in which I was interested'. William Rees Davies enjoyed 'The turmoil of a great party debate followed by a perilously small majority in the Division Lobby', and Labour's Frank Goldstone relished 'The concluding speeches on the "great occasions"; the successful speeches of my political friends'. The Conservative Harry Hope found that 'For me it was an interest and a pleasure to watch the personalities fighting in the H of C. When the Irish Members left [in 1918], the House was the poorer by their absence – as they were many of them great Parliamentarians'. The Conservative Felix Cassel simply enjoyed 'Listening to good speeches', as did Harry Brodie, while Samuel Whitbread and Gilbert McMicking enjoyed observing the debating skills of Asquith and Balfour.

Only a few claimed to enjoy speaking in debates, among them the Liberal barristers Edward Hemmerde and Alexander Boulton, the Liberal Malcolm Kincaid-Smith and Labour's William Brace. The Irish Nationalist Michael Flavin enjoyed most 'Fighting for Ireland's freedom on the floor of the House'. Some, like Arthur Griffith-Boscawen, Gilbert Willoughby and Arthur Wilson, shared Lord Robert Cecil's liking for 'the rough and tumble of parliamentary opposition'. As Arthur Wilson said, 'When a small Opposition we were allowed to do what we liked' while William Adam most enjoyed 'To catch a political opponent tripping'. About a dozen referred specifically to their enjoyment of various types of committee work, mainly in select committees or private bill committees, while three mentioned question time. Working as a minister or parliamentary private secretary was often rewarding for those who did it, including Harold Baker, Austen Chamberlain, Anderson Montague-Barlow, Eliot Crawshay-Williams, Henry McLaren (as a PPS) and Robert Munro, while the atmosphere of the whips' offices was particularly congenial for Alexander Murray (the master of Elibank and Liberal chief whip) and Lord Wolmer.

Ten respondents said, probably sometimes with their tongues in their cheeks since they included long-serving members such as Henry Bowles (1889–1906 and 1918–22) and Thomas Nussey (1893–1910), that they most enjoyed getting away from the house of commons, whether for recesses or at the end of a sitting. George Leveson-Gower's service as Liberal deputy chief whip from 1892 to 1895 may explain why he most enjoyed 'The Recess', while Henry Webb, another former whip, most enjoyed 'the cry of "who goes home?"' and Edward Wood 'The periodic motions for the adjournment'.

About 5% of respondents to Q18 had not enjoyed their time in the House, although few gave specific reasons. Arthur Black, part of the 1906 Liberal landslide, found that 'the futilities were disappointing' and Alfred Gelder that 'It did not in many aspects appeal to me'. It did not attract Henry Gooch, especially compared with municipal life, while Miles Mattison found that 'At times it was rather boring' and John Lloyd Morgan had no regrets when he left after 20 years' service. Those responses reinforced some of the answers to Q19 ('What did you dislike most, apart from getting re-elected?'), which was answered by 220 respondents (60% of the total), most of whom also answered Q18. The likes and dislikes were not necessarily correlated and, not surprisingly, the dislikes sometimes overlapped with the general disappointment expressed in some answers to Q16, although they tended to be more specific.

For Keir Hardie parliamentary life had 'no charm' while the Conservative Michael Hicks-Beach's sister said he found that 'the life was not really to his taste' and he preferred managing the family estate. The Liberal Guy Wilson served for 11 years (1907–18) but disliked 'The whole life' as did Hilton Young, who nevertheless served for a total of 17 years in four periods between 1915 and 1935 when he was raised to the peerage. The Liberal Charles McCurdy, first elected in 1910, was deeply disappointed by the calibre of his parliamentary contemporaries and wondered whether Gladstone and Bright 'had, in reality, been bigger men than my contemporaries'. Max Aitken summarised his dislikes as 'Frustration' (he never served in government during his seven years in the house of commons). A few shared Wedgwood's assumption of a universal dislike of elections. Canvassing was not popular, although attitudes to elections were sometimes conditioned by the outcome. Labour's Fred Maddison's 'greatest dislike was my own election contests'. He added, however, that 'I was not re-elected, but if I had been it would not have been classed as a "dislike"'. George Lansbury, on the other hand, actively 'liked being re-elected, & cannot say what I dislike, a lot of humbug is talked about our sacrifices I never feel I have made any I want to be in the H of C as one who serves when I fail as very often I do it is not the fault of H of C but is in myself'. Others also enjoyed elections: Henry Staveley-Hill 'enjoyed all my three contests' while Plunket Barton 'was reelected three times unopposed and I did not dislike it'.

The greatest dislike among those who had found the house of commons addictive was having to leave. Even for the Unionist James Craig, there was 'the wrench at leaving, at the passing of the Government of Ireland Act (1920) and my election to an office of profit under the Crown, i.e. first Prime Minister of Northern Ireland'. The Liberal Joseph King disliked losing his seat and 'for the next 3 or 4 years [after 1918] I felt very keenly my absence from the House of Commons' while Herbert Samuel and Henry Webb simply disliked not getting re-elected. By contrast with those who said in answer to Q18 that they enjoyed the ability to get things done, there was also considerable frustration similar to that expressed in some answers to Q16. Bertram Falle (Lord Portsea) disliked the 'Inability to remedy all grievances' while Frederick Chance shared with several colleagues the 'certain sense of futility that the Private Member often feels on entering the House later on in life, after having lived a very active life as a leader and master of men outside'. For Franklin Thomasson, it was 'The feeling of being but a helpless and very small cog in the wheel in a relentless machine'. Edmund Harvey disliked 'the lack of touch of the private member with the work of administration & the great Government departments, and too often also with the daily life and needs of the people'.

Despite the enjoyment of the social side of life in the house of commons, there was widespread dislike of the demands of attendance at the House. Those who had other interests or occupations, like the Liberal businessmen Arthur Black and Norman Lamont, resented the enforced attendance when there were other and better things they could or should be doing. The Liberal barrister Arthur Marshall disliked 'Trying to fit in professional & family duties with a very strenuous period of Parliamentary life 1909–1918'. Those with distant constituencies, particularly the Irish, disliked the travelling and the time that had to be spent away from home. D.D. Sheehan's greatest dislike was 'the enforced absence from my home and family, for so many months every year. This was, perhaps, the most grievous sacrifice which devotion to an ideal entailed'. The Scottish advocate James Clyde disliked 'the inevitable separation from my family and the constant night travelling'. Raymond Greene disliked 'Trying to sneak past the Whips at the door in order to get away for dinner!' while Basil Peto simply said 'London' and Lord Hugh Cecil 'Regular attendance'. Sir Aylmer Hunter-Weston, not a natural rebel, disliked 'the irksomeness of having to attend the House of Commons when I had nothing definite to do there' although he overcame that by pairing as often as possible. He also shared with several colleagues a dislike of the physical conditions in the House, what Julius Bertram called the 'mephitic' atmosphere of the 'Smoking Rms and Dining Rms', Francis Mildmay the 'bad air, from lack of adequate ventilation' and Cecil Harmsworth 'The long hours of confinement in a vicious physical atmosphere', while Rowland Whitehead remarked on 'the asphyxiating & depressing airlessness of the whole Palace of Westminster'.

Some found it difficult to reconcile the demands of their constituencies with those of attendance at the house of commons, Leonard Brassey complaining that 'The combination of attendance at the House of Commons and other claims upon an M.P. from a very large number of Towns and Villages constitute a severe strain'. The demands of constituents and various aspects of constituency life were the main dislikes of 9% of respondents: Anderson Montague-Barlow was very unusual in admitting to enjoying most his close relations with his constituents. William du Pre liked 'the <u>work</u> of the house & was not given enough, but I disliked the constituency work'. Social functions in the constituency and constituency correspondence were both unpopular, particularly among the more patrician members such as Edward Wood. George Lane Fox (Lord Bingley) and Thomas Hare both disliked almost very aspect of dealing with their constituencies, including specifically 'smoking concerts'. Joseph Pease's dislike of 'Having to put my tongue in my cheek when suggesting to my constituents I was "enjoying" myself in addressing meetings and opening bazaars' was widely shared. Christopher Addison disliked 'Bazaars – and flummery of all sorts', Henry Croft 'attending every small function in my constituency', Ernest Morrison-Bell 'Attending agricultural dinners & Fetes' and William Brace 'Endless courtesy letters to constituents'. Charles Welby understandably disliked 'winter meetings in villages in non-election times – no motors then'. George Marks 'disliked the appeals for money that came from the constituency, it being assumed that the member must contribute to every cause', as did Alfred Scott.

A handful simply disliked 'the other side', the Liberal Unionist Rowland Hunt describing 'the hypocritical humbug of the Radical Party & the wobbling policy of Mr Balfour' while the Conservative Viscount Dalrymple, who served from 1906 to 1914, disliked 'The Government of that time, & a great many of its supporters'. Although the answers to Q18 suggested that many enjoyed the company of their colleagues, enforced contact with uncongenial fellow members could be tiresome, George Courthope remarking on 'The narrow and selfish views of some, with whom contact was inevitable' and John Cullinan disliking 'Parliamentarians who took themselves too seriously'. Algernon Borthwick disliked 'The men who looked on politics as a game or means of self-advancement'.

The compromises and harsh realities of politics were widely disliked, with particular resentment of party discipline and the exercise of control by party whips. Arthur Hawarth disliked 'having to vote always for my Party when I disagreed or to vote against the Government which I did on several occasions'. Frederick Whyte did not like 'the fact that there were only <u>two</u> division lobbies. I often felt I wanted to be in both at the same time: or in neither: . . . I have walked in Westminster Hall in the hope of finding there a third'. Sir Robert Newman disliked 'The attempt to interfere with freedom of conscience in giving Votes. I have never been able to accept the theory that it is "<u>best to vote wrong to make things right</u>"'. Daniel Turner Holmes and Edward Pryce Jones complained about 'The tyranny of the Whips' and Athelstan Rendall 'disliked most enforced attendance at divisions & the silence my whips requested of me & the promotion of members of my party who were not silent'. Patrick Kennedy referred to the demands of 'Irish Party discipline' even though the pledge to speak and vote in accordance with the party did not strictly apply to non-Irish matters. Most of his Irish Nationalist colleagues seem, however, to have accepted a level of party discipline that would have irked many of their colleagues in other parties.

The hypocrisy and insincerity associated with party discipline, what Eliot Crawshay-Williams called 'The humbug of it', were also resented. John Sinclair disliked 'The frailties of self-interest as seen by a Whip and private secretary, disloyalty and intrigue in one's own party' and John Norton-Griffiths 'the necessity, in all political life, of sub-merging certain of one's own convictions for the sake of party solidarity, even though the ultimate and fundamental aims of the party are sound'. Lord Robert Cecil likewise disliked 'the rigidity of Party discipline & the consequent insincerity of much of parliamentary life'. James Parker disliked the 'affectation, the obscuring of truth in debates, the jealousy & meanness shown at times by those who are seeking office & climbing to power'. Colin Coote 'hated the whole business of ingratiation', Richard Cavendish disliked 'Party wrangling', John Gilmour 'Party wire-pulling', Rowland Prothero (Lord Ernle) 'Partisanship' and Thomas Morison 'The intrigues of party politics'. John Sinclair was not the only whip to find his colleagues' behaviour tiresome: George Leveson-Gower referred to 'Having to try to persuade certain M.P.s whom I neither liked nor esteemed to go on supporting the Government when they began to jib'.

The realities of day-to-day parliamentary life were even more unpopular than the higher-level realities of politics. Attendance at divisions was particularly unpopular, partly because of their timing. Gilbert Willoughby disliked 'Having to wait until 12 o'clock at night for divisions' and Cecil Harmsworth 'the endless trudging in the Lobbies'. Divisions were also seen as unnecessarily time-consuming. Leo Money resented 'the stupidity of being counted like sheep in time-wasting divisions, which must have consumed months of my life' and Lord Duncannon 'Having to spend so many hours daily unable to concentrate on other matters owing to have to wait for the Division Bell to ring'. Henry Bowles and Austen Chamberlain disliked having to dine in the House, Chamberlain remarking that 'for 10 years I never dined out on a Government night & only very rarely on other nights' while one of Hugh Law's principal dislikes was 'the food provided by the Kitchen Committee'.

The long hours and even more the late nights were cited by 20% of respondents, Plunket Barton mentioning 'the boredom of the long hours and the weariness of the late hours' and Charles Buxton and Evelyn Cecil, like many others, 'Sitting up late at night'. Dislike of the long hours was often associated with unnecessary time-wasting (cited by 13% of respondents), particularly for backbenchers, and the boredom of hanging around. William Whitelaw was not only 'a good deal disillusioned by much of what he heard and saw in the House of Commons' but also 'not a little irritated by the appalling waste of time which parliamentary practice involved'. Evan Hayward resented the 'Restraint on one's freedom – aimlessly hanging about waiting for the "House" to be "up"' and Charles Mallet 'the desultoriness of the life', although 'when I held office for a year as an Under-Secretary this feeling was diminished'. For Cecil Cochrane, it was 'The waste of time and the feeling that I could have been doing much more useful work if I had not been tied to the House'. William du Pre disliked 'The appalling waste of time hanging about doing nothing but gossip' and Alfred Gelder 'the never ending platitudes to which I had to listen – and the growing conviction that much time was wasted at Westminster by fad-ists & extremists of all parties'. Only two respondents saw another aspect of the 'time-wasting'. Ben Bathurst found that 'The philosophy of experience reconciles one to this apparent drawback, and one recognised the necessity for a safety valve of eloquence or advertisement'. Arthur Wills disliked the waste of time and frustration, 'But one willingly pays that price as a necessary and not excessive one for the preservation of democratic liberties. The alternative is dictatorship of some sort'.

Despite the popularity of debates on big occasions, routine debates were the greatest dislike of 16% of respondents. Savile Crossley, Ian Malcolm, Edward Noel Buxton and Albert Spicer all greatly disliked making speeches in the House, while routine debates were regarded as part of the more general waste of time, repetitive and boring, particularly when they were about topics in which the respondents were not personally interested. For Robert Ambrose, 'The vast majority of speeches are nonsense and not meant to be of any purpose'. Clarence Smith 'did not find all subjects interesting, nor all speeches arresting'. James Hope disliked 'The vain repetitions of the unimaginative' and Walter Carlile 'the boredom of listening to repetitions of the same views, in phraseology specially manufactured for the ears of their constituent, and valueless from a debating point of view'. George Nicholls disliked 'Listening to speeches by Members who just talked to get reported', while for Clive Morrison-Bell speeches were too long and 'Most Members had no idea what they wanted to say, & getting done with it'. William Rees Davies' main dislike was 'Probably a dull Scotch debate when the Whips decline to allow their party to leave the House', and that of Thomas Barclay 'a speech by Mr Keir-Hardy [*sic*] who had a voice worthy of Hell and a heart worthy of Heaven'.

The House's procedures in debates were also unpopular, particularly the priority given to front-bench speakers. Both Alfred Hopkinson and Charles Corbett thought front-bench contributions 'far too frequent and too long' while 'the unofficial member had so few opportunities of expressing his views and taking part in the various parliamentary discussions'. Those who sought to speak were tried by the uncertainties of waiting to be called, Wedgwood himself citing 'Not being called on by the Speaker or Chairman'. Richard Cooper added that he 'always developed a strange form of nervousness, which prevented me from expressing myself clearly and consequently I was usually ineffective in debate'. Malcolm Kincaid-Smith disliked 'Hearing someone else say what I wanted to say myself' and Jack Seely 'Making a carefully thought out speech to which nobody paid the least attention'. Henry George Chancellor disliked the 'bitterness in debate on some subjects, Home Rule, Parliament Act, Disestablishment etc.', a dislike shared by Lord Wolmer who described 'the extreme bitterness of my political opponents, the Radicals & Irish Home rulers'.

Some dislikes related to specific parliamentary events. Edmund Bartley-Denniss was involved for several years in obstructing a private members' bill, the Plumage Bill, which was eventually passed after he had persuaded the government to amend it. According to his son, he came to hate 'even the sight' of Lady Astor who had 'accused him of being financially interested in his opposition to the Plumage Bill when he was only acting as the representative of the London Chamber of Commerce, she did withdraw the insinuation, but very ungraciously, and he never forgave her'. William Clough 'disliked most the shouting down of Mr Asquith by the Opposition on May 21 1914 on the third reading of the Home Rule Bill' and Michael Flavin (an Irish Nationalist) objected to 'The closure motion on a supplementary vote of £17,000,000 – £2,000,000 of which applied directly to Ireland – on which no Irish Member was allowed to speak, accepted by Lord Ullswater. Twelve Irish Members were suspended and removed by police from the Chamber during which I sang "God save Ireland"'. Irish issues also lay behind the Unionist Major William Allen's dislike of 'The gradual socialistic tendencies of the once great Conservative Party' while John Nugent voiced the particular frustration of Irish Nationalists at Westminster, 'The ignorance of the British Public representatives on the position in Ireland and their want of appreciation that a self-governing Ireland would be a strength, not a weakness in the Empire'.

5. Personal Achievements

Whatever the dislikes of their parliamentary careers, nearly two-thirds (around 65%) of the 205 respondents to Q23 ('What was your best piece of work?) identified a parliamentary achievement of some kind as their best piece of work. It is, however, often impossible to assess whether the achievements cited were as significant as their perpetrators claimed and some of the answers suggested an element of self-promotion. Like other cases where they were invited to judge themselves, a significant number (27 or 18%) could not or would not identify a specific achievement, often preferring to leave the judgment to others. As the Conservative Sir Robert Newman, first elected at a by-election in 1918, feared, 'my work in Parliament was rather the case of doing those things which one ought not to have done and leaving undone those things that one ought to have done so in my case I shrink from suggesting what was my best piece of work. I am thankful not to be asked what was my worst'. Another Conservative, Sir Aylmer Hunter-Weston, identified his best piece of work as 'trying to make myself as little of a nuisance as possible!' and Robert Brassey named his as 'Solvitur ambulando [remaining on my feet] and remaining silent'.

Others expressed disappointment at what they saw as their non-achievements. The Liberal Eliot Crawshay-Williams, who served for only three years from 1910 to 1913 and resigned following a divorce, remarked sadly that 'I only did a certain amount of spade work in various causes, or helped to organise certain political bodies. My career ended before I had opportunity to do what I aimed at doing'. Another Liberal, Arthur Wills, had 'no piece of work I could call my own. I merely rallied support for a Liberal Government on "Proposed Purchase of the Liquor Trade", Parliamentary Committee for settlement of ex-soldiers on the land etc etc.'. Labour's Fred Maddison 'often thought none of it could warrant being called best' while the Liberal Charles Mallet could not 'lay claim to any valuable piece of work in Parliament'. The Irish Nationalist Denis Cogan had 'done nothing to boast of' while the Conservative Philip Sassoon preferred 'to leave the selection to others', as did, among others, Austen Chamberlain, for whom 'Posterity, if it is interested, must decide'. There were some mysterious choices, or non-choices. Why did the Liberal George Lambert, who served from 1891 to 1945, with a break from 1924 to 1929, find after nearly 30 years' service that it was 'All commonplace'? To whom was Austin Hopkinson referring when he said 'Getting X.Y. to resign'? (He must have assumed that Wedgwood would know the answer.)

The best achievements of over 20% of respondents were non-parliamentary, although they were almost all in public life of some kind. For some, like Alfred Gelder, Arthur Black, Emslie Horniman, George Lansbury and Charles Welby, it was their work in local government. Lansbury also considered that he was 'a fairly good agitator & propagandist', including his 'work for Women's suffrage & public propaganda on behalf of what I thought was religion & tradition'. Arthur Crosfield's best public work was 'for the National Playing Fields Association . . . and . . . as Chairman of the Kenwood Preservation Committee' and that of Daniel Turner Holmes 'in Schoolmastering'. For Harry Hope, 'The welfare of agriculture – not merely to improve the farmer's financial profit – but as a means of maintaining a healthy stock of manhood – born and brought up – in our rural districts was, ever, what I aimed at, and pleaded for, and I had a general response and approval from the people'.

Wedgwood himself cited 'Establishing the Land Tenure system in Northern Nigeria in 1918' and 'The arming and landing from the River Clyde at Gallipoli, Apr 25 – MAY 8, 1915'. Other former soldiers such as William du Pre and Gilbert McMicking cited their efforts for the Territorials. Sir Samuel Scott described how, 'in conjunction with the late Lord Roberts, the late Lord Lovat and the late Col a'Court Repington we were able . . . to lay facts before the Govt regarding German preparations which Mr Asquith then P.M. thought of sufficient importance to call a special mtg of the Imperial Committee of Defence to consider'. A handful selected achievements overseas. Percy Molteno cited 'Assisting in & securing support of Self-Government for Transvaal and Free State', Lord Ronaldshay 'I suppose my administration in Bengal', Jack Seely 'My small share in the South African Union' and Lord Wolmer his service 'as High Commissioner for South Africa from 1905 to 1910 working for the Union of South Africa'.

Several cited their work for their parties and in getting themselves elected. Keir Hardie, probably not at heart a parliamentarian, 'was always proud of the privilege enjoyed in sharing the formation and upbuilding of the Labour and socialist movement . . . making it possible to win justice for & prevent special privilege for any'. Algernon Borthwick was responsible for the inauguration of the Primrose League and James Craig persuaded Edward Carson 'to undertake that heavy responsibility' of leadership of the Ulster Loyalists in 1911. Savile Crossley 'worked hard' as chairman of the Liberal Unionist Council 'for a number of years'. Before entering parliament, Rowland

Whitehead 'was an active member of the Liberal League which supplied Mr Asquith Sir Edward Grey Mr Haldane & others with a backing which prevented their exclusion from Liberal office'. The Conservative George Younger was closely involved, in and out of parliament, in the organisation of the Scottish Conservative Associations and in the break-up of the Lloyd George Coalition, although 'in this particular crisis greatness was thrust upon him'. The Conservatives Clive and Ernest Morrison-Bell both cited their work at elections. At 'Bye Elections', Clive Morrison-Bell would 'sometimes be there, with a motor, for a week or 10 days . . . fitting in whenever the agent wanted me' while his brother's achievement was 'Winning a seat for the Conservatives that had always been Liberal, and looked upon as a very safe seat at that'. Lord John Joicey-Cecil, elected as a Conservative in 1906, said simply 'Winning the seat' and James Majendie, elected in 1900, said 'Winning a doubtful seat'. Henry Wyndham-Quin's 'best work was put into my own constituency of South Glamorgan . . . I won it from the Liberals & may claim to be the only Tory who ever represented it'. The Liberal Arthur Hawarth 'looked back on that contest (in the 1918 "Coupon" election) with more satisfaction than anything else in my political career'.

Of those whose best achievements were parliamentary, the Conservative Viscount Dalrymple saw his main achievement as opposition to the other side, 'Assisting on showing the 1905 Majority that they were not quite impotent'. The best piece of work of the Liberal William Clough was 'constant attendance [between 1906 and 1918] and for many sessions my voting record must have been in the first dozen'. Others claimed to have used parliament successfully as a platform for causes they favoured, although they seldom judged the results of their efforts. Alfred Hopkinson 'would take up some special subject & get it up thoroughly & speak on it. The "Preservation of Commons" for example was one on which a Private Member could do really useful work of lasting value'. Theodore Taylor 'led the Anti-Opium movement and devoted hundreds of hours over it from 1907 to 1917'. He also 'led the successful fight in the House, first to defeat the so-called Premium bonds proposal and second to turn down the War Charities Lotteries Bill which had passed the House of Lords in 1918'. Allan Bright 'was largely instrumental in abolishing flogging in Military Prisons' in 1905. The Liberal Willoughby Dickinson's most useful piece of work was 'in relation to the reform of the franchise in 1916–18 and in particular to Women's Suffrage'. Robert Ambrose chose his efforts 'to make the tiller of the soil – the tenant farmer and the agricultural labourer – the owner of his holding [in Ireland]' and Edmund Harvey his 'endeavour to defend the right of obscure individuals against oppression by the state or by powerful interests'.

The Liberal Edward Hemmerde cited his 'general work & speeches on the Land Question', the Conservative Walter Carlile chose 'Old Age Pensions' and Richard Cooper his work 'in widening the minds of the people for fair trade and more generous remuneration for the worker'. Arthur Brookfield claimed responsibility for 'Reviving and reorganizing the almost dead interest in the Army'. The former teacher Frank Goldstone was 'Chairman of the Parliamentary Labour Party's Education Committee & membership of the Departmental Ctee whose recommendations formed the basis of the Education Act of 1918'. The former miners' agent John Sutton listed 'assisting to help the miners to receive a Minimum wage in 1911' and his fellow trade unionist Will Thorne cited his efforts to organise 'wage earners into the Trade Union & Socialist movement & every possible assistance I could give that cause by virtue of being an M.P.'.

Members were not then invariably closely involved with their constituencies, but the greatest achievement of the Liberal Bertrand Watson was 'Answering every letter received from my constituents' (he did not say how many he received). There were claims of successful special pleading for constituency causes. The Liberal member for Reigate from 1906 to 1910, Harry Brodie, persuaded 'Mr John Burns [then president of the board of trade] to agree to favourable financial terms for a loan for the Dorking District Council'. His Conservative constituency neighbour, Stuart Coats, claimed that 'By constantly pressing ministers I had an enquiry made into the state of the Oxted Tunnel, which caused it to be totally reconstructed, and thus probably saved many lives, as it was in a very dangerous condition', and Arthur Bignold, Conservative member for Wick, got a grant for the 'Dingwall and Cromarty Railway Scheme'.

The largest category of achievement listed was in relation to legislation of various kinds, although some of the claims for personal achievements were far-fetched. Hubert Carr-Gomm, for example, used a private members' bill in 1911 to argue the case for reform of London government but it is impossible to say whether that meant, as he claimed, that 'the scheme was finally accepted in the subsequent Local Government Act of 1933'. Private bills were then numerous, particularly in connection with railways, and several respondents cited their work in connection with private bill committees, including Henry Hobhouse, who had served as 'Chairman of Private bill Comtees 1895–1905', and Henry Bowles, who cited 'Some of my Committee reports to the House'. Franklin Thomasson thought that 'The only work I did in Parliament which ever seemed to me worth while, was that done on Private Bill Committees'. The Liberal Edgar Jones must have had a considerable impact when he carried an amendment in committee 'which compelled the withdrawal of the first Railway Amalgamation Bill in spite of previous agreement between the Government and the Labour interests'. Julius Bertram cited his membership of the Cardiff Railway Bill committee in 1909, William Collins his work in 'Piloting through Parliament the Metropolitan Ambulances Act 1909', and George Lane-Fox his 'defeat of a private Bill, sponsored by the City of Leeds – which attempted to include much of my constituency [Barkston Ash] in their area'.

Some mentioned their support for such measures as the Trade Disputes Bill, while others cited back-bench achievements in getting government bills amended and in promoting private members' bills. The Conservative lawyer Felix Cassel claimed to have succeeded in 'Getting one of Lloyd George's Finance Bills ruled out of order . . . The Speaker & all the authorities of the House deliberated for a long time until the Speaker finally decided in my favour'. Similar claims were made by Henry Montgomery 'In getting Lloyd George to withdraw his intention to tax common clay' and Henry George Chancellor in 'Saving the country from a fresh vested interest on second reading of the first Petroleum Production Bill 1917 . . . which caused it to be dropped and royalties excluded from the Act of 1918'. George Marks 'helped very fully to alter the old Patent Laws . . . when the amended Patent Acts were going through'. The Conservative Raymond Heath cited how, 'In conjunction with the late Col. Eyre, Capt Edwardes Heathcote, the Late Lord Manners, then Lord Newark', he brought in a bill 'granting free education, stifled at birth by the Whips, but the principle afterwards carried into law by a Conservative Government'. Hubert Carr-Gomm moved amendments to the 1918 Representation of the People Bill introducing the principle of proportional representation for university seats. The Liberal Herbert Jessel both moved 'substantial amendments to the London Government Act 1900 and [killed] proportional representation proposed in the Bill for Representation of the People in 1918'.

The Irish Nationalists tended to stick with Irish causes but claimed similar successes. William Duffy helped 'to pass "The Ward Town Tenants' Act". An Act which saved from eviction & kept in their shops or homes innumerable house-holders in all the passing years'. Michael Joyce, a Shannon river pilot before entering the House, claimed his part in 'The passage of the Pilotage Bill of 1913 into an Act of Parliament'. Patrick Kennedy cited 'The day seven of us disobeyed the Irish Party Whip & voted for A.J. Balfour's Education Bill', an action directly against his party's rule that its parliamentary representatives should speak, act and vote as a block.

Private members' bills were a procedural minefield but could provide opportunities for the persistent or lucky backbencher. The Liberal Arnold Herbert's 'best piece of work was getting through the Bill to amend the cost of distress as a private member's bill without having won a place in the ballot. It taught me a good deal about Parliamentary procedure'. The Conservative Charles Tyrrell Giles' best work 'was in starting & advocating amongst Agricultural MPs the introduction of a Bill to extend the Workmen's Compensation Act to agricultural labourers. It became the Workmen's compensation Act 1900'. Raymond Greene introduced 'the first old age Pension Bill to obtain a 2nd Reading in the H of C'. Arthur Griffith-Boscawen's housing work led to 'my Housing Bill of 1911 . . . I proposed the principle of State aid for housing & slum clearing, since adopted by all parties'. Walter Rea was responsible for 'Getting Medical Inspection of children to 3rd Reading stage when the Government took it up' and John Lloyd Morgan 'got a Bill through unopposed to do away with Juries being locked up all night in cases of felony except murder'.

Although few respondents to Q23 had achieved senior ministerial positions, several thought their best achievements were as ministers in getting legislation through the House. The Liberal Herbert Samuel, who served in a succession of ministerial posts between 1905 and 1916, had been responsible 'mainly or partly, for the conduct through the House of Commons of between twenty and thirty bills', including the Children Act 1908, which was 'the most useful', while 'the framing of the Finance Clauses in the Irish Home Rule Bill of 1911 was perhaps my most difficult task'. For the Scottish Liberal lawyer Graham Murray, 'Asquith once said I was the best man in the House for dealing with a Govt Bill in Committee' and the Conservative John Gilmour listed his part in the Local Government Scotland and Wheat Acts. Thomas Shaw, when solicitor-general for Scotland, was asked to help John Morley, then chief secretary for Ireland, 'with the land bill of the day. Perhaps my exposition of the land system of Ireland in defence of drastic reform was my best. But who knows?'

A few respondents cited their work on parliamentary committees. Anderson Montague-Barlow cited 'Presiding (as a private Member) over the Select Cee & securing a unanimous Report which settled the then outstanding difficulties of pension scales & administration & whose recommendations were accepted in their entirety by the Govt'. Lord Robert Cecil included his service on the Marconi select committee (also mentioned by Albert Spicer, who chaired the select committee, and Labour's James Parker). Joseph Larmor mentioned serving as a member of the Speaker's committee on electoral reform and Hugh Law thought that, bearing in mind the self-imposed restrictions on the activities of Irish Nationalist members, 'If I was able to do any good work at all, it was, I suppose, upon Committees of various kinds'. The Liberal Eugene Wason's 'good working knowledge of both Scotch, and English Law' meant that he was 'a distinct success as Chairman of the many Committees, over which he presided'. William Young served on several select committees including those on the 'Putumayo atrocities',[2] the 'Proposed Purchase of the Liquor Trade' and on the 'settlement of ex-soldiers on the land'. The former teacher and Labour member Frank Goldstone served as 'Chairman of the Parliamentary Labour Party's Education Committee & membership of the Departmental Ctee whose recommendations formed the basis of the Education Act of 1918'.

Some respondents' most notable achievements were connected with the First World War, including opposition to the general conduct of the war. The Liberal (later Labour) Charles Trevelyan cited 'Opposing the continuation of the war without any attempt at negotiation' and his fellow Liberal John Whitehouse 'Resistance to the Government during the War, particularly in relation to the treatment of conscientious objectors and Free Speech'. Evan Hayward constantly worried over '"Field Punishment No 1" in the Army, I like to think I had something to do with its abolition'. Edward Smallwood served only from 1917 to 1918 but cited his achievement of 'Championing the men at the Front. Claiming fair treatment for wounded and tired long service men & a drastic "comb out" of home service and safe men'. Edgar Horne sat on the 'Public Expenditure Committee' (the first national expenditure committee) and on a sub-committee 'which had the duty of examining into, and reporting upon, the Army, Navy and Air Force expenditures; the subject was of course one utterly beyond our powers, but I think we did a certain amount of good'.

Among ministers, the then Liberal Christopher Addison cited his achievements at 'organisation work – first as under Secretary and then as Minister of Munitions 1915–1917'. Lord Robert Cecil served as minister of blockade from 1916 to 1918 and included 'perhaps the Blockade during the War' while Harry Verney thought it was 'When Parliamentary Secretary to the Ministry of Agriculture at beginning of the War 1914, organising women to work in agriculture instead of taking small boys prematurely from school'. Labour's George Barnes, who served in 1916–17 as minister of pensions, cited 'My pleading for pensions, civil and military' while J.R. Clynes listed 'The work I did in the later part of the War as Food Controller. That work was started with many signs of public apprehension. The work of the Ministry ended amid popular approval'.

6. *Leaving the House of Commons*

The answers to the final question about parliamentary careers – Q24: 'If you are no longer in Parliament, why did you leave?' – confirmed that leaving the house of commons could be a severe blow, particularly following electoral defeat. Nearly 50 (18%) of the 265 respondents gave detailed accounts of the circumstances of their departure, often implying that they felt guilty about their unsuccessful careers or that they had been innocent victims of events beyond their control. Many also mentioned their often

---

[2] An investigation into claims by Roger Casement about the treatment of Peruvian Indians employed on British-owned rubber plantations in Peru.

strenuous efforts to return. Reactions to leaving the house of commons depended to some extent on how the respondents felt about their parliamentary careers. Those who were disappointed or frustrated, like the Irish Nationalist Robert Ambrose and the Liberals Thomas Barclay and Franklin Thomasson, mostly retired of their own volition and without regrets. Robert Brassey 'did not come back to Parliament because he did not agree with payment of Members nor with votes for women'. The majority who had, on balance, enjoyed themselves or felt that they had achieved something worthwhile (including government office) were far more likely to regret having to leave, for whatever reason, including old age.

Just over a third (36%) of the 265 respondents (73% of the total) left for good involuntarily because of electoral defeat, which often created continuing resentment about their fate at the hands of an ungrateful electorate or as a consequence of party machinations. Arnold Herbert 'was ejected [in 1910] by the electors of S. Bucks' while another Liberal, Frank Newnes, left 'Because in Jan 1910 there were 300 more voters in Bassetlaw who preferred my opponent to me'. The Lib–Lab Fred Maddison 'left Parliament for one reason only [in January 1910] – because I could not get returned'. George Leveson-Gower, Liberal deputy chief whip in the early 1890s, recounted how 'Sir William Vernon Harcourt's speech at the 1895 Election, advocating Local Option, plus the generous distribution of liquor by the brewers and publicans in my district [Stoke on Trent], persuaded a majority of 200 of my constituents that they would be better pleased if I no longer represented them'. Harcourt's policies were also partly blamed by Samuel Whitbread for his defeat in 1895: 'After Harcourt's two Vetoe [*sic*] Bills . . . the organised Temperance Party made it quite impossible for anyone connected with the Brewing Trade to contest a Parliamentary election on the Liberal side. It became unfair to the party and the constituency and utterly impossible for candidates'. Another Liberal, Arthur Crosfield, 'did not leave. I was beaten at the second election in 1910. With his brother Harold as candidate, F.E. Smith – as he then was – brought down all his artillery and just enabled his brother to capture the seat by a narrow margin'. Alfred Scott attributed his defeat in December 1910 to 'the corruption of the then Mr Max Aitken now Lord Beaverbrook' but gave no more details.

The political and party upheavals in the years that followed the First World War accounted for many defeats from which parliamentary careers seldom recovered, particularly among Liberals. Willoughby Dickinson lost his seat 'when the Liberal Party was betrayed in the "Coupon" election of 1918' while John Whitehouse's constituency was, like numerous others, 'wiped out in the Redistribution Bill of 1918. I was defeated [five times] in other constituencies'. Daniel Turner Holmes experienced the combined consequences of the 'coupon' election and boundary redistribution: 'As an "uncouponed" candidate, I was defeated in Dec. 1918. In some degree my defeat was due to the redistribution of seats which detached from my constituency of Govan, the district of Govanhill'. Labour's Frank Goldstone was similarly defeated in 1918 because he 'did not receive one Mr Lloyd George's "coupons"' and 'Opposed the "Hang the Kaiser" crusade'. Joseph King left 'because at the General Election of 1918 my constituency ceased to exist, and I failed to be nominated in any electoral area'. Ernest Morrison-Bell's departure in 1918 showed that boundary redistribution did not affect only Liberals. His constituency 'was done away with in 1918, and the bigger half absorbed into Totnes, so that I, naturally, gave way to Frank Mildmay [a Liberal]'.

Arthur Wilson left 'Because unfortunately in 1923 my constituents did not think I was attending to my duties properly & turned me out'. J.A.R. Marriott, first elected in 1917 at the age of 58, 'left Parliament only because I was turned out [in 1929] by York . . . & at 70 was too old for election contests under modern conditions though I would go back to Parliament tomorrow, could I get there without a contest'. Jack Seely, originally elected as a Conservative in 1900, joined the Liberals in 1904, serving as secretary of state for war from 1912 to 1914, as well as in other government positions. He described how 'An electorate, momentarily misguided, failed to return me to the House of Commons in 1924, to which they had elected me twenty-four years previously'.

Electoral defeat, however initially unwelcome, could be a blessing in disguise, particularly for those who had reached an age or stage where they were daunted by the prospect of reselection and fighting more elections. The Conservative Arthur Griffith-Boscawen lost his seat in 1922 and was defeated again in 1923. Those 'political disasters' were 'a heavy blow' although he became 'happy & contented', having been engaged in 'lots of public work' and 'in my old age I do what I ought to have done in my youth – earn a little money'. John Stirling-Maxwell 'was not sorry' when he lost his seat in 1905 as he disagreed with his constituents' support for tariff reform and 'after one more very uncomfortable general election in which I was again beaten I retired from the fray'. Reginald McKenna, who had been Liberal member for North Monmouthshire for 23 years and served as both home secretary and chancellor of the exchequer during the First World War, 'was defeated at the Election of 1918. I fought to win, but I was not sorry to be defeated. My enthusiasm had waned in the experience of 23 years of Parliamentary work'. Arthur Murray's 'health after the War was not what it was before, and I found it increasingly difficult to attend to the House of Commons; to the needs of a large constituency . . . and to business preoccupations. So my defeat in 1923 came very opportunely!' Harry Brodie, by his own account never a particularly enthusiastic politician, 'was defeated in 1910 – & I had just got married & had more expenses so did not intend to stand again for a few years. Then the War came & after the War I have had to work harder in business'.

The Conservative Arthur Black found that 'My business claims were very pressing & being defeated in 1918 I accepted dismissal with releif [sic]'. Henry Gooch found after defeat in January 1910 that 'Parliamentary life . . . did not really attract me. So I returned in January 1911 to my municipal life, which attracted me from every point of view, and in which I have found my life's work'. Raymond Greene was defeated in 1923 '& glad to sieze [sic] the chance of being free'. Sigismund Mendl 'lost my seat in the 1900 General Election & have never felt any desire to return. In addition, business & family reasons have prevented my doing so'. Similarly, Labour's James Parker 'was defeated in 1922 & as I was 59 years of age & very tired I determined to retire. I enjoyed my Parliamentary life yet I have no wish to return'.

Some left because they disliked being in parliament or had had enough. After 17 years, the Irish Nationalist Robert Ambrose retired in 1910 because 'I was sick of it'; Alfred Hutton was similarly 'Fed up' in 1910 after 18 years' service. Julius Bertram, who served only from 1906 to 1910, 'Had enough of the Lib: party & disliked the others even more'. Franklin Thomasson 'felt out of place and hopeless of ever accomplishing anything, so refused to seek re-election' in 1910. William Barton, first elected in 1910, found that by 1922 he was 'No longer useful', while Charles Buxton 'thought I could do more useful work outside it' in 1931. William Clough, first elected in 1906, found that parliamentary life in wartime made him 'most unhappy' and did not stand in 1918. Max Aitken departed in 1917 from frustration at the age of 38 after seven years' service, 'because I failed to get office' (he was immediately given a peerage and became minister of information).

Old age and ill-health between them accounted for 17% of departures; surprisingly few respondents (around 5%) claimed to have left solely on grounds of age rather than ill-health, suggesting the need for a specific reason to justify leaving. Old age led to Charles Carew's retirement in 1922 when he was 69, and Basil Peto's in 1935 at 73; Labour's John Sutton was defeated in 1931 when he was 69 and 'decided to retire on account of advancing years'. Edward Fielden and Albert Spicer both retired in their seventies because of 'Age & deafness' and John Hodge left at the age of 68 'To spend the evening of life quietly with my wife'. Alfred Hopkinson's retirement at the age of 68 was 'on account of age fearing to be in the House with a small majority on the Govt side and when always wanted to attend divisions, tho' late, fearing Govt defeats'. Sir Aylmer Hunter-Weston 'thought that being seventy-one years of age, and having been thirty-five years in the Army and nearly twenty years in Parliament, it was time for me to make room for younger and better men'.

Some wanted or needed, often for financial reasons, to pursue other activities. By 1929, Evelyn Cecil 'had had enough after 31 years, and was anxious to retire [at 64] while I could still do useful work'. Frederick Chance served between 1905 and 1910 and retired at the age of 49 'largely because he did not really care for Parliamentary life & felt he could do more useful work outside the House'. Henry McLaren, first elected in 1906 at the age of 27, retired in 1922 because 'Business interests attracted me more'. The Conservative Ben Bathurst, whose political career had started when he was 21, decided not to stand in 1918 when he was only 46 'because I found a large constituency and Parliament demanded too much time, and after 25 years as a candidate or member I thought private affairs might come into some consideration'. Lionel de Rothschild was first elected in 1910 at the age of 28. 'Unfortunately, partly owing to old age [he was 41] and partly owing to the war in 1923 I found myself alone with my brother in the firm and the work rendered it quite impossible for me to justify my continuing to sit in the House of Commons and I had, with great regret, to announce my decision not to contest the seat again'.

Some of the 12% who retired allegedly because of ill-health were only in their thirties or forties and ill-health may have been no more than an excuse. They included Miles Mattison, first elected at his fourth attempt in 1888 when he was 34 and who served until 1892. He was 'under no necessity of retiring except that the late hours of those days were affecting my health & I was not in entire sympathy with my party'. Walter Carlile 'was never beaten, but retired, on account of Health and Expense' in 1906 when he was 44. Lord John Joicey-Cecil found at the age of 41 that 'The sedentary life made me ill' and that 'expenses were too great'. Richard Cooper was 'Worn out' at the age of 48 while Alexander Murray (the master of Elibank and Liberal chief whip from 1910 to 1912) retired from politics in 1912 at the age of 42 'after an illness' to pursue a business career (he died in 1920 at the age of 50).

Ill-health took its toll of numerous respondents in their fifties, including Labour's Albert Smith, who resigned in 1920 at the age of 54, and Anderson Montague-Barlow who 'left Parliament in 1924 owing to ill health' when he was 56. Stuart Coats was 54 in 1922 and left because of his wife's ill-health '& I also found the strain of the bad air, & irregular hours of the H of C very trying'. Others who retired in their sixties often blamed ill-health rather than old age. Thomas Salt retired 'on account of health' in 1892 at the age of 62, having served for most of the 30 years since he was first elected in 1859 at the age of 29. Henry Bowles retired in 1922 at the age of 64 'Because my Doctor said I must have all my teeth out'. Clive Morrison-Bell was 62 when he retired in 1931 and it clearly still rankled: 'my health broke down in 1930. I should not have been opposed . . . in 1931, and it would have completed my "Jubilee" in 1935, but before the 1931 General Election came, they had got another candidate and, though restored to health, I could not very well butt in again'.

The demands of parliamentary life, particularly when combined with other activities, sometimes brought pressures that led to retirement. The Irish Nationalist Denis Cogan 'resigned voluntarily [in 1907 at 58] as my health was breaking down through overwork'. James Fortescue-Flannery was 71 when he left 'as the work of the House and the Constituency and my professional occupation was so arduous as to be undermining my health'. Joseph Larmor, who sat for Cambridge University, 'Finally retired in 1922 on grounds of health and pressure of occupation as Lucasian Professor [of mathematics at Cambridge]'. Ernest Jardine, first elected in 1910 at the age of 51, described the pressures (admittedly self-inflicted) that he faced:

> I lived, and live, in Nottingham; my constituency was East Somerset, 186 miles away − 130 miles from Westminster and from Westminster to Nottingham 124 miles. . . . The strain of running business, keeping in close touch with my constituency and Parliamentary work, was too great. The Re-distribution Bill came into force [in 1918] . . . My doctor said I was overworking and this redistribution gave me the opportunity to retire.

The pressures of combining parliamentary and business careers similarly led George Touche to stand down in 1918: 'his doctors advised that the overstrained state of his heart made it essential for him to do so'. For Robert Wallace, 'Not being physically strong I found the double life of the Bar & House of Commons too much for me & Herbert Gladstone pressed me to become Chairman of London County Sessions'.

Wallace was among the 11 respondents to Q24 (4%), all barristers, who left the house of commons on appointment to legal positions, some overseas. These included John Bigham, appointed to the English high court in 1897, two judges in the Irish high court (Plunket Barton in 1900 and William Moore in 1917), a judge advocate general in the army (Felix Cassel in 1916) and four Scottish judges (Graham Murray in 1905, Thomas Shaw in 1909 and Robert Munro and Thomas Morison in 1922). Of the nine respondents who left for other public positions, six were appointed to posts overseas, including Edward Wood, appointed in 1925 as viceroy of India, and Lord Ronaldshay who became governor of Bengal in 1916. Nearer home, Labour's David Shackleton 'was offered a post in the Civil Service [as Senior Labour adviser to the home office] which I accepted with the approval of the Weavers Amalgamation, whose President I was at that time [in 1910]' while William Brace was appointed in 1920 as 'Chief Labour Adviser to the newly created Mines Department'.

Inheriting a peerage accounted for nine departures; a further nine left because they were raised to the peerage. Those who inherited peerages did not always go willingly. Lord Wolmer recounted how 'George Curzon, St John Brodrick, and I had agreed that whoever's father died first would test the case whether he could be forced to quit the House of Commons for the House of Lords. The lot fell on me [in 1895] & I tried it, but the House of Commons turned me out'. Another Curzon, Francis (later Earl Howe), was elected only in 1918 for Battersea South. He inherited his father's earldom in 1929 but thought that otherwise he 'could probably say I should still be its Member. . . . I can only look forward to the so-called Reform of the House of Lords and hope against hope'.

Even the well connected could not always sustain indefinitely the expense of getting elected and keeping a seat in the house of commons. For 20 respondents, money accounted wholly or partly for the decision to retire and that did not include those who left to look after their business interests or family estates. Arthur Brookfield retired in 1903 because he 'could barely live on the income of a consul still less on the pension such a person had time to earn'. George Montagu sat from 1900 to 1906 and 'did not stand again on account of financial reasons'. Henry Montgomery retired in 1910 because he did not have the money to keep a local party organisation going while Rowland Whitehead, having been defeated in January 1910, then 'lost the financial backing on which I relied' and did not stand again. John Starkey simply found parliamentary life 'too expensive' in 1922. George Lane-Fox found in 1931 that the 'Expense [was] too great for an income much reduced by heavy war taxation and after 25 years membership, I had done all that I could hope to do'.

A significant group of departures in 1918 was precipitated by developments in Ireland. Seventeen Irish Nationalists answered the question and two, Patrick Kennedy and Robert Ambrose, had left before 1918. Of the remainder, four retired in 1918 while the others were defeated and some clearly still felt considerable unhappiness at the circumstances of their departure. Hugh Law was determined as early as 1910 that he would not stand again because 'I was not of the timber from which successful, or even very useful, Parliamentarians are made'. However, he also acknowledged that 'thanks to the change in Irish ideas consequent upon the teaching of Sinn Fein, and of the Ulster Covenanters – this determination of mine altered nothing one way or the other'. Another retiree, John Boland, blamed 'Carsonism [which] gave such power to Sinn Fein that constitutional methods were superseded by physical force', while Daniel O'Leary 'left in compliance with the altered view of the Irish people as to the methods to be adopted to attain independence for Ireland'. Michael Flavin attributed his departure to 'The 1916 Rebellion in Ireland' and William Duffy his defeat to his remaining 'a loyal member of John Redmond's party. . . . the Electorate were so maddened at the non-performance of the promises made to Mr Redmond regarding Home Government that it was another case of false promises & betrayal & expelled from the British Parliament every supporter of Mr Redmond'.

Chapter 5. Personal and Political Finances

1. *Introduction*

Wedgwood's desire for a fully rounded picture of his colleagues extended to seeking details of their financial circumstances both before and after they entered parliament. He asked three questions about money and personal finances – Q9: 'Annual income, earned and unearned, when first you stood for Parliament'; Q17: 'How did being an M.P. affect your earning capacity?'; and Q14: 'What did it cost you then [i.e. when first elected] to contest? And how much yearly while M.P.?' As with his questions about their formative influences, he appears to have sought this information not primarily from prurience, although some of the correspondence suggests an element of that, but from genuine curiosity and because he recognised the importance of money as a determinant of political careers. Because his 'sample' was so unsystematic, the data he collected on financial matters were not statistically robust. The replies to those questions did, however, provide anecdotal information about the personal finances of his subjects which complements the findings of later more systematic studies of the socio-economic backgrounds of members of parliament in that period.[1] Similarly, they largely confirm the findings in subsequent studies of detailed aspects of electoral and party funding in the late 19th and early 20th centuries.[2]

The replies illustrated how the financial circumstances of members of parliament were gradually changing in the years before the First World War, even though politics was still largely the preserve of the well endowed. Most members of parliament from the two major parties still had independent means of some kind, if not always enough to support a political career without needing to earn. Rich patrons continued to kick-start and sustain the careers of their protégés, if on a reduced scale; a significant proportion of Liberals and Conservatives still depended to some extent on financial help from family and friends to finance their parliamentary careers. There were, however, increasing numbers, mainly among the Liberals, who depended on their own earnings. For them, going into parliament could mean significant financial hardship (Lloyd George was among the most notable examples). Most Labour members depended entirely on trade union or similar sources of funds, or on the parliamentary allowance after its introduction in 1912. Even after that, most members of parliament were personally out of pocket, partly as a result of meeting the cost of maintaining their constituencies.

---

[1] See Thomas, *House of Commons 1832–1901*, especially the analysis of occupational backgrounds in ch.1; Guttsman, *British Political Elite*, especially ch. IV; and Rush, *Role of the Member of Parliament since 1868*, ch. 4.

[2] See in particular T.O. Lloyd, 'The Whip as Paymaster: Herbert Gladstone and Party Organization', *English Historical Review*, lxxxix (1974), 785–813; and Kathryn Rix, '"The Elimination of Corrupt Practices in British Elections?" Reassessing the Impact of the 1883 Corrupt Practices Act', *English Historical Review*, cxxiii (2008), 1–30.

2. *Income and Occupation*

In his own questionnaire, circulated with the first round of chasing letters, Wedgwood was very open about his personal financial circumstances but the correspondence showed that the question about income when first a candidate still caused some respondents a good deal of anguish. In the circumstances, and given the attitudes of the time, the total number of responses to that question (224) was surprisingly high. Many did their best to be informative despite some obvious (and understandable) confusion between 'when first you stood for Parliament' and 'when first elected'. Some answered reluctantly and 14 respondents asked for the details not to be made public. That was far more than in response to any other question and included such high-profile figures as Edward Wood and Eric Geddes (Lord Geddes). Several also asked for the previously supplied details to be removed when their biographies were sent to them by Wedgwood for checking.

Wedgwood pressed some of those who had failed to answer the question to 'give a guess' at their incomes but that did not always work. Ben Bathurst, Conservative member for Cirencester from 1895 to 1906 and 1910 to 1918, replied to a follow-up request from Wedgwood for details of his income:

> As to my income in 1895, I did not put it in because I did not think it of much interest or concern from the point of view of being able to judge the position of an individual – I was living either with my brother or step-mother, and would not have managed to live independently. . . . You will . . . agree that my own personal income hardly serves as to what could be done by anybody else differently situated [so] . . . I think it better not to insert this.

Robert Brassey simply ignored a similar request while Julius Bertram thought his income could be left out: 'it was & is variable – at least the "earned" part of it "I have always had to pay surtax" might be substituted, if you want to include the informn. You will get more lies printed in the replies to this enquiry than in all the rest of your publication'.

Sixty-five respondents gave no figures but commented, usually in vague terms, on the level of their incomes – 'Several thousand pounds per annum' (Stuart Coats) or 'No record to show but his means were ample for his needs' (Thomas Salt's son), while Max Aitken contented himself with 'Big income'. It is difficult not to empathise with Thomas Nussey's description of his income when first elected as 'sufficient for my needs but not enough to satisfy my tastes' or to speculate about the lifestyle of Thomas Bethell who said he had a 'comfortable income for a bachelor'. About two-thirds gave specific details; of those who did, 58 gave figures of their earned income, 45 of unearned income (there was a high level of overlap between the two) and 80 gave a combined figure.

The other two financial questions caused much less anguish but the answers to all three undoubtedly suffered from the ambiguous wording of the questions as well as the unreliability of the subjects' memories about their personal finances 30 or more years earlier. Their families were even less reliable. Some people had clearly kept personal records, particularly of their election expenses, or used the official published returns of their election expenses. Others may have happened to remember facts of that kind fairly accurately, while many took refuge in generalisations. Since the respondents were not a representative sample in terms of age, party or date of first candidacy/election, the overall picture that emerges, particularly of personal incomes, is at best an indication of orders of magnitude, although there is no evidence of the lies predicted by Robert Brassey.

The question about pre-parliamentary incomes and their sources asked for separate details of earned and unearned incomes but many respondents chose to combine the two. The replies showed that by the late 1890s/early 1900s the range of incomes from all sources was very wide, probably wider than earlier in the 19th century when members of parliament came from a narrower range of backgrounds. There were also significant differences between the parties, which reflected the changes in the personal and occupational backgrounds of members of the house of commons following the reform of electoral practices in 1883, the third Reform Act of 1884 and other changes of the period between 1885 and 1918. Before the passage of the Corrupt and Illegal Practices Act of 1883 candidates from either of the major political parties had to be personally rich, or have the backing of a wealthy patron or organisation, to be able to afford to contest parliamentary elections. The 1883 Act reduced the financial burdens on individual candidates but there were still serious problems for the parties, especially the small socialist parties, in financing elections for candidates without private means. The Social Democratic Foundation and the Independent Labour Party were both largely financed by donations from wealthy supporters, while Lib–Lab candidates were mainly working-class men who ran with Liberal support, usually with additional financial backing from individual trade unions. In 1900, the formation of the Labour representation committee (which adopted the name 'Labour Party' in 1906) provided a mechanism for both financing candidates and supporting working-class MPs once elected. Candidates still, however, had to pay their share of the returning officers' charges, which were a substantial proportion of total spending for Labour candidates.

The number of Labour members grew rapidly from 1900 onwards, with 29 first elected in 1906. With a few exceptions, they came from very different occupational backgrounds from those of their parliamentary contemporaries and their financial circumstances could not have been more different. Most were trade union officials, originally from largely manual occupations, and they had few, if any, other sources of income apart from occasional writing. Few of them had unearned incomes. Wedgwood himself was a notable exception but he did not join the Labour Party until 1919. He was first elected in 1906 as a Liberal, so his declared unearned income of £2,500 in 1904 cannot be compared with the incomes of Labour Party members elected at the same time.

All the 11 Labour members who answered the question about incomes gave specific details of their earnings, as did the four Lib–Labs. Those incomes were all very small, especially compared with those of their contemporaries in other parties. The highest among Labour members was that of Frank Goldstone, a former teacher and trade union official, who said he had a total of earned and unearned income of £360 a year. George Lansbury, who had a long career as a writer and journalist as well as being in business in a small way, had £150, all earned, plus a house, in 1894 – but he also had a wife and six children. James Parker, originally an unskilled labourer who had held an astonishing variety of jobs, said he had an earned income of 30 shillings a week (£75 a year).

The Irish Nationalists, of whom 15 answered the question, came from a wider range of occupations with corresponding variations in incomes. Hugh Law 'had then an independent income of some £1,500 a year' and Sir Walter Nugent had 'whatever I earned'. He admitted in answer to Q8 to being 'U.S.A. banking & general Business . . . Landowner in Ireland'. Most were not affluent, even if they were not to be directly compared with Labour members. Michael Joyce, who described himself as a river pilot on the Shannon, had £200 a year and Matthew Keating, who described himself as having been a 'pit-boy' and subsequently as having a 'commercial career', earned £300 a year working in London. Stephen Gwynn described himself as a writer earning £1,000 a year (mainly from journalism – a large sum for the time), while John Boland was earning £1,500 at the English bar, which suggests that he was moderately successful.

The replies from the members of the two large parties showed that, even allowing for the effects of the 1883 Act, those first elected in 1906 and 1910 still included significant numbers with substantial unearned incomes, particularly among the Conservatives. The highest incomes (£5,000 a year or more) were found among Conservatives and, where they did not distinguish between the sources of their incomes (earned or unearned), there is often other evidence to confirm that they must have had private means, sometimes ample ones. Taken with the answers to the question about occupations (Q8), the replies show that many of the 79 Conservatives who answered the question about incomes were not actually working at their nominal occupations when they became candidates or first entered parliament. Many depended entirely on inherited or unearned wealth (the distinction is not invariably clear), although from rather different sources than earlier generations. In distinct contrast with the position only 50 years earlier, there were only a small number of landowners (seven), two of whom admitted to very large incomes (Sir George Sitwell, first a candidate in 1884 and elected in 1885, had £5,000 a year and Lord Ninian Crichton Stuart £10,000 a year when first elected in December 1910). Leonard Brassey (a descendant of Thomas Brassey, the celebrated railway contractor) gave no details of his income but 'had independent means and no definite trade or profession. I was and still am an Agricultural Landowner'.

A noticeable feature of the Conservatives' sources of income concerned the 14 who said they had allowances from their parents, usually their fathers and often of unspecified amounts. They presumably depended on those allowances since they declared no other sources of income. In some cases the allowances must have been large, although few gave details of the amounts and such allowances cannot always be distinguished from unearned incomes. Mark Sykes' son described his father as a 'considerably wealthy man . . . At the age of twenty-one he was given an allowance of £4000 a year by his father'. Rowland Whitehead could not recollect precisely but 'I think "earned" £1200, unearned £600 and a handsome "allowance" which was £1200 a year when I was in Parliament'. Unlike his barrister brother Robert, Lord Hugh Cecil had no specific occupation but an allowance of £800 a year. Francis Mildmay had no income of his own but 'My father, a partner in the commercial firm of Baring Bros & Co, made me an allowance'. George Ormsby-Gore (first elected in 1901 and who succeeded his father as Lord Harlech in 1904) simply had 'an allowance' and his son William, first elected in 1910, had '£400 allowance from my father'. Viscount Dalrymple's pay as an army officer was supplemented by an allowance from his father.

The three main occupations among Conservatives were army officers (20, 25%), barristers (17, 21%) and company directors (14, 18%). With the single exception of W.A. Adam, who admitted to no other income than £700 earned, all the army officers had substantial unearned incomes. Wilfrid Ashley, who had been a lieutenant-colonel in the grenadier guards, was first elected in 1906 with an income of £10,000 a year, most of which could not have been his army pay. Lieutenant-Colonel John Newman, first a candidate in 1906 and elected in 1910, also had an income, unearned, of £10,000. Archibald Weigall, first a candidate in 1910 and elected in 1911, had £1,500 earned income, presumably his army pay, and 'about ten times as much' unearned. Lord Ninian Crichton-Stuart's widow described him as a 'soldier and army officer' but he was also a farmer/landowner whose £10,000 a year presumably came from his family estates. Sir Aylmer Hunter-Weston, a former career soldier first elected in 1916, had a total income of £8,000, of which his army pay can have been only a small part and the rest came from his family estate. Viscount Dalrymple, who was first elected in 1906, gave no figures but said he had an allowance from his father because 'my military pay never covered necessary expenditure, except when on active service abroad'.

Only four of the 17 Conservative barristers appear to have been practising by the time they were first candidates. They were all earning significant amounts: Lord Robert Cecil between £3,000 and £6,000 when he was elected in 1910; and Felix Cassel, elected in the same year, was earning £5,000; he had no unearned income but knew that his uncle [the financier Sir Ernest Cassel] 'would always see I had what I required'. Edmund Bartley-Denniss' son could not give figures of his father's income but 'my mother had good private means and at one time he was making a good income at the Bar in general practice – he would never touch criminal work, he was very emphatic about that'.

Then, as now, the position of 'company director' meant many different things and of the 14 Conservatives within that category, only eight gave specific details of their incomes. These ranged from the £12,500, probably mostly earned and among the highest of the incomes given, of Robert Williams, a director of Williams Deacon's bank since 1874 and first elected in 1895, to the £400 earned and the same amount unearned a year of Henry Croft, first elected in 1910 when he had just left Cambridge and entered his family business of maltsters. Benjamin Cohen, a stockbroker first elected in 1892, was said by his son to have had an income of £10,000. Angus Hambro, of the banking family and first elected in 1910, said that he was 'farming at the time' and earning £1,700 a year, but did not mention any unearned income. Plunket Barton gave no details but described his personal financial circumstances as 'easy', with a 'rising professional practice' (from the bar) and a directorship of the Guinness brewery, 'owing to a family connexion with the Guinnesses'. Perhaps most remarkable of the professional incomes was the £20,000 of the surgeon, Sir William Cheyne, first elected in 1917 at the age of 65 when he had just retired and who must previously have had an extremely successful career.

The 94 Liberals who replied to the question generally gave more specific information about their incomes than the Conservatives. They were in fairly similar occupations but the distribution between the occupations was rather different. With a few exceptions, they were at least moderately affluent but depended more on earned rather than inherited or otherwise unearned wealth. There were only nine army officers (9.5% of respondents) but 25 each (27%) barristers and company directors, only four landowners and five writers/journalists. Only three of the army officers gave details of their incomes and they all had substantial private means. Austin Hopkinson was first elected at a by-election only two months before the 1918 general election and had an unearned income from his family business of £8,000; Malcolm Kincaid-Smith was first elected in 1906 with an unearned income of £2,500 and Leslie Renton first stood in 1900 with a total income of £3,000. John Bethell, a surveyor who was first a Liberal candidate in 1894, then had an income of £3,000. There were few other large incomes, especially when compared with the Conservatives. Even Charles Trevelyan, whose income was entirely unearned, had only 'about £500 a year till I married. But my father paid all my election expenses'. When Graham Murray, an advocate and later Lord Dunedin, first stood for parliament in 1883 or 1884 his income was 'quite small' and his father paid all his expenses but by the time he was first elected in 1891 his father had died and with his professional earnings he had an income 'of about £9000 a year'. He was, however, an exception even among the barristers in his party, although some were successful. The son of the Liberal Unionist and barrister John Bigham said that when his father entered the House in 1895 he was earning 'from £12000 to £15000 a year'. Nathaniel Micklem, who served from 1906 to 1910, was earning £1,000 when first elected but also had £2,500 unearned, while Thomas Morison, an advocate first elected in 1917, was earning £3,500. By contrast, Edgar Jones, first elected in 1910, claimed to have had an income as a barrister of £200 a year.

With one exception (Norman Lamont with £400 a year) the Liberal company directors who gave details had incomes of £1,000 or more. They were therefore reasonably successful if not as seriously rich as some of their Conservative equivalents. They were also predominantly from manufacturing industry or commerce rather than the financial sector favoured by the Conservatives. Courtenay Warner, who first stood unsuccessfully in 1885, was in the property business and had an income, according to his son, of £6,000. William Barton, who was in the cotton textile business and first elected in 1910, had an income of £5,000. Richard Holt, from a Liverpool ship-owning family, first stood at a by-election in 1903 with an earned income of £2,500 plus the same amount unearned. Athelstan Rendall, a solicitor and also company director who was first elected in 1906, earned £1,800 but also had £1,000 from his wife. The small number of writer/journalists (five) included Cecil Harmsworth who first stood at a by-election in 1901 and had an earned income of £2,000 and nothing unearned, although he later acquired what he called 'independent means'. There were only two medical practitioners among the Liberals: William Chapple, a surgeon first elected in 1910 with an income of about £3,000; and Christopher Addison, also first elected in 1910, who had been a professor of anatomy with an earned income of £750 and about £1,000 unearned, 'mainly wife's income'.

3. The Impact of being in Parliament on Earning Capacity

The question about the effect of being in parliament on earning capacity (Q17) was understandably difficult to answer with any precision. Most respondents could not give specific answers, although 213 replied. It is not clear whether Wedgwood deliberately chose the term 'earning capacity' rather than asking about actual earnings or incomes but the answers suggest that many took it as meaning the latter. Archibald Weigall, among others, answered the question literally, saying that being in parliament 'ended [his earning capacity] entirely'. Forty-two per cent claimed that their earnings had stayed the same or not been affected, although that figure included those who said that the MPs' allowance of £400 from 1912 onwards cancelled out any additional costs associated with being in the House. For many, being in parliament was not necessarily a full-time occupation but they had no other, presumably because they did not need to earn. In some cases, such as Wedgwood's own, being in parliament was undoubtedly a full-time occupation although Wedgwood also found time for plenty of non-parliamentary activities, including his historical work, but it was unpaid. Many of his colleagues did not do that – few can have had his energy – but may have attended to managing their wealth and similar activities rather than undertaking paid work.

It is seldom clear whether those who continued in other occupations while serving as members of parliament did so because they wanted to or because they needed to earn. Nineteen per cent said that their earnings were adversely or severely affected by being in parliament and almost 20% said that their earnings from business or professional work were reduced, while 8% had to resign from business or professional interests. Hilton Young certainly thought it unrealistic to expect that members of parliament could increase their earning capacity by being there. Some of his colleagues would have disagreed but he asked: 'How the devil can being an M.P. increase an honest man's earning capacity? It is as much as to ask, how big a swindler were you'. In answer to a later question (Q24) about their reasons for leaving parliament, 20 respondents claimed to have left the house of commons at least partly because of their financial circumstances. George Montagu said simply that he did not stand again in 1906 'for financial reasons', while George Lane-Fox retired in 1931 because the 'Expense [was] too great for an income much reduced by heavy war taxation'.

As might be expected, many of those who found that being in parliament made little, if any, difference to their earning capacity had inherited or unearned wealth and some admitted that their ability to earn money had never really been put to the test. This suggests that in the early 20th century the process of 'professionalisation' of members of parliament had not advanced very far; for many, politics might have been an expensive luxury but it was one that they could clearly afford. Frederick Guest's earning capacity was unaffected because 'I never had any', while Robert Brassey 'had no profession', so no loss of income, Malcolm Kincaid-Smith 'Never earned anything' and William du Pre said it made no difference because except as a soldier he too had never earned anything. Henry Bowles 'never earned I only spent' and for Charles Carew being in parliament had 'no effect'. James Majendie had 'never earned a shilling', so it made no difference and Lord Wolmer 'remained entirely dependent on my father's generosity & affection'. For Sir George Sitwell, however, things were rather different, despite his ample wealth and his relatively brief parliamentary career: 'It led me to neglect my private affairs. I ought to have attended much more closely to the development of my landed and mineral property'.

For 10% of the respondents, mainly those who undertook such outside activities as writing or lecturing, or who were journalists, being in parliament actually increased their incomes. William Brace found that 'Being M.P. gave me improved status and consequently larger fees for newspaper and other writings, on industrial and economic questions'. Frank Goldstone's earning capacity was increased 'to some small extent'. John Boland, an Irish Nationalist, 'contributed occasionally to the Press. Being an M.P. was a helpful introduction to some editors'. D.D. Sheehan, another Irish Nationalist, found that as a journalist being in parliament 'definitely helped'; he never had any difficulty in placing articles and 'the columns of the "Daily Express" were always open to my contributions'. Colin Coote, a Liberal and later editor of *The Times*, who went straight into the house of commons from army service during the First World War, earned 'quite a lot' as a freelance journalist and owed his subsequent employment to the recommendation of Martin Conway (later Lord Conway). George Barnes earned about as much from journalism (£200) as his salary as secretary of his union, even though 'most of my writing was done for nothing – for Labour Journals'. George Wardle, of the 1906 Labour intake, found that being in parliament gave him an opportunity to earn 'a little extra' as a journalist; he was subsequently invited to become a fellow of the Institute of Journalists. Fred Maddison, a print worker who later became an editor and first stood as a Lib–Lab candidate in 1892, 'carried on outside occupations with limited salary, but public speaking earned me more than if I had not been in Parliament. I was a trifle to the good'.

Journalists did not, however, invariably find it easy to continue to earn money while in parliament and their careers could be seriously interrupted. William O'Malley, an Irish Nationalist and journalist first elected in 1895, found that 'Parliament distracted me from work' while Wedgwood's close friend and Liberal contemporary Leo Money initially faced conflicts of interest. For him, being in parliament:

> led to my leaving the staff of a newspaper, but this I surmounted. I found complete independence preferable to staff work. I have had no difficulty in earning a simple livelihood, save that my resignation from the War Government in 1918, after the Armistice . . . meant a sudden cessation of income, because I had laid down my profession for two years and had cancelled all contracts in December 1915, when I took office. I solved this problem by selling up my beautiful home at Highgate and retiring to a tiny flat until I had recovered my profession.

Carlyon Bellairs, elected as a Liberal in 1904 but who later became a Conservative, argued that it was important for 'a conscientious M.P. to have an occupation outside Parliament. Apart from journalism and lectures it would be mere surmise on my part to assume that I could have earned anything outside Parliament'.

Those whose earning capacity was most adversely affected by being in parliament were either in the professions (mainly lawyers) or had been actively engaged in running businesses. Solicitors (of whom there were few, especially compared with barristers) had difficulty in maintaining their earnings: Lloyd George noted that 'But for the fact that I had a very self-sacrificing brother who kept the practice going, with very occasional assistance, it would have very substantially reduced my income'. Evan Hayward, another solicitor first elected in 1910, found his income 'materially lessened' as he had to dispose of his solicitor's practice in West Hartlepool. Robert Ambrose, a medical practitioner and Irish Nationalist, said that 'Naturally it injured my practice. No man can serve two masters viz his professional duty and his duty to his constituents', although his position was also undoubtedly affected by the time required to travel to and from Ireland. William

Collins, another doctor and Liberal first elected in 1906, said that 'as a medical man' his income was 'necessarily reduced'. Reginald Blair, a Scottish accountant and Conservative elected at a by-election in 1912, found that his earning capacity was considerably hindered by his being in parliament. For the architect Alfred Gelder it 'Reduced it as there were many professional matters in my life that I could not delegate'.

Some professionals, such as army officers, gave up their careers altogether and their incomes were reduced accordingly; that was presumably why Archibald Weigall found that being in parliament completely destroyed his earning capacity. Sir Aylmer Hunter-Weston, another who could hardly have pleaded poverty, claimed that 'becoming a Member of Parliament caused me to lose the military pay which I should have probably been able to draw for several years'. Academics such as Hastings Lees-Smith, a Liberal first elected in 1910, could take only part-time posts while the historian J.A.R. Marriott, who was first elected as a Conservative in 1917, resigned all his Oxford university appointments so his earning capacity was 'greatly reduced' by his election to parliament.

London-based barristers could in theory continue to practise while in parliament but did not necessarily do so. Reginald McKenna, first elected as a Liberal in 1895 and who held a series of ministerial offices from 1905 until 1918, gave up the bar altogether after becoming a candidate and Thomas Nussey 'gave up the Bar shortly after I entered the House', as did Henry Hobhouse, first elected as a Liberal as early as 1885. Jack Seely, a Conservative barrister when first elected in 1900 (he later joined the Liberals), became 'too immersed in House of Commons affairs to try to earn anything at the Bar or elsewhere'. Charles Buxton, a Liberal who fought numerous elections and by-elections between 1910 and 1931 and served in the House for three short periods totalling around five years, found that being in parliament 'destroyed' his earnings from the bar. Thomas Shaw, first elected as a Liberal in 1892, immediately lost two-thirds of his earnings but 'owing to unexpected circumstances, a vacancy occurred in the Solicitor Generalship and that helped'.

Those such as Willoughby Dickinson, Charles Tyrrell Giles, Alfred Lyttelton and Lord Robert Cecil who had worked at the parliamentary bar prior to election to the House had to give up that particular area of their practices and some of them lost substantial earnings; Lord Robert estimated that his earnings dropped by four-fifths. Edward Hemmerde found that 'Being an active Left Wing Liberal, & afterwards Labour was very detrimental to my practice as a Barrister'. Henry Hobhouse, a barrister first elected as a Liberal in 1885, 'had to give up my profession' while Alfred Hopkinson found that 'Being in Parliament to some extent injured my practice & the double work was almost killing at times'. Arnold Herbert, of the 1906 Liberal intake, served only for that parliament and also found that 'Parliamentary life was a decided obstacle to professional success unless one was physically very strong'.

Constituencies distant from Westminster, plus the existence of a separate Scottish bar, often reduced barristers' earnings, especially for the Scots and Irish. Arthur Wills, elected for Dorset North in 1905, found that 'being a Liberal candidate or M.P. for a distant rural constituency meant a whole-time job. Indeed, as it proved, it was rather more than I could manage'; he lost the seat in 1910. Two Scots – Robert Munro (Lord Alness) and Graham Murray (Lord Dunedin) – both initially made substantial financial sacrifices by entering the house of commons, although both later at least partly retrieved their positions. Munro was at first 'seriously' affected as he depended on his junior practice at the Scottish bar, which he had to give up and take silk. 'Subsequently, my ministerial salary eased the position.' Plunket Barton, first elected for Armagh in 1891, found that constant attendance during his first four years in parliament deprived him of the whole of his professional income. 'For the next two years when my party was in office [he was solicitor-general for Ireland], I was able to earn about half my professional income by living in the train backwards and forwards between Dublin and London.' Daniel O'Leary, a Nationalist member for Cork West, had to give up his professional work to attend to his parliamentary duties.

For those in business, being in parliament had mixed financial consequences. Some respondents obviously felt ambivalent about the wisdom of having abandoned what might otherwise have been successful and/or lucrative non-parliamentary careers. It is impossible to know whether Austin Hopkinson was correct in his belief (in 1936) that he 'could still make a large income if I tried. But I do not try'. Some, such as Leo Amery, explicitly used their position in parliament to earn money from a career in business, although Wedgwood observed in his draft biography that Amery's business career was not conspicuously successful, at least financially. George Lansbury was sure that being in parliament 'helped me earn money in business' while John Norton-Griffiths' son said that his father's position as an MP helped him to gain overseas contracts, although 'scrupulous attention to Parliamentary duties . . . cost him, on at least two occasions, losses running into hundreds of thousands of pounds'. George Marks, a consulting engineer and patent agent from the 1906 Liberal intake, found that his professional fees were not affected by being an MP 'but my status was widened'. The Conservative George Courthope thought that being in parliament probably increased his earnings by 'bringing directorships which might not otherwise have been offered to me'.

Most of those actively engaged in business found that being in parliament did their earnings no good, mainly because of the demands on their time, and they sometimes paid a high personal as well as financial price. As Benjamin Cohen's family put it, 'Being in Parliament certainly checked earning capacity, less time being devoted to business [as a stockbroker]; partners did more, and expected larger share of profits'. In a different occupation (banking), Angus Hambro found that being in parliament 'prevented me spending the time I ought to have to my business', while for Arthur Black, a Liberal first elected in 1905, being in parliament had an adverse effect on his income: 'My business needed me & I frequently travelled daily to & from Nottingham while I was in Parliament'. William Mitchell-Thomson, a Conservative first elected in 1904, was a businessman for whom parliament 'extinguished' his earning capacity. 'I had to resign my job in business and for 26 years had practically no outside emolument.' Edward Noel Buxton 'lost my salary. Politics would have allowed of a half-time job; but brewers thought temperance bills damaging to them, so I resigned my directorship and about £1800 a year'. Edward Strauss found that being 'a Liberal MP did not increase my income as a Hop Merchant. My brewer customers being mostly Tories'.

William Barton, from the Lancashire textile industry, saw a 'Cumulative decline' in his earning capacity and Henry George Chancellor, of the 1910 Liberal intake, who was in the newspaper business, 'lost much through giving time that might more profitably have been given to business, and I never used my membership to influence business'. Alfred Pease, from a large quaker family-owned group of diverse businesses in north-east England, found that 'It was all lost – & no gain' while his brother Joseph 'had to decline several very attractive remunerative posts in the business world' in order to remain in parliament. Allan Bright, a Liberal shipowner who first stood as a candidate in 1899, served for only two years (1904–6) but found that the ten years he 'gave up to Politics diminished my income as it took my attention from business'. Henry Croft estimated that he 'could have made a substantial income if I had concentrated on my business & kept out of politics' and Lord John Joicey-Cecil, a Conservative elected in 1906, 'refused many directorships'.

The Irish Nationalists' personal finances appear to have suffered particularly harshly, although they were often supported in parliament by funds raised through the National Irish League. John Nugent's income was affected 'Rather adversely, as [being in parliament] took me away from home and the conduct of my own business'. Michael Flavin, who served briefly following a by-election in 1891, claimed that he 'sacrificed all business interests for the love of Ireland'. Vincent Kennedy, first elected in 1904, 'lost money when I would otherwise have got a good living and made provision for the future'. Perhaps the saddest was William Duffy who served from 1900 until 1918. He was 'a shopkeeper in my native town' and being in parliament meant 'Ruin – absolute ruin. I was in a sound financial position – when taken away from my shop – I did not weigh the consequences of living in London for at least half of each year . . . All our personal resources were exhausted in honourably attending each session. I left Westminster a Poor man'.

4. *The Cost of Politics*

The replies to the two-part question (Q14) about the cost of being a candidate and how much it cost yearly while an MP suggested that a few respondents had kept detailed personal records or possibly copies of their own electoral returns. Otherwise William Clough, a Liberal first elected in 1906, could not have known that he had spent such a precise sum as £1,386 or Frank Goldstone that his election in 1910 cost £810. Most, however, relied on their memories and gave avowedly imprecise answers. A total of 244 of the respondents (68%) gave some sort of answer but of those only 176 (72%) gave specific figures for one or other of the questions. Of those who did reply, however, many commented in some detail even if they did not give figures.

The comments confirmed that, despite the 1883 Act and the subsequent growth of national political parties, during the late 1890s and 1900s it took some time for electoral practices and party and constituency funding to shake off pre-1883 patterns. Until the parties became more organised at national level, the cost of contesting an election remained high enough to be a significant deterrent to those without sufficient personal wealth or friends, family or party supporters willing to help towards the cost. Getting elected to parliament therefore remained largely the province of those with independent means, preferably ample ones. Several respondents remarked on how standing for parliament drained their resources. John Cator had to borrow from the bank the whole of the £1,200 it cost him to contest North Norfolk as a Conservative in 1892. Francis Neilson, a Liberal first elected in 1910, recounted how he 'became a candidate for the Newport Division of Salop in 1902 and before the January election of 1906 I had practically spent all my savings', while Ernest Jardine claimed that being in parliament had cost him 'More money than I should like to put down in writing'.

The practice in both major parties of not contesting 'unwinnable' seats gradually diminished with the growth of national parties, but uncontested elections still happened up to the end of the First World War, particularly at by-elections. That greatly reduced the cost to candidates.[3] Miles Mattison, who first stood as a Conservative candidate for Carlisle in 1880 and was elected for Liverpool Walton in 1888, said that his election was uncontested (but did not say which), so 'the cost was not serious'. John Lloyd Morgan, first elected as a Liberal at a by-election in 1889 for West Carmarthenshire and who retired in 1910, said that getting elected cost £400 because he was 'generally returned unopposed'. Colin Coote and Eric Geddes were both first elected, uncontested, at by-elections during the First World War. At the December 1910 general election, only ten months after the previous general election, 98 seats in Great Britain and 64 seats in Ireland were uncontested, mainly because of straitened party finances.

Irish Nationalist seats were often uncontested because the real battles were not fought at elections, but between different party factions during the selection process. Among the Irish Nationalists, John Boland had only one contested election during 18 years in parliament while Denis Cogan had to pay 'only the Sheriff's fees' of £300, and John Cullinan's son said his father had always been elected unopposed, as was Michael Flavin, whose first election cost him only £20. Vincent Kennedy said getting elected for the first time cost him £25 and 'I was 5 times elected unopposed. Cost me between £25 and £116 which was probably the rock bottom price for an Irish County Election'. Candidates in other parties in Ireland could have similar experiences: Plunket Barton, who served for mid Armagh as a Conservative from 1891 until appointed as a judge in 1900, never had a contest. 'I was elected unopposed, and was three times re-elected', although each election still cost him £250.

Studies of the effect of the 1883 Act have shown that, as the national parties grew, there may have been a marked overall reduction in candidates' election expenditure in 1885 and in subsequent elections, but 'election accounts did not always give the full picture'.[4] Spending beyond the permitted limits persisted quite widely. Wedgwood did not ask for a detailed breakdown of election expenses but if the replies were anywhere near the truth, they showed that the maximum allowed by the Act could not have been strictly followed by candidates or rigidly enforced, even when due allowance is made for inadequate records or imperfect memories. Even in the largest county constituencies, under the Act's rules very few would have qualified for expenses above £1,500, but of the 174 respondents (48.3% of the total) who gave the cost of being a candidate, 39 claimed to have spent £1,500 or more when they were first elected. The Conservative barrister Walford Green said that both the elections in which he stood (in 1895 and 1900) cost £2,000 while ten respondents said they had spent over £2,000 and the highest amount claimed by any respondent at any time was the £4,500 that the Liberal John Bethell said he had spent on what he described as 'the enormous Romford Division' in the election of 1906 and each of the two elections in 1910. When, however,

---

[3] See Michael Pinto-Duschinsky, *British Political Finance 1830–1980* (Washington, DC, 1981), especially ch. 2.

[4] Rix, 'Elimination of Corrupt Practices', 77; see also Lloyd, 'The Whip as Paymaster', 790.

he was first a candidate for the same, but then much smaller, constituency in 1894 he spent only £1,500. Another Liberal, Julius Bertram, who stood at Hitchin in 1906, claimed to have spent £3,000 but did not reveal who paid that very large sum or how he got away with such an apparently flagrant breach of the rules. At the other end of the range, but including those in uncontested seats, 23 respondents spent £450 or less (eight spent less than £100), nine spent £500, a further nine spent £800, 27 spent £1,000 and 16 each spent £1,200 and £1,500.

Expenditure by candidates did not differ substantially between the two major parties, although the average spent by the 84 Conservatives who gave specific information was slightly higher than that by the 97 Liberals. The lowest specific figure given for expenditure by a candidate from either party was £96 9s. 7d. by a Conservative, Charles Carew, who was elected at a by-election, almost certainly uncontested, in November 1915. The major differences were determined more by the size and nature (borough or county) of the constituency than the party and the majority in both parties spent somewhere between £1,000 and £1,500. As the Liberal Thomas Bethell, brother of John, remarked, 'County Elections were very costly thirty years ago'. Only four of the 12 Labour respondents to the question gave any details of their expenditure and they spent between £250 and £900. The large number of uncontested seats meant that the Irish Nationalists were very frugal: Daniel O'Leary said it cost him £400 to get elected at a by-election in 1916 and the remainder spent much less. John Campbell, elected in 1900, claimed that it cost him nothing to get elected. 'Friends clubbed 1900. No costs thereafter.'

Sometimes the lack of detailed information arose because candidates did not necessarily pay all, or indeed sometimes any, of their own election expenses. That was the norm for Labour candidates, for whom the cost of getting elected had always been literally prohibitive in the sense that they could not have afforded to meet any of it from their own resources and did not have wealthy friends or patrons. Their expenses were met from a range of sources, mainly trade unions but also other party supporters. The election expenses of Fred Maddison, first elected as a Lib–Lab candidate in 1897, 'were always paid by my nominees. This was a condition I had to make, and was well known'. For Keir Hardie, the costs of early elections were met 'by funds voluntarily raised by the workers'. George Lansbury's 'first elections cost _me_ very little money was always subscribed . . . I have always been extravagant'. James Parker's 'election expenses [were] paid by the party I contributed possibly £5'. David Shackleton's election expenses 'were paid by the Textile Factory Workers Association' and for Albert Smith 'The Textile Factory bore the union expense. My loss would be only a few pounds'. George Wardle's 'election expenses were guaranteed & paid by the Union & if I remember rightly my first election was just over £500'. The 'two to three hundred pounds' that it cost George Barnes to contest was 'mostly paid by my Trade Union', while the expenses of Philip Snowden (unspecified) and of John Hancock (£900) were all paid by the Labour Party. For J.R. Clynes, 'Any heavy charges in a contest were met by collections, or subscriptions and in later years by sufficient grants from my Trade Union'.

Liberals and Conservatives mostly expected to pay at least part of their own election expenses and there was clearly some truth in Harry Hope's description of politics as 'an expensive luxury'. Many, however, received financial support from families and friends or, occasionally, other patrons in the traditional manner, otherwise they could not have

afforded to stand. There was sometimes resentment when financial help was lacking and
the candidate was expected to bear all the cost of an election. The Liberal George Marks'
first election in 1906 cost him 'about eleven hundred pounds as the local association
never contributed any expenses then or for the nineteen years I was in Parliament'.
Henry Montgomery, who served only during the 1906 parliament, said that his election
cost him about £2,000 (one of the largest amounts mentioned for any Liberal) and he
won a seat that had never previously been Liberal. 'I received scarcely any help from my
constituency, and less when I had won the seat. "Now he's won it he can keep it" was
their attitude.'

   Lionel de Rothschild, first elected as a Liberal Unionist at a by-election in 1899,
illustrated some of the hazards faced by wealthy candidates with well-known names
when he said that, although it was impossible to provide the information, 'In all cases I
know it was strictly within the law as with my name one had to be particularly careful
in this respect, but with all my family living in the constituency my own expenses were
not very great'. The family of the 3rd marquess of Salisbury likewise drew heavily on
family resources: Lord Hugh Cecil 'was paid for by relations' while the expenses of his
brother Lord Robert 'were paid by my eldest brother'. That eldest brother, James, Lord
Cranborne, could not remember 'what the contest cost me – or rather, cost my father'.
Lord Cecil Manners was the son of the 7th duke of Rutland and all his election expenses
when first elected in 1900, as well as all his other expenses, were paid by his father. Eliot
Crawshay-Williams thought his election expenses had been 'over £1,000 a time . . . one
way or another. My people paid'.

   Charles Tyrrell Giles' experiences when he was first elected as a Conservative in 1895
showed how candidates could still depend on patronage or contributions from friends.
'I think the contest cost me about £600 . . . I did not receive anything from Headquarters, but the Duke of Bedford and Lord De Ramsey were good supporters to my
Conservative Association and personal friends'. He did not say how much the supporters
contributed. Rather later, Edmund Harvey, first elected as a Liberal in 1910, said: 'My
impression is that my first election cost about £700. The expenses were borne by
my father, with a contribution, I think of 350, from Lord Airedale, & no contribution
from Liberal Headquarters'. The family of John Sinclair, first elected as a Liberal for
Dumbartonshire in 1892, said that he was 'assisted there by Lord Overtoun'.

   The Conservative Arthur Griffith-Boscawen's first election in 1892 cost him nothing,
'a friend paying for me' and of the Liberal Arthur Haworth's £700 election expenses in
1906, 'a number of friends subscribed, without my asking, a considerable proportion'.
Similarly, the cost to Greville Verney of his election in 1895 'was found without difficulty
for him by some friends'. Carlyon Bellairs, also part of the 1906 Liberal intake, preferred
not to answer the question 'except that my expenses were paid for me at King's Lynn'
and added: 'I am ashamed of the comparison between my own expenditure & expenses
and those of my socialist opponents'. Bellairs was not alone in having his election
expenses paid by individual constituents (as opposed to the local party), although the
practice certainly dwindled. The Conservative Arthur Brookfield, who was first elected
in 1885, recounted that 'My first election, which I paid for out of my own "Privy purse"
cost me £1660. My supporters, when I told them I must retire, (on being told to stand
again about three months later,) voluntarily paid all my expenses, amounting to £150
(I think)'. Harry Brodie received 'a contribution from the Liberal Party Fund & various

constituents also contributed' towards the £1,800 it cost him to get elected in 1906. Brodie was one of the few respondents to refer to a contribution from the party, even though such contributions were not unusual. One study has found that as many as 113 Liberal members in the 1906 parliament had been helped from the party's election fund.[5]

Of the total who answered the questionnaire, 149 respondents (41.4%) gave some information about what it cost them to be an MP, although the replies often did not say what was included in those costs, probably because the question did not ask for such details and there were no legal limits on that type of expenditure. The annual cost varied widely: of those who gave figures (some of which can only have been guesses), seven (4.7%) spent £100 or less annually, 12 (8.1%) spent £200, 20 (13.4%) spent £400, 19 (12.8%) spent £500, ten (6.7%) spent £600 and 13 (8.7%) spent £1,000, while five claimed to have spent over £1,000 with four of them spending £2,000. As might be expected in view of their generally greater wealth, almost all the bigger spenders were Conservatives; of the 18 who spent £1,000 a year or more, only two were Liberals. Conservatives' average expenditure was also higher, with the majority spending annually between £500 and £1,000 compared with the Liberals, most of whom spent between £300 and £600.

Where detailed information about annual expenditure was given, the replies showed that sitting members, and candidates, were often expected to subscribe to local clubs, party organisations and a range of other good causes, sometimes on a significant scale. The extent of the practice varied a good deal but it was still fairly widespread in both major parties up to the end of the First World War. 'Nursing' of this kind was seen by some, including Campbell-Bannerman, as a serious danger to the political system since it meant that members of parliament were effectively 'buying' their seats.[6] One respondent seems to have bucked the trend: William Rees Davies, first elected for Pembrokeshire in 1892 and whose father had earlier sat for a Bristol seat, said that his 'yearly contributions, as compared with those of my father which throughout his membership were munificent, were not large. An M.P. in those [i.e. his father's] days was expected to figure prominently in his Constituency's subscription lists'.

Others, however, remarked on the expense. Thomas Hare, first elected as a Conservative for South West Norfolk in 1892, included membership subscriptions in his additional outgoings of an average of £1,000 a year while a member. Colin Coote's original election may have cost him nothing but he remarked somewhat ruefully that his constituency (Wisbech) 'had been spoilt by a succession of wealthy members and the annual charge was heavy – say £600 a year'. Raymond Heath, a Conservative first elected for Louth in 1886 and defeated in 1892, recorded 'an annual subscription of £150 to the local organisation subscription [sic], a great many small amounts to cricket clubs, chapels & so on perhaps £200 a year'. George Marks, first elected for Launceston in 1906, included in his annual expenses 'charities, public institutions, churches' and Sir Robert Newman, a Conservative first elected for Exeter at a by-election in 1918 and who lived near his constituency, 'continued my usual subscriptions to Hospitals, Clubs etc.'. Leslie Renton, first elected as a Liberal for Gainsborough in 1906 and who switched

---

[5] Lloyd, 'The Whip as Paymaster', 790–1.
[6] Rix, 'The Elimination of Corrupt Practices', 94–6.

the following year to the Liberal Unionists, claimed that his annual expenses reached £600 because 'The calls on me, especially from Nonconformists, were very many', possibly because Renton himself was a presbyterian.

Labour members were rarely troubled by the need to pay subscriptions and some members of other parties, mainly Liberals, took a robust attitude to the practice, especially in the period before members of parliament were paid an allowance. The Liberal Edward Hemmerde 'never subscribed to any clubs charities etc in any constituency which I contested or represented and except at Crewe, when I was receiving £400 a year salary, I never subscribed to the support of the organisation'. Charles Mallet, also of the 1906 intake, said that 'With a few exceptions, we took the line that we could not subscribe widely to local charities. Our constituents generally supported us in this, but it was not popular in all quarters'. Leo Money found that the yearly cost of being an MP (for a London seat) was small 'as it was known that my means were moderate and entirely earned and that I could not purchase votes'. Harry Verney, several times a Liberal candidate between 1906 and 1922 and first elected in 1910, said his annual expenses were less than £350 a year because he 'always refused ordinary constituency subscriptions', while Richard Winfrey, first elected in 1906, although he first stood as a candidate in 1895, 'tutored my constituents not to expect subscriptions from me – always quoting the attitude that John Bright took, and they loyally fell in with my views. This lasted until M.P.'s began to receive the parliamentary allowance, then I found I was expected to help many good causes in my constituency and I could not refuse to do so'. Eliot Crawshay-Williams, first elected in 1910 but who retired in 1913, 'made a definite rule that I would not give indiscriminate subscriptions' and introduced a private members' bill to ban the practice.

There were several specific references to the cost of supporting the local party organisation, including sometimes paying for an agent. George Touche, first elected as a Conservative for Islington North in 1910, 'contributed substantially to the local Conservative Association while M.P.' while Anderson Montague-Barlow, first elected as a Conservative for Salford in 1910, claimed that 'Being a very poor area all expenses fell on the member, which came (for agent, room, printing etc) to about £500–£600 annually'. Edmund Harvey 'contributed £100 yearly to the Leeds Liberal Federation towards organisation expenses & donations to the annual municipal election funds' and Arthur Hawarth 'gave the [Liberal] Association £100 a year for registration' as well as other subscriptions. Frank Goldstone, first elected for Labour in 1910, said that the £500–£600 annual cost of being a member included 'salary of an agent & expenses of organisation', although he did not say where the money came from. Herbert Jessel, a Liberal Unionist first elected in 1896, pointed out that 'the whole cost of looking after the register was incurred by the local organisation i.e. the M.P. with slight local help'. Sir George Sitwell claimed that being a candidate or member cost him a third of his annual income: 'I paid the whole cost of the Conservative organisation, paid the losses on the newspaper, and made many subscriptions'. Richard Cooper, a Conservative first elected for Walsall in 1910, claimed that being an MP cost him around £2,000 annually, 'but I ran a local paper and was always very active in the Constituency'. Frank Newnes, of the 1906 Liberal intake, found that the 'Liberal Association had small funds & I had to pay nearly everything' while Henry Montgomery, who won a seat in 1906 that had never previously been Liberal, found that he 'hadn't the money to keep a county organization going' and retired in 1910. Among Irish members, few gave details of their expenditure but Robert Ambrose found that parliament cost him a good deal because he 'had to subscribe to the Party funds'.

Even at a time when frequent visits to constituencies were not the norm, the cost of travel to and from London could be high. Irish members were at a particular disadvantage in that respect as, to a lesser extent, were those from Scotland and Wales. Despite the scale of his independent income, Hugh Law, who sat for West Donegal from 1902 to 1918, found the overall cost of being in parliament 'very heavy', including travel between London and his constituency. His fellow Nationalists often literally paid a high price to serve their cause in the house of commons. Their constituencies were distant and travel both time-consuming and expensive, so many could afford only infrequent visits to their homes. Their lives in London were often uncomfortable. They lived in cheap lodgings and often spent most of their time in the house of commons, partly in order to benefit from the cheap food available there.[7] Harry Hope, a Scottish Conservative who was first elected for Bute in 1910, did not mention the cost but said that 'In the 20 years which I served in the H of C I had to travel every weekend to Scotland, as, after my Father's death, I carried on a large farming business and made a point of never neglecting it, but it was not easy. 2 nights in the train every week and never a rest when in London, or at the home end'. Similarly, the weekly return railway ticket to and from Caernarvon cost Ellis Davies, a Liberal from Carmarthenshire first elected in 1906, 28s.

There were surprisingly few references to the cost of maintaining a second home, whether in London or in the constituency, or to the extra cost of living in London. For Walter Carlile, the annual expense 'inclusive of a London House' was about £1,000 while Rowland Whitehead, Liberal member for South East Essex from 1906 to 1910, calculated his 'extra annual expenditure while in Parliament while supporting local associations, providing agent or Secretary, subscriptions, travelling & usually renting a house in the constituency . . . at £800 a year'. Similarly, Joseph King calculated that his expenses of £600–£700 a year 'included living in London & visits to Somerset'. Raymond Heath, member for Louth in Lincolnshire from 1886 to 1892, remarked that 'in a constituency like that, & at that period the Conservative member had to entertain a good deal'. George Courthope's expenses included 'a room & food in London' while the Liberal Ellis Davies painted a vivid picture of the lifestyle of an impecunious backbencher with a distant Welsh seat who needed to keep the family business going:

> During my first Session I stayed at the Welsh club in Whitehall Court paying about 6/- to 7/- for bed and breakfast. My other meals I had in the House. Lunch, a pot of tea, bread and butter and an apple cost me 6d. or 7d with 1d. tip to the waitress. Tea was about the same generally 5d. and tip. Dinner was provided for 1/- in the House, and a tip of 2d., no more, to the waiter. A glass of milk or a cup of tea finished the day. I came home to Caernarvon Friday as I had to be in the Office on Saturday the Market day.

Wedgwood did not ask about the effect on members' finances of the introduction in 1912 of an allowance of £400 a year. The measure was the result of a deal between the

---

[7] For a detailed description of the lives of Nationalist MPs at Westminster, see James McConnel, 'The Irish Parliamentary Party in Victorian and Edwardian London', in *Victoria's Ireland? Irishness and Britishness, 1837–1901*, ed. Peter Gray (Dublin, 2004), 37–50.

Liberal and Labour Parties before the December 1910 election. It was at least partly intended to encourage more Labour candidates to stand by providing financial support for those who managed to get elected. The allowance was generous compared with both the very low pre-parliamentary earnings of almost all the early Labour or Lib–Lab members and the generally small salaries that they had previously been paid, once elected, mainly by their trade unions. It therefore significantly improved their overall financial position, although its full impact was not apparent until after the First World War. As some of Wedgwood's respondents implied, it reduced the financial burdens for most members even though it caused problems for those who were expected to contribute more lavish subscriptions. Edmund Bartley-Denniss' son knew that his father welcomed the £400 a year as 'a great help in his expenses'.

The existence of the allowance was, however, by no means universally supported, particularly among Conservatives. Some members, such as Thomas Ashton, refused to claim it at all while William du Pre did not claim it during the First World War. In the debate on the government resolution on the allowance on 10 August 1911, Arthur Lee, shadow chancellor of the exchequer, spoke for many, including some Liberals, when he argued that payment of members would mean that parliament would lose its 'moral authority' in the eyes of the public because members would become the 'mere paid delegates of their constituency rather than their free and independent representatives'. Others felt strongly that payment of members of parliament would lead to widespread corruption. The motion was nevertheless approved by a substantial majority but opposition to the allowance continued for some time.[8]

Several respondents to the questionnaire specifically referred to the introduction of the allowance and among the 149 who gave specific details of the annual cost of being a member, 58 (39%) said that it was between £300 and £500. That suggests either that the level of the allowance was in practice enough for many needs or that at least some members tailored their expenditure more or less to match the allowance; others still exceeded it. Wedgwood himself said that his expenses amounted to £400 until the First World War. Percy Alden, of the 1906 Liberal intake, found that 'when Members of Parliament were paid it absorbed practically the whole of the payment to maintain the constituency' and Henry George Chancellor's yearly expenses 'about used up Parliamentary salary'. For another Liberal, William Clough, the average yearly cost after 1912 was £257 'in addition to the salary'. The Conservative Charles Carew claimed that his expenses cost him around £250 a year over the £400 allowed and John Cator found that his annual expenses were 'my Parl Salary & more besides'. Even among Labour members, no one claimed to have saved any money from the allowance.

---

[8] In 1920, there were still some members who opposed any payment although by then most of the arguments were about whether the payment should be called an allowance or a salary and what expenditure it should cover. See evidence to the Select Committee on Members' Expenses (1920) HC 255, particularly by Sir John Rees (Q.464) and Sir Herbert Nield (Q.560).

Chapter 6. Speeches, Speech-Making and Voting Behaviour

1. *Introduction*

Wedgwood's subjects were all first elected to the house of commons in the late 19th and early 20th centuries towards the end of what was widely seen, both then and since, as a golden age of parliamentary oratory. As a recent observer has noted, in the late 19th century 'the perceptions and the realities of parliamentary speech were more than mere symbols and far from unimportant in themselves'. The growth in the scale and scope of government legislation in the second half of the 19th century led to significant changes in the style of parliamentary speech-making and debate: 'more people were speaking in the House of Commons and they were speaking more frequently'.[1] Making speeches in the house of commons was in the process of becoming a largely inescapable part of the member of parliament's job; participation rates in debates in the early 20th century were relatively high, although some way below the levels of the 1880s.[2] Wedgwood's inclusion in his questionnaire of three questions about different aspects of speech-making showed that for him, and almost certainly for the majority of his parliamentary contemporaries, speeches in the House were an important element of parliamentary life.

A significant proportion of the replies to the question (Q20) on what the subjects considered their best speech confirmed that there was no shortage of more or less willing speakers, including Wedgwood himself, and for them making a good speech could be a source of some personal satisfaction. More than half the replies showed, however, that for Wedgwood's subjects, who were reasonably representative of their peers, the tradition of the silent, or largely silent, member had by no means entirely disappeared. Speaking in the House remained a more or less optional activity, at least for backbenchers: if they disliked speaking, or thought they were bad at it, they did not have to do it to any significant extent. The answers to Q21 about the greatest speech the subjects had ever heard showed that great speakers and great speech-making were much admired but members could, if they wished, resist pressures to speak, from whatever source, without suffering undue consequences. The same applied to other sorts of parliamentary activity

---

[1] Joseph S. Meisel, *Public Speech and the Culture of Public Life in the Age of Gladstone* (New York, 2001), 105. Ch. 2, 'The House of Commons', contains a detailed analysis of the development of parliamentary speech-making in the second half of the 19th century. See also Cannadine, *In Churchill's Shadow*, ch. 5, 'Language: Churchill as the Voice of Destiny' for an account of the evolution of Winston Churchill's oratorical style in the early stages of his political career.

[2] Meisel, *Public Speech and the Culture of Public Life*, 74–5. See also Rush, *Role of the Member of Parliament since 1868*, 140–1 and table 6.2, 148. Meisel's and Rush's figures of participation in debates are differently calculated but broadly support each other.

© *The Parliamentary History Yearbook Trust and The History of Parliament Trust 2012*

such as asking questions or membership of committees, but Wedgwood's questionnaire did not include those activities.[3]

2. *What was Your Best Speech?*

The question on members' own best speeches was not specifically worded but most respondents assumed that it referred to parliamentary speeches and answered accordingly. Wedgwood gave his subjects no help in making their choice because he gave no criteria for what constituted a good (or bad) speech in terms of context, content, style, delivery or impact. Of the 210 respondents to the question, nearly half (94) identified a specific speech as being their best. Some themes can be discerned in the choices but few, even among the more analytical of the respondents, attempted to define what they meant by their 'best'. The majority gave simply the topic or nature of the debate concerned (such as debates on the Address), or both, and 18 of the 94 said that their best speech was on legislation of some kind. Only six (Leonard Darwin, Alan Haworth, Joseph King, Arthur Richardson, John Sinclair, Alan Sykes and George Wardle) identified speeches they had made which had, in their view, had a significant impact through influencing the course of events or changing the minds of the government or their colleagues. Sometimes length played a perverse part in the choice: the Labour member George Barnes thought his best speech was 'at any rate the longest' on the king's civil list in 1910, while at the other extreme the Conservative Sir John Gilmour simply said: 'The shortest – $2^1/_2$ minutes' but gave no more details; the Unionist William Allen's best speech was simply 'a short one'.

Frequent speakers such as Joseph King, who claimed that he spoke 'too often' to choose, Francis Neilson, who 'made so many I never had the chance of thinking which was the best', and Thomas Nussey said they could not decide. Wedgwood listed three possibilities among his own speeches but boasted that he had 'made more speeches than any of my contemporaries save Lloyd George & Winston Churchill'. Carlyon Bellairs, however, complained that in his own speeches he was generally 'too long-winded & would have succeeded better if I had spoken shortly and oftener [*sic*]'. Several other respondents pointed out the difficulty of judging their own speeches because, like Miles Mattison and Charles Trevelyan, they were 'no judge of my own speaking'. Henry Bowles 'never thought about it', while Stuart Coats 'spoke seldom and [was] unable to form an opinion'. Austen Chamberlain, among numerous others, could not say and Fred Maddison could not very well assess the value of his own speeches but claimed that the 'one which my friends . . . would say was my best was the one in which I answered Balfour's "There is a limit to human endurance speech" in connection with the disgraceful riot during the Boer War'. Clive Morrison-Bell gave no details but claimed it was 'The one the House thought my worst'. Edgar Jones could not say himself but 'The House seemed to regard a speech I made on the Irish Language Question during the Home Rule Committee Stage as the best'.

[3] For a more detailed analysis of general levels of 'parliamentary participation' (speaking, asking questions and voting), see chs 6 and 7 of Rush, *Role of the Member of Parliament since 1868*. See also G.W. Cox, *The Efficient Secret: The Cabinet and the Development of Political Parties in Victorian England* (1987), ch. 7.

For those who did choose, praise from others, especially senior or prominent colleagues or opponents, could determine the selection. Carlyon Bellairs described how 'Asquith complimented me warmly on a speech I made about the Defence Committee' for which he had no notes and was 'entirely unaware' that the subject was to be raised. Somewhat surprisingly, the Irish Nationalist William Duffy, who introduced a private members' bill to expropriate the property of Lord Clanricard, an ancestor of the earl of Harewood, claimed with obvious pride that afterwards 'I was sent for & had the honour of receiving compliments from Prime Minister Bannerman, Lloyd George, Sir E Grey & other great statesmen'. Similarly, Richard Cooper, a Conservative, quoted Philip Snowden's remarks in his autobiography about Cooper's speech in the debate on the Address in 1913. Snowden referred to Cooper's 'wise words' and said that 'if the Government had acted on this policy a great deal of trouble would have been saved'. William Rees-Davies' speech on Welsh disestablishment led to his receiving 'kindly congratulations from prominent opponents'. Charles Mallet listed two speeches, one on free trade and the other opposing women's suffrage, in 1908 or 1909. 'Should I confess that the opinions of them which I liked best came from the Prime Minister and the Speaker? There were no two men whose favourable opinions I valued more.' Richard Winfrey's speech on the introduction of the Small Holdings Bill in 1907 'caught the ear of Sir Henry Campbell-Bannerman and brought me in close touch with him – an experience I much enjoyed'. Praise from a rather different source influenced Edward Smallwood, who was first elected in 1917. His maiden speech, on the 'Soul-lessness of the War Office', was based on his wartime experiences. It was published 'verbatim' in the *Daily Mail* and 'Nearly 2000 letters resulted'.

A reason commonly advanced for the success of a speech was the speaker's knowledge of the subject. That did not invariably lead to a 'great' speech but may have secured an attentive or respectful audience and possibly have influenced the outcome of a debate or the course of events. For Arthur Brookfield, '[t]he best speech I ever made was about the old Volunteer Force. For I knew my subject & spoke almost without any notes, for quite an hour'. Walter Carlile found that 'one, on the Old Age Pension Bill, was the only one worth listening to, as I knew my subject from A to Z'. Arthur Murray was a director of the North British Railway company and as such was asked 'to voice the views of Scotland on the original proposals of the [Railways Amalgamation] Bill' which he though his best speech in the House. John Norton-Griffiths' son claimed that, although his father was a poor speaker in the House, he was 'always listened to with respect as he only spoke on subjects with which he was fully conversant' and Michael Hicks-Beach was 'a rare but quietly effective speaker on subjects of which he was always fully master'. Knowledge of the rules could also play a part: Julius Bertram claimed that his best speech was made on an amendment to the Address in 1906 'because it was wholly "in order": & every one else got pulled up for transgression'.

Knowledge of a subject through constituency involvement also led to some successful speeches. John Bethell's Romford constituency was directly affected by an East Ham Corporation Bill and he made a speech which led to a government defeat on a key provision of the Bill. Reginald Blair, another member for two different seats in the East End of London, chose a speech on London local government about which he had considerable knowledge. Arthur Bignold was the Conservative member for Wick and his widow chose a speech 'in the cause of the Scottish line sea fishermen in the debate in the International Law governing the Three Mile Limit in 1907'. The family of another Scot, John Sinclair, said that he had been 'Considered successful in moving the 2nd Reading of the Small Landowners Scotland Bill' in 1907, which eventually became law in a modified form in 1911.

Strength of feeling on a particular issue, particularly relating to Ireland, the Great War and matters of conscience, sometimes led to what were regarded as good speeches. Not surprisingly, Irish members often cited their contributions on Irish matters, although most of them seldom spoke on any other topic and several of the speeches cited were made outside parliament. John Boland chose a speech during Balfour's administration 'on the need for a University for Irish Catholics in Ireland', while Michael Flavin chose 'the introducing of an Irish Land Bill'. Plunket Barton listed three speeches of which the first was in June 1893 'in Committee on Home Rule Bill arguing that a proposed safeguard, which was based on "due process of law" was futile'. Although Stephen Gwynn took no interest in his own speeches, 'one abt old age pensions as reflected by Irish vital statistics was all right'. Although a Roman catholic, Mark Sykes was not an Irishman but his son said there was no doubt that his best speech was in the House on 31 March 1914 on 'the Irish question'. Edward Wood, despite claiming that he had never made a good speech, recollected 'the feeling of having said more or less what I meant in condemnation of Lloyd George's policy in Ireland, at the time of the Black and Tans'.

Sir Aylmer Hunter-Weston, a serving front-line general when first elected in 1916, recounted in some detail the impact of his speech on 24 January 1918 in a debate on army manpower:

> Its success and value was not so much due to me as to its circumstances and setting. In a crowded House, with the galleries full, a figure in uniform was voicing the cry of the men in the trenches at a critical moment of the War. . . . Never before . . . had a Member of Parliament been simultaneously a Commander of an Army Corps in the Field.

Among issues of conscience, Lord Hugh Cecil cited his speech in 1917 on conscientious objectors, often said by colleagues to be among the greatest parliamentary speeches they ever heard. Henry George Chancellor chose a speech on 9 February 1915 'which challenged and mitigated the bullying of soldiers who refused to obey illegal orders to undergo vaccination or inoculation'. Edmund Harvey suggested two possibilities: 'either a speech made in the Conscription Bill in 1916 on moving an amendment to provide for conscientious objectors to military service or one at a later stage of the war on behalf of a peace of understanding'.

Maiden speeches were (and still are) often seen as an unpleasant but unavoidable ordeal for new members but several respondents cited their own maiden speech as their best. Daniel Turner Holmes thought his maiden speech in 1912 on a Scottish temperance bill – a topic that often aroused strong feelings – was his best, as was that of John Sutton in 1910 on the Parliament Act. Greville Verney's sister said that 'The newspapers reported that his first speech was received with "laughter and applause"; the kindness invariably shown to maiden speakers, especially to young ones, seemed to have been extended to him; but he always possessed the happy knack of amusing his audiences'. Sir Walter

Nugent claimed that 'My first made the most impression on myself'. By contrast, Carlyon Bellairs argued that 'It is easier to know my worst speech. My maiden speech offended all canons of taste and delivery. I believe that the views & arguments were correct but as a model it was the worst maiden speech on record'.

Around half the respondents were at best ambivalent about their parliamentary performances and often harboured considerable doubts about them, sometimes blaming the particular difficulties of speaking in the House. The barrister Robert Wallace found that, in the house of commons, 'not knowing when you had a chance of speaking was very disturbing & so I seldom tried'. Another barrister, Willoughby Dickinson, could never do well in the House because the 'mental atmosphere of the House is critical and my mind is very responsive to the occult influence of an audience'. Thomas Barclay, who served for ten months between the two elections in 1910, spoke only once 'and I was so disgusted at speaking to empty benches, that I never spoke again'. J.A.R. Marriott claimed that, while he might have made 'a number of fairly good speeches' in the House, 'I was never as completely at ease in the House as I was on the platform', where, he said, he was thought a very effective performer. Wedgwood's close friend Leo Money 'made not a single speech in Parliament worthy of me; all my utterances were lame; I do not know why' and Edwin Montagu's sister described how her brother's 'nervous temperament made him acutely conscious of his responsibilities, and he was often plunged into very fearful depression after what appeared to be in public a great parliamentary success'.

Numerous other respondents refused to identify their best speech because they shared the feelings of Max Aitken who claimed that he made 'No good speeches'; they often also shared Patrick Kennedy's declared dislike of speaking. Sir Samuel Scott 'didn't speak often and was a bad speaker', Archibald Weigall was 'Equally disappointed with all' and Edward Wood 'Never made a good one!' Sir Arthur Crosfield felt that 'The best speech I ever made would really be nothing to boast about'. Hugh Law could not recollect having made any good speeches and 'like Dr Johnson's Latin verses, some were no doubt worse than others' while Reginald McKenna 'never made a good speech and consequently never made a best'. Malcolm Kincaid-Smith may well have spoken for many when he said 'None good, except in cab going home'.

Over-preparation was sometimes blamed for unsuccessful speeches. Carlyon Bellairs claimed that 'Practically all my speeches were carefully prepared & they were all failures so probably my acquired dislike of oratory is just sour grapes'. Joseph King made several speeches during the First World War 'with passionate conviction and prepared with great care but as they fell on deaf or dead ears & made no difference to anyone but myself, as far as I knew at the time, I cannot call them, any of them, good at all'. Illness was also claimed on occasion to have affected parliamentary performances. Percy Alden's worst speech was made 'when I had the greatest opportunity of moving a resolution on Unemployment but I was seriously unwell at the time'. Viscount Dalrymple 'always so intensely disliked making speeches, that I have always been glad to forget them. I probably had the unique experience of being called . . . when I was feeling very ill, & had given up rising'. Walter Rea said that he 'never made any of any account: in extenuation . . . I was a Whip for most of the time'.

The replies to other questions, particularly Q21 on the greatest speeches by others, showed how accomplished speakers could be much admired but many seem to have concluded that it was not worth trying to emulate them. Some, like the Irish Nationalist Robert Ambrose, simply saw making speeches as a waste of time. William Bridgeman's son said that his father 'spoke very rarely considering the length of time he was in the House, and set very little store by his speaking'. Another Irishman, Denis Cogan, 'worked rather than spoke in Parliament', an approach shared by Sir Aylmer Hunter-Weston who was 'of opinion that my most effective speech was my complete <u>Silence</u> during the latter part of my Parliamentary career! I soon learnt how futile, except on rare occasions, are the speeches of Back-benchers, most of their speeches being directed to their constituents, or being a means of self-advertisement'. He recognised that this lost him 'all Parliamentary self-advertisement, but I fortunately required none' and mostly preferred to work behind the scenes to find 'practical solutions' and 'by this means [was] able to get a large number of useful things done'.

The replies do not suggest that the infrequent speakers were subject to any pressure to speak; if they were, they must have ignored it. The only evidence of the whips' activities showed how such pressures could, when applied, have unsought consequences. John Stirling-Maxwell recounted how he spoke 'at the request of the whips in order to prolong a debate on Welsh Museums, and so keep back another motion they wanted to block. The effusive thanks of the Welsh members, who little guessed the object of my speech, filled me with shame and I never again joined in obstruction'. Among the respondents were four who claimed never to have spoken in the House but none implied that this caused them significant difficulties, although two served for only short periods. Sir George Sitwell never spoke during two short terms in the House in the 1880s and 1890s: 'I hoped some day for a great opportunity, but dissolutions in those two short Parliaments came earlier than expected'. Robert Brassey served only for ten months between the two 1910 elections during which he 'maintained silence'. John Deans Hope 'Sat 22 years in Parliament & <u>never spoke</u>'. In expiation, he claimed that he 'Served 17 years on Kitchen Committee and 9 Parliamentary Commissions'. The barrister John Bigham never spoke during his two years in the House because by the time he was elected his practice was so large that 'he had very little time to devote to Parliament and could only get there at the end of a very long day'. Henry Montgomery, who served from 1906 to 1910, claimed that 'In 1906 there was little chance of making speeches' although that certainly did not hinder many of his contemporaries, including Wedgwood. Angus Hambro said his best speech was his 'one & only' in 12 years in the House and Alan Sykes described himself as 'practically a silent Member'.

3. Speeches and Voting Behaviour

The widespread doubts about the value of making speeches, particularly for backbenchers, were to some extent confirmed by the replies to the second question on the topic, Q22: 'Did speeches affect your vote?' In the 247 replies to the question, 41% said that speeches never affected how they voted and a further 33% said they did so only rarely. Only 2% said that their views were often affected while 20% said sometimes; only 20, or well under 10% of respondents, said that speeches by others had ever changed their minds on major issues. Of those, 15 mentioned specifically the impact of front-bench speakers. In other words, for around three-quarters of the respondents, regardless of party, the speeches they heard made little if any difference to how they voted at the end of a debate. It is therefore not surprising that many of them questioned whether it was worth making speeches themselves, especially as backbenchers, although Alfred Gelder grumbled that he considered 'then & now that too much time is taken up by a very limited number of members'.

In theory there was much more scope for frontbenchers to influence votes – they tended to speak relatively frequently, often on major issues of the day, and at times when there were large numbers present – but in practice party loyalties meant that that did not often happen. The Liberal Alexander Boulton must have spoken for many of his colleagues from all parties when he claimed that the speeches of his party leaders (Asquith and Lloyd George) 'only confirmed my opinions'. Of the 15 references to the impact of speeches by front-bench speakers, three were to Sir Henry Fowler in the 1890s, described by Alfred Hopkinson as 'the most effective opposition side . . . Dull generally & nearly always worth hearing'. Others referred to the sometimes perverse impact of Lloyd George's speeches. The Conservative Wilfrid Ashley claimed that 'Lloyd George twice made me vote against my own party' while the Liberal Julius Bertram 'voted constantly against my party as a result of speeches by Ll. George'.

Most respondents' comments confirmed that by the end of the 19th century party loyalties were sufficiently well established for them to vote with their parties most of the time, if sometimes reluctantly. In particular, at least on Irish matters, the Irish Nationalist members always voted as a block, whatever rebellious inclinations they may personally have had. John Hayden could be influenced 'on other than Irish questions' but John Boland, acting chief whip of the party before its dissolution in 1918, repeated the famous Irish Party Pledge 'to sit, act and vote with the Irish Party'. Patrick Kennedy described how 'While in Irish Party – Mechanical – after left it (or rather name erased ex Party List) – voted on merits of speeches'. Hugh Law was 'far too much afraid of the Whips and imbued with perhaps exaggerated sense of the ultimate effect of any particular vote on general policy & the fortunes of the Government of the day. We had been elected to win Home Rule for Ireland. To that object all other things must be secondary'.

Several respondents from other parties testified that party loyalties meant that voting against their own party was not something to be undertaken lightly, if at all, however persuasive the arguments advanced by the other side. The Conservative George Montagu found that 'Loyalty to the party was very strong at the beginning of the century' while Labour's Ben Tillett said that 'The Parliamentary Party system' prevented voting other than in accordance with his party. The Liberal backbencher Evan Hayward put the party loyalists' case when he said that speeches rarely altered his convictions and, even if they did,

> they would not affect votes unless some vital matter of principle was involved, because a member would not jeopardise the whole aims and programme of his party for the sake of some subordinate issue. Those who did so only kicked over the traces at the expense of the 'loyal' men who they knew would be relied upon to save them from the logical result of their 'independence'.

Arthur Wills, a Liberal, claimed that he was sometimes influenced by speeches but ultimately on important issues party loyalty had to prevail. 'It would have required an overwhelming case to make me imperil a government I considered the best of modern times. Such a case would have implied that I no longer thought the Government worthy of support. It never arose.' The Liberal Willoughby Dickinson similarly felt that the government was 'carrying through a programme of reform with which I was in entire agreement'. Charles Buxton, originally a Liberal who later joined the Labour Party, and the Conservative Plunket Barton were both in general agreement with their parties and therefore did not vote against them, while the Conservatives John Randles and Richard Cooper found that if they wished their party to remain in power they had better support it consistently.

There were several witnesses to the influence, not invariably welcome, of the party whips. Wedgwood's 'sample' was not systematic, particularly in terms of party breakdown, but the answers generally confirm other findings that, by the early 20th century, whipping was very consistent and party cohesion correspondingly high. The influence of the whips may also have been enhanced because members were increasingly voting on matters about which they had relatively little information and were therefore in greater need of guidance.[4] Percy Alden, a Liberal who later joined the Labour Party, admitted that once or twice he would have voted differently 'if the Whips had been taken off', and Sir Robert Newman found it 'difficult under our strict party system to be much influenced by a party speech'. The Conservative Felix Cassel said simply that speeches 'very rarely' affected his vote because 'The whips saw to that'. Arthur Brookfield claimed that 'sometimes, in a rhetorical way, my feelings were so far affected that I should, if possible, have escaped from the House. As it was, I think I only voted about twice against my own party, or for the other side'. William du Pre testified to the difficulties when there was no whip in operation: his votes were 'very seldom' influenced by speeches 'except when the Government Whips were taken off, & then very often one was at a loss which lobby to go into'. Colin Coote, who was first elected in the early days of the Lloyd George coalition during the First World War, found that in those particular circumstances he was 'very much' influenced by speeches: 'Party discipline was exceedingly loose during the first Coalition, and issues extremely confused'.

There were a few genuinely independent-minded members who made up their minds (or said they did) on the merits of the issues, regardless of the whips' promptings. It is noticeable that, despite his record of independent-mindedness, Wedgwood did not include himself among their number and few went so far as the Liberal Ellis Davies who claimed he was unaffected by speeches and 'often disagreed with my Party and voted with its opponents'. The Scottish Liberal Arthur Murray could not recall a speech that actually influenced how he voted but asserted that he repeatedly told his constituents that he 'refused to go to the House of Commons as a mere vote-registering machine'. For the Liberal William Clough, 'speeches never affected my vote in any matter upon which I had definitely committed myself in my election addresses'. The Liberal Jack Seely was influenced by speeches in the early stage of his career and 'constantly voted accordingly until I became a Minister, when alas!, this privilege vanished'. Alfred Gelder, by contrast, was not often influenced by speeches but 'I generally voted my own convictions for which very often I found myself in trouble with the party Whips'.

[4] John D. Fair, 'Party Voting Behaviour 1886–1918', *Parliamentary History*, v (1986), 65–82; and Cox, *The Efficient Secret*, 65.

Algernon Borthwick's daughter claimed to know that 'if any man had been able to convince my father that the side he was about to take was wrong, he would have voted according to his conscience regardless of anything else'.

Party loyalty and discipline may have been the principal determinants of voting behaviour, especially on the floor of the House, but about half the respondents nevertheless claimed that there were circumstances, albeit limited ones, when they felt they could exercise some discretion about how they voted. In those circumstances, speeches could be influential. Nearly 10% of respondents claimed to have voted occasionally for the other side (the Liberal Harold Baker said he did so on '5–6 occasions from 1910 to 1914'), although not necessarily as a result of hearing speeches. Apart from the effect of Lloyd George's speeches on Wilfrid Ashley and Julius Bertram, Alfred Hopkinson also claimed that 'Speeches often decided me to vote against the speaker's view especially Harcourt's'. For Leo Money, 'Yes [speeches could be influential], as is shown by the fact that on a number of occasions this particular sheep was found in the opposition [Conservative] lobby'. Charles Venables-Llewellyn, who served as a Conservative only between the two elections in 1910, claimed that speeches did influence him 'when they threw fresh light upon a subject' while another Conservative, George Courthope, claimed that speeches 'frequently' influenced his vote.

Raymond Greene (a Conservative), Edmund Harvey and Daniel Turner Holmes (both Liberals) were among those who welcomed the greater freedom from the whips allowed for votes in committee; that applied even for the Irish, as Hugh Law, among others, remarked. Wedgwood himself claimed that 'Of course in Committee, speeches affected votes and party action much more and every day'. Austen Chamberlain, who had held high ministerial office, spoke from experience when he said that speeches 'often modify or change the decision of a Government in Committee'. There were similar opportunities for speeches to affect votes in debates on private bills and private members' bills. Others distinguished between major and minor party issues, usually without saying where they would draw the line. Arnold Herbert remarked how 'Occasionally my views on minor points were altered by speeches in Parliament but when that was so the change was generally wrong'. Sir George Sitwell described how:

> On the great political issues men's minds are made up, but on what are supposed to be minor issues some votes will always be influenced by a well-reasoned and sympathetic speech. I voted for the shortening of the hours of labour in coal mines, for the opening of churchyards to Nonconformist burials, against the party use of secret service funds, and against compulsory examination of prostitutes. In these, as in other cases, the Conservative Whips were in the other lobby.

Some remarked that speeches could make their influence felt in other, more subtle, ways even if they did not affect votes as such. As Wedgwood put it, 'They affected my mind, and therefore must have affected my future votes' and for Lord Cranborne, 'they very often to a certain extent shook my opinion'. For James Hope, speeches did not often immediately affect his vote 'but they sometimes set going new trains of thought. Often however preconceived notions not amounting to convictions, were completely dissipated in debate. Except for set party wrangles, nowhere is the truth better elicited (and "stunts" confuted) than in the House of Commons'. Herbert Spender-Clay thought that members might be so influenced that they brought 'pressure to bear on the Leaders of the Party to modify or withdraw proposed legislation'.

4. *Great Speeches*

Many of the 204 replies to Wedgwood's third question about speeches – Q21: 'What was the greatest speech that you remember hearing?' – confirmed that individual speeches (and speakers) may have been admired but were not necessarily viewed in terms of their impact on events. Again, Wedgwood offered no criteria for judging what constituted 'the greatest' speech his subjects had heard but most assumed that he was interested in parliamentary speeches and answered accordingly. Relatively few of them attempted, however, to justify their choice. As the Liberal Evan Hayward remarked, 'the qualities of speeches vary so much – one may have excellencies in one respect and another in others'. Similarly, the Conservative William Whitelaw pointed out that the word 'greatest' might mean several different things and many avoided choosing by identifying more than one speaker or speech. The Irish Nationalist John Campbell refused to answer, claiming that oratory 'does not flourish' in the house of commons and that 'Your only orators have been Irish'. Others either could not say, sometimes because they had heard too many speeches, or said they could not remember what they considered to be the greatest speech they ever heard.

Many respondents identified those whom they regarded as great speakers rather than individual great speeches, although others did both. Gladstone, surprisingly, was hardly mentioned in general terms as a great speaker – perhaps it was taken for granted – but for those who had had opportunities to hear him his speeches obviously made a great impact, even among his opponents. Many of his admirers claimed to remember actual speeches they had heard. George Lansbury (who can only have been a teenager at the time but must have heard the speech from the Strangers' Gallery when Gladstone was probably at the height of his powers) claimed that 'The greatest speech I ever heard was by Mr Gladstone in 1875 or 76 when he closed with a magnificent peroration about Montenegro. No one in these days comes near him as an orator who convinced his hearers by eloquence and apparent sincerity'. Austen Chamberlain remembered his father's view, shared with Balfour, that 'given the circumstances, Gladstone's speech on the first of his Bulgarian resolutions in 1878 (?) was the finest parliamentary effort they had heard'. Richard Winfrey recounted how, in 1881, 'then a young man in London, I sat in the Strangers' Gallery from 4 p.m. till midnight and heard Mr Gladstone introduce the first Irish Land Bill in a speech of some 4 hours'.

Lord Wolmer chose 'Mr Gladstone's speech on the Bradlaugh case in (?) 1881', as did Nathaniel Micklem who heard the speech from the gallery. S.F. Mendl, among several others, including Henry Hobhouse, who strongly opposed home rule, chose Gladstone's contributions to the Irish home rule debates in the 1880s; there were half a dozen who chose the home rule debates in the 1890s. William Rees-Davies described Gladstone's introduction of his second home rule bill as 'a marvellous effort for an octogenarian' while Arthur Griffith-Boscawen cited 'Gladstone's introduction of the Home Rule Bill in 1893, after which I was a Home Ruler for 10 minutes. But Sir E. Clarke's wonderful reply quickly re-converted me'. Joseph Pease recalled 'Mr Gladstone one night in the

House of Commons in 1893 hammering Mr Chamberlain on his attitude towards conceding self-government to the Irish people'. Eliot Crawshay-Williams remembered 'A few words spoken by Gladstone on July 11th 1893 when he quelled a fierce row in the House. It showed the immense power he had and his tremendous force of character'.

Twenty-nine respondents (nearly 14%) either singled out Asquith as a speaker or chose individual speeches by him. They confirmed Asquith's reputation as a speaker who could have a powerful impact on a parliamentary audience, possibly as much for the style and manner of his delivery as for the content of his speeches. Most of his admirers did not identify a specific speech as the greatest they had heard, possibly because his long service in senior positions (he was chancellor of the exchequer and then prime minister between 1905 and 1916) meant that he spoke relatively frequently. For Frederick Whyte, he was, however, 'the master of debate', one of a handful of speakers for whom Whyte 'would always desert dinner to hear'. John Cator found him a 'finished orator' while Harry Hope saw him as 'dignified and persuasive', Hugh Law cited the 'solidity' of his arguments and Max Aitken simply answered 'Asquith'. Arthur Wills regarded him as 'certainly supreme in the House of Commons' and Percy Alden described 'one of the ablest and best worked speeches of a classical type' by Asquith on home rule. Two of his individual speeches were specifically mentioned, one in 1913 following the death of Alfred Lyttelton (described by Leo Amery as 'the best valedictory speech') and the other following the death of Sir Henry Campbell-Bannerman in 1908 (cited by Thomas Wiles).

Lloyd George attracted significant support as a speaker, with 12 respondents referring to him in general terms as a great speaker or identifying specific speeches. He was also singled out as a platform speaker. Several testified to his powers of persuasion but he could arouse mixed emotions, even on his own side. His fellow Liberal Guy Wilson remarked that the greatest speech he heard was probably by Asquith and 'certainly none of Lloyd George's'. The Conservative Harry Hope commented on his 'powerfully dramatic style' and he was one of several speakers who 'deeply impressed' the Lib–Lab William Brace, while the Irish Nationalist Hugh Law thought him 'the most beguiling orator I ever listened to, though as time went on I began to suspect a nigger in the woodpile'. Richard Cooper, a Conservative, remembered a speech in 1915 'on the shortage of shells on the Western Front and generally known as his "Too Late" speech. It was a masterpiece of oratory and was the dominant factor which broke Asquith'. Thomas Owen Jacobsen simply recalled 'Lloyd George on the War' and Daniel Turner Holmes chose a speech in 1918 in the so-called Maurice debate:[5] 'For brilliancy, dexterity, art & artfulness this was a marvellous effort'. Edward Archdale, Conservative member for Fermanagh North, remembered 'Lloyd George defending his conduct in the war' while George Nicholls, a Lib–Lab member from 1906 to 1910, cited the 1909 Budget speech, as did the Liberal George Gooch but who also remarked that 'as it was read, perhaps it hardly qualifies'.

Another admired former prime minister was Arthur Balfour, thought by Plunket Barton to be 'comparatively ineffective' in opening several Irish debates but when

---

[5] The debate was about allegations in a letter to *The Times* by the recently dismissed General Sir Frederick Maurice, director of military operations at the war office, that Lloyd George had lied to the house of commons about the strength of the British army in France.

winding up 'with his back to the wall', 'he was a marvellous parliamentary swordsman'. He was also Leo Money's 'favourite parliamentary speaker' and struck Henry Wyndham-Quin as 'the most effective speaker in my day'. Ellis Davies, although a Liberal, 'was more impressed by the speeches of Balfour than any other'. Other highly rated frontbenchers included Joseph Chamberlain, Richard Haldane, as secretary of state for war, Sir John Simon as both law officer and home secretary, Winston Churchill and Michael Hicks-Beach. Haldane's speech in 1906 on the army estimates was described by William Clough as 'the masterpiece of a master – fluent, rapid and entrancing'. Chamberlain was notable for the range of topics on which he made memorable speeches. Hugh Law singled out Chamberlain's 'histrionic power of making any least point tell' and Raymond Heath his 'rapier play, all the time' in debates on the 'Irish Question' while Thomas Hare recalled a speech (unspecified) on home rule. Chamberlain was responsible for what Leo Amery called the 'finest debating speech' he could remember in a motion on South Africa in 1896, a speech also chosen by Walford Green. James Majendie, who served from 1900 to 1906, was, possibly surprisingly, the only person specifically to choose Chamberlain's contributions to debates on free trade, although James Parker remembered the 'great Free Trade debates in 1906. The whole series of Front rank men who took part spoke wonderfully'.

Because of his position, Sir Edward Grey often spoke on a wide variety of topics throughout his service as foreign secretary between 1905 and 1916. There were few references to his general abilities as a speaker but he made the single speech most frequently chosen by Wedgwood's respondents (37 from all parties or around 17%) as the greatest they heard. Technically, it was a statement, not a speech, on 3 August 1914, the day before the outbreak of the First World War, when Grey succeeded in winning for the government the support of a previously deeply divided House and party. It made a profound and lasting impression on all who heard it. In his memoirs Speaker Lowther called it 'the greatest and most thrilling occasion I ever witnessed in the House'[6] while Lord Hugh Cecil (a Conservative and initially one of Grey's critics) found it 'the greatest example of the art of persuasion that I have ever listened to'.[7] The contributions by Asquith and John Redmond on the same occasion were also singled out, Redmond's by, among others, the Irish Nationalist John Hayden specifically for its effect on the House while the Liberal Unionist Herbert Jessel remembered Asquith as saying 'We shall not sheath the sword'.

A few other occasions provoked widely remembered speeches from the front benches, of which the most notable was during the 1909 Budget debate when Balfour accused the solicitor-general, Alexander Ure, of telling lies about old age pensions. The Liberal Thomas Barclay described hearing Balfour vindicate 'his right to use strong language when necessary' while Edward Hemmerde remembered Ure's reply 'to a speech charging him with "having uttered a frigid & calculated lie"'. Sir Walter Nugent, an Irish Nationalist, remembered hearing Ure 'defending his honour' against Balfour and George Wardle described the 'dramatic intensity' of Ure's speech, while Alexander Boulton simply referred to Ure's speech as the best he remembered, as did Walter Rea.

---

[6] James Lowther, Viscount Ullswater, *A Speaker's Commentaries* (2 vols, 1925), ii, 167.
[7] Quoted in G.M. Trevelyan, *Grey of Fallodon* (1937), 265.

For backbenchers, it was clearly much more difficult to make a lasting impression as a speaker, partly because of the dominance of the front benches, both government and opposition, in terms of debating time. Of the few who did, the most notable was Lord Hugh Cecil, a 'high tory' who served from 1895 to 1906 and from 1910 to 1937 and was on Frederick Whyte's list of speakers for whom he would always desert dinner. Charles Trevelyan (at that time a Liberal) claimed that for him 'more than one of Lord Hugh Cecil's in the 1900 parliament were [*sic*] perfect, though I sometimes disagreed with him profoundly'. Fifteen respondents from all parties cited speeches by Lord Hugh as the greatest they heard, of which the most frequently mentioned (by seven respondents) was his contribution to a debate in 1917 on a proposal in the Representation of the People Bill to disenfranchise conscientious objectors (Lord Hugh also chose it as his own best speech). It was unquestionably a memorable performance but on that occasion, as on others including during the passage of an education bill in 1902, Lord Hugh may have dazzled his audience but he failed to win the argument, a measure of how difficult it was (and has remained) for backbenchers' speeches to have tangible results. As Henry Wright, a fellow Conservative, remarked, 'Hugh Cecil's speech on the Disestablishment of the Church in Wales was the most moving speech I ever heard, & kept the House enthralled, but made not the smallest difference to anybody's vote'. The other frequently cited back-bench speech (mentioned by six respondents) was F.E. Smith's maiden speech in 1903 although Percy Alden remarked obscurely that it might have been the cleverest speech he heard 'but of course it was not a great speech'. It could have no impact on events but it undoubtedly made Smith's reputation as a speaker at an early stage in his parliamentary career.

Wedgwood did not ask his subjects to explain their choices but they provided some clues about the qualities thought to contribute to a great house of commons speaker or speech. Charles Mallet singled out three people – Sir Edward Grey, Jack Seely and George Cave – as having what he called 'conspicuously the special House of Commons gift' and there were several speakers who were specifically admired for their debating (as opposed to platform) skills, including Joseph Chamberlain (by Leo Amery in particular), Arthur Balfour (by, among others, Plunket Barton), Sir William Robson, as solicitor-general (by Hubert Carr-Gomm) and Bonar Law (by Ellis Davies). Hugh Law also singled out Sir Henry Campbell-Bannerman's 'extraordinary skill' in tariff reform debates in the early 1900s 'in a kind of dialectic exactly suited to each occasion'. William Clough praised highly Richard Haldane's fluency, while Vincent Kennedy recalled Haldane's ability to speak for nearly five hours without notes on a subject with which he was not wholly familiar.

Clarity of exposition, as demonstrated by speakers such as Asquith, Balfour and Sir John Simon, had a strong appeal, while Samuel Whitbread noted John Redmond's 'clearly reasoned speeches' in his 'annual plea for the Irish political prisoners'. Wit, as shown by Augustine Birrell, was also popular. Lloyd George won many plaudits for his dramatic speaking style and, on occasion, his persuasiveness, as did several Irish speakers, including Tim Healy and John Redmond. Lord Hugh Cecil's reputation for high-mindedness may explain why he was one of the few speakers known for how they could appeal to the emotions on issues of principle while the ability to find the right words on difficult occasions at least partly explains why Grey's statement on 3 August 1914 was so compelling and memorable. He was not known as a dramatic orator but he could always be relied on to say whatever was required and for that reason was often called upon to speak in debates when the government was in difficulties. He could not have been more aware of the significance of that particular occasion but, as he explained in his memoirs, when it came to the point he knew what he had to do and was not nervous. 'In a great crisis, a man who has to act or speak stands bare and stripped of choice. He has to do what is in him to do . . . and he can do no other.'[8]

---

[8] Quoted in Trevelyan, *Grey of Fallodon*, 263.

Chapter 7. The Biographies

Wedgwood's intention had been that the questionnaire would provide a basis for his respondents to write their own autobiographies. To include biographies written by 'the man himself' would, he had thought, add a special ingredient to his proposed late 19th- and early 20th-century volumes of the *History* project, one which would be unavoidably lacking from those covering earlier periods. He largely failed, however, in his objective of getting his subjects to supply their own biographies. Only 25 (about 8%) of the 294 who supplied their own answers to the questionnaire did as he asked and provided structured biographies based on the topics in the questionnaire. A further eight biographies were provided by *History of Parliament* staff or the subjects' families; some of those supplied by families were lengthy hagiographies which did not follow the topics in the questionnaire.

The remaining respondents were probably deterred by a mixture of reluctance to undertake literary composition and the vagueness of the preamble to the questionnaire. They gave varying amounts of information in their answers, sometimes with additions in correspondence with Wedgwood that were probably not intended for publication but were nevertheless used. He was therefore left with a substantial task in preparing the biographies, probably involving much more drafting and editing than he had originally expected. He had no hesitation in adding his own gloss or interpretation of events to complete the picture given by the raw material supplied by his subjects. His attachment to parliament and its members gave him a very particular view of his colleagues although otherwise his biographies generally followed the pattern laid down in the questionnaire.

Wedgwood appears to have started to prepare the biographies based on the answers to the questionnaires in about September 1936 when he claimed to be doing four in a day.[1] He made relatively slow progress until the end of the year, saying in a letter of 1 January 1937 to Henry McLaren that he had written 35. In January 1937, he went on a sea voyage of about three weeks, during which he must have prepared about two-thirds of the 130 that he compiled. That was well under half the number of completed questionnaires in the files, including those completed by families, and there are no signs that he subsequently prepared any more biographies. Once typed, he mostly kept to his undertaking to allow his subjects to approve his 'censored summaries' which were sent to them for comment and correction. It is not always clear from the files which individual biographies were sent for correction but over a hundred certainly were sent and returned.

The correspondence shows that the biographies completed during the sea voyage were sent to their subjects mainly in the course of February and March 1937; Wedgwood continued to exchange correspondence about them at least until May 1937 and in a few cases rather later. He told Henry McLaren that he had chosen the subjects for his biographies from among the people he knew, 'on pretty scanty information', although in

---

[1] HoP MSS: J.C. Wedgwood to Charles Cochrane-Baillie, 29 Sept. 1936.

a letter of 9 February 1937 to Lord Robert Cecil he said he was 'having great difficulty with those biographies of people I know. It is much easier to do those I don't'. The preponderance of biographies of subjects with surnames beginning in the first half of the alphabet suggests that he started by working through the replies to the questionnaires in alphabetical order but was sometimes diverted into doing those of friends such as Hilton Young.

As far as he could, Wedgwood used the answers to the questionnaires more or less as they stood as the basis of the biographies. The answers by no means invariably contained what he sought, which was something pithy and epigrammatic. The manuscript and typed drafts of his biographies show how he joined extracts, often lengthy, from the answers to the questionnaires into more or less seamless accounts, with additions based on his own knowledge. By using quotation marks, he generally showed when he was quoting directly from the answers. In a few cases, he ignored his 500 word limit but the results were often much shorter. As he had acknowledged to Henry McLaren, the lack of information in the questionnaires could mean that he had to make bricks with very little straw. For Lord Ernest Hamilton, for example, he constructed a 100-word biography from a short letter and a couple of his own sentences. For Harry Lawson he used some very brief notes supplied by Lawson's brother and his own knowledge, possibly supplemented by information provided by *History of Parliament* staff, to compile a detailed 500-word biography. Even allowing for the bias inherent in any selection process, he was much less cavalier with the raw material than might have been expected from his earlier correspondence with Colonel Murray and A.E.W. Mason or, indeed, from his own 'casual attitude to facts and figures'.[2] On the other hand, he had no hesitation in drawing on his personal knowledge and even more his opinions of his subjects and the events in which they were involved. His additions were mostly but not always flattering and could be both lengthy and tendentious, particularly when he knew the subjects well.

Some biographies bore signs of hasty drafting, with extracts from the replies to the questionnaires strung together without a clear narrative, and there was no consistency about the use of the first or third person. There were, however, some sharply drawn pen portraits. Lord Hugh Cecil 'had achieved nothing, save in the minds of men' and was described as 'the anarchist, who moves where he will, alone through the heavens', sitting in the corner seat below the gangway where 'he twists his hands in agony as he straightens out his arguments'. George Lansbury's biography was skilfully selected from a characteristically lengthy and rambling questionnaire and ended: 'It is George Lansbury and the truth as he sees it . . . The complete absence of selfishness in Lansbury . . . is indeed remarkable'. In some biographies, such as those of Henry Bowles and Rowland Hunt, he captured both the humorous tone of the answers to the questionnaire and the personality of the subject. Some of the very short ones, such as those of Joseph Bliss, Leonard and Robert Brassey, Sir Charles Barrie, Alfred Hutton and Sir Ernest Jardine, used limited information and some personal knowledge to provide brief but clear accounts of their subjects, to the extent that Leonard Brassey said he 'could not improve on this'. The short biography of Thomas Hare ended with a telling

---

[2] Mulvey, *Political Life of Josiah C. Wedgwood*, ix. Murray completed a questionnaire but there is no biography while Mason did not complete a questionnaire.

sentence: 'He was made a baronet in 1905, as was fitting in the useful and normal public career of the English country gentleman'. Another, of John Deans Hope, encapsulated the fate of Scottish Liberal politics: 'For twenty-two years he sat in Parliament and never made a speech. This was the quintessence of the strong silent Scottish radicalism of the pre-Clydeside era. When John Deans Hope left, Maxton arrived. The men of the Covenant are gone'.

Many of the biographies were not what his subjects had been led to expect. Wedgwood's personal input was not always well received, even by his friends who were often taken aback by his comments on them and their careers. As Percy Harris remarked tartly in response to the draft of his own biography:

> I thought the record you were making for this Parliamentary History was to be historical and mere statement of facts. Instead of that, you have thought fit to put in your personal impressions of myself which you are entitled to have, and if you like to sign them and put them in as your personal impressions, I have no right to take any exception, but if this statement is supposed to be historical, I object very strongly. . . . I don't think you have any right to introduce your own personal predilections in a book that is subscribed for by all Members of Parliament. . . . I should prefer you to limit your statement to the facts that I gave you and omit comments which no doubt will be indulged in my Obituary Notice.[3]

In notes attached to a letter to Wedgwood of 15 February 1937, it was evident that J.R. Clynes shared Percy Harris' views when he said that he particularly resented being described as 'not really a socialist'. He also complained that 'You may, of course, say that I am a poor speaker . . . but I know of no one else who has said it', quoting Philip Snowden's view of him in support. He ended that his notes were 'a comment on a few of your statements which I have underlined, touching questions of both fact and opinion. You may decide in what way the points in my notes can be used'. Wedgwood agreed, as he almost invariably did, to make the alterations but added that if he were writing for 20 years hence his version would be much more picturesque.

In his biographies, Wedgwood by no means always accepted his colleagues' judgments of themselves and their achievements as expressed in their questionnaires. Some, such as the Conservative Charles Tyrrell Giles, took the opportunity when checking their own biographies to correct what they had said about themselves in their questionnaires while others, much more often, corrected what Wedgwood had said about them. The results of the corrections and redrafting could be duller than what Wedgwood sought (or wrote) but he appears to have accepted most of the subjects' corrections and changes without demur. Cecil Cochrane, Ellis Davies, Walter Essex's daughter, Sir Aylmer Hunter-Weston, Weston Jarvis, Norman Lamont and John Ryder were among those who substantially rewrote Wedgwood's efforts, thereby achieving indirectly what he had originally wanted, the words of 'the man himself'.

Others made significant changes or deletions. Joseph King, a well-known pacifist, corrected a reference to his allegedly being imprisoned for corresponding with a friend in Switzerland. He offered Wedgwood a choice of two versions of the truth that he had

---

[3] HoP MSS: Percy Harris to J.C. Wedgwood, 5 Mar. 1937. There is no corrected version of Harris' biography in the files.

been prosecuted and fined, but not imprisoned, for writing a letter containing military information to a friend in New York. Lord Robert Cecil saw his biography as 'far too laudatory' and took Wedgwood to task for his description of his subject's differences with Lloyd George, saying that 'I cannot complain of L.G.'s treatment of me. . . . The truth is that I could never work with the Conservatives or with the Ramsay Labour people & the Liberal Party perished with Asquith and Grey'.[4] Wedgwood was also firmly rebuked by Frances Stevenson on Lloyd George's behalf for saying that Lloyd George 'never knows his case, he refuses to read, his ignorance exasperates both Treasury and colleagues'. Although Lloyd George was notorious for not reading his briefs and the biography was otherwise generally favourable, she told Wedgwood that:

> As a matter of fact, there is no one who takes more trouble with his briefs as Mr. Lloyd George. He gives a great deal of time to reading up the facts and, although it is a common legend that he does not read, there is absolutely no foundation for this fallacy. Mr. Lloyd George reads a great deal of every kind of book, both contemporary and classical, and, as I have already said, it would not be possible for anyone to take more trouble in reading up the papers connected with any subject upon which he is to speak or write.[5]

Frederick Guest simply removed without comment a final Wedgwood sentence saying that 'Probably Guest always thought of himself first, but it was not a bad first'. According to Wedgwood, Arthur Griffith-Boscawen's parliamentary career 'closed in disaster', a description amended by Griffith-Boscawen to 'came to an untimely end'. Willoughby Dickinson crossed out a paragraph describing him as 'too gentle and sensitive for the rage of party warfare'; and Ellis Davies deleted a description of himself as 'the little Welsh attorney'. James Craig made an insertion to emphasise that, whatever their public political differences, he was personally on good terms with all his fellow Irishmen. He also corrected Wedgwood's terminology on Irish politics ('Protestants' became 'Ulster Loyalists' and the 'Irish below the gangway' became the 'Nationalists opposite').

Philip Sassoon replaced a paragraph in which Wedgwood had described him as possessing 'a modesty or shyness which excludes both ambition and comfort' and continuing: 'Between him and all the rank and file of the House there is a great gulf, fixed by him. Across it we only see a sad smile as of apology for not having been killed in the War'. Sassoon's version described how, as undersecretary of state for air, he had learned to fly and 'visited almost every flying station at home and overseas'. Wedgwood described the bland alternative as 'a great improvement on the original'. His old friend George Lane-Fox disliked being represented as mean: the biography implied that he had left the House because of the expense whereas he had stood in nine elections at a personal cost of around £1,000 a time. He added, however, that he did not mind being called stupid, a reference to Wedgwood's description of him and certain fellow Conservatives as 'Perhaps stupider, but much better for England and for Democracy than the quick, clever, bitter brains of the preceding generation'.[6]

---

[4] HoP MSS: manuscript note on returned copy of Lord Robert Cecil's biography.
[5] HoP MSS: Frances Stevenson to J.C. Wedgwood, 21 Apr. 1937.
[6] HoP MSS: George Lane-Fox (Lord Bingley) to J.C. Wedgwood, 5 May 1937.

Some subjects, such as Plunket Barton and Austen Chamberlain, were clearly embarrassed by Wedgwood's flattery,[7] although they seldom asked for it to be removed. Edmund (Ted) Harvey sought the removal of two final sentences: 'Ted Harvey was the nearest approach to completely unselfish sainthood that we had in the House in this period. He was too gentle'. Edward Noel Buxton wrote 'Absurd!' beside Wedgwood's remark that 'for complete altruism he had no match in the House, save perhaps the Cecils', but left it in place. Felix Cassel, who left the house of commons in 1916 to serve until 1934 as judge advocate general, had 'no corrections or alterations to make. The draft is far too complimentary and generous but I feel it is not for me to interfere with your generosity'. Ben Bathurst, described as 'a popular and decorative figure', thought the biography was good 'except of course the last little compliment!! Which I accept from your hand'. Harry Brodie accepted a description of him as 'very naïve and very loveable . . . We missed him badly, for his sensitive ambition never showed itself in sneer or jealousy'. George Gooch, a close friend, similarly left in a sentence saying that 'he has the courage of the martyr in the cause which he thinks right'.

Hubert Carr-Gomm, who became parliamentary private secretary to the prime minister, Sir Henry Campbell-Bannerman, almost immediately after he was first elected in 1906, did not object to Wedgwood's description of him as the 'model – in dress and deportment – if not in orthodoxy' for all the other 40 PPSs at the time, although he did remove another sentence describing him as 'the perfect product of Eton'. Ian Malcolm and George Wyndham were described as 'the handsomest and best dressed men of their day'. Wedgwood claimed that Malcolm might not have been a great speaker 'but he always looked and probably was the perfect diplomatist', a description which, Malcolm told Wedgwood, 'Couldn't be better'.

The biographies revealed Wedgwood's enduring interest in military careers and achievements. Most of the war office's statements of the military service of members of the house of commons in the First World War were not available when he was compiling his biographies and he seems to have made little use of those that had been supplied. Instead, he appears to have relied mainly on his own memory or other sources of information and rarely failed to refer to wartime or other military service whenever an opportunity arose. He went out of his way to include references to the war service of, among others, the Irish Nationalist Stephen Gwynn, the Conservatives Leo Amery, Viscount Dalrymple, George Hamilton, Sir Aylmer Hunter-Weston and George Lane-Fox, and the Liberals Austin Hopkinson and Hastings Lees-Smith.

Despite being a committed Zionist, Wedgwood also could not resist commenting on apparently Jewish aspects of some of his colleagues including Leo Amery, Frank Goldstone, Herbert Jessel and Percy Harris. The first part of Leo Amery's biography was closely based on Amery's questionnaire but Wedgwood made a lengthy addendum starting 'So writes Leo Amery of himself. It is too modest'. He went on to highlight in some detail other aspects of Amery's career, particularly his war service, ending with a claim that 'It has not been democracy that has spoilt Amery's life. It has been the ridiculous whispers that his name was Emerich and he a Jew. There was no truth in it; if he had stood 6 feet in his stockings he could have laughed the fools out of court. No one else cares; but the damned story has blighted his self-confidence and his career'.

[7] HoP MSS: Austen Chamberlain to J.C. Wedgwood, 27 Feb. 1937.

Amery, who was a small man and whose Jewish connections through his mother were 'generally known if unremarked',[8] must have been sent a copy for correction since he wrote to Wedgwood on 10 February 1937 saying that he had 'put off answering your commentary on my answers to the questionnaire. I am not sure that I entirely concur in its conclusions. But that is a matter which we might discuss together in the House one of these days rather than attempt to deal with by correspondence'. There is no corrected version of the biography in the files.

From his schooldays, Wedgwood had supported Irish independence.[9] The questionnaires provided a good deal of personal information about the Irish Nationalists but he compiled biographies of only three of the 22 who had completed questionnaires: Stephen Gwynn, a Roman catholic but born into a unionist family and who switched to the nationalist cause when 'obliged to think about Ireland and resent much I heard' while at Oxford University; Hugh Law, the protestant son of a former lord chancellor of Ireland, who likewise became a supporter of the nationalist cause and a Roman catholic convert; and Denis Cogan, 'provision merchant', businessman and a more typical Irish Nationalist than Gwynn or Law who were both English educated. Wedgwood's correspondence with both Gwynn and Law suggested that he knew them well and also showed his sympathy for the nationalist cause. Their personal backgrounds and history were hardly typical of their party but Wedgwood may have felt more comfortable doing their biographies than those of some of their colleagues whom he knew less well. Law's answers to the questionnaire were lengthy and detailed and Wedgwood simply instructed the typist to include almost the entire text as it stood with, unusually, no embellishments from him.[10] Gwynn did not mention his own war record in his questionnaire but Wedgwood's biography drew particular attention to it, ending 'when we mourn over the vanishing of the Old Party, it is of those very gentle and brave men we think – Stephen Gwynn and William Redmond, the Protestant and the Catholic, who went to the trenches for the honour of Ireland'.

The relatively few cases where Wedgwood did not adopt a laudatory approach were often marked in the files, but not in Wedgwood's handwriting, 'Not to be sent for correction'. It is not clear who was responsible for this caution, but it was most unlikely to have been Wedgwood. A handful of biographies stand out for their intemperate language, lack of discretion and the strength of Wedgwood's prejudices about his subjects. 'Mystery' was said, for example, to surround the arrival of Max Aitken at Westminster and 'the manner whereby he won that Liberal seat at Ashton', he had an 'unpleasing' voice and his politics after the First World War were 'mostly wrong', although Wedgwood gave him unqualified credit for his energy and unwillingness to admit defeat, his part in establishing the first coalition and then Lloyd George's government during the First World War as well as for the success of his newspapers. The draft was sent to Aitken but there is no corrected version in the files.

Among the least flattering biographies was that of Edward Hemmerde KC, another parliamentary contemporary and one-time close collaborator over the land tax, but with

[8] See *ODNB* entry on Amery by Deborah Lavin.

[9] C.V. Wedgwood, *Last of the Radicals*, 30, 115.

[10] Law's handwriting was very difficult to read and the typist transcribed only the biographical facts about him.

a chequered political and personal career. Hemmerde wrote briefly but amiably to Wedgwood on 17 September 1936 when returning his questionnaire. Wedgwood's biography, however, ended with a paragraph based entirely on his personal knowledge of Hemmerde and not on his questionnaire:

> Conceit and intense ambition inspired Hemmerde. He had all F.E. Smith's brains without his bonhomie. Most M.P.s are conceited and strenuously conceal it; a touch of orientalism and a handsome person betrayed Hemmerde's failing, and he was never 'F.E.' – never known by his christian name. He got his recordership, got into financial troubles, lost his safe Denbighshire seat, and became a liability to the party he had served so well. They mud-raked his past and present, and all the time Hemmerde remained a child who never grew up – ever optimistic and ever more bitterly resenting lack of appreciation. Nobody loved him, Labour would not give him office, and he never understood. A queer financial kink in the brain destroyed the greatest adventurer in modern politics.

The paragraph was all the more remarkable because Hemmerde was still alive. The biography was among those never sent to the subjects for their comments.

Surprisingly, given his extensive experience as both author and editor, Wedgwood seriously underestimated how long preparing the biographies would take. To almost anyone else, especially given his other commitments, his output in September 1936 of four a day would have seemed remarkable but it proved unsustainable. His declared intention to complete the biographies based on the questionnaire by June 1937 (almost certainly a self-imposed deadline) was always unrealistic[11] and seems to have taken no account of how his biographies would need to be merged with those being prepared by *History of Parliament* staff. By about May 1937 he had completed 130 biographies, from a total of around 355 questionnaires, of which over 100 were sent to their subjects for correction. After that he prepared no more although he was still conducting correspondence about the questionnaire late in 1938.[12]

Wedgwood's determination to carry forward his *History* to 1918 was not confined to the biographies based on the questionnaire. The three staff that the informal committee of members of the two Houses had agreed in February 1936 could be employed had started work by the summer of 1936. They helped with some of the practical tasks of the questionnaire, including keeping records, checking the factual parts of the biographies and some editorial work. They also worked on biographies of members of parliament who had served between 1868 and 1885 and in the earlier part of 1885–1918, including some of those whose questionnaires had been completed by their families. They used mainly published sources such as Hansard, *Dod*, *Who's Who*, *The Times* and other newspaper obituaries and periodicals such as *Truth* to prepare biographies, following a template probably devised by Wedgwood. The files show that he sometimes played an active editorial role. Together, they also conducted a considerable amount of correspondence with the families of dead members who could be traced, starting early in 1937 and

[11] See HoP MSS: J.C. Wedgwood to Duff Cooper, secretary of state for war, 2 Dec. 1936.
[12] See, for example, HoP MSS: J.C. Wedgwood to Daniel Sheehan, 1 Dec. 1938.

continuing sporadically throughout 1938 and into 1939. By then, most of the correspondence was being done by *History of Parliament* staff, mainly by Wedgwood's assistant,
Miss Menna Jones.

The staff's achievements between late 1936 and some time in the first half of
1940 were considerable. Apart from the main sequence of 354 questionnaires, there is a
separate sequence of 130 biographies, compiled by staff, of deceased members for
1885–1918 for whom questionnaires were completed by their families. It is not obvious
why they were filed separately rather than with the 'Wedgwood' questionnaires which
include 60 completed by families. The files also contain approximately 1,000 biographies
for 1868–85 and 600 for 1885–1918, all listed during late 1940. None of the staff-
compiled biographies has the qualities of Wedgwood's but their style shows his editorial
influence. They are in very varying states of completion. A few have nothing more than
a name and very limited personal information while others are more or less complete
with meticulously listed published sources and signs of having been edited, often with
considerable care and in a few cases in Wedgwood's handwriting. For those covering
1885–1918 in particular the surnames beginning with earlier letters of the alphabet
are much more thoroughly worked than the rest. Like the material related to the
'Wedgwood' questionnaire, those biographies were probably sorted and filed in the early
1940s. The archives also contain numerous meticulously prepared lists of election results
and members of successive administrations between 1885 and 1918. Those lists, which
represented a great deal of work, were almost certainly intended for inclusion in the
planned volumes for that period.

Even if Wedgwood was, as his niece suggested, trying to have some entertainment at
his colleagues' expense,[13] his questionnaire undoubtedly had a serious purpose. His belief
in the importance of recording the lives of members of parliament for the benefit of
future generations was strongly held. There is nothing in the correspondence, his memoir
or his last published work – *Testament to Democracy*, published in 1942, in which the text
of the questionnaire is reproduced – to indicate why he stopped work on the biographies
after the middle of 1937. The tone of the correspondence and the vigour with which
it was conducted suggest that, despite occasional brushes with present and former
colleagues, he at least initially enjoyed the work associated with the biographies. An
exchange with his Conservative friend and parliamentary contemporary, George Lane-
Fox in May 1937 suggests, however, that even he may have become discouraged in his
dealings with his subjects and, possibly, by the magnitude of the task he had taken on.
In a letter of 10 May 1937, written after receiving Wedgwood's reactions to his
comments on his biography, Lane-Fox asked: 'Why this despairing letter? You had
written nothing about me that I resented . . . If I have given a different impression please
forget it. I must have expressed myself very badly. . . . And do go on with your book. I
shall look forward to reading about my friends . . . so long as you don't get involved in
libel actions this will be great fun'.

By the late 1930s Wedgwood's health was beginning to deteriorate. His involvement
in numerous other causes must have made substantial demands on his time and energy

---

[13] C.V. Wedgwood, *Last of the Radicals*, 170; Wedgwood himself asked, rhetorically: 'If the reader should
think them inquisitive, reflect what we would not now give to have had answers to such questions from
those Parliament-men who sat under Elizabeth, Cromwell or Queen Anne!' J.C. Wedgwood, *Testament to
Democracy*, 18.

while events in the outside world were becoming increasingly ominous. If indeed he had become discouraged with the biographies, there were ample reasons for him to divert his energy elsewhere, even if he always intended to return to the biographies when life allowed. The 'self-biography' project fizzled out and there was no further progress with the large number of biographies initially drafted by members of staff. The carefully prepared lists of members of late 19th- and early 20th-century administrations, the statements of wartime service and accompanying lists, which all represented a substantial body of work, were never used. The promised 19th- and 20th-century volumes were not completed, and Wedgwood's ambition to create a public memorial to his colleagues' wartime achievements was never realised. The questionnaires and related material were listed, sorted and filed, with the statements of service, early in the 1940s, probably around the time that the History of Parliament Trust was created in December 1940.

Had they been completed on the lines that Wedgwood seems originally to have envisaged, those volumes would have contained about 294 biographies compiled by him from the questionnaires and about 2,000, possibly more, compiled by staff from questionnaires completed by families and from published sources (the exact number would have depended on the period that the volumes covered, which was never finally determined). The result would have been a curious mixture. If the drafts in the *History of Parliament* archives are any indication, the staff-compiled biographies would have been standard scholarly contributions to a work of reference, dry and lacking any personal touch, but based on accurately recorded published sources. Wedgwood's approach to his biographies was completely different and not what he had led either the professional historians or his subjects to expect. He was a skilled editor and his personal gloss on many of his subjects and their careers has its own interest. It was, however, more like the product of a sketch-writer or cartoonist than of the scholar he often purported to be. He seems to have seen no inconsistency in inviting his subjects to provide their own biographies ('No biographer, only the man himself, can answer such questions') and then adding his own editorial interventions which often contradicted or even overrode the original contributions.

It is impossible to know what the reactions would have been to the 19th- and 20th-century volumes, had they been completed and published. Some of Wedgwood's subjects and the wider public might have shared George Lane-Fox's view that the result was 'great fun'. Sales of the medieval volumes were disappointing[14] but there might have been more interest in biographies of those who were still alive or only recently dead. There are no signs that he had attempted to draft the sort of general conclusions to those volumes that had brought him into such contention with the historians in connection with the medieval volumes, although he probably intended to do something of that kind.[15] His political views, as documented shortly before his death in *Testament to Democracy*, had become increasingly unfashionable but his romantic attachment to parliament was undiminished. He would have relished building a composite picture of his colleagues, and the parliaments in which they served, as he had done in his first medieval volume. One extract from the introduction to his first medieval volume is in itself almost an accurate summary of Wedgwood's own career:

---

[14] Mulvey, *Political Life of Josiah C. Wedgwood*, 176.

[15] Probably in connection with his *Staffordshire Parliamentary History*, Wedgwood had prepared summary accounts of the parliaments from 1885 to 1918, but they were never used.

Each time the country loved it – the excitement, the news, the trip to town, the gossip and the exaggerations. . . . They mixed, they talked, they petitioned; they made public opinion. . . . After a few weeks, when they had had enough of town and talk and bills, and wanted to go home, they were not allowed to go until they had voted a subsidy of half a tenth and a fifteenth, which they did on the last day. Then Parliament was prorogued or dissolved, and the Members had spent an enjoyable time. . . . Generally they returned somewhat uncomfortably, feeling that the story they had to tell would not be well received. Most grievances would be unredressed, most promises unfulfilled.[16]

[16] History of Parliament, *Biographies: Commons 1439–1509* (1936), introduction, iv–v.

Appendix 1: Respondents to Wedgwood's Questionnaire

The table below lists the names of all the 354 respondents to the questionnaire that Wedgwood sent to members of parliament and former members of parliament in July 1936 who supplied information, or about whom information was supplied, which can be treated as a response to at least one question in the questionnaire. As explained above (p. 115) it does not include the separate sequence of biographies, compiled by staff, of deceased members for 1885–1918 for whom questionnaires were completed by their families.

Column 1 lists the surnames of respondents in alphabetical order in the form in which they were used by Wedgwood and the *History of Parliament* staff. Surnames listed in bold are those for whom Wedgwood or *History of Parliament* staff compiled a biography. Surnames in italics are those for whom families or friends completed the questionnaire or otherwise supplied information.

Column 2 lists the first name used, or titles in the case of peers.

Column 3 lists the date of first election of the respondents to the house of commons; as in column 4, dates given with a month are those of by-elections, with the exception of 1910, when there were two general elections (in January and December) and the list indicates which of those two elections was involved.

Column 4 lists the date of final departure of the respondents from the house of commons, whether by death, retirement, elevation to the peerage or electoral defeat.

Column 5 lists the respondent's party at first election to the house of commons, using the party names in Stenton and Lees' *Who's Who of British Members of Parliament* and Michael Rush's database of United Kingdom members of parliament 1832–2001.

Columns 6 and 7 list years of birth and death as given by Stenton and Lees.

Surname	First name used	Date of first election	Date of exit	Party at first election	Year of birth	Year of death
Adam	William	1910 (Jan.)	1910 (Dec.)	Conservative	1865	1940
Addison	Christopher	1910 (Jan.)	1935	Liberal	1869	1951
Agar-Robartes	Thomas	1905 (Mar.)	1915 (Sept.)	Liberal	1880	1915
Aitken	Max	1905 (Mar.)	1916 (Dec.)	Conservative	1879	1964
Alden	Percy	1906	1924	Liberal	1865	1944
Allen	William J.	1917	1905 (Apr.)	Unionist	1837	1903
Allen	William	1892	1900	Liberal	1870	1945
Ambrose	Robert	1893	1910 (Jan.)	Nationalist	1855	1940
Amery	Leo	1911	1945	Conservative	1873	1955
Anderson	George	1918 (Aug.)	1918	Conservative	1854	1941
Archdale	Edward	1898	1903 (Mar.)	Conservative	1853	1943
Ashley	Wilfrid	1906	1932 (Jan.)	Conservative	1867	1939
Ashton	Thomas	1895	1906 (June)	Liberal	1855	1933

Surname	First name used	Date of first election	Date of exit	Party at first election	Year of birth	Year of death
Baden-Powell	George	1885	1898 (Nov.)	Conservative	1847	1898
Baggallay	Ernest	1885	1887	Conservative	1850	1931
Baker	Harold	1910	1918	Liberal	1877	1960
Baker	John	1892	1909 (Nov.)	Liberal	1828	1909
Barclay	Thomas	1910	1910 (Dec.)	Liberal	1853	1941
Barlow	Anderson Montague	1910 (Dec.)	1923	Conservative	1868	1951
Barlow	Percy	1906	1910 (Jan.)	Liberal	1867	1931
Barnes	George	1906	1922	Labour	1859	1940
Barran	Rowland	1902	1918	Liberal	1858	1949
Barrie	Charles	1918 (Oct.)	1940 (Jan.)	Liberal	1875	1940
Bartley	George	1885	1906	Conservative	1842	1910
Bartley-Denniss	Edmund	1911	1922	Conservative	1854	1931
Barton	Plunket	1891	1900	Conservative	1853	1937
Barton	William	1910 (Jan.)	1922	Liberal	1862	1957
Bathurst	Ben	1895	1906	Conservative	1872	1947
Bellairs	Carlyon	1906	1931	Liberal	1871	1955
Bertram	Julius	1906	1910 (Jan.)	Liberal	1866	1944
Bethell	George	1885	1900	Conservative	1849	1919
Bethell	John	1906	1922	Liberal	1861	1945
Bethell	Thomas	1906	1910 (Jan.)	Liberal	1867	1957
Bigham	John	1895	1897 (Oct.)	LU	1840	1929
Bignold	Arthur	1900	1910 (Jan.)	Conservative	1839	1915
Black	Arthur	1906	1918	Liberal	1863	1947
Blair	Reginald	1912 (Nov.)	1945	Conservative	1881	1962
Bliss	Joseph	1916 (Mar.)	1918	Liberal	1853	1939
Boland	John	1900	1918	Nationalist	1870	1958
Borthwick	Algernon	1885	1895	Conservative	1830	1908
Boulton	Alexander	1906	1910 (Jan.)	Liberal	1862	1949
Bowles	Henry	1889	1906	Conservative	1858	1943
Brace	William	1906	1920 (Nov.)	Lib–Lab	1865	1947
Brassey	Leonard	1910 (Jan.)	1929	Conservative	1870	1958
Brassey	Robert	1910	1910 (Dec.)	Conservative	1875	1946
Bridgeman	William	1906	1929	Conservative	1864	1935
Bright	Allan	1904 (July)	1906	Liberal	1862	1941
Brodie	Harry	1906	1910 (Jan.)	Liberal	1875	1956
Brookfield	Arthur	1885	1903	Conservative	1853	1940
Brunner	John	1906	1910 (Jan.)	Liberal	1865	1929
Bryce	James	1885	1907 (Feb.)	Liberal	1838	1922
Buxton	Charles	1910	1910 (Dec.)	Liberal	1875	1942
Buxton	Edward Noel	1905 (June)	1930 (June)	Liberal	1869	1948
Calley	Thomas	1910 (Dec.)	1910 (Dec.)	LU	1856	1932
Campbell	John	1900	1906	Nationalist	1870	unknown
Carew	Charles	1915 (Nov.)	1922	Conservative	1853	1939

Surname	First name used	Date of first election	Date of exit	Party at first election	Year of birth	Year of death
Carlile	Walter	1906	1919 (Nov.)	Conservative	1852	1942
Carr-Gomm	Hubert	1906	1918	Liberal	1877	1939
Cassel	Felix	1910	1916 (Oct.)	Conservative	1869	1953
Cator	John	1910 (Jan.)	1918	Conservative	1862	1944
Cavendish	Richard	1895	1906	LU	1871	1946
Cecil	Evelyn	1898	1929	Conservative	1865	1941
Cecil	(Lord) Hugh	1895	1937 (Jan.)	Conservative	1869	1956
Cecil	(Lord) Robert	1906	1923	Conservative	1864	1958
Chaloner	Richard	1895	1900	Conservative	1856	1938
Chamberlain	Austen	1892	1937 (Mar.)	LU	1863	1937
Chance	Frederick	1905 (July)	1910 (Jan.)	Liberal	1852	1932
Chancellor	Henry	1910	1918	Liberal	1863	1945
Channing	Francis	1885	1910 (Dec.)	Liberal	1841	1926
Chapple	William	1910	1924	Liberal	1864	1936
Cheyne	William	1917	1922	Conservative	1852	1932
Clough	William	1906	1918	Liberal	1862	1937
Clyde	James	1909 (May)	1920 (Mar.)	Conservative	1863	1944
Clynes	John	1906	1945	Labour	1869	1949
Coats	Stuart	1916 (Apr.)	1922	Conservative	1868	1959
Cochrane	Cecil	1916 (Mar.)	1918 (Oct.)	Liberal	1869	1960
Cochrane-Baillie	Charles	1886	1890	Conservative	1860	1940
Cogan	Denis	1900	1907 (June)	Irish Nat.	1859	1944
Cohen	Benjamin	1892	1906	Conservative	1844	1909
Collins	William	1906	1910 (Dec.)	Liberal	1859	1946
Cooper	Richard	1910	1922	Conservative	1874	1946
Coote	Colin	1917	1922	Liberal	1893	1979
Corbett	Archibald	1886	1910 (Jan.)	LU	1856	1933
Corbett	Charles	1906	1910 (Jan.)	Liberal	1853	1935
Courthope	George	1906	1945	Conservative	1877	1955
Cox	Harold	1906	1910 (Jan.)	Liberal	1859	1936
Craig	Charles	1903 (Feb.)	1922	Conservative	1869	1960
Craig	James	1906	1921	Unionist	1871	1940
Cranborne	(Viscount)	1893	1903 (Aug.)	Conservative	1861	1947
Crawshay-Williams	Eliot	1910 (Jan.)	1913 (June)	Liberal	1879	1962
Crichton-Stuart	Ninian	1910 (Dec.)	1915 (Sept.)	Conservative	1883	1915
Croft	Henry	1910 (Jan.)	1940 (May)	Conservative	1881	1947
Crosfield	Arthur	1906	1910 (Dec.)	Liberal	1865	1938
Crossley	Savile	1900	1906	LU	1857	1935
Cullinan	John	1900	1918	Irish Nat.	1858	1920
Curzon	(Viscount)	1885	1900 (Sept.)	Conservative	1861	1929
Dalrymple	Hew	1915 (Feb.)	1918	Unionist	1857	1945
Dalrymple	(Viscount)	1906	1914 (Dec.)	Conservative	1879	1961

Surname	First name used	Date of first election	Date of exit	Party at first election	Year of birth	Year of death
Dalrymple White	Godfrey	1910 (Jan.)	1923	Conservative	1866	1954
Darwin	Leonard	1892	1895	LU	1850	1943
Davies	Ellis	1906 (June)	1929	Liberal	1871	1939
Davies	Richard	1868	1886	Liberal	1818	1896
Davies	William Rees	1892	1898 (Feb.)	Liberal	1863	1939
Dickinson	Willoughby	1906	1918	Liberal	1859	1943
Dixon	Daniel	1905 (Sept.)	1907 (Mar.)	Conservative	1844	1907
Du Pre	William	1914 (Feb.)	1923	Conservative	1875	1946
Duckworth	James	1897 (Nov.)	1900	Liberal	1840	1915
Duffy	William	1900	1918	Irish Nat.	1865	1945
Duncannon	(Viscount)	1910 (Jan.)	1910 (Dec.)	Conservative	1880	1956
Emmott	Alfred	1899 (July)	1911 (Oct.)	Liberal	1858	1926
Essex	Walter	1906	1910 (Jan.)	Liberal	1857	1941
Everett	Robert	1906	1910 (Jan.)	Liberal	1833	1916
Falle	Bertram	1910 (Jan.)	1934 (Jan.)	Conservative	1859	1948
Fielden	Edward	1900	1906	Conservative	1857	1942
Flavin	Michael	1896	1918	Irish Nat.	1866	1944
Fortescue– Flannery	James	1895	1906	LU	1851	1943
Freeman– Thomas	Freeman	1900	1906	Liberal	1866	1941
Geddes	Eric	1917 (July)	1920 (Mar.)	Conservative	1875	1937
Gelder	Alfred	1910 (Jan.)	1918	Liberal	1855	1942
Giles	Charles	1895	1900	Conservative	1850	1940
Gilmour	John	1910 (Jan.)	1940 (Mar.)	Conservative	1876	1940
Goldstone	Frank	1910	1918	Labour	1870	1955
Gooch	George	1906	1910 (Jan.)	Liberal	1873	1968
Gooch	Henry	1908 (Mar.)	1910 (Jan.)	Conservative	1871	1959
Green	Walford	1895	1906	Conservative	1869	1941
Greene	(Walter) Raymond	1895	1923	Conservative	1869	1947
Griffith– Boscawen	Arthur	1892	1906	Conservative	1865	1946
Guest	Frederick	1910 (Dec.)	1922	Liberal	1875	1937
Gurdon	Robert	1886	1886	Liberal	1829	1902
Gwynn	Stephen	1906 (Nov.)	1918	Irish Nat.	1864	1950
Hackett	John	1910 (Jan.)	1918	Irish Nat.	1865	1940
Hambro	Angus	1910 (Jan.)	1922	Conservative	1883	1957
Hamilton	(Lord) Ernest	1885	1892	Conservative	1858	1939
Hamilton	George	1885	1906	Conservative	1845	1927
Hancock	John	1909 (July)	1923	Labour	1857	1940
Hardie	Keir	1900	1915 (Sept.)	Labour	1856	1915
Hare	Thomas	1892	1906	Conservative	1859	1941

Surname	First name used	Date of first election	Date of exit	Party at first election	Year of birth	Year of death
Harmsworth	Cecil	1906	1910 (Jan.)	Liberal	1869	1948
Harris	Percy	1916 (Mar.)	1945	Liberal	1876	1952
Harvey	Edmund	1910 (Jan.)	1922	Liberal	1875	1955
Haworth	Arthur	1906	1912 (Mar.)	Liberal	1865	1944
Hayden	John	1897	1918	Irish Nat.	1863	1954
Hayward	Evan	1910 (Jan.)	1922	Liberal	1876	1958
Heath	Arthur	1886	1892	Conservative	1854	1943
Hemmerde	Edward	1906 (Aug.)	1924	Liberal	1871	1948
Herbert	Arnold	1906	1910 (Jan.)	Liberal	1863	1940
Hicks-Beach	Michael	1906	1916 (Apr.)	Conservative	1877	1916
Hobhouse	Henry	1885	1906	LU	1854	1937
Hodge	John	1906	1923	Labour	1855	1937
Holmes	Daniel	1911 (Dec.)	1918	Liberal	1863	1955
Holt	Richard	1907 (Mar.)	1918	Liberal	1868	1941
Hope	Harry	1910 (Jan.)	1931	Conservative	1865	1959
Hope	James	1900	1929	Conservative	1870	1949
Hope	John Deans	1900	1922	Liberal	1860	1949
Hopkinson	Alfred	1895	1929	Conservative	1851	1939
Hopkinson	Austin	1918 (Oct.)	1945	Liberal	1879	1962
Horne	Edgar	1910	1922	Unionist	1856	1941
Horniman	Emslie	1906	1910 (Jan.)	Liberal	1863	1932
Hunt	Rowland	1903 (Dec.)	1918	LU	1858	1943
Hunter	William	1910 (Jan.)	1911	Liberal	1865	1957
Hunter-Weston	Aylmer	1916 (Oct.)	1935	Conservative	1864	1940
Hutton	Alfred	1892	1910 (Jan.)	Liberal	1865	1947
Idris	Thomas	1906	1910 (Jan.)	Liberal	1842	1925
Illingworth	Albert	1915 (Nov.)	1921 (May)	Liberal	1865	1942
Jacobsen	Thomas	1916 (Mar.)	1918	Liberal	1864	1941
Jardine	Ernest	1910 (Jan.)	1918	LU	1859	1947
Jarvis	Alexander	1886	1892	Conservative	1855	1939
Jessel	Herbert	1896	1906	LU	1866	1950
Joicey-Cecil	John	1906	1910 (Jan.)	Conservative	1867	1942
Jolliffe	Hylton	1895	1899 (Oct.)	Conservative	1862	1945
Jones	Edgar	1910 (Jan.)	1922	Liberal	1878	1962
Jowett	Frederick	1906	1931	Labour	1864	1944
Joyce	Michael	1900	1918	Irish Nat.	1854	1941
Kay-Shuttleworth	Ughtred	1869	1902	Liberal	1844	1939
Keating	Matthew	1909 (Aug.)	1918	Irish Nat.	1869	1937
Kennedy	Patrick	1900	1906	Irish Nat.	1864	1947
Kennedy	Vincent	1904 (June)	1918	Irish Nat.	1876	1943
Kincaid-Smith	Malcolm	1906	1909 (Apr.)	Liberal	1874	1938
King	Joseph	1910 (Jan.)	1918	Liberal	1860	1943
Lambert	George	1891	1924	Liberal	1866	1958

Surname	First name used	Date of first election	Date of exit	Party at first election	Year of birth	Year of death
Lambert	Richard	1910 (Dec.)	1918	Liberal	1868	1939
Lamont	Norman	1910 (Jan.)	1910 (Jan.)	Liberal	1869	1949
Lane-Fox	George	1906	1931	Conservative	1870	1947
Lansbury	George	1910 (Dec.)	1940 (May)	Labour	1859	1940
Larmor	Joseph	1911 (Feb.)	1922	Conservative	1857	1942
Law	Hugh	1902	1918	Irish Nat.	1872	1943
Lawson	Harry	1905 (Jan.)	1906	LU	1862	1933
Lawson	Wilfrid	1886	1900	Liberal	1829	1906
Lees-Smith	Hastings	1910 (Jan.)	1941 (Dec.)	Liberal	1878	1941
Legh	Thomas	1886	1898	Conservative	1857	1942
Leveson-Gower	George	1885	1895	Liberal	1858	1951
Lewisham	(Viscount)	1885	1891 (Aug.)	Conservative	1851	1936
Lloyd George	David	1890	1945	Liberal	1863	1945
Lowther	Henry	1915 (Oct.)	1922	Conservative	1869	1940
Lyttelton	Alfred	1895	1913	LU	1857	1913
Maddison	Fred	1897	1910 (Jan.)	Lib–Lab	1856	1937
Majendie	James	1900	1906	Conservative	1871	1939
Malcolm	Ian	1895	1906	Conservative	1868	1944
Mallet	Charles	1906	1910 (Dec.)	Liberal	1862	1947
Manners	Cecil	1900	1906	Conservative	1868	1945
Marks	George	1906	1924	Liberal	1858	1938
Marriott	John	1917 (Mar.)	1929	Conservative	1859	1945
Marshall	Arthur	1910 (Jan.)	1923	Liberal	1870	1956
Mattison	Miles	1888	1892	Conservative	1854	1944
Maxwell	Herbert	1880	1906	Conservative	1845	1937
McCurdy	Charles	1910 (Jan.)	1923	Liberal	1870	1941
McKenna	Reginald	1895	1918	Liberal	1863	1943
McLaren	Francis	1910 (Jan.)	1917 (Aug.)	Liberal	1882	1917
McLaren	Henry	1906	1922	Liberal	1879	1953
McLaren	Walter	1886	1912	Liberal	1853	1912
McMicking	Gilbert	1906	1910	Liberal	1862	1942
Mendl	Sigismund	1898	1900	Liberal	1866	1945
Micklem	Nathaniel	1906	1910 (Jan.)	Liberal	1853	1954
Mildmay	Francis	1885	1922	Liberal	1861	1947
Mitchell-Thomson	William	1906	1932	Conservative	1877	1938
Molteno	Percy	1906	1918	Liberal	1861	1937
Money	Leo	1906	1918	Liberal	1870	1944
Montagu	Edwin	1906	1922	Liberal	1879	1924
Montagu	George	1900	1906	Conservative	1874	1962
Montagu	Samuel	1885	1900	Liberal	1832	1911
Montgomery	Henry	1906	1910 (Jan.)	Liberal	1863	1951
Moon	Edward	1895	1906	Conservative	1858	1949
Moore	Newton	1918 (Oct.)	1932	Conservative	1870	1936

Surname	First name used	Date of first election	Date of exit	Party at first election	Year of birth	Year of death
Moore	William	1899	1906	Unionist	1864	1944
Morgan	John	1889	1910 (Dec.)	Liberal	1861	1944
Morison	Thomas	1917 (Jan.)	1922 (Feb.)	Liberal	1868	1945
Morrison-Bell	(Arthur) Clive	1910 (Jan.)	1931	Conservative	1871	1956
Morrison-Bell	Ernest	1908 (Jan.)	1918	Conservative	1871	1960
Munro	Robert	1910 (Jan.)	1922 (Oct.)	Liberal	1868	1955
Murray	Alexander	1900	1912 (Sept.)	Liberal	1870	1920
Murray	Arthur	1908 (Apr.)	1923	Liberal	1879	1962
Murray	Graham	1891 (Oct.)	1905 (Feb.)	Conservative	1849	1942
Neilson	Francis	1910 (Jan.)	1916 (Mar.)	Liberal	1867	1961
Newman	John	1910 (Jan.)	1923	Conservative	1871	1947
Newman	Robert	1918 (May)	1931	Conservative	1871	1945
Newnes	Frank	1906	1910 (Jan.)	Liberal	1876	1955
Newnes	George	1900	1910 (Jan.)	Liberal	1851	1910
Nicholls	George	1906	1910 (Jan.)	Lib–Lab	1864	1943
Norton-Griffiths	John	1910 (Jan.)	1924	Conservative	1871	1930
Nugent	John	1915 (June)	1918	Irish Nat.	1869	1940
Nugent	Walter	1907 (Apr.)	1918	Irish Nat.	1865	1955
Nussey	Thomas	1893	1910 (Jan.)	Liberal	1868	1947
O'Donnell	John	1900 (Feb.)	1910 (Jan.)	Irish Nat.	1870	1920
O'Leary	Daniel	1916 (Nov.)	1918	Irish Nat.	1875	1954
O'Malley	William	1895	1900	Nat. (A-P)	1857	1939
O'Neill	Arthur	1910 (Jan.)	1914 (Nov.)	Conservative	1876	1914
O'Neill	Hugh	1915 (Feb.)	1922	Unionist	1883	1982
O'Neill	Robert	1885	1910	Conservative	1845	1910
Ormsby-Gore	George	1901 (May)	1904 (June)	Conservative	1855	1938
Ormsby-Gore	William	1910 (Jan.)	1938	Conservative	1885	1964
Parker	James	1906	1922	Labour	1863	1948
Pease	Alfred	1885	1902	Liberal	1857	1939
Pease	Herbert	1898	1923	LU	1867	1949
Pease	Joseph	1892	1900	Liberal	1860	1943
Peto	Basil	1910	1945	Conservative	1862	1945
Prothero	Rowland	1914 (June)	1919 (Oct.)	Conservative	1851	1937
Pryce-Jones	Edward	1895	1918	Unionist	1861	1926
Randles	John	1900	1906	Conservative	1857	1945
Rawson	Richard	1910 (Jan.)	1918 (Oct.)	Conservative	1863	1918
Rea	Walter	1906	1935	Liberal	1873	1948
Rendall	Athelstan	1906	1924	Liberal	1871	1948
Renton	Alexander	1906	1910 (Jan.)	Liberal	1868	1947
Rice (Rhys)	Walter	1910 (Jan.)	1911 (June)	Conservative	1873	1956
Richardson	Albion	1910 (Dec.)	1922	Liberal	1874	1950
Richardson	Arthur	1906	1910 (Jan.)	Lib–Lab	1860	1936
Ridley	Samuel	1900	1906	Conservative	1864	1944
Robson	William	1895	1910 (Oct.)	Liberal	1852	1918
Rolleston	John	1900	1906	Conservative	1848	1919

Surname	First name used	Date of first election	Date of exit	Party at first election	Year of birth	Year of death
Ronaldshay	(earl of)	1907 (June)	1916 (Nov.)	Conservative	1876	1961
Rothschild	Lionel de	1899 (Jan.)	1910 (Jan.)	LU	1868	1937
Royds	Edmund	1910 (Jan.)	1922	Conservative	1860	1946
Runciman	Walter	1899 (July)	1937 (June)	Liberal	1847	1937
Salt	Thomas	1886	1892	Conservative	1830	1904
Samuel	Herbert	1902 (Nov.)	1935	Liberal	1870	1963
Sanders	Robert	1910 (Jan.)	1923	Conservative	1867	1940
Sanderson	Lancelot	1910 (Jan.)	1915 (Oct.)	Conservative	1863	1944
Sandon	(Viscount)	1898 (July)	1900	Conservative	1864	1956
Sassoon	Philip	1912 (June)	1939 (June)	Conservative	1888	1939
Scott	Alfred	1906	1910 (Jan.)	Liberal	1868	1939
Scott	Charles	1895	1906	Liberal	1846	1932
Scott	Samuel	1898 (Feb.)	1922	Conservative	1873	1943
Seely	John	1900	1918	Conservative	1868	1947
Shackleton	David	1902 (Aug.)	1910 (Nov.)	Labour	1863	1938
Shaw	Charles	1892	1910	Liberal	1859	1942
Shaw	Thomas	1892	1909 (Feb.)	Liberal	1850	1937
Sheehan	Daniel	1901 (May)	1918	Irish Nat.	1873	1947
Sinclair	John	1897 (Jan.)	1909 (Feb.)	Liberal	1860	1925
Sitwell	George	1885	1895	Conservative	1860	1943
Smallwood	Edward	1917 (Oct.)	1918	Liberal	1861	1939
Smith	Albert	1910 (Dec.)	1920 (June)	Labour	1867	1942
Smith	Clarence	1892	1895	Liberal	1849	1941
Snowden	Philip	1906	1931	Labour	1864	1937
Spender-Clay	Herbert	1910	1937	Conservative	1875	1937
Spicer	Albert	1892	1918	Liberal	1847	1934
Stanley	George	1910	1929	Conservative	1872	1938
Starkey	John	1906	1922	Unionist	1859	1940
Staveley-Hill	Henry	1905 (July)	1918	Conservative	1865	1946
Stevenson	Francis	1885	1906	Liberal	1862	1938
Stirling-Maxwell	John	1895	1906	Conservative	1866	1956
Strauss	Edward	1906	1939 (Mar.)	Liberal	1862	1939
Sutton	John	1910 (Jan.)	1931	Labour	1880	1945
Sykes	Alan	1910 (Jan.)	1922	Unionist	1868	1950
Sykes	Mark	1911 (July)	1919 (Feb.)	Unionist	1879	1919
Talbot	Edmund	1894 (Aug.)	1921 (Apr.)	Conservative	1855	1947
Taylor	Theodore	1900	1918	Liberal	1850	1952
Terrell	George	1910 (Jan.)	1922	Conservative	1862	1952
Thomas	John	1900	1906	Liberal	1850	1935
Thomasson	Franklin	1906 (Mar.)	1910 (Jan.)	Liberal	1873	1941
Thorne	William	1906	1945	Labour	1857	1946
Tillett	Benjamin	1917 (Nov.)	1931	Ind. Lab.	1860	1943
Tobin	Alfred	1910 (Jan.)	1915 (June)	Conservative	1855	1939
Touche	George	1910 (Dec)	1918	Conservative	1861	1935
Trevelyan	Charles	1899 (Mar.)	1931	Liberal	1870	1958

Surname	First name used	Date of first election	Date of exit	Party at first election	Year of birth	Year of death
Tryon	George	1910 (Jan.)	1940 (Apr.)	Conservative	1871	1940
Turton	Edmund	1915 (Feb.)	1929 (May)	Conservative	1857	1929
Venables–Llewellyn	Charles	1910 (Jan.)	1910 (Dec.)	Conservative	1870	1951
Verney	Harry	1910 (Dec.)	1918	Liberal	1881	1974
Verney	Richard	1895	1900	Conservative	1869	1923
Wallace	Robert	1895	1907 (Feb.)	Liberal	1850	1939
Warde	Charles	1892	1918	Conservative	1845	1937
Wardle	George	1906	1920 (Mar.)	Labour	1865	1947
Warner	Courtenay	1896 (Feb.)	1923	Liberal	1857	1934
Wason	Eugene	1885	1918	Liberal	1846	1927
Watson	Bertrand	1917	1923	Liberal	1878	1948
Wedgwood	Josiah	1906	1942 (Jan.)	Liberal	1872	1943
Weigall	Archibald	1911 (Feb.)	1920 (Feb.)	Conservative	1874	1952
Welby	Charles	1900	1906	Conservative	1865	1938
Wheler	Granville	1910 (Jan.)	1927 (Dec.)	Conservative	1872	1927
Whitbread	Samuel	1906	1910 (Jan.)	Liberal	1858	1944
White	James	1906	1910 (Dec.)	Liberal	1866	1951
White	Patrick	1900	1918	Nat. (P)	1860	1935
Whitehead	Rowland	1906	1910 (Jan.)	Liberal	1863	1942
Whitehouse	John	1910 (Jan.)	1918	Liberal	1873	1955
Whitelaw	William	1892	1895	Conservative	1868	1946
Whitley–Thomson	Frederick	1900	1906	Liberal	1851	1925
Whyte	Frederick	1910 (Jan.)	1918	Liberal	1883	1970
Wiles	Thomas	1906	1918	Liberal	1861	1951
Williams	Robert	1895	1922	Conservative	1848	1943
Willoughby de Eresby	(Lord)	1894 (Jan.)	1910 (Dec.)	Conservative	1867	1951
Wills	Arthur	1905 (Jan.)	1910 (Jan.)	Liberal	1868	1948
Wills	Gilbert	1912 (Nov.)	1922	Conservative	1880	1956
Wilson	Arthur	1900	1922	Conservative	1868	1938
Wilson	Guy	1907 (Nov.)	1918	Liberal	1877	1943
Wilson	Leslie	1913 (Nov.)	1922	Conservative	1876	1955
Winfrey	Richard	1906	1924	Liberal	1858	1944
Wolmer	(Viscount)	1910 (Dec.)	1940 (Nov.)	Conservative	1887	1971
Wood	Edward	1910 (Jan.)	1925	Conservative	1881	1959
Wright	Henry	1886	1895	Conservative	1839	1910
Wright	Henry	1912 (Mar.)	1918	Conservative	1870	1947
Wyndham–Quin	Windham	1895	1906	Conservative	1857	1952
Yate	Charles	1910 (Dec.)	1924	Conservative	1849	1940
Young	Edward Hilton	1915 (Feb.)	1922	Liberal	1879	1960
Young	William	1910 (Jan.)	1922	Liberal	1863	1942
Younger	George	1906	1922	Conservative	1851	1929

Appendix 2: The Questionnaire

The text given here is that of the original version of the questionnaire sent out in July 1936. Material incorporated in square brackets is omitted or altered in the second version. The notes indicate amendments made in the second version. See Chapter 2 for a discussion of the questionnaire, especially pp. 12–14.

Biographies of Living Members of Parliament

In 1929 the Prime Minister (the Right Honourable Stanley Baldwin, M.P.) appointed a Committee, presided over by Colonel the Right Honourable Josiah Wedgwood, D.S.O., M.P., to examine the material available for a record of the personnel and politics of members of the House of Commons from A.D. 1264. The Committee reported that the task of preparing and publishing such a record was possible and should be undertaken.

It has been suggested that it would be desirable for living Members or [ex-Members of Parliament][1] to assist in the compilation of their own biographies. Below are questions which ought to be dealt with. [It would be useful to have answers to these from our predecessors and contemporaries; they will inform and guide our contemporaries and successors in this and other lands.][2]

[No biographer, only the man himself, can answer such questions.][3]

[Please write your answers in the space provided.][4]

Committee on History of Parliament,
1, Queen Anne's Gate Buildings,
Dartmouth Street, S.W.1.

---

1. When did you first become interested in national politics? Why?
2. What influence started you on this line of thought?
3. What books formed your political views?
4. What were your religious convictions?
5. Which was then your favourite newspaper?
6. Why did you want to be an M.P.?
7. What or who first led you to think of it as a career?

---

[1] 'or their surviving relations' in the second version.

[2] 'It would have been useful to have answers to these from our predecessors' in the second version.

[3] This sentence was omitted in the second version.

[4] In the first version of the questionnaire, there were no spaces between the questions but the questions were attached to three blank pages intended for the response. Following complaints about the layout, the second version contained this sentence and the questions were spread over three (foolscap) pages with spaces between them for the answers and a blank fourth page.

8. What was your trade, profession or occupation?
9. Annual income, earned and un-earned, when first you stood for Parliament?
10. Had you experience of public work – if so, what?
11. How did you first get a seat?
12. What was your chief political interest?
13. On what did you, in fact, concentrate most in Parliament?
14. What did it cost you then to contest? And how much yearly while M.P.?
15. Who, at that time, was your ideal living British statesman, or dead statesman of any land?
16. How did Parliament modify your views?
17. How did being an M.P. affect your earning capacity?
18. What did you enjoy most in Parliamentary life?
19. What did you dislike most, apart from getting re-elected?
20. Which speech do you think was your best?
21. What was the greatest speech you remember hearing?
22. Did speeches affect your vote?
23. What was your best piece of work?
24. If you are no longer in Parliament, why did you leave?
25. [What books have you written, and what books have been written about you?][5]

Answers to all these questions are optional. If it is desired that answers be treated as confidential, they should be enclosed in brackets; these will remain unpublished for 100 years.[6]

Please supply also the usual bald facts from 'Who's Who' or any other work of reference so as to save the compilers trouble.[7]

---

[5] This question was not included in the first version and was answered by very few of the respondents who had received the second version.

[6] These sentences were moved to the introductory remarks in the second version.

[7] This sentence was also included in the introductory remarks in the second version.

Appendix 3: Wedgwood's Own Completed Questionnaire

BIOGRAPHIES OF MEMBERS OF PARLIAMENT

Replies by Colonel the Right Honourable Josiah Wedgwood, D.S.O., M.P.

In 1929 the Prime Minister (The Right Honourable Stanley Baldwin, M.P.) appointed a Committee, presided over by Colonel the Right Honourable Josiah Wedgwood, D.S.O., M.P., to examine the material available for a record of the personnel and politics of members of the House of Commons from A.D. 1264. The Committee reported that the task of preparing and publishing such a record was possible and should be undertaken.

It has been suggested that it would be desirable for Members or their surviving relations to assist in the compilation of these biographies. Below are questions which ought to be dealt with. It would have been useful to have answers to these from our predecessors.

---

1. When did you first become interested in national politics? Why?
   At school (Clifton) in house debates. My father's politics were Liberal and I, therefore, supported that point of view.

2. What influence started you on this line of thought?
   I suppose my father and mother. But Clifton was Liberal under Canon Wilson, the Headmaster, to whom I was attached.

3. What books formed your political views?
   Macaulay's works; "Looking Backward"; after 1905 Henry George's works.

4. What were your religious convictions?
   Agnostic and puritanical, mixed.

5. Which was then your favourite newspaper?
   "Daily Chronicle" (1904), and "Manchester Guardian" (1906 onwards).

6. Why did you want to be an M.P.?
   I thought it the finest thing to be, and it is.

7. What or who first led you to think of it as a career?
   My work in South Africa had to stop when my wife's health broke down; we met Mrs. Runciman at Grand Canary, September, 1904, and she suggested it.

8. What was your trade, profession or occupation?
   Naval architect till 1899; soldier 1899–1901; Resident Magistrate of Ermelo 1902–4; none thereafter.

9. Annual income, earned and un-earned, when first you stood for Parliament?
   £2,500 unearned; earned nil.

10. Had you any experience of public work—if so, what?
    Only as Resident Magistrate of Ermelo, Transvaal.

11. How did you first get a seat?
    The Liberal candidate at Newcastle-under-Lyme struck a bad patch of trade and withdrew; as there was a Wedgwood available, prepared to spend £400 a year, he got it. (January, 1905.)

Figure A3.1: Copy of the printed questionnaire, with Wedgwood's answers, as circulated by Wedgwood in 1936

12. What was your chief political interest?
    Taxation of Land Values.

13. On what did you, in fact, concentrate most in Parliament?
    On that, on the interests of Indian freedom, and the protection of Natives, till the war; then, winning the war; then, saving the world from tyrants and the weak from oppression.

14. What did it cost you then to contest? And how much yearly while M.P.?
    £850 (1906); £300 (1929). About £400 a year till the war. About £100 a year since. Nothing during the war.

15. Who, at that time, was your ideal (a) living British statesman, (b) dead statesman of any land?
    (a) Sir Edward Grey. (b) Cromwell or Lincoln.

16. How did Parliament modify your views?
    I know now that the vested interests are too strong for justice; and that one can only hope to moderate injustice and protect such liberties as we have.

17. How did being an M.P. affect your earning capacity?
    I was earning nothing. I could have got journalist articles to write, or directorships of the guinea-pig class, but I didn't.

18. What did you enjoy most in Parliamentary life?
    Having made a good speech.

19. What did you dislike most, apart from getting re-elected?
    Not being called on by the Speaker or Chairman to speak when I wanted to.

20. Which speech do you think was your best?
    On the Declaration of War? Secret Session on Paschendaele? Urging going off gold standard, 1931? India in 1907? But I have made more speeches in Parliament than any of my contemporaries, save only Lloyd George and Winston Churchill, and amid so much excellence I find it difficult to choose!

21. What was the greatest speech that you remember hearing?
    Either Hugh Cecil on Conscientious Objectors (1917?) or Rosslyn Mitchell in the first Prayer Book debate.

22. Did speeches affect your vote?
    They affected my mind, and, therefore, must have affected my future votes. Of course, in Committee, especially Grand Committee, speeches affected votes and party action much more and every day.

23. What was your best piece of work?
    Establishing the Land Tenure System in Northern Nigeria in 1908. The arming of and landing from the " River Clyde " at Gallipoli, April 25 to May 8, 1915.

24. If you are no longer in Parliament, why did you leave?

25. What books have you written, and what books have been written about you?
    " The Road to Freedom," " The Future of the Anglo-Indian Commonwealth," " Essays and Adventures of a Labour M.P.," " The Seventh Dominion," " Local Taxation in the British Empire," etc. About me, none worth referring to.

JOSIAH C. WEDGWOOD,
28th July, 1936.

Figure A3.1: *(Continued)*

Appendix 4: Sir Henry Bowles' Questionnaire, Biography and Correspondence

Figure A4.1: Bowles to J.C. Wedgwood, covering completed questionnaire, 1 December 193[6]

written by J.C. Wedgwood·

BOWLES, Sir Henry Ferryman Bart.

Returned

BIOGRAPHIES OF MEMBERS OF PARLIAMENT

In 1929 the Prime Minister (The Right Honourable Stanley Baldwin, M.P.) appointed a Committee, presided over by Colonel the Right Honourable Josiah Wedgwood, D.S.O., M.P., to examine the material available for a record of the personnel and politics of members of the House of Commons from A.D. 1264. The Committee reported that the task of preparing and publishing such a record was possible and should be undertaken.

It has been suggested that it would be desirable for Members or their surviving relations to assist in the compilation of these biographies. Below are questions which ought to be dealt with. It would have been useful to have answers to these from our predecessors.

Answers to all these questions are optional. If it is desired that answers be treated as confidential, they should be enclosed in brackets; these will remain unpublished for 100 years.

Please supply also the usual bald facts from " Who's Who " or any other work of reference so as to save the compilers trouble.

Please write your answers in the space provided.

COMMITTEE ON HISTORY OF PARLIAMENT,
1, QUEEN ANNE'S GATE BUILDINGS,
DARTMOUTH STREET, S.W.1.

1. When did you first become interested in national politics ?   Why ?

    In November 1873 when Mr. Dorrington (Sir John Dorrington) beat Sir Henry Havelock (Sir Henry Havelock Allen) at Stroud, this was before the Ballot Act.   Elections were some sport in those days.

2. What influence started you on this line of thought ?

    I joined the Constitutional Union when I left Cambridge with many of my Friends.

3. What books formed your political views ?

    I inherited my Political views and I have tried to keep my Party on the Main Line and not side tract,

4. What were your religious convictions ?

    I was Baptised into the faith of the Church of England, which has always been good enough for me.

5. Which was then your favourite newspaper ?

    Punch, as in those days it had a sense of humour.

6. Why did you want to be an M.P. ?

    I wanted to be of some use to my Country.

Figure A4.2: Bowles' completed questionnaire

7. **What or who first led you to think of it as a career?**

   I never regarded being a Member of Parliament as a career,
   now M.P's are paid Civil Servants it may be different.

8. **What was your trade, profession or occupation?**

   I was an M.A., Cambridge, a Captain of Militia and a Barrister-
   at- Law and a Husband of a charming wife.

9. **Annual income, earned and un-earned, when first you stood for Parliament?**

   What my Father gave me.

10. **Had you any experience of public work—if so, what?**

    I was a County Councillor.

11. **How did you first get a seat?**

    My Constituents asked me to return from my Honeymoon and my
    wife's charm made it a cert, although the Government were
    losing seats at the time.

12. **What was your chief political interest?**

    Private Bill Legislation.

13. **On what did you, in fact, concentrate most in Parliament?**

    Private Railway Bills of which for many years I was Chairman
    of the Committee.

14. **What did it cost you then to contest? And how much yearly while M.P.?**

    About £1,200 each Election and on Political organisation £500
    a year.

15. **Who, at that time, was your ideal (a) living British statesman, (b) dead
    statesman of any land?**

    Lord Beaconsfield and Mr. Joseph Chamberlain.
    (a)

    (b)

Figure A4.2: (*Continued*)

16. **How did Parliament modify your views?**

    I learnt there was some good in all Parties, more in some less in others.

17. **How did being an M.P. affect your earning capacity?**

    I never earned I only spent.

18. **What did you enjoy most in Parliamentary life?**

    Parliamentary recesses.

19. **What did you dislike most, apart from getting re-elected?**

    Dinner in the Members Dining Room.

20. **Which speech do you think was your best?**

    Never thought about it.

21. **What was the greatest speech that you remember hearing?**

    Sir James Agg-Gardner on the Kitchen Committees Estimate.

22. **Did speeches affect your vote?**

    Only once, Mr. Joseph Chamberlain on Free Education.

23. **What was your best piece of work?**

    Some of my Committees reports to the House.

24. **If you are no longer in Parliament, why did you leave?**

    Because my Doctor said I must have all my teeth out.

25. **What books have you written, and what books have been written about you?**

Figure A4.2: (Continued)

Colonel Sir Henry Fenyman Bowles (Bart) Created 1926

JP. DL. Middlesex MP. Conservative 1889 – 1906 & 1918 – 1922

Born 19 Dec 1858 Educated at Harrow & Jesus College Cambridge

MA — Lt. Col 7 Batt Rifle Brigade (militia)

Hon Colonel 7 Batt Middlesex Regiment (Territorial)

and County Commandant Middlesex (Vol) during

great war Barrister-at-law Inner Temple 1883

Middlesex County Councillor 1889 – 1909 Alderman 1909

High Sheriff Middlesex 1928 Address Forty Hall Enfield

Eldest Son of H.C.B. Bowles of Myddelton House Waltham Cross

and of Forty Hall Enfield

a Member of the Court of the Worshipful Company of Goldsmiths

City of London.

Fellow of the Royal Society of Arts — the Royal Horticultural

Society — the Zoological Society of London — The Marine

Biological Association.

Was Chairman of the Edmonton Division of Justice from

1915 — 1936 and has been chairman of the

Governors of the Enfield Grammar School from 1908

Was Chairman of the National Union of Conservatives

1903 – 04   Patron of Woughton Parish Church Bucks

Figure A4.2: (*Continued*)

BOWLES, Col. (Sir) HENRY FERRYMAN (1858-19); of Forty Hall,
Enfield. M.P. MIDDLESEX (Enfield) 1889-92, 1892-5, 1895-1900, 1900-5.
(Contested 1906,) 1918-22, 1922-3, 1923 (Conservative).
b. 19 Dec. 1858, s. of H.C.B. Bowles of Enfield Myddleton House, Enfield,
and ; m. 1889 Florence, da. of J.L. Broughton of Almington,
Staff; issue 1 da.   Educ., Harrow & Jesus, Camb. M.A.
Hon. Col. 7th Rifle Brigade; sheriff, Mdsx., 1920-9; cr. a baronet 1926.

His interest in politics dates from Nov. 1873 when Dorrington beat
Havelock Allen at Stroud, — before the Ballot Act. "Elections
were some sport in those days". The Church of England "has
always been good enough for me", and "Punch" had a sense of
humour. "I was an M.A. Camb., a Captain of Militia and a
Barrister at Law, & a husband of a charming wife". He was also a
County Councillor and had "what my father gave me". He got
his seat because "my constituents asked me to return" - in
.. .. time". His chief interest in the House was "Private
Ry. Bills, ... Committee". Each election cost about
£1200 to £500 a year. What he alledges that he liked
most by were the recesses; and disliked most, dinner in the
Members Dining Room. So that the greatest speech he
remembers was "Agg-Gardner on the Kitchen Committee
Estimates". His best work was "some of my Committees
reports to the House". And he left Parliament "because my
Doctor said I must have all my teeth out".

So, if this is Bowles alive, one can understand completely
both why he was elected & why all wish he were back.
The romance of his story can be completed, for his wealth came
all from a quarter share in the New River Co, formed by
Hugh Myddleton M.P. in 1630. His grandson, with the Bowles
surname, is in the Blues and a grand daughter keeps him
completely happy.

Figure A4.3: J.C. Wedgwood's handwritten draft biography of Bowles

BOWLES, Col. (Sir) HENRY FERRYMAN; of Forty Hall,

Enfield. M.P. (Cons.) Middlesex (Enfi eld) 1889-92, 1892-5,

1895-1900, 1900-5. Contested 1906; ~~MP~~ 1918-22.

B. 19 Dec. 1858, s. of H.C.B. Bowles (1830) of

Myddleton House, Enfield, and *Cornelia dau of George Kingdom R N*

m. 1889 Florence, da. of J.L. Broughton of Almington, *Staffs.*

1 da. *who married Eustace Son of Revd the Honble Algernon Parker and took the surname of Bowles*

Educ. Harrow and Jesus, Camb., (M.A.). Hon.Col. 7th Rifle Brigade;

sheriff, Mdsx., 1928-9; created a baronet 1926.

His interest in politics dates from Nov. 1873 when

Dorrington beat Havelock Allen at Stroud - before the Ballot

Act. "Elections were some sport in those days." The Church

of England "has always been good enough for me", and "Punch"

had a sense of humour. Beaconsfield and Chamberlain were his

ideals. "I was an M.A., Cambridge, a Captain of Militia and a

Barrister-at-Law, and a husband of a charming wife." He was

also a County Councillor and had "what my Father gave me". He

got his seat because "my constituents asked me to return from

my honeymoon and my wife's charm made it a cert, although the

Government were losing seats at the time." ~~His~~ "My chief interest

in the House were Private Railway Bills of which for many years

I was Chairman of the Committee." Each election cost £1,200

and £500 a year. What he alleges that he liked most were the

recesses; and disliked most, dinner in the Members' Dining

Room. So that the greatest speech he remembers was "Agg-Gardner

on the Kitchen Committee Estimates". His best work was "some

of my Committee's reports to the House". And he left Parliament

"because my Doctor said I must have all my teeth out".

So, if this is *Colonel* Bowles at 78, one can understand both why

he was elected and why all wish that he were back. The romance

of his story can be completed, for his wealth came from ~~a quarter~~

~~a~~ a share in the New River Co., founded by *Sir* Hugh Myddleton, M.P. *Bart 1630*

which his Father gave him on his marriage & he sold it for
£115,000 before the Government collared them for £76,000

Figure A4.4: J.C. Wedgwood's typed draft as amended by Bowles (part)

BOWLES

TELEPHONE.
ENFIELD 0099.

FORTY HALL,
ENFIELD.

Feb 16ᵗ 1937

My dear Wedgewood.

I return you my answer of which
you seem to approve showing you have not lost your
sense of humour. I did not know Sir Hugh
was an M.P. he gave a share in the new
River to the Goldsmiths Company you must
come & dine some night & see the Cups he gave
us that Good Queen Bess drank out of at her
Coronation The Company did not sell so they
only get £2280 a year Who goes in Pensions to
daughters of Goldsmiths.

Sincerely yours

ansd.

Henry. F. Bowles.

Figure A4.5: Bowles to J.C. Wedgwood, 16 February 1937

BOWLES.

18th February,1937.

My Dear Bowles,

I am so glad you liked it. I did too.
By all means ask me to come and dine some
night, but you will have to ask my wife as
well if it is to be at Enfield.

As a matter of fact, you ought to come
down to Staffordshire and pay us a car visit.

Yours sincerely,

Col. Sir Henry Ferryman Bowles, Bart.,
Forty Hall,
Enfield.

Figure A4.6: J.C. Wedgwood to Bowles, 18 February 1937

Appendix 5: The Biographies

Editorial Note

Printed here are all the biographies prepared for publication by Wedgwood or his staff on the basis of either a questionnaire or other texts supplied by the subject or his family. They are all contained in the sequence of alphabetical files containing the completed questionnaires and Wedgwood's biographies (for an explanation of the sequence of files, see above, pp. 14–16). Not included are biographies constructed by the *History of Parliament* staff without the involvement of either Wedgwood or the subject (or subject's family), and completed questionnaires or separate biographies written by the subject (or his family), but not prepared for publication. Also excluded is one biography on which Wedgwood began work, but which was never completed (Michael Hicks Beach).

The form of the name given is that used by Wedgwood or the *History of Parliament* staff for the biography, which can be a peerage title rather than the family name. The text is generally that of whatever appears to be the last version of the biography, and contains any corrections included in that biography. This usually means that it is the text sent by Wedgwood and his staff to the subject, with the subject's (or the subject's family's) amendments included. In a few cases, the subject or his relations have re-edited and retyped the biography. In such cases, either the retyped version or Wedgwood's draft may be used as the text for the entry, normally whichever is the fullest version: the version adopted is indicated in the notes.

As far as possible, the existing format of the biography has been retained. This means that wherever Wedgwood has left spaces for the subject to insert information, these spaces have been preserved. No attempt has been made to standardise Wedgwood's conventions or to correct mistakes in his use of his own conventions. Typists' errors have been silently corrected where they are egregious or evident from the original draft of the biography. Wedgwood's errors, including spelling mistakes, have been left unamended, and editorial contemporary corrections on the typescript or manuscript have been made. Where the subject, or a relative of the subject, has made changes to the text of a biography, these will normally have been incorporated within the text, but the nature of these changes is indicated in a footnote.

Passages within square brackets are editorial.

The Biographies

ADAM,[1] Major WILLIAM AUGUSTUS, contested Woolwich 1906; M.P. (U) Woolwich Jan.–Dec. 1910; contested Dec. 1910.

---

[1] Written by JCW; corrected by the subject.

<u>B</u>. 27 May 1865, e.s. of Rev. B.W. Adams D.D. (1830–1886). Resumed family name of Adam, 1907. <u>M</u>. (1) 1912 Antonia (<u>d</u>. 1927) da. of 1st Earl de Montalt of Dundrum; (2) 1928 Queenie, only da. of Sir Stephen Penfold.

Educ. Harrow, Dublin University, M.A. (Honours, Classics and Modern History) and Sandhurst; Regiment, 5th Royal Irish Lancers 2nd Lieut. 1887, Capt 1893, served in S. Africa 1899–1902, defence of Ladysmith (2 medals, 6 clasps); Major 1903; on Gen. Staff, War Office 1907–10, being placed on half-pay on election.

The atmosphere of his home made him a politician; Gibbon and Mill's *Political Economy* shaped his mind; strong Church of Ireland were his convictions; residence in Russia showed Parliament as the way. By a miracle[2] he defeated Will Crooks in Jan. 1910. It cost £1,500 and £200 a year. Balfour was his living ideal; Pitt and Lincoln in the past. The Army estimates (June 1910) provided his best speech; one by Lord Salisbury at the Albert Hall, the best he heard; and he loved to catch an opponent tripping. His best work was getting a murderer (late Sergeant R.A.) released, and paying his passage to his friends in Canada. He was beaten in Dec. 1910 'by a Government publication which deprived me of my profession and of all further activity – an infringement of every Member's constitutional right to free speech in Parliament.'[3]

He was on active service again 1914–17. He was a brilliant linguist, wrote many books including poetry; and his statement of his case may be found in '*Whither? Or the British Dreyfus Case,*' 1920.

ADDISON,[4] RT. HON. CHRISTOPHER, M.D., F.R.C.S. of Gt. Missenden, Bucks.

Parl. Sec. Board of Education 1914–15; to Ministry of Munitions 1915–16; P.C. 1916; Minister of Munitions 1916–17; Minister for Reconstruction 1917–19; Minister of Health 1919–21; Minister without Portfolio 1921; ParL. Sec. Board of Agriculture 1929–30; Minister of Agriculture 1930–1. M.P. (Lib.) Hoxton 1910–18, 1918–22. Contested N. Hammersmith as Labour 1924; M.P. (Lab.) Wilts. (Swindon) May 1929–31 (when defeated), and Oct. 1934–5 (when defeated).

---

[2] 'By a miracle' marked with a pencil question mark in the margin. Adam's letter of 6 Mar. 1937 (addressed to 'Dear Sir Josiah Wedgwood') asks Wedgwood to 'reconsider this, as there was no miracle? I was adopted by the old united Borough of Woolwich as a Candidate (Cons.) in 1905, when there was a majority of over 4000 against the party, a large one before women had the vote. At the General Election in 1906 I reduced the Labour Majority, Woolwich being, I believe, the only Constituency in the Kingdom where this occurred, as 1906 was the great Lib-Lab. Victory. I continued to steadily nurse the Constituency, speaking in the evenings at four or five meetings a week after my daily work on the Head Quarter Staff at the War Office was over for the day. Woolwich is a large military station, and I got the military vote solid, turned over some lukewarm and even ardent Socialists, got a 95 per cent poll, and won the seat in January 1910 by a majority of 400 odd. In August 1910, the War Office published the official communiqué, which was in 1914 found by the High Court to be a "false and malicious libel". In December 1910, having lost the whole of the military vote (about 1000), I lost the seat by 200 odd. I was in fact beaten by the official use made of what is now admitted to be a forged document'.

[3] A footnote indicator points to a note at the bottom of the sheet saying 'Foot-note (?)'. Adam's letter to Wedgwood says: 'You ask me for a foot-note. On what, please? The enclosed appeal gives the details, and you can write anything you like, but perhaps, if you do, you would be good enough to let me see it before it goes to print'. The file contains two printed papers, dated 1937 and 1938, referring to his grievance over his attempts in the house of commons in 1910 to raise the issue of the treatment of officers of the 5th Lancers, the removal of his army commission as a result and his libel action against the Army Council the same year.

[4] Written by JCW; heavily corrected by the subject.

B. at Hogsthorpe, Lincs., 19 June 1869; s. of Robert Addison (3 s. 4 d.) and Susan, da. of Charles Fanthorpe. M. 1902 Isobel (d. 1934) da. of Archibald Gray; sons 2, Christopher and Michael, and 2 da. Educ. Harrogate and 'Barts' hospital; Hunterian professor (1901), Professor of Anatomy, and many other high medical posts.

Talk in the home and Gladstone's speeches made him a politician; inspired by his mother and her father Charles Fanthorpe. Macaulay, and Carlyle's *French Revolution*, helped, and he was of puritan nonconformist stock. He wanted to get into the House because the health of the poor was utterly neglected, (1890). With an income of £750 earned and £1000 unearned, he was selected for the Tory seat at Hoxton and won it. It cost £700 and £350 a year. His chief interest, health, became vital in the National Insurance Bill (1911–12). This brought him into close contact with Mr Lloyd George and he acted continually between the Minister and the doctors. His living ideal was Lloyd George; or Cromwell and Bright among the dead. He liked the struggle forwards; disliked most, bazaars and the 'flummery' of being M.P.; also he had to give up his professorship and salary because of Parliamentary work. He thinks his best speech was moving the 2nd reading of the Agricultural Land Utilisation Act, 11 Nov. 1930, his best work, the organisation of munition supply 1915–17, and in inaugurating a National Scheme of re-housing in 1919 and in the introduction of organized agricultural marketing by the act of 1931 for which he was responsible.

He has written much on anatomy, but his most important works are *Politics from Within* 1924, dealing with the years 1912 to 1919 and his record of the war years in *Four and a half years*, 1934, and *Religion and Politics*, 1931.

Some Members disliked Dr Addison because he was promoted too easily – was 'a Lloyd George man'. It was largely jealousy, for he was a supremely honest politician, lacking perhaps the show of firmness needed to impress[5] the public.[6]

AGAR-ROBARTES,[7] HON. THOMAS REGINALD, V.C. (1880–1915); of Lanhydrock, Bodmin. M.P. (L.) Cornwall (Bodmin) 1906, but unseated on petition.[8]

M.P. (L.) Cornwall (Mid. or St. Austell) Feb. 1908*[9]–Jan 1910–Dec.* 1910–Sept. 1915.

B. 22 May 1880; e.s. of Thomas Charles Agar-Robartes, 6th Viscount Clifden of Gowran (M.P. 1880–2), of Lanhydrock, Bodmin, by Mary, dau. of Francis Henry Dickinson.

Educ. Eton; Christ Church, Oxford.

Unmarried.

Brought up in the Liberal tradition, his father and grandfather having been Liberal Members of the Commons, Agar-Robartes interested himself in politics at Oxford, and

---

[5] Addison has deleted the words 'colleagues and', and added the note 'I have omitted "colleagues" above as I got on very well with them & was made chairman of many Cabinet Committees'.

[6] Wedgwood's last sentence – 'He was rightly blamed for remaining Minister without Portfolio, but let not others with inadequate incomes who cling to office throw the first stone.' – is deleted by Addison, with his note, 'Private to J.W'. 'Please omit this. It would be injust that this went down to History. It is certainly wrong. I only held the post 3 months until the matters in dispute were settled one way or the other & when they were settled against me I resigned the same day.'

[7] Written by HoP staff; corrections by JCW and others.

[8] Note on original: 'Unseated June 1906 on ground that his agent had acted corruptly'.

[9] Asterisks indicate unopposed election.

on leaving the University, accepted in 1903 the candidature for Bodmin. It was in support of his campaign in Bodmin in Nov. 1905 that Rosebery declared his sorrow that Sir Henry Campbell-Bannerman had adopted the cause of Irish Home Rule, and that he himself would not support Home Rule. Robartes then stated that he would follow Rosebery's lead, and throughout his Parliamentary career he consistently opposed Home Rule. He was prepared to oppose any measure irrespective of party which he felt he could not wholeheartedly support.[10]

In the House 'Tommy' Robartes was one of the most popular of the younger members. Neil Primrose (q.v.)[11] was his greatest friend and they always sat together on the 3rd bench below the gangway on the Government side. His main interest in the House was opposition to Home Rule; and his great achievement was the carrying of a Land Tenure Bill for which he had the luck of the ballot. He conducted it dashingly onto the Statute Book before he was unseated.[12]

At the outbreak of the War in 1914 he joined the Royal Bucks Yeomanry, but finding himself still in England in Jan. 1915, he obtained a transfer to the Coldstream Guards as Lieut., and went out to France in Feb. 1915. He was first wounded in May, but went back as Captain in June. In September he was at Loos. His company attacked on the night of the 27th. 'During the attack he behaved fearlessly and never could be persuaded to take cover of any sort.' The next day he was fatally wounded, when, in face of heavy machine gun fire, he left his trench to bring in a severely wounded serjeant. For this he was mentioned in despatches and awarded the V.C for conspicuous gallantry. Two days later, on 30 Sept. 1915, he died of his wounds.

The gross value of his unsettled property was valued at £3,638.

AITKEN,[13] (Rt. Hon.) Sir WILLIAM MAXWELL, Knt. & Bart., (1879–   ); of Cherkley, Surrey. Chancellor of the Duchy 1918. M.P. (Cons.) Ashton-u-Lyne 1910–16. Lord BEAVERBROOK 1917 onwards.

B. 25 May 1879, 2nd. s. of Rev. Wm. Aitken, (18 –   ) Scottish Minister at Newcastle, New Brunswick by Jean (Noble) of Vaughan, Canada; m. 1906 Gladys (d. 1927) da. of Gen. Chas. Wm. Drury, C.B., of Halifax, N.S.

Mystery surrounded his arrival at Westminster and the manner whereby he won that Liberal seat at Ashton. At 31 he came from Canada with a self-made fortune in the financing of cement, and a devotion to protective tariffs. His voice was unpleasing; his speeches on banking and finance failed to convey the sincerity of his convictions; but he had bought and developed the 'Daily Express' and in four years he had achieved for it and himself success and power. The War saw him for a time with the Canadian Forces in France as Canadian Govt. representative. He was a member of the Other Club, and

---

[10] Note on original: 'The motive for his actions can be summed up in his own words – "Is there not some responsibility resting on a Member to examine a thing, and to find the truth, and to risk his seat in order to maintain the truth."' These words are taken from his brother, Viscount Clifden's note in answer to the questionnaire, which states that they were found in notes for a speech among his papers.

[11] *Sic* in original. There is no biography of Primrose.

[12] As amended by JCW. The original sentence said: 'His main interest in the House was agricultural reform, and his great achievement was his Land Tenure Bill, which became law in 1906 under the title of the Agricultural Holdings Act, 1906'. A marginal note in pencil says 'NO! unseated *June*, Bill > Law *Dec*.'

[13] Written by JCW but not sent for correction; some corrections by JCW.

it was in Whitehall, backing Mr Bonar Law, that he, more than any other save the protagonists, established the first coalition (1915) and Mr Lloyd George's government (1916). His *Politicians and the War* is a good account both of four years underground work and of that combination of patriotism and ambition in which he excelled. Bitterly disappointed at not getting cabinet office, he resigned from the Commons, 1916, and took a peerage as Lord Beaverbrook in 1917. In 1918 they made him Chancellor of the Duchy, Minister of Information and Privy Councillor.

Since the War his politics have been mostly wrong, but furiously energetic. He is the Churchill of the Press. Controlling the Evening Standard, Daily Express, Sunday Express and a varying host of provincial papers, Max shouts at us still from a thousand hordings.[14] He has not yet unhorsed Mr Baldwin, not yet isolated us from Europe, though he has driven us out of Iraq and almost out of Palestine. But he has beaten the loyal Berry press, and even that other crypto-fascist Rothermere press, at their own business of selling their papers. Next to The Times, his opinion counts most. Respectables and Responsibles rage and splutter with indignation, but his friends in all camps outnumber those of other men, and the 'reddest' forgive all of his unforgivable past each time they see Low's cartoons, or on finding that the august Times can be drawn into vituperation with the Evening Standard over the King's right to marry the lady.

He never speaks in the Lords; he has cast off Parliamentary and Executive ambitions, but the free-for-all political fight has never delighted him more than it does today; and, whatever it may be that he set out to do, he knows that he has not failed.

ALDEN,[15] (Sir) PERCY (1865–   ) M.P. (Rad.) Tottenham 1906–10, 1910, 1910–18; S. Tottenham (Lab.) 1923–4.

<u>B</u>. at Oxford 6 June 1865 s. of Isaac & Harriet E. Alden; <u>m</u>. 1899 Dr Margaret Pearce and has 4 da. Before entering Balliol coll he had come under the influence of Thomas Hill Green & Arnold Toynbee. After graduating (Lit. Hum:) he went to Mansfield Coll. For 2 years under Dr Fairbairn of non-conformist fame. He started a[16] settlement in the East End and his whole life was spent in such-like philanthropic social reform work. He had heard Henry George and was influenced by *Progress and Poverty*, but was essentially a Fabian socialist. Alden had no income save what he made by lecturing all over the world, and twenty times he toured America successfully. He was a member of the West Ham Borough Council, 1892–1901; coopted member of the London School Board 1903; edited the *Echo* 1901–2. Then he won the enormous Tottenham division in 1906 as a Radical.

In the House he was secretary to Sir Charles Dilke's Radical Committee which met daily before Questions – keeping the peace amongst us all. He moved the first resolution on self-government for S. Africa. During the War he was a moderate pacifist, and therefore got no coupon and lost his seat. He came back during the short Labour Parliament, forgotten among the new crowd. He is still Chairman, Bursar and Secretary of several Social Service Organisations in and around the London he has served so long and well. He was knighted in 1933.

---

[14] *Sic.*

[15] Written by JCW; corrected and partly rewritten by the subject.

[16] The original text of the biography up to this point has been replaced with this passage written on a separate piece of paper by Alden.

He was too mild and good for politics; he had been taught by Jowett & Nettleship at Balliol to see both sides of a question. This is fatal in the House of Commons.[17] His speeches lacked fire, for he attacked nobody. Indeed he supported too many virtuous reforms; worked without thought of self; and yet actually achieved more for the poor than all the rest of the enthusiasts of 1906. He admired Campbell-Bannerman most, but his books were on 'Unemployed', 'Unemployable', and 'Housing' 'Democratic England'.[18] Certainly he was a Socialist in Liberal clothing.

ALLEN,[19] Capt. WILLIAM, K.C. (1870–   ); of Woodhead by Cheadle, Staffs. M.P. (Liberal) Newcastle-under-Lyme 1892–5, 1895–1900; Burslem (National) 1931–5.

S. and h. of William Shepherd Allen, M.P. (–   ); m. (1) 1893 Jeannette, da. of John Hall of Leek by whom his s. and h.; (2) 1929 Mrs Oliver Riley.

Educ. at Emmanuel, Camb., and elected to Parliament while still an undergraduate for which father's seat and by his father's wish. For his father had voted against Home Rule and was classed as a Liberal Unionist. Young Allen, partly under Dilke's influence, worked specially at Labour Legislation and the Miners' Eight Hour Bill, which affected his constituency. He had much to do later with the setting up of the Licencing Commission, and he was one of the Commissioners. He was thought to have gone over to the brewers, to have a doubtful interest in the trade. Consequently the temperance interest in the borough refused to support him in 1900, and while absent, fighting as a Captain with the New Zealand troops in S. Africa, he lost the seat (1900). Then for many years he practised on the Oxford Circuit; was Recorder of Ludlow 1928–32, of Newcastle 1932 onwards. K.C. 1930; defeated Maclaren (Labour) for Burslem 1931.

An hereditary rather than a convinced politician. Of the £1,500 class and necessarily wedded to the calls of the Law and the hunger for briefs. A rather lonely person with a feeling of failure.

ALLEN,[20] Lt.Col. Sir WILLIAM JAMES, formerly a linen manufacturer of Lurgan, Co. Armagh.[21] M.P. N.Armagh 1917–18, 1918–22; County Armagh 1922–3, 1923–4, 1924–9, 1929–31, 1931–5, 1935– . Conservative.[22]

B. at Lurgan Oct 1866 s. of Joseph (18   –   ) and Catherine, da. of John Phoenix.[23]

---

[17] 'he had been taught . . . House of Commons.' inserted by the subject.

[18] Last title inserted by the subject.

[19] Written by JCW; probably corrected by him. A note on the file by Wedgwood says 'Copy not to be sent to Wm. Allen'.

[20] Written by JCW; extensively corrected by the subject. Wedgwood's note sending him the draft ('Will you improve & return the enclosed. Even enliven it') asks for a 'guess at your income in 1917'. Allen's response says: 'I really cannot say anything about my income. It was a business privately owned by myself, a business that had 3 bad years prior to the war, & which were taken as the standard years in determining excess P.D. 1917 was a good year in business, and you can guess what happened under E.P.D. [Excess Profit Duty] finance'.

[21] Words 'formerly a' added, and 'Lurgan Co Armagh and' substituted for 'Belfast' by the subject.

[22] 'Conservative.' substituted by the subject for 'Unionist'.

[23] 'at Lurgan' and 'John Phoenix' added by the subject, who also changed the date of birth from 1870, but did not supply dates of birth and death for his father.

M. 1892 Maria, eld. da. of John Ross; one da. (one son died after war service)[24] Educ. Lurgan College. Vice Chairman of[25] the Armagh County Council; J.P. and D.L. Co. Armagh; D.G.M. Grand Orange Lodge of Ireland.[26] Joined army as Lieut.[27] 14 Nov. 1914; served in France from 1 Oct. 1915; major 16th Royal Irish Rifles, Sept. 1916 Lt. Colonel April 1918 to command the Battalion[28] (despatches 4 times); Chevr. Legion of Honour, D.S.O. 1918; K.B.E. 1921.

'In Ulster we take in our politics with our mother's milk; we read Witherow's *Siege of Derry* and the lines of the brilliant pioneers whose deeds created the Empire,[29] and are staunch[30] Protestants. I wanted to be an M.P. to maintain our position in the British Empire and the union between Britain and Ireland. My regiment was at the Front when William Moore[31] was made a judge and I was called home to fill the vacancy so caused, and then returned to my unit in France.' Edward Carson was his ideal statesman. What he liked was the good-fellowship of all parties; and disliked the 'gradual socialistic tendency of the once great Conservative party.' 'Parliament only intensified my views; and[32] I was bitterly disappointed with the so-called Conservatives, who bartered away the lives, liberties and properties of a people whose only fault was their loyalty to King and Constitution.'[33] His best speech was against 'the Empire wrecking Statute of Westminster'. The best he heard was Joynson-Hicks against the change in the C. of E.[34] Prayer Book.

And these answers might have been made by all that survives of Protestant Ulster. Fifteen[35] years over military age, the linen manufacturer goes out to fight as they did at Derry, serves not on the Staff but in his Ulster[36] regiment, and survives even the Somme.

AMERY,[37] RT. HON. LEOPOLD CHARLES MAURICE STENNETT (1873–). Asst. Secretary, War Cabinet, 1917–18; Political Secretary to Supreme War Council 1918; Under Secretary for the Colonies 1918–21; Financial Secretary to the Admiralty 1921–2; First Lord of the Admiralty 1922–4; Secretary of State for the Colonies 1924–9. M.P.[38] (Cons.) S. Birmingham 1911–18; Sparkbrook divn, 1918–22,1922–3, 1923–4, 1924–9, 1929–31, 1931–5, 1935–

[24] '(one son died after war service)' added by the subject.
[25] 'Vice Chairman of' substituted for 'on' by the subject.
[26] 'Of Ireland' added by the subject.
[27] 'as Lieut.' added by the subject.
[28] 'Lt. Colonel April 1918 to command the Battalion' added by the subject.
[29] 'and the lines . . . created the Empire,' added by the subject.
[30] 'staunch' substituted for 'black' by the subject.
[31] 'William' supplied by the subject.
[32] 'and' substituted for 'but' by the subject.
[33] 'to King and Constitution' added by the subject.
[34] 'C of E.' added by the subject.
[35] 'Fifteen' substituted for 'five' by the subject.
[36] 'Ulster' substituted for 'Belfast' by the subject.
[37] Written by JCW; not corrected by the subject, who wrote to Wedgwood on 10 Feb. 1937 that 'I have been very busy and have put off answering your commentary on my answers to the questionnaire. I am not sure that I entirely concur in its conclusions. But that is a matter which we might discuss together in the House one of these days rather than attempt to deal with by correspondence'.
[38] Wedgwood has inserted a footnote indicator at this point; but there is no footnote.

B. 22 Nov. 1873; s. and h. of Charles F. Amery ( ) of Lustleigh, Devon, by Elizabeth (Leitner); m. 1910 Florence, sister of Hamar Greenwood M.P.,., and has two sons.

'I was born in India where my father was in the Forestry Service and remember hearing about Indian affairs from early childhood. My mother had spent her early girlhood in Turkey at the time of the Crimea and I used to hear a great deal about foreign politics from her, and about the interest and importance of the Diplomatic Service. Consequently I grew up with the idea that I should go into the Diplomatic Service and then at some time or other leave it for political life. My interest was first mainly in foreign affairs and India, but on my 13th birthday my mother gave me Froude's *Oceana*. This and Seeley's *Expansion of England*, which I read shortly afterwards, settled my political views and made the closer union of the British Empire the object to which I wished to devote my career.

I gave up the idea of the Diplomatic Service when I was offered the Assistant Foreign Editorship of The Times in 1899. I was on the staff of The Times until 1909. I had no immediate or definite plans about Parliament until 1903 when Joseph Chamberlain's campaign for Imperial Preference at once enlisted me on his side. Up to that time, though strongly Imperialist, I had not taken a definite party line and had many affiliations on the Liberal side and also with the Fabian variety of Socialist (I had actually joined the Fabian Society while at Oxford). I was first adopted as Liberal-Unionist candidate for E. Wolverhampton in May 1905 and fought my first election in the following January.

My work on The Times, and in particular my part as chief of The Times correspondents in S. African war and writing the Times History of that war afterwards brought me a great deal in contact with public affairs. I had also done a certain amount of social work at Toynbee Hall. My chief interest was in Imperial affairs, and more particularly at that time in the campaign for Imperial Preference and Tariff Reform. I had also concentrated a great deal on defence questions. Besides the History of the S. African war I published in 1903 a book on Army Reform (The Problem of the Army).

I suppose of dead statesmen Odysseus, Themistocles, Julius Caesar, Chatham (were my ideals). Of my contemporaries I looked up most to Lord Milner and Joseph Chamberlain.

Parliament has taught me patience and made me realise how long it takes to get things through. I cannot say it has modified my views, though it may have made me more tolerant of the views of others.

The finest debating speech I can remember was one by Joseph Chamberlain answering a motion of Leonard Courtney's on South Africa in 1896. The best valedictory speech Asquith's tribute to Alfred Lyttelton. The most eloquent political speaker I have heard was Deakin, the Australian Prime Minister.'

So writes Leo Amery of himself. It is too modest. He has left out the spectacular double First at Oxford, ending in the Fellowship at All Souls. He has left out the battle of Ypres and his decorations. Alas he has left out the story of how he hid in the locker and escaped capture when the 'Caledonian' was torpedoed and all the rest were taken. He has even left out Mrs Amery and the Wednesday parties at which the Secretary of State picked the brains and picked out the interests of every official home on leave; it was their best piece of work at the Colonial Office. And he has bracketed, to be left unmentioned, everything concerning £.s.d. as hardly decent – a reticence which dates him.[39] One can only hope that he is doing better in the City than he did (financially) in politics. Worst of all he has left out all his dreams of the future of the race and Empire. For he is a dreamer, a sad, rather sobered dreamer. Fighting for Tariff Reform with all the boys behind you was so exciting and so different from solitary dreaming of the Roman Empire with Mussolini as August Caesar. Adolf Hitler has something in him of Alfred Milner, and the Empire of Amery's dreams is not always a democracy. It has not been democracy that has spoilt Amery's life. It has been the ridiculous whispers that his name was Emerich and he a Jew. There was no truth in it; if he had stood 6 feet in his stockings he could have laughed the fools out of court. No one else cares; but the damned story has blighted his self-confidence and his career.

ANDERSON,[40] GEORGE KNOX, of Bridge Hill, Canterbury. M.P. Canterbury Aug.– Nov. 1918. Conservative.

<u>B</u>. Nov. 6 1854, s. of John Andrew Anderson J.P. of Faversham, Kent and[41]

<u>M</u>. 1883 Mary Ada, da. of John T. Prall of Rochester; one s., one da. Educ. Privately.[42]

D.L., J.P. for Kent[43] member of Church Assembly, and of Central Board, Church Finance 1920–30; hon. treas. Canterbury Diocesan Board from formation. He writes: – 'For some years I had devoted myself, while living in another part of the County, to public work in the County and districts, including political affairs as a Conservative. When I came into residence here in 1912, I carried on in the same way and found I was fairly well known and[44] I had all sorts of work during the War chiefly as a member of the Kent Territorial Association (1908 to 1928).[45] In 1918, following the death of the Member for Canterbury, I was approached and consented to be nominated as a Candidate to enable me to bring together the Unionist party which had been divided into two sections. I stipulated, however, that I should not seek re-election at the General Election when the City of Canterbury would be merged into the County Division. My candidature received the expressed support of all parties and I was elected, unopposed, on Aug. 9, 1918 and sat from Oct.11, 1918 until Nov. 21 1918. . . . My short connection with the House of Commons was a very happy episode in my life, delightful to me, but it exists only as a memory now.' This letter, written in a firm, clear hand by the last Member for Canterbury at the age of 82, can only be compared to that of Major Darwin written at 85.

[39] i.e., in Amery's responses to the questionnaire. Amery also bracketed the answer to the question about religion.

[40] Written by JCW; corrected by the subject. The draft was sent to Anderson on 18 Feb. 1937 with a query: 'Amongst particulars we have received from the War Office concerning Members of the War Parliament, the following remark appears against your name – "?Lieut. Indian Army." Perhaps you would be good enough to confirm this information'. Anderson's response written on the letter says 'This, as far as I am concerned, is an error'.

[41] Birth and details of his father filled in by the subject, who did not fill in details of his mother after 'and'.

[42] 'Privately' inserted by the subject.

[43] 'D.L., J.P. for Kent' inserted by the subject.

[44] 'and' substituted by the subject for 'as'.

[45] 'chiefly as a Member . . . (1908 to 1928)' inserted by the subject.

ARCHDALE,[46] RT. HON. Sir EDWARD MERVYN; of Ballinamallard, Fermanagh. P.C. (Ireland) 1921; Minister of Agriculture (N. Ireland) 1921–33. M.P. N. Fermanagh 1898–1900, 1900–3, 1916–18, 1918–21. M.P. (N. Ireland) Fermanagh & Tyrone 1921–29; Enniskillen 1929 onwards,[47] Conservative.[48]

B. 26 Jab. 1853, s. of   of the same (   ) and[49] m. 1880 Alicia Bland (d. 1924), da.[50] of Quintin Fleming of Liverpool; issue[51] killed in the War,

Educ. Naval School, Portsmouth; entered Royal Navy 1866, retired Lieut. Comdr. 1880;[52] sheriff of Fermanagh 1884; Baronet 1928.

The Archdales went from Norfolk to Fermanagh c. 1600; an (Archdale) heiress m. Nicholas Montgomery who thereupon took the name of Archdale, so that Archdales have ever sat for the County. 'When I retired from the Navy I took up farming on 1,000 acres and saw the necessity of strong government and close connection with Great Britain. I did not want to be an M.P. and only stood in consequence of repeated requests to keep out undesirables. I resigned in 1903, but was re-elected in 1916. The best speech I heard was Lloyd George defending his conduct in the War.'[53]

ASHLEY,[54] RT. HON WILFRID WILLIAM of Broadlands, Romsey,[55] Hants. Parl. Sec. Ministry of Transport 1922–3; Under Sec. for War 1923–4; Minister of Transport Nov. 1924–June 1929. M.P. Cons Blackpool 1906–10, 1910, 1910–18; Lancs. (Fylde) 1918–22; Hants (New Forest) 1922–3, 1923–4, 1924–9, 1929–32 (created Lord Mount Temple 1932).

B. 13 Sept. 1867; s. and h. of Rt. Hon. Evelyn Ashley, M.P., (b. 1836–d. 1907)[56] by Sybella, da. of Sir Wm. Farquhar 3rd Bart; m. (1) 1901 Maud (d. 1911), only child and heir of Rt. Hon Sir Ernest Cassel by whom 2 da. who m. respectively Lord Louis Mount Batten and A.S. Cunningham-Reid, M.P.; (2) 1914[57] Hon. Mrs. Forbes Sempill.

---

[46] Written by JCW; not corrected by the subject. In a note sent to Wedgwood on 18 Feb. 1937 Archdale enclosed a sheet which appears to be intended to correct or add to the information given in the biography (see notes below).

[47] Archdale's note crosses out 'Fermanagh & Tyrone 1921–29' and substitutes for 'Enniskillen 1929 onwards' 'Enniskillen Division from 1921'.

[48] Archdale's note adds 'Honorary LL.D Queen's University Belfast'.

[49] Archdale's note says 'Born 26 January 1853 eldest son of Nicholas Montgomery Archdale JP, DL of Crock na Crieve and Adalaide his wife'.

[50] Archdale's note says 'youngest dau:'.

[51] Archdale's note says 'had 5 sons and 1 dau. The sons all served in war. One [word illegible] killed in E. Africa. Dau. Married P.M. Tottenham Inspector General of Irrigation in Sudan'.

[52] Archdale's note says 'Educated [Knights?] Southsea. Passed into Britannia Dec. 1866 retired as Lieut. 1880'.

[53] Archdale's note adds: 'In 1885 Wm Archdale uncle of Sir Edwd the sitting MP for Fermanagh county resigned on account of old age thus breaking a continuous membership of the county by members of the Archdale family in direct descent for 154 years. His great grandfather Col. Marvyn Archdale MP for the county from 1761 to 1800 was one of the 3 conservatives from Fermanagh who voted against the Union'.

[54] Written by JCW; corrected by the subject.

[55] 'Broadlands, Romsey' substituted by the subject for 'Lee'. Mount Temple also deleted the vital dates given by Wedgwood, probably by accident.

[56] Dates supplied by the subject.

[57] Date supplied by the subject.

Educ. Harrow and Magdalen, Oxford; Grenadier Guards 1889–98; J.P., D.L., member of Romsey Town Council,[58] and Alderman, Hants. C.C. His interest in politics and his strong Protestantism came from his father and he went into Parliament, having been Campbell-Bannerman's private sec. 'because politics are the most interesting of all things.' Nevertheless he got his safe seat as a Conservative being 'friend of the son of the Chairman of the Blackpool Conservative Assocn.' Income then £10,000 a year; election cost £1,200; annual cost £500. He spoke on Army matters, became a Conservative Whip 1911–13, and was one of the handsomest men in the House. In the War he raised and commanded in England the 20th King's Liverpool Regt.; and organised the 'Comrades of the Great War' – his best piece of work. He took office from 1922 onwards, but without much enthusiasm, being quite content to rule in Hants. Indeed he was the personification of one of Ouida's languid guardsmen with a non-committal smile for everyone; perhaps too conscious of Ashley superiority to be really genial, or the perfect Whip; too Liberal in tradition to be the perfect 'junker' He says he has moved to the right, but he could never fit in with Mosley. For years, he has guided the destinies of the Anti-Socialist & Anti-Communist Union.[59]

ASHTON,[60] THOMAS GAIR, 1st BARON ASHTON OF HYDE (cr. 1911), 1855–1933); of Vinehall, Robertsbridge, Sussex. Cotton manufacturer. Unitarian. M.P. (Lib.) Cheshire (Hyde) 1885–1886: <u>contested same (G.L.) 1886, 1892</u>. M.P. Bedfordshire (Luton) 1895–1900–1906–Jan.1910–Dec.1910–June 1911.

B. 5 Feb. 1855, e.s. of Thomas Ashton, J.P., D.L., LL.D., of Hyde, and of Ford Bank, Manchester, by Elizabeth, dau. of S S Gair, of Penketh Hall, Liverpool.

Educ. Rugby; Univ. Coll. Oxford (B.A. 1878: M.A. 1882; Hon. Fellow)

M. 1886, Eva Margaret (d.), dau of John Henry[61] James, of Kinswood, Watford, Herts.; issue, 2 sons, 2 dau.

After leaving Oxford, Ashton became partner in the two large family concerns, the merchant firm of Thomas Ashton & Sons, Manchester, and the cotton manufacturing firm of Ashton Bros. & Co., of Hyde. The family's connections with the cotton industry dated from the 18th century and early in the 19th they were the largest cotton manufacturers in the country. His father, a leading figure in business and politics, a friend of Bright, Cobden and Gladstone, was named by Hammond[62] as one of the most enlightened employers of his day. Brought up in such an atmosphere, Gair Ashton inherited, as an economist and free-trader, the traditions of the Manchester school.

His interest in public affairs began before his entry into Parliament in 1885, for he had for several years prior to that date acted as Hon. Sec. of the Manchester Liberal Association.

During the 6 years he was out of the House (1886–92) he was active in the organisation and consolidation of his party, serving as Chairman of the Executive

---

[58] 'member of Romsey Town Council' added by the subject.
[59] Last sentence added by the subject.
[60] Compiled by staff; corrected by JCW.
[61] Names 'John Henry' probably supplied by JCW.
[62] Footnote supplied on text: '*The Rise of Modern Industry*, J.L. & B. Hammond.'

Committee of the Manchester Liberal Association and Treasurer of the Manchester Liberal Union, and in local affairs filled the offices of County Councillor and Chairman of Hyde Technical Schools.

His first Election address (1885) advocated reform of the Land Laws, of Local Government, and of the House of Lords. He seldom intervened in debate, but it became his practice to speak regularly on the Budget. He shared generally in the opinions of his distinguished brother-in-law, James Bryce, and throughout his Parliamentary career he maintained keen interest in Free Trade, Education and Local Government. When differences occurred in the Liberal party over the Boer War, he followed Campbell-Bannerman. His most useful work in the Commons was done in Committees; he acted as Chairman of the Railway and Canal Traffic Committee (1909), and of the Standing Orders Committee (1910), and served on various Royal Commissions and Departmental Committees. A most loveable unselfish man.[63]

After his elevation to the Lords in 1911, Lord Ashton took little further part in politics, but during the Great War served as Chairman of the Cotton Export Committee, and in 1931 was made a Governor of Manchester University.

He died on 1 May 1933, leaving gross estate valued at £239,651, with n.p. £195,829.[64]

BADEN-POWELL,[65] Sir George Smyth, K.C.M.G. (1888), C.M.G. (1884), (1847–1898)

M.P. (C.) Liverpool (Kirkdale) 1885–1886–1892–1895–Nov. 1898.

B. 24 Dec. 1847, s. of Professor the Rev. Baden Powell, Savilian Professor of Geometry to Univ. of Oxford, and Henrietta Grace, dau. of Vice-Admiral William Henry Smyth.

Educ. St. Pauls; Marlborough; Balliol Coll. Oxford. (B.A. 1875, Chancellor's Prize 1876; M.A. 1878)

m. 1893, Frances, (d.   ) o.d. of Charles Wilson of Cheltenham; issue, 1 son, I dau.

[His interest in politics began before his undergraduate days and from its inception][66] His political outlook was influenced by his knowledge and experience as an economist and traveller. An early accident at school necessitated a long world tour before he went up to Balliol, and as a result of this tour, even while he was still an undergraduate, he advocated the formation of an Empire Parliament for all but local affairs in his book *New Homes for the Old Country* (1872).

In subsequent years he visited both officially and unofficially almost every part of the Empire. In 1877 he became private secretary to Sir George Bowen, Governor of Victoria. In 1880 he went out to the West Indies as commissioner to investigate the effects of the Sugar Bounties on the West Indian trade. In 1882 he was appointed under Gladstone's Government joint Commissioner to inquire into the administration revenue

---

[63] This sentence inserted by Wedgwood.

[64] Footnote supplied on text: 'Sources used: Private information from son; *Times* obit; Hansard Debates; *Lancashire Biographies (1917)*; *Liberal Year Books*; Dod's *Parliamentary Companion.*'

[65] Biography compiled by staff on the basis of an original draft by the subject's son, Donald Baden-Powell, and edited/corrected by JCW.

[66] Sentence in original, deleted by JCW. JCW note in margin: '?relation to Lord B.P.' The related correspondence shows that the original questionnaire was addressed to his younger brother, the 1st Lord Baden-Powell, who suggested that Wedgwood should contact the subject's son.

and expenditure of the West Indian Colonies. His work in this connection was rewarded by the conferment of a C.M.G. He repeatedly drew attention to the desirability of calling a Conference on this question until this was done in 1888.

In Jan. 1885 he went to South Africa as political assistant to Sir Charles Warren in the pacification of Bechuanaland. He afterwards made a tour of investigation in Basutoland and Zululand.

Almost immediately after his election to Parliament in Dec. 1885, he proceeded to Canada to assist in the establishment of communication with Japan by means of a line of steamers between Vancouver and Yokohama. In1887 he was appointed joint special commissioner in revising the constitution of Malta. The following year he was nominated K.C.M.G. His next important official appointment (1891) was that of British Commissioner on the Behring Sea question, and 1892 British representative on the Behring Sea Joint Commission held at Washington. He acted as adviser to the Government in the successful preparation of the British case before the arbitrators in Paris.

This varied experience served to strengthen him in his political theories – unorthodox though they might have been, because for him they were the natural expression of his observation. Thus in *Protection and Bad Times* (1879), and *State Aid and State Interference* (1882), he advocated free trade, both within the Empire and towards foreign countries. He firmly believed in the necessity of an executive union of all the members of the Empire [, even though he held that independent governments were advisable for local affairs].[67] He was opposed to the Irish Home Rule movement and set forth his views in *The Saving of Ireland, Industrial, Financial, Political* (1888).

In the Commons, Baden Powell 'was regarded on the Conservative side as the representative of Colonial interests.'[68] He was an able and frequent speaker on Colonial affairs. Lacking both a commanding presence and a commanding voice, he made no attempt at vehemence or oratory, but his speeches delivered in a competent genial style always attracted attention because they were so[69] well-informed.[70]

In his personal life he had strong convictions as an Evangelical Low Churchman, but his generous and broad-minded nature was reflected in his enormous circle of friends among whom were numbered such different personalities as Nansen and Rhodes. Although he was a popular host in London society he himself remained a teetotaller, and on account of his religious theories did not attend theatres.

He *d.* on 20 Nov. 1898 leaving gross estate of £10,870 n.p. £7,572.[71]

BAGGALLAY,[72] ERNEST (1850–1931), of Egerton Gardens, S.W. M.P. (Cons.) Lambeth (Brixton) 1885–1886–July 1887.

---

[67] Words in square brackets deleted, probably by JCW.

[68] Note on original: 'Sir Richard Temple's *Character Sketches from the House of Commons*'.

[69] The words 'it was known that they were' have been deleted and replaced by 'they were so', probably by JCW.

[70] The following words have been deleted, probably by JCW: 'and based on a fund of knowledge not derived from maps and books but from personal visits and contacts. As the representative of one of the divisions of Liverpool he naturally took interest in mercantile and shipping questions'.

[71] Pencilled note on original: 'Sources used: information from son; *Times* 21 Nov. & 5 Dec. 1899 & 21 Jan. 1899; *D.N.B.*; Dod's *P.C.*; *W.W.W.*; Hansard's debates'.

[72] Written by staff; corrected by the subject's son, E. Burrell Baggallay.

B. 11 July 1850; 3rd. son of the Rt.Hon. Sir Richard Baggallay, P.C., M.P. 1865–68, 1870–74, (q.v.); Solicitor General; Attorney-General, later Lord Justice of Appeal (d. 1888); by Marianne, dau. of Henry Charles Lacey, of Withdean Hall, Sussex, M.P. Bodmin 1847–1852.

Educ. Marlborough; Caius Coll., Cambridge. (M.A. 1875).

M. 1876, Emily Charlotte Edrica, (d. 1935), dau. of Sir Walter Wyndham Burrell, 5th Bart. of Knepp Castle, Horsham, Sussex, M.P. New Shoreham 1876–80: issue 2 sons, 2 dau.

Baggallay was called to the Bar by Lincoln's Inn in 1873 and a few years later (1877) appointed Senior Counsel to the Post Office, a position he held until 1887 when he was made Stipendiary Magistrate for West Ham. In 1907 he left the West Ham Bench to become Metropolitan Police Magistrate, and sat successively at Greenwich, Tower Bridge, and Lambeth, until his resignation in 1914.

During his short time as Member for Brixton, Baggallay spoke on two or three topics. His best speech (14 Apr. 1887) was his spirited defence of Balfour's Irish Crimes Bill which he described as 'mild as milk' compared with Lord Grey's Bill of 1883. He introduced in 1887 his Glebe Lands Occupation Bill which was intended to amend the general law relating to incumbents holding Glebe lands in their own occupation, but the measure did not proceed beyond a 2nd reading. His parliamentary career ended in July 1887 when he resigned in order to accept the appointment of Stipendiary Magistrate for West Ham.

Baggallay *d.* on 9 Sept. 1931[73] leaving 1 son & 2 daughters surviving.[74]

BAKER,[75] Rt. Hon. HAROLD TREVOR (1877–   ); Financial Secretary to War Office 1912–15; P.C. 1915. M.P. (Lib) Accrington 1910–18. Contested same 1918, 1922.

B. 22 Jan 1877, 3rd. s. of Sir John Baker M.P. Unm. Educ. Winchester and New Coll. (scholar of both); Craven scholar, Hertford Scholar, Gaisford prizeman, Eldon scholar, President of the Union. Fellow of New College 1900–07, of Winchester 1933; Warden of Winchester 1936.

He was called to the Bar; made secretary of the Royal Comn. on War Stores in S. Africa; took a large part in the foundation of the Territorial Forces & wrote a book on the subject;[76] elected for Accrington, Lancs., 1910, – a contest costing nearly £1,800.[77] He had been a liberal of the middle type[78] since his father contested Portsmouth in 1885. He spoke mainly on the Budget and House of Lords issue. He was a great friend of the Asquiths; but his work on the Territorial Force, his record and his brains marked him out quickly for office. He was made Financial Secretary to the War Office,   1912. The formation of the first Coalition in 1915 cost him his post; but at 38 he was the youngest Privy

---

[73] The original says 'leaving gross unsettled estate £15,712 with n.p. £12,382'. These words are deleted in the text and replaced by 'leaving 1 son & 2 daughters surviving'. Baggallay's son's letter of 24 May 1938 returning the draft with corrections.

[74] Note on original: 'Sources: private information from son, E.B. Baggallay; *Times* 11 Sept. 1931; *Men & Women of the Times* (1899); Dod's *P.C.*; Debrett & H of C; see Vanity Fair Album 1905 No. 972'.

[75] Written by JCW; corrected by the subject.

[76] The words 'took a large part . . . book on the subject;' have been inserted by the subject.

[77] The subject has written in his letter to Wedgwood: 'I am not absolutely positive about the £1800 for Accrington – anyway it was very near the legal limit'.

[78] The words 'the Daily News' have been deleted, and 'the middle' inserted by the subject.

Councillor, and on 8 Feb. 1916 he was gazetted Major and given work outside Parliament as Inspector of Quartermaster General's Services. From 26 June 1917 till the end of the War he was D.A.Q.M.G.[79] (Military Aeronautics). He voted against the Government on the Maurice debate, was refused the 'coupon', and was naturally defeated in 1918 and again in 1922. No more brilliant man has been excluded from public life by the extinction of the Liberal Party.

BAKER,[80] Sir John (Kt. 1895) (1828–1909); of North End House, Portsmouth.

Contested (Lib.) Portsmouth 1886; M.P. Portsmouth 1892–1895–1900; contested same 1900; M.P. same 1906–Nov. 1909.

B.   1828, Portsmouth;   s. of   by   dau. of
Educ.

M. 1870, Louisa (d. 1899), dau. of Paymaster-in-Chief Robert Crispin: issue, sons,   dau. (Son, Rt. Hon. Harold Trevor Baker, M.P., q.v.)

Baker was head of a prosperous woollen business in Portsmouth.[81] He had long experience of public work in Portsmouth[82] local politics, and his success in that sphere encouraged him to enter Parliament. For twenty years[83] he was member of the Portsmouth Corporation, twice Mayor, and senior Alderman at the time of his death. He was also Chairman of the School Board (21 Years), Member of the Hospital Committee (20 years), and Guardian of the Poor (18 years). He was made a freeman of the Borough in 1901, and in later life became Governor of Portsmouth Grammar School.

In the House Baker was not a frequent speaker, somewhat retiring but well-liked and well-informed.[84] His chief interest was elementary education, and having considerable experience of board schools he intervened with authority in their defence during the debates on the Education Bills of 1896 and 1897.

On 9 Nov. 1909 he died quite suddenly of heart failure while having breakfast. His estate was valued at £148,792 gross with £114,736 n.p.[85]

BARCLAY,[86] Thomas (Sir); barrister of Lincoln's Inn. Contested Kircaldy 1886; M.P. (L.) Blackburn Jan. to Dec. 1910.

B. at Dunfermline February 20[th87] 1853, e.s. of George Barclay, LL.D. of Cupar, Fife, (1869–1876)[88] the Foreign Editor of The Times, (called at that time Sub-Editor).[89]

---

[79] Deputy assistant quartermaster general in the Directorate of Military Aeronautics.

[80] Written by staff; corrected by Wedgwood.

[81] The words 'Storekeeper or merchant' are written in the margin, probably by Wedgwood, although it is unclear whether this is a question or a statement.

[82] *Sic.*

[83] The word 'when' has been written in the margin, probably by Wedgwood.

[84] The words 'somewhat retiring but well-liked and well-informed.' have been inserted by Wedgwood to replace the words 'but intervened occasionally to support the claims of the dockyard workers and the Naval service men in his constituency'.

[85] Note on original: 'Sources: private information from son – Rt. Hon. H.T. Baker; *Times* 10 Nov. 1909; Dod's *P.C.*; *W.W.W.*; Liberal Year Books; Hansard debates'.

[86] Written by JCW and corrected by the subject.

[87] 'February 20th' inserted by the subject.

[88] Dates inserted by the subject. They are presumably the dates of his father's editorship.

[89] '(called at that time sub-editor)' inserted by the subject.

<u>M</u>. Marie-Therese, d. of R. Teuscher, M.D., Rio de Janeiro & Jena – issue: 2 da. & only son killed in the War 1918.[90] Educ. University College, London, and Universities of London, Paris and Jena. Times correspondent in Paris 1876–82. 'My grandfather and father were disciples of Hume, and as our clergyman at Cupar was pulled up for heresy, my religious convictions were unorthodox.' His favourite authors were:[91] Erasmus, Scott and Burns. Naturally *The Times* and *Scotsman* were his papers. He was knighted in 1904 for his work as promoter of the 'Entente Cordiale'.[92] As a Unionist he was defeated at Kirkcaldy (cost £200) (income about £2000);[93] in 1910 he was returned with Snowden (cost paid by constituency), defeating Lord Robert Cecil who represented the Conservative interests. His legal work was largely international and was well paid. This was his best work as is proved by the long list of books he has written, and international offices he has held.

His Radicalism[94] was diluted[95] with conservatism; Balfour and MacDonald were his living favourites; Peel among the dead. He found that Parliament increased his earning capacity. Tea on the Terrace or a debate on Foreign business relations pleased him most; and he disliked most listening to Keir-Hardy 'who had a voice worthy of Hell and a heart worthy of Heaven.' 'I only spoke once – on Free Trade – and I was so disgusted at speaking to empty benches that I never spoke again.' Balfour, vindicating his right to use strong language if necessary, was the best speech he heard. He now lives at Versailles, where the French Government[96] made him in 1933 a Commander of the Legion of Honour.[97]

BARLOW,[98] RT. HON. Sir (CLEMENT ANDERSON) MONTAGU; barrister of Lincoln's Inn. Parl. Sec., Minister of Labour, 1920–2; P.C. 1922; Minister of Labour 1922–24. M.P. (Cons.) S. Salford 1910–18, 1918–22, 1922–Dec 1933.

<u>B</u>. <u>c</u>. 1870, s. of   Barlow (   ), Dean of Peterboro', and <u>m</u>. 1934 Doris Louise Reed, late deputy Administrator Womens' Royal Air Force. Educ. Repton (Head of School) and King's Camb. (1st Class Law, Whewell Scholar, Yorke University Prize Essay). Called to Bar, Lincoln's Inn, 1895, and practised mainly in educational and charity cases; Examiner in Law, London University. Served on London County Council as a Municipal Reformer, East Islington, 1907–10. Director or Chairman of Sothebys 1909–28. In the War he raised the five Salford Battalions, K.B.E. 1918.

---

[90] 'Marie-Therese . . . only son killed in the war 1918.' added by the subject.

[91] The words 'They too dipped him into' have been deleted by the subject and replaced with 'his favourite authors were'.

[92] The words 'for his work as promoter of the "Entente Cordiale"' have been inserted by the subject.

[93] The words '(income about £2000)' have been inserted by the subject.

[94] The word 'liberalism' has been deleted by the subject and replaced with 'Radicalism'.

[95] 'well' before 'diluted' has been deleted by the subject.

[96] The words 'they rightly' have been replaced by 'The French Government'.

[97] The subject has added at the end 'Club: Athenaeum'.

[98] Written by JCW; uncorrected. Correspondence of 18 Mar. 1937 suggests that the biography was sent to Barlow who responded: 'At present I must honestly admit it reads to me rather as the account of a somewhat foolish busybody; and I am not quite clear how to get it into a better shape. Would you be content with short statements of *fact*, on the lines of "Who's Who"? It seems to me this would be simpler'. Wedgwood responded on the same day that 'Everybody is entitled to "Who's Who" if they want it, and you shall have it without "flummery"'.

He was started on Conservative politics by his father's example, by debating at Repton and at the Cambridge Union, influenced by Macaulay's *Essays* at School and Pericles' great speech in the 2nd Book of Thucydides; and he read The Times. Sir Montagu is a strong upholder of Christianity and the Church of England. As he had a good income and was a bachelor, Parliament seemed natural and interesting; he was put in touch with three constituencies in 1909 and selected the Salford seat. His elections cost £800 to £900 and £500 a year; and on joining the Government he had to give up directorships. He got a baronetcy on leaving the Cabinet, 1924.

He enjoyed most, unlike anybody else, his close relations with his constituents, and promoting unemployment insurance while in office. He liked best his first speech as Minister of Labour, 'on which I received the public congratulations of the Leader of the Opposition, Mr H.H. Asquith.' And his best piece of work, apart from his services as Minister and Parl. Sec., was securing a suitable and unanimous report from the Select Committee on Pension Scales and Administration over which he presided. He has written: – *Essays on Church Reform*, Education Acts 1902–3, Barlow Family Records, etc. His recreations are rowing, fishing, golf, shooting and all manly sports. Yet after he left office he became Director of many Companies.

BARNES,[99] RT. HON. GEORGE NICOLL; Mechanical engineer, Trades Union Secretary. Pensions Minister 1916; P.C. 1916; Cabinet, without Portfolio, 1916–18. Contested Rochdale 1895; M.P. (Lab.) Glasgow (Blackfriars) (Gorbals) 1906–10, 1910, 1910–18, 1918–22.

B̲. at Dundee 2 Jan. 1859, so. of James Barnes of Preston[100] m̲. 1882 Jessie, da. of Thomas Langlands of Dundee; issue three sons & one daughter, one son, Henry killed in the War, Gordon Highlanders.[101]

Educ. Village school Enfield Highway and in life thereafter from 10 year old.[102] Asst. Sec. 1892, Gen. Sec., Amal. Soc. of Engineers 1896–1908.

Henry George and poverty had most to do with his awakening; religious denominations and sects very little. The Daily News suited his views, and he was pushed into Parliament against the grain by Keir Hardie. He was earning about £2 a week, but actually out of work when he stood for Rochdale. Taxation of Land Values and Old Age Pensions were his chief interest and remain so to this day. His first Glasgow election cost about £250, mostly paid by the A.S.E. Campbell-Bannerman, living, and Lincoln, dead, were his ideal statesmen. 'I found M.P.s just like other folk – better if anything, but not so clever as I had expected to find them, nor myself either for that matter.' He liked the fine spirit of courtesy among members but mildly disliked the hours. 'My best speech, at any rate the longest, was on the provision for the King's Civil List in 1910'. Asquith's at the beginning of the War, was the best he heard.

He was one of the Minister Plenipotentiaries at the Peace Conference in 1919. The Labour Party decided that the Parliamentary Party should not include any who remained

---

[99] Written by JCW; not corrected by the subject (who responded to the biography in a letter of 20 Feb. 1937: 'my record has been seen through coloured spectacles. But, at all events, I am glad of your friendship and good will'.

[100] 'James Barnes of Preston' inserted by the subject.

[101] Details of issue and son killed inserted by the subject.

[102] Details of education inserted by the subject.

in Government office. Most left office and rejoined the Party as did Clynes and Brace, but Barnes stopped on and did the Paris work. So he left Parliament in 1922. Had he come out in 1919 he would probably have been Prime Minister in 1924 and history would have been very different. For Barnes, unlike MacDonald, was essentially a Liberal and devoid of animosity. He was a man capable of great sacrifice, who wanted measures, not kudos. Common action with Liberals was very possible in 1924. Since 1922 he has devoted himself to League of Nations, collective action and the International Police Force sponsored by Lord Davies.

The path to victory of the Trades Union leader is strewn with the corpses of competitors. The successful use of elbows develops self-assertion and confidence rather than the gentler virtues. On arrival he is apt to arm himself with suspicion and a cautious determination not to 'give himself away'. They do not as a rule make comfortable colleagues. How then can one account for such as Tom Burt and George Barnes, with their quiet soft voices, and all that modesty and courtesy which endeared them to the House of Commons? They were indeed the perfect gentlemen, ever frank and yet men with whom one never trifled. Their arrival speaks well for the Northumbrian miners and engineers of fifty years ago; the districts of Blyth and Tyne and the Wear contained the cream of the working class world – there was the dawn. So George Barnes led the greatest Trades Union and was pressed into Parliament and became Chairman of the Parliamentary Party. Rival factions or loyalties raged over the vanities of Keir Hardie and MacDonald till the Party turned for peace and honesty to two unusual Trades Union leaders, that they might escape the shrillness of the combatants. Shackleton and Barnes stood out in 1910 as the rallying ground of sense and confidence; and then Shackleton retired onto a permanent Government post. Barnes had beside something which all his colleagues lacked – the sure knowledge of what was wrong with the world, and the certainty of the way out. He was firm founded on Adam Smith and Henry George with a faith that none could shake. Such a man could afford to be honest, and his comparative poverty today carries with it the dignity of a Cincinatus into private life. George Barnes remains where he was in 1892.

BARRIE,[103] Sir CHARLES COUPAR; of Airlie Park, Angus; shipowner and company director. M.P. (Lib. Nat.) Elgin Burghs 1918, Banffshire 1918–22; Southampton 1931–5, 1935–

B. Glasgow[104] s. and h. of Sir Charles Barrie (1875)[105] and Jane Ann Cathro of Arbroath, Angus.[106]

m. 1926 Ethel, only da. of Sir James Broom; 3 da. Educ. Blairlodge School, Polmont; entered his father's business as shipowner and merchant, Chas. Barrie & Sons, Dundee. Director of L.N.E.R., of Central Argentine Ry., of Mercantile Bank of India, of the Phoenix Assurance, of Cables & Wireless Ltd., etc., etc. He served during the War in an

---

[103] Written by JCW; corrected by the subject.

[104] Place of birth inserted by the subject.

[105] This date, inserted by the subject, is the date of Barrie's own birth, rather than that of his father, as intended.

[106] Details of mother inserted by the subject.

advisory capacity concerning shipping at Admiralty,[107] and represented the Ministry of Munitions during the Peace Conference. C.B.E. 1918; K.B.E. 1921. A Member of the Supreme Economic Council and Chairman of the Disposal Board and Navy Army & Air Force Institutes.[108] He is also a Member of most Advisory Councils, but even[109] with all these activities he finds[110] time to give to Parliament & be a Chairman of Committees.[111] He entered Parliament 'with a desire to play a part in our country's welfare' but never aspired to office.[112] He lives at Airlie Park, near Broughty Ferry, Angus.

BARTON,[113] Rt. Hon. Sir (DUNBAR) PLUNKET, Bart., K.C.; Solicitor-General for Ireland 1898–1900; Judge of High Court (Ireland), 1900–4, Chancery 1904–18.

M.P. (C) Mid-Armagh 1891–1892; 1892–1895; 1895–1898; 1898–1900.[114]

B. 29 Oct. 1853, s. of T.H. Barton (1816–1878) and Charlotte,[115] 3rd da. of 3rd Baron Plunket; m. 1900, Mary Tottenham (d. 1928), da. of Joseph Manly. Educ. Harrow and Corpus College, Oxford (President of the Union 1877); called to Irish Bar 1880 (Q.C. 1889); to the English Bar[116] at Gray's Inn, 1893. He was Private Secretary to the Lord Lieut. (Duke of Marlborough) 1880–85, and to the Lord Chancellor of Ireland 1885–8.

Educated at Harrow. With G.W.E. Russell and Walter Sichel, he edited the 'Harrovian'. Home atmosphere and family tradition made him a moderate Conservative; David Plunket, Lord Rathmore, his uncle, was a second father to him. He was also connected by family ties and by friendship with[117] the Guinnesses, and was a director of the Guinness Brewery Company.[118] 'Disraeli's ideas[119] inspired me as a young man with the hope of reconciling tradition with progress, peace with honour, imperialism with freedom, and the happiness of the people with the preservation of the monarchy and our institutions, and these ideas still seem to offer[120] good dreams for youth to indulge in.' Of the then living statesmen he particularly admired[121] Lord Salisbury and Cecil Rhodes who was his greatest friend at Oxford.

[107] The words 'at Admiralty' inserted by the subject.

[108] The words 'and Navy Army & Air Force Institutes' inserted by the subject.

[109] 'but even' substituted by the subject for 'and'.

[110] 'he finds' substituted by the subject for 'has little'.

[111] The words '& be a Chairman of Committees' inserted by the subject.

[112] The words 'but never aspired to office' inserted by the subject.

[113] Written by JCW; heavily corrected by the subject, who wrote in a letter to Wedgwood of 2 Mar. 1937 that 'I have made it more modest', and asked to see a new draft.

[114] The dates have been corrected by the subject, who wrote in his letter: 'I was elected (unopposed) at a byelection in December 1891 – I was reelected (unopposed) at the general elections of 1892 and 1895 and again (unopposed) on appointment as Solicitor General. Four unopposed elections in 8 years was something like a record'. The words 'Contested East Tyrone 1890' have been deleted in the same blue pencil as has been used to write 'BARTON' at the top.

[115] Date of birth, dates of father and name of mother inserted by the subject.

[116] The words 'to the English Bar at' inserted by the subject.

[117] 'connected by family ties and by friendship with' substituted by the subject for 'related to'.

[118] 'the Guinness brewery company' substituted by the subject for 'the brewery'.

[119] The subject has deleted the words (taken from his original responses to the questionnaire) 'and phrases (however vague, florid or even turgid they might have been'.

[120] 'offer' substituted by the subject for 'me to be'.

[121] 'particularly admired' substituted by the subject for 'put first'.

Barton was an Irish Loyalist[122] and a Protestant, but without sectarian bigotry,[123] regarding sectarian differences[124] as accidents of birth. When he stood for Parliament he had a particular desire to keep Great Britain and Ireland united.[125] He was in easy circumstances,[126] besides his[127] income at the Bar. His constituency cost c. £350 a year. The House taught him to respect and appreciate the motives of[128] political opponents.[129] He enjoyed[130] 'the adventure and excitement of the Parliamentary conflict, and the occasional comedies which relieved the routine.' The most effective[131] debating speeches of that time[132] were Mr Arthur Balfour's replies at the end of several Irish debates. Mr Balfour[133] was comparatively ineffective at opening a debate, but 'with his back to the wall' he was a parliamentary swordsman.[134]

His own best speeches were on the proposed safeguards in the Home Rule Bill,[135] 15 June 1893, on the Address, 15 Feb. 1892, and in moving the reply to the Address, 8 Aug. 1892. His best work was during the War when he resigned his judgeship and devoted nearly three years to settling Labour differences and promoting[136] industrial peace in Ireland. He has written[137] books on various branches of[138] the Law, a Biography of Bernadotte, on Links between Shakespeare and the Law, and between Ireland and Shakespeare, and Memories of[139] 'Tim' Healy. He has written the[140] replies to these questions at the age of eighty-three.

BARTON,[141] Sir WILLIAM (1862–19); of Manchester; manufacturer. M.P. (Lib.) Oldham 1910–1918; 1918–22.

---

[122] 'an Irish loyalist' substituted by the subject for 'Unionist'.

[123] 'without sectarian bigotry' substituted by the subject for 'not bigoted'.

[124] 'sectarian differences' substituted by the subject for 'religion'.

[125] This sentence, amended by the subject, originally read: 'When he stood for Parliament it was pleasantly, a desire to do something worthy of his ancestors'.

[126] 'in easy circumstances' substituted by the subject for 'rich enough'.

[127] 'his' substituted by the subject for 'making a good'.

[128] 'most' deleted by the subject.

[129] 'and increased my admiration for the constitution and our national character' deleted by the subject from the end of the sentence (the quotation, from the subject's questionnaire, originally began with 'to respect').

[130] 'enjoyed' substituted by the subject for 'liked'.

[131] 'effective' substituted by the subject for 'amusing'.

[132] 'of that time' inserted by the subject.

[133] 'Mr Balfour' substituted by the subject for 'he'.

[134] 'he was a parliamentary swordsman' substituted by the subject for 'a marvellous parliamentary swordsman'.

[135] 'on the proposed safeguards in the Home Rule Bill' substituted by the subject for 'on Home Rule'.

[136] 'and devoted nearly three years to settling Labour differences and promoting' substituted by the subject for 'in order to maintain'.

[137] 'many' deleted by the subject.

[138] 'various branches of' inserted by the subject.

[139] 'Memories of' inserted by the subject.

[140] 'He has written the' substituted by the subject for 'but none so good and illuminating as his'.

[141] Written by JCW; not corrected by the subject (note on the file says 'draft not returned').

B. in Scotland, 5 Aug. 1862, s. of Robert Barton (18   –   ) and Annie (Gray); m. (1) Jessie (d. 1915) da. of Jas Boyd, merchant of Manchester; (2) 1918 Olive Ruth, matron of the Red Cross Hospital, Flanders, da. of Oliver Bryson of Ilfford; one da. by each marriage.

Educ. Glasgow University: a Manchester Guardian man, outwardly Evangelical, inwardly agnostic. About 1885 he moved to Manchester and became a cotton textile manufacturer and shipper. With a 'hereditary taint of Communism' dating back to the Robert Owen period, Liberalism came his way. With Adam Smith and Mill as guides, he became – and remains – a convinced Free Trader, and he was spurred on by seeing the low wages of unskilled labour. Indeed he was out of the Employers Association for speaking his mind. So he was made in 1900 secretary to the newly formed Liberal Association at Oldham and elected there in 1910. Barton was averaging £5,000 a year; the election cost £1,200 and annual expenses ran to £1,000 a year. He had done much health and housing work on the Manchester City Council 1906–9, but in the House his best work was on the Public Accounts Committee. For this he was kntd. in 1917. He got the coupon in 1918, but his business suffered and he could not modify sufficiently his established Free Trade views; so he retired in 1922. He now lives at Colwyn Bay.[142]

BATHURST,[143] Lt. Col. Hon. ALLEN BENJAMIN M.P. (Cons.) Glos. (Cirencester) 1895–1900, 1900–5; (Contested 1906); 1910–18.

B. 25 June 1872, 3rd s. of 6th Earl Bathurst (18   –   ) and Meriel, da. of 2nd Lord de Tabley; m. 1902 Augusta Ruby, e. da. of Lord Edward Spencer-Churchill; one s.

Educ. Eton and Agricultural Coll., Cirencester. Served in Gloucestershire Militia 1891–1913, Lt.Col.; employed in St Helena during Boer War; Lt.Col. 5th Glos. Territorials 30 Sept. 1914; transferred to Territorial Force Reserve 9 Mar. 1916.

His forefathers for five generations had sat in the Commons, and naturally family tradition sent him there too; he accepted the offer of the Cirencester division on his 21st birthday. Lord Apsley M.P.[144] makes the seventh generation of the family on the green benches. 'I found Committee work on Private Bills very interesting, perhaps for the reason that one felt one was doing real work, whereas an enormous time seemed to be wasted in the House. The philosophy of experience reconciles one to this apparent drawback, and one recognises the necessity for a safety valve of eloquence or advertisement. As a body I found the House of Commons a marvellous assembly of varied interests, for from its members it would be possible to find experts on every imaginable subject. For this reason conversation could always be profitable, and there was always a sensation of being very near to the centre of affairs.

I think that speeches had but little influence over my vote, at any rate, unless information of a sudden nature were contained in a speech I should think it rare that it should have the effect of changing one's attitude.

---

[142] The words 'and pays me the most delightful of compliments' have been deleted. In his letter enclosing the completed questionnaire Barton wrote: 'If you like you can most truthfully add that of the very few original thinkers "Josh Wedgwood" was one.'.

[143] Written by JCW; corrected by the subject.

[144] Lt. Col. Allen Algernon Bathurst, Lord Apsley (1895–1942), MP Southampton 1922–9, Bristol Central 1931–42. Apsley's wife succeeded him at Bristol 1943–5.

I did not stand in 1918 because I found a large constituency and Parliament demanded too much time, and after 25 years as candidate or member I thought private affairs might come into some consideration.'

He published *Letters of Two Queens* in 1924. This is an inadequate account, for 'Ben' Bathurst added a popular and decorative figure to the great roll, well maintaining the traditions of his house.

BERTRAM,[145] JULIUS (1866–   ); of Abington Hall, Cambs.; solicitor of Lincoln's Inn, M.P. (Lib.) Herts. (Hitchen) 1906–10.

B. 8 Nov. 1886; s. of Julius Alfred Bertram (b.   –d.   ) and Martha Janet, da. of Capt. Jas. Gammell of Ardiffery, N.B.; m. Marjorie, da. of Hon. Mr.[146] Justice Sutton; one s.

Educ. Repton and New College,[147] Oxford, B.A. 1889. He says he was never guided by anything but prejudices, & that he always refused compliance with what he did not understand. As his prejudices and understandings included Adam Smith, Arthur Young, Bastiat and T.H. Buckle, the grounding was good enough. Though we believe him to be organist, bibliophile and foxhunter,[148] he alleges that he is a solicitor, so the rest had better be *ipsissima verba*. Favourite newspaper? The old *Westminster Gazette* and the *New States-man*. Favourite Statesman? Living, Campbell-Bannerman; dead, Pym or Pericles. Political interest? Free Imports and anti-Imperialism.[149] How did I get a seat? I wanted to divert the Tories from retaining a near-by constituency (E. Herts.) where they had only a majority of 40. So I invented the organisation and obtained support by saying I would contest the seat if no one else would do so. It cost £3,000 and £200 a year thereafter. In the House I always tried to secure a final appeal by any aggrieved person to the High Court of Justice. The House gave me a dislike of manoeuvring and little else. I liked the friendships I made, and disliked most the atmosphere – smoking rooms and dining rooms – all mephitic. My best speech was on an amendment to the address in 1906 because it was wholly in order, and everyone else was pulled up for transgression. The best I heard was S.H. Butcher on secondary education in Ireland. I voted constantly against my party as a result of speeches by Lloyd George, and I did not stand again because I had had enough of the Liberal Party and disliked the others even more. My best piece of work was on the Cardiff Railway Bill (Committee) – six weeks in a temperature of 80° in[150] 1909.

We all thought his best piece of work was the delight and amusement of his friends; and his worst, in spite of Bastiat, his obstinate[151] opposition to the taxation of land values.

---

[145] Written by JCW; corrected by the subject. A letter from Bertram of 3 Feb. 1937 says: 'I return the cameo. I have scarce ventured upon any re-touching. I find however that in my anxiety to "confess myself" rapidly I omitted one of my guiding prejudices – a strong anti-clericalism which has deepened & been intensified every day! But it may not be worth adding to yr dissection of me. I think my income can be left out – it was & is variable – at least the "earned" part of it. "I have always had to pay surtax" might be substituted, if you want to include the informn'.

[146] 'Mr' substituted by the subject for 'Sir Henry'.

[147] 'College' substituted by the subject for 'Coll.'.

[148] 'foxhunter' substituted by the subject for 'pianist'.

[149] The subject has deleted a sentence concerning his income when he entered the House. See Note 145 above.

[150] The words 'six weeks in a temperature of 80° in' have been inserted by the subject.

[151] JCW amended the original 'pig-headed' to 'obstinate'. The subject has written in pencil 'I prefer "pig-headed"'.

BETHELL,[152] Sir JOHN HENRY, of Bushey House, Bushey, Hertfordshire. Contested Romford, Essex 1894, 1895; West Ham N. 1900. M.P. (Lib.) Essex (Romford) 1906–10, 1910, 1910–1918; East Ham North 1918–22. Lord Bethell of Romford 1922.

B. 23rd Sep. 1861, eldest[153] son of George Bethell of Woodford, Essex, died Aug. 26, 1908, who married Frances daughter of Robert Tipper of Scarborough, Yorksh.[154]

m. 30 May 1895 Florence daughter of James Woolley Wyles of Essex House, East Ham, Essex.[155]

3 s. Lieutenant Frank Harry (Killed in action 1915), John Raymond, William Gladstone. 3 da.[156]

Gladstone was his ideal statesman and he took an active part in supporting the Liberal candidates at Romford in 1885 and 1886. He was Church of England and read the 'Daily News', sat on the West Ham Council from 1886 (Mayor 1893 and 1900)[157] and moved to the left on Social Reform as years passed on. He was a surveyor.[158]

His contests cost him in 1894, £1500; 1895, £1500; 1900, £800; and the three 1906–1910 elections for the enormous Romford Division, £4500 each; East Ham in 1918, £750.

His best speech was in 1913[159] when he[160] opposed the findings of the local Government Committee on the East Ham Corporation Bill, and he succeeded in the face of the strong opposition of Mr. John Burns, then President of the Local Government Board, in carrying a motion by a majority of 47 in a full House, referring the Bill back to Committee with instructions to re-insert the clause granting full County Borough powers to the Borough of East Ham. The Bill afterwards became law.

The best speech he heard was Grey in Aug. 1914. He was knighted in 1906, created a baronet 1911, and a peer Nov. 1922. He had the 'coupon' in 1918. He is a Director of Barclays Bank, of the Royal Exchange Assurance Corporation, of the British Land Co, and Chairman of the Frederick Hotels Ltd.[161]

His brother also sat in the House 1906–1910. Both were sound sturdy Liberals, good to the Whips, but naturally not inclined to the taxation of land values.

---

[152] Written by JCW; the subject had typed out a new and slightly amended version. The subject's corrected version is reproduced here, with significant divergences from the original noted.

[153] 'eldest' supplied by the subject.

[154] 'died Aug. 26, 1908, who married Frances daughter of Robert Tipper of Scarborough, Yorksh.' supplied by the subject. The address was given in a letter of 23 June 1937 and inserted in the biography by the staff.

[155] Address of wife's father supplied by the subject, who has also expanded contractions. This was supplied as in Note 154.

[156] Details of children expanded by the subject (JCW had only '1s. (John Raymond), 3 da.'.

[157] Dates supplied by the subject.

[158] The sentence 'By 1894 he was making £3,000 a year.' has been omitted from the subject's version of the biography.

[159] Year supplied by the subject.

[160] The original version of this paragraph quoted the subject's original questionnaire and was in direct speech. The quotation marks have been removed and the paragraph converted to indirect speech.

[161] Wedgwood's version of this sentence read: 'He is a Director of Barclay's Bank, and of the Royal Exchange Assurance Co., deputy chairman of Frederick Hotels, and of the British Land Co., which he controls'.

BETHELL,[162] (Sir) THOMAS ROBERT (1867–); barrister of Middle Temple; company director. M.P. (Lib.) Essex (Maldon) 1906–10, contested 1910; contested Eye 1924.

B. 1867, yr. bro. of Lord Bethell (q. v.); m. 1925 Edith Lillie, da. of Geo. Tabor of Highbury. No issue.

Educ. Haversham Grammar School; called to the Bar 1897. The two Bethells developed the North East of London. They were Times and Church of England men, but with the liberalism of Sir Henry Campbell-Bannerman and the traditions of Oliver Cromwell. Sir Thomas served apprenticeship on his Local Authority, acquired a comfortable fortune in bricks and mortar, and found his way into Parliament as being the right thing to do. Then his work was mostly on Housing and Public Health; his best speech on the 2nd reading of the Old Age Pension Bill. In 1910 he was defeated; kntd. 1914. He was induced to come forward again for the Party in Oct. 1924, but was defeated at that 'Red Letter' election in the Eye division of Suffolk. He still lives in the Temple and dines at the Reform, but he directs the County of London Electricity Supply and a dozen other companies. A safe, comfortable, successful man.

BLACK,[163] Sir ARTHUR WILLIAM, of Nottingham; lace-manufacturer. Contested Doncaster 1900; M.P. (Lib.) Beds. (North) 1906–10, 1910, 1910–18; contested Mid. Beds. 1918.

B. at Nottingham 28 Feb. 1863, s. of Wm. Edw. Black (18 –) and Annie, da. of Frederick[164] Hatton; m. 1887 Helen, y da. of John Spence of Paisley; issue one daughter.[165] Educ. Nottingham and started business 1888; city councillor 1895–1907; Sheriff 1898–9; mayor 1902–3; kntd. 1916.

'My father was a Liberal. I still remember the thrill and fun of the election in 1874. I was then 11 years of age and was interested in every election thereafter.' Black[166] was a Methodist local preacher from the age of 17 onwards, read the *Daily News*, and was influenced most by Morley's *Life of Cobden*. Asquith and Cobden were his ideals. He was a[167] prosperous manufacturer of the £2,500 a year class, & his business increased from year to year,[168] and tried to carry on business and Parliament together. His elections cost about £1,100 a time, every penny paid by himself,[169] and some £400 a year. The waste of his time, one of a 400 majority, annoyed him; he concentrated rather on agricultural wages, or says so.[170] We[171] remember him as a first-rate radical committee

---

[162] Written by JCW; not corrected by the subject. In this biography, Wedgwood spells the name 'Bethel', despite using 'Bethell' in his brother's. It has been amended here.

[163] Written by JCW; corrected by the subject. Pencil corrections may be either by Wedgwood or by staff.

[164] 'Frederick' supplied by the subject.

[165] 'one daughter' supplied by the subject.

[166] Altered in pencil from 'He'.

[167] After 'a' the word 'medium' has been deleted and substituted with 'fairly' in pencil. This word has also been deleted by the subject.

[168] '& his business increased from year to year' inserted by the subject.

[169] 'every penny paid by himself' has been substituted by the subject for 'largely of course found by the Party'.

[170] 'or says so' has been underlined in pencil.

[171] 'We' substituted in pencil for 'I'.

man. He puts F.E. Smith's maiden speech as the best he heard, which is generous. His best work was evidently outside Parliament as Chairman of the Nottingham Education Committee, and he did not get the coupon in 1918. He sat on the first bench[172] behind Liberal[173] Ministers, and was a credit to Nottingham Nonconformity. In fact few knighthoods were more popular.

BLAIR,[174] Sir REGINALD; Member of the Institute of Accountants and Actuaries.[175] M.P. (Cons.) Bow and Bromley Nov. 1912–22; contested Kensington 1923; M.P. Hendon, Middlesex 1935 with largest single Member majority 41,000.[176]

B. 8 Nov. 1881, so. of George MacLellan Blair, J.P., Engineer, of Glasgow and Jean Scott of Cadder.[177] M. 1905 Mabel, daughter of George Bradley Wieland, Chairman of the N.Brit.Rly. and Forth Bridge Co.; 2 s., 1 da. Educ. Kelvinside Academy and Glasgow Univ.; kntd. 1921.

Church of England and agreed with politics of the 'Morning Post' with a strong belief in the Unity of Empire. Carson was his ideal and gave him great encouragement.[178] His wife, and before that his father, urged him to enter Parliament. Lansbury sensationally resigned his seat in 1912 to test the opinion of his constituency on women's suffrage at Bow and Bromley and was supported by many Liberals. Blair who was opposed to women's suffrage and advancing Conservative policy, won the seat, and held the seat for a second time against Lansbury in 1918. Each election cost him about £800 and he spent in the Constituency about £1,000 a year.[179] For many years he was on the Public Accounts Comn. and spoke[180] on the estimates. He was 10 years Chairman of London Municipal Society under Lord Farquhar and Capt. Jessel as he was then.[181] He served in the Great War with the Expeditionary Force 1914–16 (despatches) as a field cashier, and later on the Paymaster-in-Chief's staff at the War Office with the temporary rank of Major.[182] Earned income, which was about £1,000 a year, was reduced considerably by being M.P.[183] He disliked most the cadging for subscriptions to which he was subjected. He was likened to Relieving Officer in his constituency and it has been mooted that his Scotch voice was difficult for his constituents to understand.[184] His association with his fellow M.P.s pleased him most. He puts Grey's 1914 speech as the greatest he has

---

[172] 'on the first bench' has been inserted in pencil, probably by Wedgwood.

[173] 'Liberal' inserted by the subject.

[174] Written by JCW, but redrafted by the subject. The text here is that of the subject's redrafted biography, which uses the same words but the phrasing is altered in many places; only very significant departures from the original are noted.

[175] 'Member of the Institute of Accountants and Actuaries' substituted for 'Chartered Accountant' by the subject.

[176] 'with largest single Member majority 41,000' inserted by the subject.

[177] Profession of father and mother's name added by the subject.

[178] Sentence inserted by the subject.

[179] JCW's version of the sentence reads: 'It cost him £800 and the immense sum of £1,000 a year'.

[180] 'often' omitted by the subject.

[181] Sentence added by the subject.

[182] 'with the temporary rank of Major' added by the subject.

[183] JCW's version of the sentence reads: 'Earnings from his profession were reduced by being M.P.'.

[184] Sentence inserted by the subject.

heard.[185] Perhaps his hardest work was on the first National Expenditure Committee, 1918. He did not stand in 1922 as he was hostile to Mr. Lloyd George's Coalition Government. During the thirteen years he was 'out', he devoted much of his time behind the scenes to Local Government work in London.[186] He was appointed the first Chairman of the Racecourse Betting Control Board which established the tote in England in 1928 and served 5 Home Secretaries as their nominee on such Board.[187] He was devoted to his work as Chairman of the great Middlesex Division of Hendon and on the elevation of the sitting member, Sir Philip Cunliffe-Lister to the peerage, the Association unanimously invited him to be the candidate.[188]

BLISS,[189] JOSEPH; merchant banker. Contested Lancs. (Lonsdale) 1906, 1910 (twice). M.P. (Lib.) Cumberland (Cockermouth) 1916–18; contested North Lonsdale[190] 1918.

B. Leyland, Lancs.[191] 1853, e.s. of Rev. J. Bliss of Brampton, Cumb. and[192]

m. 1891 Margaret, d. of J. McClymont Esq. of Borque House,[193] Kirkcudbright; 3 da. Educ. Silcoates and Edinburgh Univ.

He went out to Turkey as a merchant in 1871 and became interested in Near East politics – the Russo-Turkish and Egyptian wars. His paper was the 'Daily News' 'when its contents were more solid and less sensational, and less as it is today.' He retired from business in 1902, took an active part in Lancashire[194] local government and school board work (J.P. etc.); but Chamberlain's tariff reform campaign made him try for Parliament, for Gladstone and Asquith were his ideals. When at last he got it, Peace & International settlement after the War[195] became his interest; and naturally he did not take[196] the Lloyd George[197] coupon and was defeated in 1918.

BOULTON,[198] ALEXANDER C. FORSTER; barrister. M.P. (Lib.) Hunts. (Ramsey) 1906–10; contested same 1910; Christchurch[199] 1923, 1924.

---

[185] JCW's version of the sentence reads: 'Of course he puts Grey's 1914 speech as the best and prefers his own one on London Local Govt.'.

[186] 'he devoted much of his time behind the scenes to Local Government work in London' is substituted by the subject for 'he did much work for the Conservative Party, and was given a safe seat at Hendon on Cunliffe-Lister's elevation to the peerage'.

[187] Sentence added by the subject.

[188] Sentence added by the subject.

[189] Written by JCW; corrected by the subject. Bliss wrote to Wedgwood on 22 July 1937 returning the corrected article, but saying that he had not included the income statement Wedgwood had asked for 'as I don't see the need of it. Whether much or little it was earned by hard work & exile!'

[190] Inserted by the subject.

[191] Place of birth inserted by the subject.

[192] Left blank for insertion of details.

[193] 'Esq. of Borque House' substituted by the subject for 'of'.

[194] 'Lancashire' substituted by the subject for 'Cumbrian'.

[195] '& International settlement after the war' inserted by the subject.

[196] 'take' substituted by the subject for 'get'.

[197] 'Lloyd George' inserted by the subject.

[198] Written by JCW; corrected by the subject.

[199] Altered by the subject from 'Hants (Christchurch)'.

B̲. 1862[200] at Port Hope, Ontario, o.s. of James Forster Boulton, barrister, of Ottawa and of Moulton Lincs. and of Jane, da. of Col. Graham, 75th Regt. and gdau of Lt. Gen. Graham governor Stirling Castle;[201] m̲. 1891 Florence (d̲. 1903) o. child of Henry Harms;[202] one da. Educ. Trinity College, Toronto; called to Canadian Bar 1885, to Inner Temple 1895 and practised on the[203] South East Circuit. Counsel to the Post Office 1906–31; J.P. Surrey 1908 sitting on the Dorking-Reigate Bench.[204]

He became interested in politics as a Home Ruler and Gladstonian admirer. Church of England, but in favour of disestablishment – basing his views generally on Canadian practice. Moreover he was for breaking the drink monopoly; and read the *Daily News*. He practised law here mainly as a specialist in Dominion Law, and earned in 1906 as a Consultant[205] some £400 a year. His election expenses were £900 and £150 a year.

'The best speech I remember in the House of Commons was by Alexander Ure, the Lord Advocate, in reply to A.J. Balfour's statement that Ure was telling lies about the old age pensions. The best work I did in the House was in pushing the Small Holdings Bill and Act in my own Constituency. The great enjoyment I got out of Parliamentary life was in speaking in the House and outside the House. . . . The speeches of Asquith and Lloyd George only confirmed my opinions. I have always been a democrat since I was old enough to think for myself.'[206]

BOWLES,[207] Col. (Sir) HENRY FERRYMAN; of Forty Hall, Enfield. M.P. (Cons.) Middlesex (Enfield) 1889–92, 1892–5, 1895–1900, 1900–5. Contested 1906; M.P. 1918–22.

B̲. 19 Dec. 1858, s. of H.C.B. Bowles (1830[208]–) of Myddelton House, Enfield, and Cornelia dau of George Kingdom R.N.[209] m̲. Florence, da. of J.L. Broughton of Almington, Staffs. 1 da. who married Eustace son of Revd. the Hon. Algernon Parker and took the surname of Bowles.[210]

Educ. Harrow and Jesus, Camb. (M.A.). Hon. Col. 7th Rifle Brigade; sheriff, Mdsx., 1928–9; created a baronet 1926.

---

[200] '1862' inserted by the subject.

[201] 'and gdau of Lt. Gen. Graham governor Stirling Castle' inserted by the subject.

[202] 'one s.' deleted by the subject.

[203] 'practised on the' inserted by the subject over words in pencil.

[204] 'sitting on the Dorking-Reigate Bench' inserted by the subject.

[205] 'as a Consultant' inserted by the subject.

[206] The subject has deleted the words 'He has now retired to Shirley Holmes, Newdigate, Surrey' from the end of the paragraph. In a letter to Wedgwood from Shirley Holmes of 20 Feb. 1937 containing his corrections, Boulton added: 'I am the 3rd generation born on Canadian soil – my grandfather one of the first judges in Canada appointed 1805. I am still practising in Dominion Law in the Temple (1 Essex Court) my son who was in the I.C.S. died last April at Gib on the way home – my other son a midshipman R.N. was killed at Coronel 1914 – Personally I am cross at the failure of Labour & Liberal to join with Cripps & form a united front – I wish there were more like yourself in Parliament'.

[207] Written by JCW; corrected by the subject.

[208] Year inserted by the subject.

[209] 'Cornelia dau of George Kingdom R.N.' inserted by the subject.

[210] 'who married Eustace son of Revd. the Hon. Algernon Parker and took the surname of Bowles.' inserted by the subject.

His interest in politics dates from Nov. 1873 when Dorrington beat Havelock Allen at Stroud – before the Ballot Act. 'Elections were some sport in those days.' The Church of England 'has always been good enough for me', and 'Punch' had a sense of humour. Beaconsfield and Chamberlain were his ideals. 'I was an M.A., Cambridge, a Captain of Militia and a Barrister-at-Law, and a husband of a charming wife.' He was also a County Councillor and had 'what my father gave me'. He got his seat because 'my constituents asked me to return from my honeymoon and my wife's charm made it a cert, although the Government were losing seats at the time.' 'My[211] chief interest in the House were[212] Private Railway Bills of which for many years I was Chairman of the Committee.' Each election cost £1,200 and £500 a year. What he alleges he liked most were the recesses; and disliked most, dinner in the Members' Dining Room. So that the greatest speech he remembers was 'Agg-Gardner on the Kitchen Committee Estimates'. His best work was 'some of my Committee's reports to the House.' And he left Parliament 'because my doctor said I must have all my teeth out'.

So, if this is Colonel Bowles at 78, one can understand both why he was elected and why all wish that he were back. The romance of his story can be completed, for his wealth came from[213] a share in the New River Co., founded by Sir Hugh Myddelton, Bart., M.P. 1630 which his Father gave him on his marriage & he sold it for £115,000 before the Government collared them for £76,000.[214]

BRACE,[215] RT. HON. WILLIAM (1865–19   ); coal miner. Under Secretary Home Office 1915–18; P.C. 1916; Labour Adviser Ministry of Mines, 1920–7. M.P. (Lib.-Lab.) S. Glamorgan 1906–10, (Lab.) 1910, 1910–18; Monmouth (Abertillery) 1918–20.

B. 23 Sept. 1865, s. of   Brace (18 –   ) and   . m. Nellie, dau. of Wm. and Harriet Humphreys, s. da.   .

Educ. Risca Board School. As he managed to vote Liberal in 1880,[216] as he was a Baptist local preacher, as Reynold's was his light reading, and all of Henry George as well as Thorold Rogers formed his serious politics, so he soon moved from the pit face to responsible office in his Trades Union; got onto the Board of Guardians and the Glamorgan County Council. He was President of the South Wales Miners' Federation in 19 . His Union put him up for Parliament in 1906 and paid expenses (£1,500). His salary was then about £200 a year. Gladstone, Lloyd George and Campbell-Bannerman were his ideal statesmen, but Parliament made him more pro-Labour. He certainly liked Parliament and the work, and Parliament liked him. Moreover 'being M.P. gave me improved status and consequently larger fees for newspaper and other writings on industrial and economic questions.' He puts his speech on Nationalisation of the Mines as his best, and Grey's on the Russian Duma as the best he heard. In 1918 the Labour Party decided to exclude all M.P.s who remained Ministers in the Coalition Government. Brace gave up office and rejoined the feeble opposition. But throughout Brace was

---

[211] 'My' substituted by the subject for 'His'.

[212] *Sic.*

[213] 'a quarter of' deleted by the subject.

[214] 'which his Father . . . £76,000' inserted by the subject.

[215] Written by JCW; not corrected.

[216] Note in JCW's text: 'His name was on the voters' list in error, & he large enough'.

a liberal, and he cannot have enjoyed post-war post-office politics. In 1920 therefore he accepted a good Government post outside Parliament, and we saw no more of the formidable black moustachios and the mild smiling eyes of the great miner from South Wales. Like Burt and Hartshorn, William Brace had the manners of a gentleman, the candour of a child, and the complete honesty of the chapel.

BRASSEY,[217] Sir (HENRY) LEONARD (CAMPBELL);[218] of Apethorpe, Northants. M.P. (Unionist) North Northants 1910, 1910–18; Northants (Peterborough) 1918–22, 1922–3, 1923–4, 1924–9; contested 1929.

B. 7 Marc. 1870, s.[219] of Henry A. Brassey, M.P., and .

m. Violet[220] Mary Gordon Lennox, da. of 7th Duke of Richmond; 3.s.

As all Brasseys were in Parliament, he was always in politics. Chamberlain's fiscal reform campaign brought him in actively, for Disraeli and Chamberlain were his ideals. He owned some 3,000 acres in his constituency, had a commission in the Yeomanry, and some experience of Local Government. Naturally Agriculture and Imperial questions interested him most. His election cost him £1,000 and £500 a year. He enjoyed the life, finding 'the proceedings of Parliament and many debates were full of interest – also companionship of men of experience in many different walks of life. To be in the heart of things was gratifying. The combination of attendance at the House of Commons and the social and other claims upon an M.P. from a very large number of towns and villages constitute a severe strain.' But he had been a member of the Jockey Club since 1898, and he left the House for the turf without a qualm after 20 years. He was created a baronet in 1922.

BRASSEY,[221] Capt. ROBERT BINGHAM, of Cottesbrook, Northants; 17th Lancers. Contested ? Banbury 1906; –1914[222] M.P. (C) Oxfordshire (Banbury) 1910. Jan–Dec 1910.[223]

B. at Heythrop[224] 18 Oct. 1875, only s. and h. of Albert Brassey, M.P., (18 –) and Matilda Bingham, O.B.E., da. of 4th Lord Clanmorris; m. (1) 1904 Violet (d. 1919) da. of A.H. Lowry-Corry; 1.s., 3 da.; (2) Lady Dalmeny, (3) 1927 Constance (Britten).

He took his politics from his father, his religion from his conscience, and his facts from *The Times*; and he fought in Jan. 1910 to relieve his father of the contest against Eustace Fiennes. Each contest cost £1,500 and £1,000 a year (including his secretary). He admired Bismarck in the past, Chamberlain, Balfour, Salisbury, Redmond,[225] Carson and Cecil Rhodes.[226] He enjoyed good debates, disliked the illiteracy of so many members,

---

[217] Written by JCW; corrected by the subject (who has written on the bottom: 'I cannot improve on this. LB 22 Feb. 1937'). 'Major' deleted by the subject.

[218] Brackets inserted by subject around the word 'Campbell'. A note in blue pencil at the top of the page says 'BARON 1938'. Brassey became a peer (Baron Brassey of Apethorpe) in Jan. 1938.

[219] The subject has deleted '2nd' before 's'.

[220] 'Lady' deleted by the subject before 'Violet'.

[221] Written by JCW; corrected by the subject.

[222] '–1914' inserted by the subject.

[223] 'Jan–Dec 1910' inserted by the subject.

[224] 'Heythrop' inserted by the subject.

[225] 'and' deleted by the subject.

[226] 'and Cecil Rhodes' inserted by the subject.

and concluded that his best work *solvitur ambulando* through the lobbies. He did not come back to Parliament because he did not agree with payment of Members nor with votes for women. And when the War came he had his work, being Brigade Major of 2nd Welsh Border Mounted Brigade[227] 1915–16.[228]

BRIGHT,[229] ALLEN HEYWOOD, of Liverpool, shipowner. Contested Exeter 1899, 1900; Oswestry 1901; M.P. (Lib.) Salop (Oswestry) 1904–6; contested 1906; contested Stalybridge Jan. & Dec. 1910.

B. at Liverpool 24 May[230] 1862, so of Henry Arthur Bright (1830–1884)[231] and Mary Elizabeth eldest daughter of Samuel H. Thompson D.L., J.P. of Thingwell Hall, Lancs.[232] m. (1) 1885 Edith (d, 1929) da. of Alfred Turner J.P., of Liverpool; (2) 1929 Kelburn Milroy, da. of James Ramsay of Auchencairn; one da. by each wife. Educ. Harrow; J.P.

'When I was at Harrow I became a strong Radical, following Mr Gladstone in his views on the Eastern question and intensely disliking the imperialism of Lord Beaconsfield. I followed Mr Gladstone when he declared for Home Rule for Ireland. My life in Liverpool was that of a merchant and shipowner. When the Boer War came, I strongly opposed the policy which led to it. In the Autumn of 1899 I contested Exeter and although the war was raging I increased the Liberal poll. I again contested Exeter 1900. In 1901 at the request of the late Herbert Gladstone I fought a bye-election at Oswestry. Although I was called 'pro-Boer', I again polled the full Liberal vote. I believe I have addressed more turbulent meetings than any man living except Lloyd George.'

'In 1904 there was again a bye-election in Oswestry and this time I won the seat. The contest was mainly on protection, a policy I still oppose. My political interests and my speeches in the House of Commons were confined to two points – personal freedom and sound finance. Altogether I fought seven elections in little more than ten years. My object in each case, however, was to further certain views which I considered right. I suppose each contest cost me about £1,000 – but I had help from friends and sometimes from the Liberal Party. I think, however, I spent in one way or another out of my own pocket about £10,000 in politics. The ten years I gave up to politics diminished my income as it took my attention from business. For a short time I was chairman of the Liberal Party in Liverpool.

The statesmen with whom I had most sympathy were Fox, Cobden, and John Bright, who was no relation, and in my own time Campbell-Bannerman; the best speech I ever heard was made by Gladstone in Liverpool during the Home Rule campaign; my best piece of work in Parliament was abolishing flogging in Military Prisons (see Hansard, 1905).

I am a Fellow of the Society of Antiquaries and have written a book on Piers Plowman. I left Liverpool in 1920 when I came to reside at Barton Court, Colwall, Heref.'

[227] '2nd Welsh Border Mounted Brigade' inserted by the subject.

[228] The following paragraph added at the end by the subject: 'I had an allowance from my father until I married in 1904. I served in the SA war with the 17th Lancers. I left them when they went to India in Sept 1905 & was in the Reserve of Officers I rejoined 5th Reserve Regt of Cavalry on mobilisation in 1914'.

[229] Written by the subject; edited by JCW and corrected by the subject.

[230] '24 May' inserted by the subject.

[231] Dates inserted by the subject.

[232] Name and other details of mother inserted by the subject.

BRODIE,[233] HARRY CUNNINGHAM, of London; colonial merchant. M.P. (Lib.) Surrey (Reigate) 1905–10; contested 1910.

<u>B</u>.   1875, s. and h. of John Brodie of Hansell, Sussex (18   ) and   .
<u>m</u>. 1909 Mabel, da. of Sir Robert Hart, Bart.

Educ. Winchester and abroad; a partner in Findlay, Durham and Brodie; Major, Middlesex Yeomanry; served in Egypt 1915–6, in France 1917.

Winchester debates and a love of history started him with the ambition of the young; but the easy course of the family business deflected him from diplomatic dreams, though it did allow of entry into Parliament at 27 with the £2,000 a year with which his business provided him. His marvellous election cost £1,800, though most did not fall on him; annual cost, £400 a year. His liberalism was mild – Free Trade – Small Holdings – but he went Left, becoming a Home Ruler. He thought his speeches in the House poor, but all he could dislike was waiting in a crowd in division lobbies. 'It was the best time of my life, I enjoyed every moment of it. I also liked electioneering and I became genuinely fond of large numbers of people in the constituency. I used to be very worried – one seemed to be able to do so little to repay them for their enthusiasm and all the help they gave. I do not think I was cut out for a politician, I am too uncertain of my opinions; I always see the other side of any argument.'

Churchill on the grant of self-government to the Transvaal (1906) was the best speech he heard. After 1910 he went out. 'My father had no objection to my being a Liberal but my other partner resented it very much and this used to weigh on my mind.' 'All the people with whom my Firm did business in South Africa hated the Liberal Government.'

Harry Brodie was very naïve and very lovable. He collected perorations for the benefit of his constituents, and frequently strung together several before resuming his seat. We missed him badly, for his sensitive ambition never showed itself in sneer or jealousy.

BUXTON,[234] EDWARD NOEL (Rt. Hon.) (1869–19   ); of Aylsham. Minister of Agriculture Jan.–Nov. 1924, 1929–30. P.C. M.P. Yorks. (Whitby) (Lib.) 1905–6; Norfolk (North) 1910–18; (Lab.) 1922–3, 1923–4, 1924–9, 1929–30. Lord Noel Buxton 1930 onwards.

<u>B</u>. Jan 9 1869; 2nd. s. of Sir Thos. Fowell Buxton, M.P., 3rd. Bart. <u>m</u>. Lucy Edith (M.P. 1930–31), da. of Major Pelham Burn, 3s, 3 da.

Educ. Harrow and Trinity, Camb. (History Honours) M.A.; A.D.C. to his father Governor of S. Australia 1896; served on Whitechapel Board of Guardians, and Home Office Comn, on Lead Poisoning.

With his father he became Liberal-Unionist in 1885. 'In 1893 I was given time for travel and went to New Zealand. While there I was attracted by democratic social equality. Nobody was a speechless subordinate like the villagers at home. The Home-rule of Australia made me keen on the Home-rule bill for Ireland, of which I got news while travelling. . . . Reflection restored my natural (family) liberalism.' Mazzini, Morley and Gladstone formed his political views, and the Daily News became his paper, which he

---

[233] Written by JCW. There is no evidence of it having been corrected by the subject.
[234] Written by JCW; corrected by the subject.

joined Cadbury in buying. Canon Barnett, E.N. Buxton, and his brother and sister got him to stand for Parliament 'because it was a family tradition, and to indulge my taste for reform.'

He was a Major in the Territorials, and a Director of Truman's Brewery, with an unearned income of £2,000 a year when he contested Ipswich in 1900. He won Whitby for the Liberals (for the first and only time) in 1905. But temperance was one of his 'Causes', and to sit in Parliament he gave up his directorship and £1,800 a year. The election cost him £1,200, sitting cost around £400 a year. After 1910 he concentrated on foreign affairs and peace, moving more to the Left. When the War came he and Charles (q.v.) went to Bulgaria, where they had long been justly popular, to try to prevent that country joining Germany against us. A Turkish agent shot him at close quarters, but he survived, Oct. 1914. For the next four years he advocated consistently a peace by understanding; lost his seat accordingly in 1918, but continued and still continues to do all possible for an understanding with Germany. When he returned as a Labour Member in 1922, he and his brother were obviously the best friends African natives had in the House. Because he was one of the few Labour Members with an agricultural constituency, Macdonald sent him to the Ministry of Agriculture and his most successful piece of work was passing the Agricultural Wages Regulation Act of 1924. But he probably liked Cabinet Office less than most. Salary meant nothing to him even after he was married. 'What I liked best was the sense of being an M.P.; dealing with things that matter; justifying my existence. I was never well fitted for the life itself, being ill-equipped with the right social gifts.' Illness caused him to retire from office in 1930, when he accepted a peerage.

For complete altruism he had no match in the House, save perhaps the Cecils. But seeing good in everybody, even in Hohenzollerns and Hitlers, exasperates mankind. It is very doubtful if toleration is the virtue it was thought to be in Victorian days. Noel Buxton would defend Communists and Fascists, sadly but firmly as a saint might do. He was a convinced Protestant Evangelical, and he 'combined it with the social side of the teaching of Gore and the Christian Social Union'; when forced to the issue he voted for the new Prayer Book. He is reserved and incalculable; but he requires no man (or woman) to make up his mind; he says and thinks no harm of anyone; and all would turn to him in trouble.

CAREW,[235] CHARLES ROBERT SYDENHAM, of Tiverton. M.P. (U) Devon (Tiverton) 1915–18, 1918–22.

B. 7 June 1853, s. and h. of Rev. R.B. Carew of Collipriest (1833[236]–1899) and A.E. Daniel.[237]

m. 1891 Muriel Mary, da. of Sir John Heathcoat Amory, 1st Bart.; 1 s., 3 da. Educ. Blundell's and St John's, Camb. (B.A.)

He was interested in tea and rubber plantations; was for many years Master of Harriers, in religion Church of England, and his favourite newspaper was the Daily Telegraph. He was on the Tiverton Town Council, had a comfortable income of £4,000

[235] Written by JCW; corrected by the subject.
[236] '1833' inserted by the subject.
[237] 'A.E. Daniel' inserted by the subject.

a year, was invited by Conservatives and Liberals to stand for Parliament. His only contest was in 1918.[238] The seat cost however about £650 a year. Salisbury,[239] Disraeli and Balfour were his ideal statesmen; winning the War and holding Ireland his objects: if Carew voted against the Government on the debate on Amritsar, it was because they had not adequately backed up General Dyer. He springs from a direct line of ancestors who at the Conquest resided at Carew Castle, Pembrokeshire.[240]

CARLILE,[241] Sir WALTER, of Gayhurst, Bucks. Contested N. Bucks. 1892; M.P. (C) Bucks. (Buckingham) 1895–1900, 1900–05.

B. 15 June 1862, s. of J.W. Carlile[242] of Ponsbourne, Herts., and Gayhurst, Bucks.[243] m. 1886 Blanche, da. of Rev. E. Cadogan. Educ. Harrow and Clare, Camb.

As a landowner, he wanted to frustrate the revolutionary tactics of Joseph Arch. The Church of England, the social side of English history, and *The Times* and *Telegraph*, made him the Tory democrat he became later.[244] An election cost £1,500, and the annual expense, inclusive of a London house, was about £1,000. Old Age Pensions became his chief subject, just as Chamberlain was his ideal statesman. Parliament, he says, made him less Tory and more Socialistic in the best sense'. He enjoyed the companionship of interesting and older men. What he disliked was 'the waste of time and the boredom of listening to repetitions of the same views, in phraseology specially manufactured for the ears of their constituents, and valueless from a debating point of view. Also the want of freedom, and restraint. I seldom spoke, but one speech, on the Old Age Pension Bill, was the only one worth listening to, as I knew my subject from A to Z.'

He retired in 1906 on account of health and expense; but re-emerged in the War to help Gen. Fabian Ware with the Missing Bureau in France.[245] He received the O.B.E. in 1920, and was[246] created Baronet in 1928. Also the Mons Star with bar & usual decorations.[247]

---

[238] This sentence substituted by the subject for 'and never had a contest'. An asterisk refers to the following note: 'I fought a general election Decr – 1918
Result.

Carew Charles	9598
Penton Sir Edward (Asquithian)	4827
Fraser, Revnd Donald (Labour)	2377.

[239] 'Salisbury,' inserted by the subject.

[240] This sentence substituted by the subject for 'He still writes a firm hand and shoots straight; and he springs from a long line who knew Devon and Parliament'. Carew has added at the bottom of the page: 'N.B No member of the Carew family have ever sat in Parliament with the exception of Nicholas de Carew who signed the Barons letter to the Pope in 1300 and General Sir Reginald Pole-Carew, whose ancestor (Pole) took the name on marrying an heiress'.

[241] Written by JCW; corrected by the subject.

[242] The subject has deleted Wedgwood's skeleton dates ('(18 –)'), but inserted at the bottom: 'Father J.W. Carlile born Sept 5th 1823 Died Dec. 5 1909. Mother Mary daughter of Walter Whiteman of Glengall Co. Argyll N B who died July 1892'.

[243] 'Gayhurst, Bucks' inserted by the subject (in the space intended for the name of his mother).

[244] The subject has deleted the following sentence against which Wedgwood had put a pencilled question mark: 'He and his father both stood in 1895/1892, and his father was defeated but paid his son's expenses'.

[245] 'in France' inserted by the subject.

[246] 'He received the O.B.E. in 1920, and was' substituted by the subject for 'O.B.E. 1920'.

[247] Last sentence inserted by the subject.

CARR-GOMM,[248] Capt. HUBERT WILLIAM (1877–19   ); of Rotherhithe. M.P.
(Lib.) Rotherhithe 1906–10, 1910, 1911–18.

B. 2 Oct. 1877[249] at Ootacamund, S India, s. and h. of F.C. Carr-Gomm (b. 1834
d.1918)[250] of the Madras Civil Service [;] of[251] Farnham Royal, Bucks., by Emily
Blanche dau. of A. Morton Carr[252] heiress of Rotherhithe. Married (1) Kathleen
McNeale Rome (divorced 1913) (2) 1916 Eleanor Margaret only dau. of Norreys
Russell of 43 Westbourne Terrace.[253] No children.

Educ. Eton and Oriel, Oxford; M.A., and became interested in politics by taking part
in House debates at Eton, his father then representing Rotherhithe as a Progressive on
the L.C.C (1889–92).[254]

And this father 'coached me with the idea of eventually standing for Parliament'. The
Carr-Gomms nursed Rotherhithe both politically and manorially. Thence came their
wealth and there were their responsibilities. On the death of his mother, Carr-Gomm
succeeded her as lord of the manor of Rotherhithe, and in 1905 he was adopted as
Liberal candidate. Meanwhile he was private secretary to Winston Churchill, then a
Conservative Free Trader, and (later) devilling for Geake, editor of the Liberal Magazine
and manager of the Liberal Publication Dept. Of course he won Rotherhithe for which
no other Liberal has ever sat. He was undoubtedly orthodox, Church of England, and
his favourite newspaper was the *Westminster Gazette*, when he entered the House at the
age of 29. The Prime Minister always has two Parliamentary Private Secretaries.
Campbell-Bannerman chose Carr-Gomm (1906–08), and all the forty other P.P.S.s took
their junior for their model – in dress and deportment – if not in orthodoxy.

With other London members he urged the need for a reform of London Government
and, with the object of calling public attention to the matter, brought forward on a
private members day in 1911 a London Government Bill based on the recommendations
agreed upon by Majority and Minority Reports of the Poor Law Commission. Though
opposed and derided in official quarters in those days the scheme was finally accepted
in the subsequent Local Government Act of 1933.

In a speech on the second reading of the Port of London Bill and in an amendment
in Committee, he successfully pressed the Government to include, as members of the
P.L.A., two direct representatives of Labour Organizations in the Port.

With H.J. Craig, M.P. for Tynemouth, he proposed amendments introducing the
principle of Proportional Representation for University Seats in the Representation of
the People Bill, 1918.[255]

[248] Written by JCW; corrected by the subject.

[249] Exact date inserted by the subject.

[250] Dates inserted by the subject.

[251] JCW's original text read 'of Farnham Royal, Bucks.,'. The subject has inserted 'the Madras Civil Service of'.

[252] 'by Emily Blanche dau. of A. Morton Carr' inserted by the subject.

[253] Details of marriages substituted by the subject for 'Twice md.'.

[254] '92' inserted by subject.

[255] The three paragraphs 'With other London members . . . Representation of the People Bill, 1918.' are
written by the subject to be inserted at this point. In a letter to JCW from Luxor, dated 11 Jan. 1937,
Carr-Gomm asks if he would 'be so good as to see that the three sentences I have added are inserted.
Otherwise it wd appear as if, except for achieving an attitude of complete orthodoxy I had never interested
myself in anything at all nor effected anything whatsoever!'

He says that the best speech he heard was Sir Wm. Robson (Solicitor Gen.) on the right of the Commons to control finance, during the Committee stage of the Parliament Bill, 1910.[256] He joined up when the War started; Captain in the 2/22 London Regt. (Queen's) 1914–17, and served on the Western front[257] in 1916 and in Salonica 1917. In Dec. 1918 he did not receive the coupon and losing the seat in a three-corner competition[258] retired from Parliament. For a few years he was[259] a director of John Lane, The Bodley Head Ltd., publishers, and he remains the perfect product of Eton.

CASSEL,[260] Capt. Sir FELIX (Bart. 1920), (1869–19); L.C.C 1907–10; Judge Advocate General 1916–1934. Contested C. Hackney[261] Jan. 1910, (Cons). M.P. West St Pancras 1910–16.

B. 1869[262]

m. 1906 Lady Helen Grimston, da. of 3rd Earl of Verulam; 3 s., 2da.

Educ. Corpus Christi, Oxford; called to the Bar, Lincoln's Inn, 1894; K.C. 1906, Bencher of Lincoln's Inn 1912, Treasurer of Lincoln's Inn 1935.[263] He started politics with debating at the Union, 'I intended to go to the Bar, and thought this a good opportunity to learn speaking.' Living with his uncle, Sir Felix Cassel, reading *The Times*, he was naturally a Conservative. Thanks to Sir Ernest, he was completely independent, but soon made a good income; took silk 1906, and was earning £5000[264] a year when he entered Parliament. His election for his Parliamentary[265] seat, at St Pancras West,[266] which he only won by nine votes on a scrutiny, cost £750 and thereafter some £500 a year.

Cassel came in with the honest 'hope that I might acquire distinction in the House', and for four years he was a familiar figure rising from the 3rd bench above the gangway, fighting the land taxes, setting embarrassing puzzles to Mr Speaker, and confounding the Government front bench. His private practice went to pieces; and then his Parliamentary work ceased too. As a Lieut. In the 19th London Regiment (aged 45) he vanished into France, Jan.1915. In Sept. 1916 they saved his life and got the best Judge Advocate General. There are few posts which cannot be better held by an M.P. than by a layman. Cassel could not of course continue to sit in Parliament, but he could and did supervise and correct the schoolboy justice of old Army officers sitting in judgment on new Army civilians. He probably dealt with more Court Martial cases than all other Judge

---

[256] A sentence 'But thereafter Carr-Gomm took little part in the House.' has been deleted by the subject.

[257] 'on the Western front' substituted by the subject for 'continuously in France'.

[258] 'losing the seat in a three-corner competition' inserted by the subject.

[259] 'For a few years he was' substituted by the subject for 'He continues as'.

[260] Written by JCW; corrected by the subject.

[261] Wedgwood had written 'Hacking'.

[262] Year of birth supplied by the subject. He has deleted Wedgwood's skeleton 'son of (b. d.) and'.

[263] 'K.C. 1906 . . . Lincoln's Inn 1935' inserted by the subject; 'contested Central Hackney Jan. 1910' deleted.

[264] '5000' substituted by the subject for '4,000'. In the questionnaire, Cassel had originally written 4,000, and changed it to 5,000.

[265] 'Parliamentary' substituted by the subject for 'L.C.C.'. Cassel talked in the questionnaire of having been chairman of the parliamentary committee of the LCC.

[266] 'at St Pancras West' inserted by the subject.

Advocates before and since, and if record of his life's work is wanted, it can be found for ever in the long series of books of his Rulings kept in the Judge Advocate's office.

If he had remained M.P. and survived the Somme, he would now be Lord Chancellor, for he had a safe seat. The country is probably better serviced by his hard choice in 1916.

CATOR,[267] John, of Woodbastwick, Norfolk. Contested N. Norfolk 1892, S. Hunts 1910 Jan.; M.P. (C) Hunts (South) 1910–18.

B. 24 Sept. 1862, s. & h. of Albemarle Cator (–1906) and Mary Molesworth, da. of C.A. Mohun-Harris of Hayne, Devon; m. 1895 Maud, da of Henry J. Adeane of Babraham, Cambs., one s., one da. Elizabeth Margaret, m. Michael Bowes Lyon, s. of 14th Earl of Strathmore. Educ. Eton and Christ Church, Oxford (B.A.).

When he contested Norfolk in 1892, the voters were 'Church' and 'Chapel' and he was 'Church'. 'I had a fairly liberal allowance from my father and many friends in Parliament. Politics seemed the natural outlook. After my marriage I was on the London School Board and for a time acted as private secretary (unpaid) to Mr Henry Chaplin. Mr Aylwin Fellowes was instrumental in getting me adopted as Unionist candidate for South Hunts in 1908 . . . I stood as a Tariff Reformer. The 1892 election cost c. £1200 – I borrowed the money from the Bank: later elections cost rather less; annual expenses somewhat over the salary. In 1892 Beaconsfield was the model for all Unionist candidates, in 1910 Chamberlain for Tariff Reformers.'

' He liked 'the general interest of political life as well as the social life in the House of Commons. . . . Asquith impressed me most as a finished orator, and Lord Hugh Cecil on the occasion of the Education Bill (?) made one of the finest speeches I have ever heard in the House of Commons.' 'Under the Redistribution Bill, S. Hunts and N. Hunts were merged into one County seat. This I felt disinclined to contest, so I left Parliament, having enough to occupy my time in overlooking the management of estates in Norfolk, Beckenham, Kent, and Blackheath.' 'Incidently[268] I became a Director of the Alliance Assurance Co. about the year 1900 and acted as chairman of the local Unionist Association for several years from about the same date, as well as doing other County work.'

CAVENDISH,[269] Rt Hon. Lord RICHARD FREDERICK, of Holker in Cartmel, Lancs. M.P. (Lib. U.) Lancs. (North Lonsdale) 1895–1900, 1900–05; contested 1906.

B 31 Jan. 1871, 2bd s. of Lord Edward Cavendish (1840–1892)[270] and Emma Lascelles.[271]

m. 1895 Moira, da. of 10th Duke of St Albans, 1 s. 4 da. Educ. Eton and Trinity Camb.

Politics were in the blood and his uncle, Lord Hartington, made those politics Whig and Liberal-Unionist. 'Anyone in a position to go into Parliament, should do so.' 'In my family it was the natural thing', and in due course he was invited to stand. Chamberlain

---

[267] Written by JCW. Not corrected: a note on the file says 'Not returned'.

[268] *Sic.*

[269] Written by JCW; corrected by the subject.

[270] Dates supplied by the subject.

[271] Name of mother supplied by the subject.

living, and Fox dead, were natural ideals. The maintenance of the unity of the Empire was object enough in 1895. He liked 'the many friendships it enabled me to make'; objected to the 'Party wrangling'. The best speech he heard was Bromley Davenport on the Penrhyn Quarries strike. Of course he was defeated in the Chinese Labour election of 1906. Lord Cranborne M.P. and Lord Balniel M.P. married Lord Richard's daughters. Lord Hartington M.P. is his nephew.

CECIL,[272] Rt. Hon. Lord HUGH, (1869–19); P.C. 1918, M.P. (Cons.) Greenwich 1895–1900, 1900–5; Oxford Univ. 1910, 1910–18, 1918–22, 1922–3, 1923–4, 1924–9, 1929–31, 1931–5, 1933–1937 (Jan.).

B. 14 Oct. 1869, 5th s. of Robert Cecil, Marquess of Salisbury (q.v.) by Georgina (Alderson) unmd.

Educ., Eton and Univ., Oxford; Fellow of Hertford. Private Secretary to his father when Prime Minister.

What Lord Hugh says of himself is − that he admired Macaulay and Burke; that his religious convictions were Church of England, Tractarian; that the Times was always his favourite newspaper; that in 1895 he had an allowance of £800 a year; that his election expenses were paid for him by the family; that Church questions were his chief political interest; that what he liked most was his Parliamentary friends, and that he disliked most regular attendance; and that his best speech was on conscientious objectors in 1917, − a speech which so many think was the best they ever heard.

One cannot help putting all this down, for it is right that what he says of himself should be in the history of Parliament. Elsewhere we can look for him in his writings and speeches. He wrote a book on 'Conservatism', which is rather a book on liberty. He was a Free Trader, for liberty, a Tractarian, for liberty, an inspirer of conscience, for liberty. He has achieved nothing, save in the minds of men. It is right that he should have joined the Air Force in 1915 and learnt to fly at the age of 46. It is right that he should never have held office. For him the State cannot make things right or wrong; he is the anarchist, who moves where he will, alone through the heavens. From the corner seat below the gangway he twists his hands in agony as he straightens out his argument. He makes but one speech in three years, yet he is through patient sincerity and persuasive logic the chief acknowledged master of Parliamentary oratory. He is the embodiment of the catholic faith, yet untouched by clericalism. His school is authoritarian, yet he is the apostle of liberty. He goes now to be a Provost of Eton. One sadly wonders why; but of course he must be right.

CECIL,[273] Lord ROBERT (Rt. Hon.) (1864–19); Under Secretary for Foreign Affairs and P.C. 1915–16; Minister for Blockade 1916–18; Lord Privy Seal 1923–4; Chancellor

---

[272] Written by JCW; not corrected by the subject. A letter to Wedgwood from Cecil dated 15 Mar. 1937 rejects the idea of writing a biography of himself, and suggests that if Wedgwood proposes to reprint any part of his 'conscientious objectors' speech, he should do so in the revised version published in a pamphlet called *Nationalism and Catholicism* in 1919. Wedgwood has written on two separate sheets of paper: 'we give extracts from two of his speeches. The first on 4 Nov. 1909 to the Associated Societies of Edinburgh University': lengthy extracts from the speech follow. There is no reference to a second speech. Cecil addressed Wedgwood in an earlier letter as 'My dear cousin Josiah'.

[273] Written by JCW; corrected by the subject.

of the Duchy Nov. 1924–Aug. 1927; President of League of Nations Union. M.P. (Cons.) East Marylebone 1906–10. Contested Blackburn 1910 (Jan.) and Cambs. (North) 1910 (Dec). M.P. (Hitchen) 1911–18, (Ind. Cons.) 1918–22, 1922–23. Visct. Cecil of Chelwood, 1923.

B. 14 Sept. 1864, 3rd. s. of Robert, 3rd Marquess of Salisbury, M.P., by Georgina (Alderson); m. 189 Lady Eleanor Lambton, da. of 2nd. Earl of Durham. Educ. Eton and Univ. Oxford, M.A., D.C.L.; private sec. to his father 1886–8; called to the Bar (Inner Temple) 1887. Q.C. 1899.

He was interested in politics from childhood, naturally. Books had little influence though he read and admired Maine, Dicey, Macaulay etc. Cecil alone names Punch as his favourite newspaper, which is strange since most of our generation draw their knowledge of political history from back volumes of Punch. He calls himself Moderate High Anglican, worked hard at the Parliamentary Bar and was making £3,000 to £6,000 a year when nominated for Marylebone in 1906. He was known even then as a Free Trader but was selected as Conservative candidate. His interests then lay in Free Trade, the Irish Question, and Ecclesiastical matters and his election expenses were met by his elder brother as in the case of Lord Hugh. Once in Parliament, 4/5th of his legal income ceased. The Parliamentary Bar was closed to him, and he rose almost hourly, a tall round shouldered question mark, from the third corner seat above the gangway. 'I was in opposition in my first Parliament – a small body – and I took a very active part speaking almost every night.' He marks as his best speech one in that Parlt. 'in which I separated myself from the tariff reform policy of the Opposition'. 'Parlt. did not modify my views except that I moved gradually to the left. I always found myself in close agreement with Sir E. Grey and more than once contemplated joining the Liberal Party on the Free Trade issue. But for Welsh Disestablishment and to a lesser degree Home Rule I should probably have done so'. He says that he enjoyed most 'the rough and tumble of Parlty. opposition', that he disliked most 'the rigidity of Party discipline and the consequent insincerity of much of parliamentary life'. That Mr. Tim Healy's speech on the Education Bill of 1906 and Sir Edward Grey's on 4[274] Aug. 1914 were the best he ever heard; and then, alas, that his best piece of work was on 'The Marconi Committee and perhaps the blockade during the war, apart from Peace work later on'.

The Marconi scandal was innocence itself compared with post war guilt in high places; the blockade of Germany, seen today to be due to inability to pay, makes our war-time efforts seem futile and misplaced. And the right work for Peace might have been done openly and effectively by a Cecil wielding the power of Great Britain. It is not Lord Robert's tragedy, but the tragedy of the whole world that he was not our Sec. of State for Foreign Affairs 1916–23, and thenceforward whatever Govt. was in power.[275] [He might have been, had it not been for the Marconi. Comn. and the useless Blockade job. Mr. Lloyd George can do many things but he cannot choose men, and he cannot

[274] JCW's draft gives 4 Aug. but the speech was on 3 Aug.

[275] 'and thenceforward . . . power' has been underlined in pencil, and marked in the margin with a question mark, probably by Wedgwood, as the same marking is on the original copy as well as the carbon copy that went to Cecil.

forgive.][276] So from 1916 for 20 years the master of Peace and Reconciliation and Collective Security has been alternately the office boy and the bogey-man of the Foreign Office and its vacillating chiefs. They have sent him in irons to Geneva, as it might be to Coventry or Jericho. Even when his great stroke of the Peace ballot had conquered Mr Baldwin, the same officials could still dodge and ruin England's name and the world's chances.

Lord Robert is not perhaps a great speaker, but he convinces for he is a great man. He has that honesty, lucidity and vision, which may annoy the dull party politician, but arouses devotion and all the best in others, here and abroad. Eden may take the place of Grey, but no one can replace Lord Cecil of Chelwood.[277]

CECIL,[278] Lord JOHN (PAKENHAM), JOICEY-, of Andover. M.P. (C) Lincs. (Stamford) 1906–10.

B. 3.3.1867,[279] y.s. of 3rd Marquess of Exeter and m. 1896 Isabella Maud, da. of Col. John Joicey, M.P. (took the additional surname of Joicey,   ). Issue, 2 s., 2 da., Eldest son a Lieut. In the Grenadier Guards. Killed on the Somme 1916.

Helping his brother Lord Burghley in 1884 brought him into politics. His father and brother were strong Conservatives. His Church was Anglican; his paper the *Times*; and he entered Parliament as a matter of duty. Disraeli and Chamberlain were his leaders; tariff reform his chief interest, or 'turning out the so called Liberal Government.' His election cost £1,600 and the seat £500 a year. In the end the sedentary life made him ill and expenses were too great so he retired in 1910. His best piece of work – he says – was winning the seat, indeed no mean task in 1906. He liked meeting people and disliked the dining room, such likes and dislikes being almost common form, for he dare not mention the all-night sittings to which he contributed from the 3rd opposition bench.

My own career.[280] Educated at Eton joined the Northamptonshire Militia 1885 – Gren Gds 1887 retired in 1898 and became Maj Leicestershire Militia which he commanded till 08 when Haldane did away with Militia. Rejoined Gren Gds 14 raised & commanded 8th Service Battn Wiltshire Regt. Later commanded 32nd Training Battn 1st (Home Service) Royal Berks. (mentioned in despatches). Formed and Cmded. 12 batt. Royal Defence Corps on completion of military service was appointed Chief Agricultural Officer. National Service. For 7 years was a member of the Andover Borough Council & retired 36 to make way for a younger man.

---

[276] The subject has bracketed Wedgwood's two sentences and inserted a pencil note: 'I cannot complain of L.G.'s treatment of me. He had promised me the succession to AJB when I resigned in 1918. The truth is that I could never work with the Conservatives or with the Ramsay Labour people & the Liberal Party perished with Asquith and Grey'.

[277] Cecil's letter to Wedgwood of 5 Feb. 1937 comments that 'Beyond the fact that it seems to me far too laudatory, I have no serious criticism', although he makes the point also made in the previous note concerning Lloyd George, and adds: 'The only other suggestion I have to make is that I should a little like you to put in some reference to the work that I did at Paris on the League of Nations Commission. I venture to enclose a copy of a note that Woodrow Wilson sent to me at the end, which will indicate the kind of part that I was able to take on the Commission'.

[278] Written by JCW; corrected by the subject.

[279] Day and month of birth inserted by the subject.

[280] This paragraph has been added in manuscript by the subject at the foot of the page.

CHALONER,[281] (formerly LONG) Col. RICHARD GODOLPHIN WALMESLEY, of Gisborough, Yorks. M.P. (C) Wilts, (Westbury.) 1895–1900; Liverpool (Abercromby) 1910–17. Cr. Lord Gisborough 1917. Born at Dolforgan Newtown. Mont. Oct. 12, 1856,[282] 2nd son of late Richard Penruddocke Long of Rood Ashton, & Wraxall, Wilts, M.P. (Chippenham, 1859, N. Wilts 1865–8.), & bro. of the Right Hon. Walter Long (Viscount Long.) M.P.[283] Took name of Chaloner under will of his great uncle Admiral Chaloner, C.B. 1888. M. 1882 Margaret[284] dau. of the Rev. W. B. Davis; 2 s. (eld. killed in great war.) 4 dau. Educated Winchester. Entered army 1878, 6th. Dragoon Guards, served in India & Afghan War, 1879–80 mentioned despatches, (medal), Adj. N. Somerset Yeomanry, 1888–1893, Commanded 1st. Batt. Imp. Yeo. S.Africa War; (Medal, & clasp.) Major 4th. Reserve Cavalry 1914–1918.

For obvious reasons, a Long took to politics. He read the *Morning Post*, & *Sheffield Daily Telegraph*, & was a Protestant. Beaconsfield & Chamberlain were his ideals. He was persuaded against his better judgment to fight a hitherto hopeless seat for his party & won it & entered Parliament as a whole hearted Tariff Reformer.[285] Being beaten in 1900 he did not stand again until 1910 when he won the Abercromby Division of Liverpool from Col. Seely, & held it again in the second 1910 election with a record majority.[286]

Parliament did not, & does not modify his views, they are those of 600 years of Wiltshire Longs, based on practical experience.[287]

CHAMBERLAIN,[288] Rt. Hon. Sir (JOSEPH) AUSTEN, Civil Lord of the Admiralty 1895–1900; Financial Secretary to Treasury 1900–2; Postmaster General 1902–3; Chancellor of Exchequer 1903–5; Secretary of State for India 1915–17; War Cabinet, April 1918; Chancellor of Exchequer, Jan. 1919–21; Lord Privy Seal and Leader of the House of Commons 1921–2; Secretary of State for Foreign Affairs, Nov. 1924 to June 1929; First Lord of Admiralty, Aug.–Oct. 1931. M.P. (U) Worcs. (East) 1892–5, 1895–1900, 1900–6, 1906–10, 1910, 1910–14; Birmingham West 1914–18, 1918–22, 1922–3, 1923–4, 1924–9, 1929–31, 1931–5, 1935.

B. 16 Oct. 1863, s. and h. of Rt. Hon. Joseph Chamberlain M.P. (18 –) and Harriet, da. of Archibald Kenrick; m. 1906 Ivy Muriel, da. of Col. Henry Lawrence Dundas; issue:-

Educ. Rugby and Trinity, Camb. His father and the talk at home made him a politician before he was 15. They were Unitarians, and his favourite newspapers were the *Birmingham Post*, *The Times*, and Escott's articles in the Standard; but all came from his father.

---

[281] Written by JCW; rewritten by the subject. The version printed here is Chaloner's, with significant divergences from Wedgwood's indicated in the footnotes.

[282] JCW: 'B. 1856;'

[283] Some details of father's name and address not given by JCW.

[284] JCW does not give name of wife.

[285] JCW: 'But he was forced to fight a hopeless seat and found himself in Parliament as a Tariff Reformer, almost by accident. His election expenses were paid for him, but being M.P. cost him about £1000 a year'.

[286] This sentence not in JCW's version.

[287] 'based on practical experience' not in JCW's text.

[288] Written by JCW; not corrected by the subject. Chamberlain returned the typescript with a note: 'My dear Jos, I really cannot write a notice about myself. Do with your material, therefore, what you like'.

'I was an undergraduate when my father offered me the choice of law, business or politics. I chose politics because I thought it an opportunity for congenial work and a noble career.'

He had spoken a good deal and was chosen as Liberal-Unionist candidate for the Border Burghs, 1888, but was actually elected at a bye-election for Worcestershire. 'I spoke little, became a whip in opposition, and Civil Lord of the Admiralty in 1895.' In 1892 he had an allowance of £300, his early elections cost £1,500 to £1,800, and about £200 a year, which of course was met by his father. That father was his ideal statesman, and among the dead he puts Chatham, Cavour, Pitt – 'but none of them *ideal*'. Of course Parliament affected his views; 'it is a Liberal education'. He liked best 'Administration', disliked most 'dining in the House, and for ten years I never dined out on a Government night and only very rarely on other nights.' He will not name his greatest speech, but others think that he improves each year. 'Balfour and my father agreed that, given the circumstances, Gladstone's speech on the first of his Bulgarian resolutions in 1878 (?) was the finest Parliamentary effort they had heard.' 'Speeches often modify or change the decision of a government in committee.'

One of the engaging features about Sir Austen is the way in which here, and ever, he refers everything to his father. The choice may be difficult yet one must prefer him to his father, and partly for this very loyalty. When he resigned office in 1917, quite unnecessarily, it was merely the duty of the son of Joseph Chamberlain. When he went out in 1922, it was loyalty to a chief whose views he did not share. The partisanship of tariffs has been replaced by a patriotism which is the glory of the House of Commons.

He liked best administration; and he would like to think that his best work was at the Foreign Office and Locarno, but to one at least, that 'best piece of work' which he would 'leave to posterity to decide' has been done from the corner seat on the third bench below the gangway, an example to all, and an influence on the mind of mankind which has ennobled politics and may still save England.[289]

Possibly he would like to think that his best work was at the Foreign Office and Locarno, but to one at least, that 'best piece of work' which he would 'leave to posterity to decide' has been done since he left office. Who shall say whether an example and influence which have already ennobled politics may not have an effect on the minds of mankind and the future of England?

CHANCELLOR,[290] Henry George (1863–19   ); paint manufacturer, of London. M.P. (Lib.) Haggerston 1910, 1910–18. Contested 1918.

B. 3 June 1863, s. of John Chancellor (18   –   ) of Walton by Glastonbury, and Louisa, da. of John Porter of Ashcott, Som.; m. 1883 Mary Dyer, da. of John Surl of Newent, Glos.; 2 s., 3 das.

Educ. Elmfield Coll., York; entered business of C. Chancellor & Co. 1883, and became sole owner. He started politics when he came to London, influenced by what he saw and learned in Sunday School and Band of Hope work. Books which taught him the one

---

[289] These last two paragraphs are alternatives: Wedgwood wrote 'either' and 'or' beside them.

[290] Written by JCW; not corrected by the subject (although Chancellor read the text and commented that the facts were correct, 'but I accept no responsibility for the last par. which is yours; though it is quite true that I care much more for causes than for Kudos').

and only remedy for poverty were a pamphlet 'The Bitter Cry of Outcast London' and 'Progress and Poverty'.[291] He started as a Methodist and became a Unitarian, read *Daily Chronicle*, then *Morning Leader* and *Star*. 'No favourite now.'[292] President of N. Islington Liberal Assocn. since 1896, and published *The Londoner*, a progressive paper, 1896–9; contested N. Islington for L.C.C., 1907.

He was making £1000 a year when he won Haggerston from the brewers on Taxation of Land Values in Jan.1910. His elections cost £800 each, and yearly expenses took his salary. He started with Land, Peace, Temperance, and in practice adopted other unpopular causes; – Humanitarianism, man's right to his own person, e.g., innoculation, vivisection, and soldiers' rights during the War. His personal ideals were 'Gladstone, champion of freedom, and Stansfield, the moral hero,' also Abraham Lincoln, abroad. Parliament showed him 'the strength of the interests to oppose progress. My liberal convictions were strengthened, my hopes were damped.' He liked the absence of snobbishness and the friendship with members of inter-party groups. He disliked the bitterness of debate, and inability to respond to innumerable appeals for financial help. His best speech was one on 9 Feb. 1915 which mitigated the bullying of soldiers.[293] His best work, with J. Dundas White in 1917, was preventing the creation of a fresh vested interest, petroleum royalties.[294] The best speech he heard was Hugh Cecil's on conscientious objectors. He lost money by being a member 'and I never used my membership to influence business'. Of course he did not get the coupon, and was defeated in Dec. 1918.

A very modest, quiet man, with grey beard and black frock coat; he was one of the small band of devoted Single Taxers, and we always knew him as 'Henry George'. Twice he was President of the League. He never thought of himself.

CHAPPLE,[295] Dr WILLIAM ALLEN (1864–1936), of Wellington, N.Z. Surgeon. M.P. (Lib) Stirlingshire 1910–18; contested 1918; Dumfriesshire 1922–3; contested 1924.

B. at Alexandra, Otago, N.Z. 14 July 1864, only s. of J.C. Chapple of same and m. 18   Sarah Douglas, da. of Thomas Turnbull of Wellington, architect; 4 da. Educ. Dunedin Univ.; practised as surgeon in Wellington until 1906. M.P. for Tuapeka in New Zealand Parliament 1907–9.

He started on politics largely through his mother's desire for social reform; they were Presbyterian. Love of politics and political power sent him to Parliament when he gave up practice. He had then a good income of £3,000 a year. He had been on the Senate

---

[291] The sentence was confused in the original draft and JCW's corrections have only partly clarified it. The sentence in Chancellor's questionnaire was 'A pamphlet, "The Bitter Cry of Outcast London", which described the conditions of slum dwellers, and Henry George's "Progress and Poverty" which taught me the one and only remedy for poverty'.

[292] i.e., no favourite newspaper.

[293] JCW note: '*Hansard*, 79, cols. 431–447'.

[294] JCW note: '*Hansard*, 98, cols. 32–36'.

[295] Written by JCW; not corrected by the subject. There is a letter in the file from Chapple to Wedgwood dated 22 July 1936, promising a reply to the questionnaire and explaining that he had spent the last ten years in New Zealand 'struggling to save a fortune in a Native Trust, which the Govt. took by Act of Parliament'. A form letter from Wedgwood with Wedgwood's own responses has a note on the bottom from Chapple's widow, explaining his death on 19 Oct.

of the N.Z. University and his interest was chiefly in Education and Public Health. In Parliament, representing Scottish constituencies, naturally Scottish affairs became his chief field. *The Times* was his newspaper; but Asquith living, and Lincoln dead, were his ideal statesmen. He enjoyed elections and the fraternity of Parliament; learnt the advantages of the team spirit. He put his speech on Scottish Home Rule as his best, and Asquith's on all subjects as supreme. His best work was for Scottish Home Rule and on Nurses' Registration.

Financial misfortune, largely due to Government action in New Zealand, prevented his contesting again after 1924; but he wrote much afterwards on temperance, and added to his works on Health. He died on 19th October 1936. He was so good a Scotsman that we never knew he was a New Zealander!

CLOUGH,[296] William (1862–19   ); of Steeton by Keighley, retired worsted spinner and manufacturer.[297] M.P. (Lib.) Yorks. (Skipton) 1906–10, 1910, 1910–18.

B. 13 May 1862, s. of Thomas Clough, manufacturer, (b. July 27, 1827) (d. March 11, 1911);[298] by Hannah, da. of Joseph Dawson;[299] m. 1886 Louisa da. of Wm. Clapham of Keighley, 1 s., 1 da.

Educ. Steeton Provident School, Keighley Trade School; Pannal College, Harrogate.

Speeches by Sir Matthew Wilson and Lord Frederick Cavendish in the 1880 election first interested him in politics. His Sunday School superintendent ripened the seed. His religious conversion to Wesleyan Methodism also occurred in 1880. The *Leeds Mercury* helped. He retired in 1892; in 1906[300] had £3,000 a year, mostly unearned, and 'wanted to be of some use and to increase his interest in life'. He was elected to the West Riding C.C. from 1903 and still so (1937). Elected in 1906, his chief interests were 'Free Trade, Temperance, Education, Abolition of the veto of the House of Lords, Irish Home Rule, Retrenchment and economy, Franchise reform, Civil and Religious equality, "Peace on Earth, good will to men" '. Election Expenses about £1,400 each, and the seat cost him £700 to £650 a year. In Parliament he enjoyed most the Question hour; 'When Wedgwood, Watt, Pringle and Hogge kept us all awake'; disliked most the shouting down of Mr. Asquith on the Home Rule Bill, 21 May 1914. His best speech, on 5 July, 1917, was against including the Co-op. in the Excess Profits duty. The best speech he remembers, Haldane on the Army Estimates, 12 July 1906. His best work, his voting record.

We certainly liked Willie Clough. He was the quintessence of virtuous liberal non-conformity; but never posed or pompous. He took the 'ragging' of bright young radicals in good part. 'Willie' we would say 'You shall vote with us. Skipton expects it'. And one on each arm he was dragged into the wrong lobby, when he would wrench himself free, with half serious excuse, and bolt back among the baronets, under the approving eye of his adored Prime Ministers.

---

[296] Written by JCW; corrected by the subject.

[297] 'worsted spinner & manufacturer' substituted by the subject for 'cotton spinner'.

[298] Father's vital dates inserted by the subject.

[299] 'Joseph Dawson' inserted by the subject.

[300] 'in 1906' inserted by the subject.

CLYDE,[301] Lord,[302] Rt. Hon. JAMES AVON CLYDE, P.C., LL.D.;[303] Solicitor Gen., Scotland 1905–6; Lord Advocate 1916–20; Lord Justice Gen. of Scotland[304] and Lord President 1920–35.[305] Contested Clackmannon and Kinross 1906; M.P. (U) Edinburgh West 1909–10, 1910, 1910–18; Edinburgh North 1918–20.

B. at Dollar, 14 Nov. 1863, 2nd. S. of James Clyde, M.A., LL.D (1821–1912)[306] and Elizabeth, da. of Thomas[307] Rigg of Whitehaven; m. 1895[308] Anna M.M., da. of P.W. Latham, M.D., Downing Prof. of Med. Cambridge; two sons.[309]

Educ. Edinburgh Academy and University (Gray Scholar 1884, LL.B. 1888); called to Scottish Bar 1889; K.C. 1901.

'I was[310] mainly influenced by my ideas of right and wrong. Books only helped me by making me critical. I read a great deal of orthodox political economy, and became ardently socialistic until I read the socialists, from Godwin to Marx, which certainly quenched my ardour, and left me chiefly individualistic, but a bit of an opportunist.' He came to Parliament 'because I desired to follow the public traditions of my profession at the Scottish Bar; and also because Parliament is a possible door to the attainment of the highest professional ambition.' When he stood first in 1906 he was making c. £5500 a year, and had £1000 a year unearned.[311] A contest cost about £700 and the constituency[312] £400 a year. He idealised no man.[313] Grey's speech at the outbreak of the War was the best he remembers hearing; but 'I never made a speech which satisfied me'. In his time in Parliament,[314] he enjoyed most 'the society of two or three of the friends I made there'; disliked most 'the inevitable separation from my family and the constant night travelling.'

His last answers shall be given in facsimile; for this Scottish lawyer of 73 combines with straightforward simplicity the best and firmest hand of them all.[315]

---

[301] Written by JCW; corrected by the subject (a note in the corner by Clyde says 'vetted in acc. With J.C.W.'s letter of 20/2/37. J.A.C. 27/2/37').

[302] 'Lord' inserted by the subject.

[303] 'CLYDE, P.C., LL.D.' substituted by the subject for 'of Kinross. K.C.'.

[304] 'of Scotland' inserted by the subject.

[305] '37' corrected by the subject to '35'.

[306] 'LLD' and father's dates inserted by the subject.

[307] 'Thomas' inserted by the subject.

[308] Year inserted by the subject.

[309] 'M.D., Downing Prof. of Med. Cambridge; two sons' inserted by the subject.

[310] 'I was' substituted by the subject for '. . .'.

[311] JCW note: 'Half his practice vanished when he came to Westminster. "It is almost impossible to keep up a professional practice in Edinburgh, and give proper attendance at Westminster"'.

[312] 'constituency' inserted by the subject.

[313] The sentence 'Indeed I think that such an idea would have to him the sound of blasphemy' has been deleted by the subject.

[314] 'In his time in Parliament' inserted by the subject.

[315] JCW's text indicates an illustration here. The answers are:
'Q22. Did speeches affect your vote? Sometimes.
Q23. What was your best piece of work? I worked hard, but accomplished little or nothing in the House. I believe my best work was done in the Scottish Office while Lord Advocate of Scotland.
Q.24. If you are no longer in Parliament, why did you leave? Because in March 1920, I was appointed Lord Justice General of Scotland and Lord President of the Court of Session.
Q. 25. What books have you written, and what books have been written about you? A translation of Sir Thomas Craig's "Jus Feudale"'.

CLYNES,[316] RT. HON. JOHN ROBERT (1869–19   ). President of National of Workers. Parl. Sec. Ministry of Food 1917–18; Food Controller 1918–19; Chairman Parl. Labour Party 1921–2; Lord Privy Seal 1924; Home Secretary 1929–31. M.P. (Lab.) Manchester (Platting) 1906–10, 1910, 1910–18, 1918–22, 1922–3, 1923–4, 1924–9, 1929–31, 1935 –

B. at Oldham, 27 Mar. 1869, s. of Patrick Clynes, Oldham.

m. 1893 Mary Elizabeth da. of Owen Harper, Bury.

'From 10 years of age to 22, when I began Trades Union work, I was a cotton operative in spinning mills. In early manhood I was influenced by industrial conditions and factory life to regard politics as a means of improvement. *Progress and Poverty* by Henry George was a first influence, together with pamphlets on Labour and Socialist questions. I cannot say that in early life I wanted to be an M.P. I attached great importance to the Trades Union work which I was then doing in Lancashire, and was pressed to stand for Parliament by friends in Platting. It cost me only small sums for personal expenses, any charges in a contest being met by collections or subscriptions, and in later years by sufficient grants from my Trades Union. The best work I did was in the later part of the War as Food Controller. That work started with many signs of public apprehension but ended amid popular approval.'

So writes J.R. Clynes, and no more. To colleagues he was always serious, steady, and a trifle suspicious[317] as though they might be trying to 'put something over him'. He is no Socialist[318] but a moderate Liberal, driven against his wish into concurring in wilder policies. In 1919 he might have retained office in the Coalition Government, but considered it more judicious[319] to remain in the Labour party with a safe seat[320] as a moderating influence. In 1921 he succeeded Adamson as Chairman of the Parliamentary party and led it better than before, in spite of being a poor speaker.[321] He even joined the Council of Action. But his moderation exasperated the I.L.P. and after the 1922 election, when the I.L.P. returned in great force, Clynes was deposed from leadership in favour of Macdonald by a very small majority – so that Macdonald became Prime Minister the following year instead of Clynes. Clynes took it remarkably well, and probably it could not have been helped though many of us afterwards regretted the votes we gave on that momentous occasion. Thereafter Clynes had no chance to make much

[316] Written by JCW; not corrected by the subject, although Clynes wrote to Wedgwood on 15 Feb. 1937: 'The enclosed notes are a comment on a few of your statements which I have underlined, touching questions of both fact and opinion. You may decide in what way the points in my notes can be used'. Clynes' responses are given in notes to this text.

[317] Clynes' note: 'I am quite unaware of being suspicious of colleagues, and can declare that I have not been'.

[318] Note by Clynes: 'I have been a Socialist since early manhood, and have never been connected with any political body other than a Socialist body'.

[319] Note by Clynes: 'My action in 1919 was not dictated by what was judicious. I have abided always by the principle of accepting Conference decisions, and so far as I argued in favour of continuing the Coalition Government it was to secure for Labour a place in making the Peace'.

[320] Note by Clynes: 'Platting has never been a safe seat, and majorities have varied from thousands to a few hundreds'.

[321] Note by Clynes: 'You may, of course, say that I am a poor speaker. I know of no one else who has said it. Snowden may be taken as an impartial judge, and you may see his opinion in the second volume of his book'.

mark in Parliament. He was content. Mrs Clynes and his family became more and more the centre of his life.[322] It would be surprising if Clynes had never been jealous of the meteoric careers[323] of Macdonald, Henderson and Thomas; but certainly he never showed such jealousy. He strongly disliked Communists[324] (he would not allow Trotsky to come to England); but he never troubled to belittle anyone – or even show much enthusiasm for friends.

COATS,[325] Sir STUART AUCHINCLOSS, Baronet. Contested Morpeth 1906, Deptford Jan. & Dec. 1910. M.P. (U) Surrey (Wimbledon) Apr. 1916–18; Surrey (Easter) 1918–22.

B. 20 Mar. 1868, s. and h. of Sir James Coats, 1st Bart.,[326] and Sarah, da. of John Auchincloss of New York; m. 1891 Jane Muir, da. of Thomas Greenlees of Paisley; two s., one da.

He was a partner in J. & P. Coats, the makers of sewing cotton. Brought up a Presbyterian, he was reconciled to the Catholic Church in 1899 and has since been Private Chamberlain of Cape and Sword to three Popes. He holds a Commandership of the Crown of Italy besides two[327] Papal Orders. Sir Stuart was educated in the U.S.A. and held various positions there in the American branch of his firm. Thence came his belief in[328] high tariffs; but a French relative first gave him the idea of standing[329] for Parliament. Once elected, economic questions and the Catholic schools held his interest. 'It made me feel that far too much power was in the hands of the House of Commons and that we required for our national safety a strong non-hereditary Upper Chamber with *real* power over matters of finance.' His best piece of work: – 'By constantly pressing Ministers I had an enquiry made into the state of the Oxted tunnel, which caused it to be totally reconstructed, and thus probably saved many lives, as it was in a very dangerous condition.' He left Parliament just before the 1922 election and went to live at Cannes for the sake of his wife's health.

COCHRANE,[330] (Sir) CECIL ALGERNON, of Gosforth, Northumberland; Coal-owner. Contested Durham City 1910; M.P. (Lib) South Shields 1916–18.

---

[322] Wedgwood has deleted here his own sentence: 'It is a relief to all of us that we need no longer fear Macdonald'.

[323] Note by Clynes: 'I can assure you that I have not been jealous about the careers of my colleagues'.

[324] Note by Clynes: 'My attitude towards Communists has not been one of dislike. In their early approach to the Labour Party many years ago I supported their admission to the Labour Party. I wish all countries could live on a community basis, but the conduct of Communists for many years past here, as in other countries, has demanded not only a working-class dictatorship, but has provoked a demand for dictatorships in other classes. To make the Communists here stronger than they are would be the short cut to Fascist success in Britain'.

[325] Written by JCW; corrected by the subject.

[326] The subject has deleted 'M.P.' and Wedgwood's markers for the dates of his father.

[327] 'two' substituted by the subject for 'many'.

[328] 'belief in' substituted by the subject for 'love for'.

[329] 'a French relative first gave him the idea of standing' substituted by the subject for 'his French stepmother made him stand'.

[330] Written by JCW; redrafted by the subject. The text here is the subject's redraft, with significant changes indicated in the notes.

B. 24th April 1869, 2nd surv. s. of William Cochrane (mining engineer) (b. 23rd Jan. 1837 d. 2th Nov. 1903) and Eliza (née Collis, b. 21st Feb. 1838, d. 23rd Feb. 1900).[331] M. 1905 Frances Sibyl, da. of Col Addison Potter C.B. of Heaton Hall, Newcastle-on-Tyne. Educ. Sherborne and Christchurch, Oxford, M.A. 1894. A Director of Consett Iron Co., Newcastle Gas Co. Bolsover Colliery Co., Blackwell Colliery Co. &c.[332]

He became a Gladstonian[333] Home Ruler at school. Was a reader of the 'Daily News'. Is a Protestant.

'Partly ambition and partly because I thought I might do some useful work' sent him to Parliament. But 1916–1918 were bad years for new private members. 'I could have been doing much more useful work if I had not been tied to the House'. He was on the Shortt and Geddes Committees. He resigned to enable Havelock Wilson to sit for South Shields.[334] Joined the Conservative Party after the war.

J.P. for Northumberland since 1908: Was Chairman of the Council of Armstrong College for 12 years and is on Senate of Durham University. Hon.D.C.L. (Durham) since 1920. Knighted 1933.

COCHRANE-BAILLIE,[335] Hon. (Sir) CHARLES WALLACE ALEXANDER NAPIER (Lord LAMINGTON from 1890); of Lamington, Lanark. M.P. (C) North St. Pancras 1886–1890.

B. 29 July 1860, s. and h. of 1st Baron (18 –1890) and Annabelle, da. of Andrew R. Drummond, of Cadlands, Hants; m. 1895 Mary H. Hozier, da. of 1st Lord Newlands; issue, Victor, M.C.; 1 da.

Educ. Eton and Christ Church, Oxford (B.A.). Assistant Private Secretary to Lord Salisbury, when Prime Minister 1885–86. In 1890–1 he travelled through from Siam to Tonquin, the first European to cross that hilly & jungly[336] barrier. Governor of Queensland 1895–1901; Governor of Bombay 1903–07, since which time he has been the protagonist of the Moslems of India and Palestine in Parliament.[337] He is Church of England and owns 12,000 acres.

A politician from youth by family and tradition. His father saw him into the Commons[338] and Lord Salisbury, for whom he worked, was his ideal statesman. He refuses to believe that he ever made a good speech, and puts first Gladstone's speeches on Home Rule. Lord Lamington was an early example of the House of Commons man making a good Indian governor. It was also good for him, giving him his mission in life.

---

[331] Subject's birth date, father's vital dates and detail of mother not in Wedgwood's draft.

[332] Wedgwood's sentence 'The Cochranes were the chief coalowners of Tyneside fifty years ago' has been omitted.

[333] Wedgwood's draft says 'committed Gladstonian Home Ruler'.

[334] Wedgwood's draft says: 'He was on the Shortt and Geddes Committees and could have got the coupon, but resigned to enable Havelock Wilson (q.v.) to sit for Shields'.

[335] Written by JCW; corrected by the subject.

[336] 'hilly & jungly' substituted by the subject for 'mountain'.

[337] The subject has inserted a note: 'But sympathise with the Jews & spoke in favour of the National Home at an overflow meeting in 1917. But travelling in Palestine in 1919 he realised it would be an embarrassing task to reconcile the different promises made to the rival parties; so greatly did he feel this that he wrote privately to Lord Curzon recommending that we should have no responsibility for Palestine'.

[338] The subject has deleted Wedgwood's parenthesis '(allowance £400 a year)', and written: 'I don't object to this reference to my gross income but it seems trivial and uninteresting'.

The virtue of our Parliamentary system is that there is always someone to champion any cause or any people in face of unpopularity.[339] So Lord Lamington believes in the followers of the Prophet.[340]

COGAN,[341] DENIS JOSEPH, of Dublin; provision merchant. M.P. (Nationalist) E. Wicklow 1900–5.

B. at Bray, Co. Wicklow[342] 1859, s. of Denis Cogan born Sept 1819 died 1909, and Mary Cogan.[343]

m. (1) 1886 Elizabeth M., da. of John Murphy of Laragh, Co. Wicklow; (2) 1915 Marie C. da. of John P. Butler of Blackrock, stockbroker.

He is governing director of D.J. Cogan Ltd., chairman of the Hibernian Fire & General Insurance Co.; a Councillor of Dublin Corporation; a member of the Dublin Chamber of Commerce, the Royal Dublin Society[344] etc. His father and grandfather before him had been militant Irish Nationalists. In religion, a Catholic; the Freeman's Journal his favourite paper. 'My only thought was to serve my people's and my country's cause in whatever sphere I might be called upon to do so.' He was making £800 a year when he first stood for Parliament. His experience of public work at that time included membership of the Dublin Municipal Council from 1885, of Rathdrum Board of Guardians from 1894, Wicklow County Council from 1899, and other public bodies. Gladstone, Campbell Bannerman and Balfour were his ideal British statesmen. What he liked most was 'being in the House of Commons'. His best speech he thinks was on the Sugar Convention.

But by 1907[345] his health was breaking down through overwork and long travelling, and he retired from Parliament in 1907.[346] He was a good type for the 20th Century Commons, if only things had worked out differently.

COOPER,[347] Sir RICHARD ASHMOLE, Bart., of Shenstone, Staffs. M.P. (C) Walsall 1910–18, 1918–22.

B. 11 Aug. 1874, s. and h. of Sir Richard Powell[348] Cooper, Bart., of same (1905–1913)[349] and Elizabeth Anne[350] da. of E.A. Ashmall of Hammerwich, Staffs.; m 1900 Alice E. da. of Rev. E. Priestland of Spondon Derbyshire;[351] 3 s. Educ Clifton Coll.; entered his father's sheep-dip chemical business; and went to America in that business. He had served on the Herts. C.C. and had £5,000 a year and expectations. During the war he

[339] The subject has deleted 'and unreason'.

[340] 'and even in the Grand Mufti' deleted by the subject. (Wedgwood's note to Lamington of 27 Apr. 1937, enclosing the draft, says: 'I suppose you will cut out the "jeer" at the end'.)

[341] Written by JCW; corrected by the subject.

[342] Birthplace inserted by the subject.

[343] Details of father and mother inserted by the subject.

[344] 'The Royal Dublin Society' inserted by the subject.

[345] '7' substituted by the subject for '5'.

[346] 'from Parliament in 1907' substituted by the subject for 'after six years'.

[347] Written by JCW; corrected by the subject.

[348] 'Richard Powell' inserted by the subject.

[349] '1905' has been inserted (incorrectly) by the subject. 1905 was the date of the creation of the baronetage.

[350] Name of mother inserted by the subject.

[351] 'Derbyshire' inserted by the subject.

sold Shenstone to James Dadman and Birmingham has since built over it. In 1922[352] he became very ill and retired.

Cooper was proud of his social reform views and votes and speeches, emphasised his independence, and was a founder of the 1917 National Party. This he contrasts with 'the purely opportunist National Party of Mr Lloyd George.' Disraeli and Chamberlain were his models, and he told both Parliament and[353] his constituents the 'unvarnished truth' at a loss to himself[354] of £2,000 a year. 'An M.P.'s education only begins when he gets into the House. If he takes politics seriously he soon learns that there are two sides to most problems. I learned very much about human nature and the "milk of human kindness". The Brotherhood amongst M.P.s is a wonderful feature of our Parliamentary System. On public matters, I disliked the wide exercise of compromise and tardy action; but in later life I see that these features appear to serve well the British public, and is to be preferred to the hasty ill-digested and ungrammatical legislation which too often reaches the Statute Book.' He liked 'helping to get things done, and the valued friendships I built up'; disliked 'waiting to be called upon to speak. I always developed a strange form of nervousness, which prevented me from expressing myself clearly and consequently I was usually ineffective in debate.' He liked best his speech on Snowden's amendment to the Address in 1913 of which Snowden speaks so favourably in his *Autobiography*. His best piece of work was 'in Parliament and in the country in widening the minds of the people for fair trade and more generous remuneration for the Worker.'

COURTHOPE,[355] Colonel Sir GEORGE LOYD, Bart., of Whiligh, Sussex. M.P. (C) Sussex (Rye) 1906–10, 1910, 1910–18, 1918–22, 1922–3, 1923–4, 1924–9, 1929–31, 1931–5, 1935.

B. 12 June 1877, s. and h. of George John[356] Courthope of the same (1848–1910)[357] and Elinor Sarah (d. 1895), da.[358] of Col. E. Loyd of Lillesden, Kent; m. 1899 Hilda Gertrude, da. of Maj. Gen. Henry Pelham Close;

Educ. Eton and Christ Church, Oxford. Called to the Bar, Inner Temple, 1901, but did not practise. Served in Volunteers or Territorials 1892–1934, and with the B.E.F. in Flanders 1915, – wounded,[359] M.C., despatches – afterwards commanding the 5th Royal Sussex and Kent & Sussex Terr. Infantry Brigade.[360]

Courthope wanted to be a soldier, but yielded to family tradition and went into Parliament. He was Evangelical, but tolerant of the views of others, and his favourite newspaper was *The Times*.

By some amazing change, Rye had 'gone radical' in 1904. It had to be won back, T.A. Brassey retired at the eleventh hour, and Courthope came in. That election cost £1,750,

---

[352] Altered by the subject from '1921'.

[353] 'both Parliament and' inserted by the subject.

[354] 'at a loss to himself' substituted by the subject for 'to the tune'.

[355] Written by JCW; corrected by the subject.

[356] Substituted by the subject for 'S.'.

[357] Father's vital dates inserted by the subject.

[358] 'and h.' deleted by the subject.

[359] Note by the subject: 'First attack by 1st Division on Aubers Ridge – 9 May 1915 – fractured skull'.

[360] 'and Kent & Sussex Terr. Infantry Brigade' substituted by the subject for 'till the end of the War.'.

but his annual expenses since have always been under £200. His income when he first stood was £670. Chamberlain was his ideal, protection for agriculture his policy. His share in establishing the British Beet Sugar industry was his best (!) piece of work; his proposing Fitzroy as Speaker, 2 Nov. 1931, his best speech. King George's Jubilee speech in Westminster Hall, the best he heard. He liked in Parliament 'the association with better brains than my own', and disliked 'the narrow and selfish views of some with whom contact was inevitable'. One knows, however, that his chief pride is that another Courthope after five centuries has again provided the oak trees for Westminster Hall.[361]

He answers in the House for the Forestry Commissioners and is an Ecclesiastical Commissioner too,[362] and we cannot give all his chairmanships, directorships, memberships and committees. Courthope of Rye was never the typical country squire nor the true Colonel Blimp, but just such another knight of the shire as Sussex has sent for seven hundred years. With them he took his place in the field and in the council chamber; the best of all the Courthopes of Rye.

CRAIG,[363] (RT. HON.) Sir James, Bart., D.L., M.P., (1871–19   ); Treasurer of Household 1916–18; Parl. Sec., Ministry of Pensions, 1919–20; Financial Sec. to Admiralty 1920–1; P.C. 1921; 1st Prime Minister of Northern Ireland 1921 and still so. Contested N. Fermanagh 1903; M.P. (Cons.) Down (East) 1906–10, 1910, 1910–18; Down (Mid.) 1918–21. M.P. in Northern Ireland Down 1921 and ever since. Viscount Craigavon of Stormont 1927 onwards. 1937, Knight of Grace of Order of St. John of Jerusalem.[364]

B. 8 Jan. 1871, 6th s. of James Craig of Craigavon and Tyrella, Co. Down (b. 1823 d. 1900)[365] by Eleanor Gilmour, da. of Robert Brown; m. Cecil Mary, da. and h. of Sir Daniel A.A. Tupper; 2 s., 1 da.

Educ. Merchiston; capt. 3rd R. Irish Rifles; served in S. African war 1900–2 with Imperial Yeomanry and Irish Horse; A.A. and Q.M.G. of the 36th (Ulster) Division 1914–15.

Everyone born in Ireland takes an interest in politics; he saw the risks confronting Ulster of Nationalist domination and separation from Great Britain.[366] Books form a small factor in a community where daily conversation turns on issues vital to Ulster Loyalists.[367] *The Times* was his chief medium in keeping in touch with public opinion and affairs further afield. 'In 1906 I succeeded in unseating an advanced Radical, and till 1920 represented my native country in the Imperial Parlt., since when North Down has

---

[361] JCW's note, taken from Courthope's questionnaire: 'I supplied the oak – c. 16,000 c.ft. – for the recent restoration of the Westminster Hall Roof after H.M. Office of Works had taken steps to protect me from penalty. The accounts of Richard II's reconstruction of the roof, which were found subsequently, record the purchase in 1394 "for the King, for his Hall of Westminster, of great oaks, from Courthope of Wadhurst", the owner of most of my present property and my direct ancestor. This Courthope appears to have been returned to Parliament in 1400 for the Cinque Port of Hastings. Some of the trees which I felled for this restoration were shown by their "annual rings" to be over 600 years old. They were therefore sturdy youngsters when their neighbours were felled to build the roof, to repair which they themselves were felled 5¼ centuries later'.

[362] 'and Ecclesiastical Commissioners alike' altered by the subject to 'and is an Ecclesiastical Commissioner too'.

[363] Written by JCW; corrected by the subject (and retyped for him).

[364] '1937, Knight of Grace of Order of St. John of Jerusalem' inserted by the subject.

[365] The subject has inserted his father's vital dates but omitted 'distiller' from Wedgwood's draft.

[366] 'and separation from Great Britain' inserted by the subject.

[367] 'Ulster Loyalists' substituted by the subject for 'Protestants'.

returned me unopposed to our local House of Commons at Stormont. Being a Peer of Great Britain is no bar under our constitution to election to the lower Chamber. My chief activities throughout have naturally been centred on Ulster's place in the United Kingdom and the British Empire and her internal interests and development. My ideal British Statesman is Stanley Baldwin,[368] was Lord Carson of Duncairn. To me the chief enjoyment of Parliamentary life was the indefinable "atmosphere" of the legislative chamber and the study of the psychology of its members, and what I disliked most was the wrench at leaving, on the passing of the Government of Ireland Act (1920) and my election to an office of profit under the Crown, i.e. first Prime Minister of Northern Ireland. The greatest speech to which I ever listened was that of Sir Edward Carson (as he then was), when he accepted the leadership of the Ulster Loyalists at the great Craigavon Demonstration in 1911. My best piece of work was persuading him to undertake that heavy responsibility.'

Craig always sat beside Carson on the 3rd seat above the gangway. Badinage with the Nationalists opposite was shared between him and William Moore. Craig, heavy, six-foot three, seldom smiled[369] (in public). He was on good terms, aside from politics, with his fellow-Irishmen.[370] He[371] was symbolical of black Ulster Protestantism. He was insepa- rable from Carson, but he himself had all the makings of an equally good leader. His friends and enemies knew ever where he stood. We used to rage and jest at what we thought was[372] his intolerance, but that was before the War and before the Government of Ireland Act, 1920.[373]

DALRYMPLE,[374] Hon. Sir HEW HAMILTON, K.C.V.O. Contested Wigtownshire 1885; M.P. (C) Wigtownshire 1915–18.

B. at Bargany, Ayrshire, 29 Sept.[375] 1857, 3rd s. of 10th Earl of Stair (John Hamilton Dalrymple K.T.) and Louisa de Coigny Hamilton, Countess of Stair.[376] Educ. Cheam School and Harrow; served in Militia Battn. Royal Scots Fusiliers, retiring as Hon. Lt. Col. in 1898. Captain in the Royal Company of Archers, King's Bodyguard for Scotland; Chairman of Board of Trustees for the National Galleries of Scotland; Vice-Chairman of National Library of Scotland; K.C.V.O. 1932; J.P. Ayrshire and D.L. and J.P. Wigtownshire.

Was Assistant Private Sec to Rt Honble Sir Henry Campbell-Bannerman when Sec of State for War 1886 till Government resigned.

---

[368] 'is Stanley Baldwin' inserted by the subject.

[369] 'seldom smiled' substituted by the subject for 'never smiled at all'.

[370] 'He was on good terms, aside from politics, with his fellow-Irishmen' substituted by the subject for 'nor ever condescended to speak to Catholic Irishmen'.

[371] The words 'even more than Carson' have been left out by the subject.

[372] 'what we thought was' inserted by the subject.

[373] 'but that was before the War and before the Government of Ireland Act, 1920' substituted by the subject for 'That was before the War. By 1937 a great many unpleasant matters have come to the forefront – cruelty, injustice, tyranny – which have made intolerance a virtue, and turned toleration into cowardice.'.

[374] Written by JCW, though his original text reproduced the very basic information given by Dalrymple in response to the questionnaire (Dalrymple wrote to him: 'I have filled in usual facts such as given in Whos Who or Kelly'). Wedgwood's request for further information was met by the corrections the subject made to his typed biography, and the notes added at the end.

[375] Day and month inserted by the subject.

[376] Father's and mother's names inserted by the subject.

I was 30 years on the County Council of Wigtownshire for some years Chairman. I entered Parliament for Wigtownshire 1915 because I was asked to do so.

I left because I did not wish to continue in Parliament, also my constituency Wigtownshire was united to Kirkcudbrightshire and now called Galloway. The member for Kirkcudbrightshire then became MP for Galloway.

DALRYMPLE,[377] Lt. Col. Viscount JOHN JAMES DALRYMPLE, M.P. (C) Wigtownshire 1906–10, 1910, 1910–14; Earl of Stair 1914.

B. 1 Feb. 1879, s. and h. of   11th Earl of Stair and Susan, da. of Sir James Grant Suttie, Bart.; m. 1904 Violet E., da. of Col. Harford; four s. two da. Educ Harrow and Sandhurst; entered Scots Guards 1898; served in S.A. War 1900–2.

'My own view of patriotism' was his politics; Salisbury and Chatham were his heroes. When he got in, one of half a dozen surviving Tories from Scotland, he was determined that the Whig dogs should not have the best of it, and his best piece of work was 'showing them that they were not quite omnipotent'. Naturally F.E. Smith's maiden speech was the best he heard. As for his own; – 'I have always so intensely disliked making speeches, that I have always been glad to forget them. I probably had the unique experience of being called by Deputy Chairman when I was feeling very ill, and had given up rising, on an occasion.' But he held other records: he voted in two divisions in one day, and in between went down to Hampshire, fished the Test, caught a 20lb salmon and cast it in the Members' cloak room while running up the stairs to catch the tale[378] of the division. Another record gave his colleagues more solid satisfaction as there was no bet on it. He went out with the Scots Guards to Zeebruge in Oct. 1914, and within the month he had taken 200 prisoners, was the first M.P. to win the D.S.O., and was himself taken prisoner by the Germans. He was at Crefeld two years, then interned in Switzerland,[379] and exchanged to England on Government parole, Sept. 1917. For the rest of the War he commanded the Reserve Battalion, Scots Guards, in London.

But he had long since become Earl of Stair and the House of Commons knew him no more. Fortunately Lord Turnour, his rival in the role of gadfly, might become Lord Winterton without leaving the proper field for their devastating tactics. Lord Stair lived[380] up to his earlier reputation by making his maiden speech in the Lords the day he took his seat. But now he is Chairman of a Milk-Marketing Board.

DARWIN,[381] Major LEONARD (1850–19   ). M.P. Staffs. (Lichfield) 1892–5 (Liberal-Unionist). Contested same 1895, 1896.

B. 15 Jan. 1850, 4th s. of Charles Darwin, F.R.S. (d. 1882)[382] by (his cousin) Emma (d. 1896),[383] da. of Josiah Wedgwood, M.P., of Etruria; m. (1) 1882 Elizabeth (d. 1898) da.

---

[377] Written by JCW; not corrected by the subject, and draft not returned.

[378] *Sic.*

[379] JCW note: 'Largely a mere matter of reprisal. He was the only Earl or M.P. whom the Germans had got, and he was 6′4″ tall; ideal for the triumphal procession which never came off'.

[380] 'and coh.' deleted by the subject.

[381] Writen by JCW; corrected by the subject.

[382] Date inserted by the subject.

[383] Date inserted by the subject.

of G.R. Fraser, (2) his cousin Charlotte Mildred, eld. da. of Edmund Langton and Emily Langton-Massingberd[384] of Gunby, Lincs. Educ. R.M.A. Woolwich; entered R.E. 1871; major 1889; retired 1890. On staff, Intelligence Dept., War Office, 1885–90.

Mill's *Political Economy*, read in 1874, made and has kept him a Free Trader. He was a Unionist from having visited Ireland in 1882 and from a dislike of surrender to crime. Sidgwick's *Methods of Ethics* influenced him on moral questions. His favourite paper, *The Times*, with reservations. Income on retirement from the army, £2000 a year. Having failed to get into the L.C.C., the Lib. Unionist Association enabled him to contest and win Lichfield by 4 votes (increased to 11 on a recount). This was a win against the tide. 'Perhaps the Duke of Devonshire was the nearest to my ideal as a statesman, chiefly because he never strove to be anyone's ideal. I also admired W.H. Smith. What I gained most by my short career in the House was the general interest which Parliament made me take in all national affairs. I wrote on Bimetallism in 1897, on Municipal Trading, 1903 and 1907 . . . Probably what I did in connection with the Parish Council Bills was my best work in Parliament.[385] The only other speech worth noting was when I seconded a motion which led Sir E. Grey to say on March 28, 1895, that the Government would regard the despatch of a French expedition to the Upper Nile as 'an unfriendly act.' 'When he (Grey) sat down, Mr. J. Chamberlain said to me that it was the most important statement he had ever heard made in the House.' 'I left Parliament because I was turned out by a brewer. He was turned out on petition, and when I stood for the third time I was severely defeated, having literally robbed a poor man of his beer.'

Major Darwin was President of the Eugenics[386] Society 1911–28, and wrote on the subject. The five brothers, William, Sir George, Sir Francis, Sir Horace,[387] and Leonard enjoyed to a remarkable degree culture, character and hereditary transmissible ability. Parliament was only a passing incident in the long and active life of Major Darwin. But it is fitting that a Darwin should have adorned Parliament.

DAVIES,[388] Ald. ELLIS WILLIAM, of Craig Wen, Caernarvon; solicitor. M.P. (Lib.) Carnarvon (Eifion) June 1906–10, 1910, 1910–18; contested 1918; Denbighshire 1923–4, 1924–9.

B. 12 Apr. 1871, s. of David Davies (son of William (Davies) Morgan who claimed descent from Henry VII through the Morgans of Penbryn, Cardigan)[389] quarry clerk of Bethesda and Catherine, da. of Ellis (Jones) Salmon.[390]

---

[384] 'and Emily Langton-Massingberd' inserted by the subject.

[385] 'in Parliament' inserted by the subject.

[386] 'Education' deleted by the subject.

[387] The subject has altered Charles to George, added Sir in front of Horace and placed William first.

[388] Written by the subject; edited by JCW (with considerable excisions); corrected by the subject. The text presented here is that of Wedgwood's draft, as corrected by the subject. The subject retyped the text, introducing further changes. These, where they are significant rather than merely stylistic, are presented in the footnotes.

[389] Davies has inserted 'son of William (Davies) Morgan . . . Cardigan' in the brackets left by Wedgwood for the vital dates of his father.

[390] Name of mother's father inserted by the subject.

m. 1901 Minnie, da. of Richard Hughes of Portmadoc; Educ. at Liverpool College; started as clerk in an insurance office; Solicitor in 1899 (First Class Honours, Law Society Prize);[391] on the County Council since 1903; alderman since 1907.

'In my childhood[392] I heard repeatedly of my grandfather's denunciation of the land laws, whilst my father,[393] a deacon[394] in the[395] Chapel was interested in the question of[396] Disestablishment.[397] Welsh politics then[398] consisted[399] entirely of the land and the Church. Social questions were little discussed, financial reform never. In 1899 I[400] settled in Caernarvon and[401] became the secretary of a Liberal Association.[402] In 1903 I was elected a Member of the County Council and[403] made Chairman of an Unemployed Committee. . . . when a vacancy occurred in the Southern Division of the county of Caernarvon I was elected unopposed in June 1906. My[404] expenses, including the Sheriff's fees, amounted to £120 – a considerable sum to a young solicitor – married with one child and earning all told about £600 a year.[405]

My first feeling in the House was one of great loneliness. My views – said to be socialistic as I advocated Old Age Pensions – did not make me a persona grata among my Welsh colleagues, particularly as Mr. Lloyd George had[406] exerted[407] his influence to prevent my selection as candidate as[408] I had[409] opposed him in his[410] campaign against the Education Act. The[411] new M.P.s had by June formed their friendships and coteries, and[412] I was struck by the remarkable ties – family, school, varsity, social – which

[391] 'Solicitor in 1899 (. . . Prize)' substituted by the subject for 'articled to a solicitor in 1894'.

[392] 'In my childhood' substituted by the subject for 'My mother Catherine Davies was the daughter of a small farmer who kept a large number of sheep on the commons. I was brought up hearing'.

[393] 'a quarry clerk,' deleted by the subject.

[394] 'and son of a deacon' deleted by the subject.

[395] 'Welsh Calvinistic' deleted by the subject.

[396] 'Welsh' deleted by the subject.

[397] Davies' retyped text omits all of the first sentence except the phrase 'In my childhood', which begins the next sentence.

[398] 'then' inserted by the subject.

[399] 'almost' deleted by the subject.

[400] 'In 1899 I' substituted by the subject for 'In 1899 I qualified as a solicitor and'.

[401] 'and' has been deleted by the subject in error. It is left here.

[402] 'and spoke at meetings' deleted by the subject. His retyped version also omits 'became the secretary of a Liberal Association'.

[403] 'was' deleted by the subject.

[404] 'My' substituted by the subject for 'As there was considerable opposition from prominent Liberals to my selection as candidate owing to what they called my Socialism, my'.

[405] Some text here intended by Wedgwood as a footnote is pasted over the text to which it was supposed to relate. The text gave a detailed account of Davies' expenses when first an MP (see p. 93 in Ch. 5). The text which it overlies reads: 'My maiden speech was made in July on the question of unemployment and the House was very friendly. I advocated work being found on the main roads which might in time of War become essential'. The footnote is included in the main text in Davies' retyped version.

[406] 'through his brother' deleted by the subject.

[407] 'all' deleted by the subject.

[408] 'as' inserted by the subject over the top of the full stop.

[409] 'publicly' deleted by the subject.

[410] 'Welsh' deleted by the subject.

[411] 'More than that,' deleted by the subject before 'The new M.P.s'.

[412] 'and' substituted by the subject for 'whilst'.

bound[413] Members of all parties.[414] I was outside all these, but I got friendly with the Land Taxers, Whitley, Trevelyan, Wedgwood, Chiozza Money and Charles Masterman,[415] whilst Sir Charles Dilke was helpful.[416] 'Sam' Evans, later the famous Admiralty Judge, gave me sound if cynical advice.[417]

In Jan. 1910 election expenses came to about £400 which my supporters paid. I was unopposed in Dec^r.

I was a member of a Joint committee on the Sale of Landed Estates presided over by Lord Haversham,[418] as I carried my proposals against the Chairman, I had to prepare the report.[419]

In 1912 Mr Lloyd George, then Chancellor, appointed me on[420] a private Committee 'The Land Enquiry', and with Richard Cross, Seebohm Rowntree and Charles Buxton [I] was responsible for the[421] report.

In 1913 I sat on the Juries Committee under Lord Mersey.[422]

During the War I favoured peace from 1916 and so earned Mr. Ll G's opposition but I acted on several committees one on[423] the acquisition of Land under Mr. Leslie Scott. In 1916 I sat on[424] [the] Franchise Committee under Speaker Lowther[425] and later on[426] the Second Chamber Conference under Lord Bryce.

In the 1918 Election the 'coupon' was given against me and I failed to get returned. I was elected for Denbigh in 1923.[427] Ill health kept me from the House during considerable periods between 1923 and 1929 when I retired, but I spoke often on the Land Question, on Foreign Affairs and[428] Taxation. I was on the Panel of Chairmen.[429]

My best speeches were on 25 Apr. 1928 on taxation and on 13th Nov. 1928 on Foreign Affairs.'[430]

---

[413] 'a large number of' deleted by the subject.

[414] 'together' deleted by the subject.

[415] 'Charles' inserted before 'Masterman', and 'and others' deleted by the subject.

[416] 'was helpful' substituted by the subject for 'was very kind and encouraging'. Davies' retyped text says 'through his Radical Group, though garrulous was helpful'.

[417] Sentence inserted by the subject. Another sentence is inserted in Davies' retyped text: 'In 1908 I joined Masterman and Wedgwood in criticising "Lulu" Harcourt's Small Holding Bill'.

[418] 'and' deleted by the subject.

[419] 'which was accepted and issued by the Committee.' deleted by the subject.

[420] 'appointed me on' substituted by the subject for 'formed' (he has also deleted the following sentence: 'I was made a member'.

[421] 'two volumes of' deleted by the subject.

[422] Sentence inserted by the subject.

[423] 'I favoured peace . . . one on' substituted by the subject for 'I acted on several committees, locally I presided over the Agricultural Production Committees, in London on the Committee for'.

[424] 'I sat on' substituted by the subject for 'I was appointed a member of the'.

[425] 'under Speaker Lowther' inserted by the subject.

[426] 'on' substituted by the subject for 'of'.

[427] 'In the 1918 . . . in 1923' inserted by the subject.

[428] 'Land' deleted by the subject.

[429] 'and presided over the Grand Committee when considering several Bills. I was also a Member of the Estimates Committee.' deleted by the subject.

[430] Davies has deleted Wedgwood's final sentence: 'So actually the little Welsh attorney fitted in very well – jammed uncomfortably between Wedgwood and Chiozza Money, with P.W. Wilson urging Christian toleration on individualist and collectivist alike'.

The ablest man in the House was A.J. Balfour while the best debater was Bonar Law, and the most persuasive speaker Mr. Lloyd George.[431]

DAVIES,[432] Sir WILLIAM REES, K.C. M.P. (Lib.) Pembrokeshire 1892–5, 1895–8.

B. 11 May 1863, s.[433] of Sir Wm. Davies, M.P., of Scoveston, Pembs.; m. (1) 1898 Florence B. (d. 1910) da. of John Birkett of Kendal, (2) 1913 Hilda K. da. of W.E. Blennerhassett Atthill of Faversham, Kent; 1 s. Wm. Rupert. Educ. Eton and Trinity Hall, Cambridge[434] (B.A.); called to the Bar, Inner Temple 1887; on South Wales Circuit; P.P.S. to Sir William Harcourt 1892–8.

He was 'cradled in Liberal politics' and took economics at Cambridge. He succeeded to his father's seat and came in 'tinged also with professional ambition' – and he did get Treasury briefs. As Harcourt's sole P.P.S. his life throughout those six years was strenuous.[435] 'Parliament has I think a mellowing effect, and although it may not affect materially the opinions of an individual, it encourages deference for the opinions of one's opponents.' He liked best 'the turmoil of a great party debate followed by a perilously small majority in the Division lobby'; and his best speech was on Welsh Disestablishment. The best he heard was Gladstone's introduction of his Second Home Rule Bill.

Then he took a Colonial Office appointment and retired. He was Attorney General, Bahamas, 1898–1902; King's Advocate, Cyprus; Attorney General, Hongkong; chief Justice, Hongkong, 1912–24. Knighted 1913.

Far more of these Colonial Office appointments should be filled from the House of Commons, for reasons which are both obvious and admirably exemplified by Sir Wm. Rees[436] Davies.

DICKINSON,[437] RT. HON. Sir WILLOUGHBY HYETT (1859–19   ); of Painswick, Glos., barrister. Contested Stepney 1895, N. St Pancras 1900; M.P. (Lib) N. St Pancras 1906–10, 1910, 1910–18; created Lord Dickinson (Nat[438] Lab) 1930 onwards.

B. 9 Apr. 1859, s. of Sebastian Stewart Dickinson of Stroud, Glos, M.P. (d. 1878), by Frances S. Hyett;[439] m. Minnie Eliz., da. of Gen. Sir Richard Meade; issue, Richard Sebastian (b. 1897, d. 1935) Desirée m. J.C. Butterwick,[440] and Joan, m. Rt. Hon. J.C.C Davidson M.P.

Educ., Eton and Trinity, Camb.; called to the Bar 1884; on L.C.C. 1889–1907, deputy chairman, and chairman 1899. Chairman of the London Liberal Federation 1900–8.

---

[431] Sentence inserted by the subject at the end of the retyped piece.

[432] Written by JCW; corrected by the subject.

[433] 'and h.' deleted by the subject.

[434] 'Cambridge' inserted by the subject.

[435] 'was strenuous' substituted by the subject for 'may be imagined'. Davies adds when returning the draft that 'although "I was Harcourt's sole P.P.S." his son Loulou was invariably with us in his Father's room at the H of C & we worked in Concert. This was of course before Loulou H became M.P. himself'.

[436] 'Rees' inserted by the subject.

[437] Written by JCW; corrected by the subject.

[438] Wedgwood wrote 'Lab'. The subject has inserted 'Nat' in front.

[439] Mother's name inserted by the subject.

[440] Son's death date and details of first daughter inserted by the subject.

On a large number of Royal Comns., and since 1915 he has been an inspirer of the League of Nations. P.C. 1914; K.B.E 1918. With two generations of Liberal M.P.s behind him, reading Mill and Charles Kingsley, with broad Church views, he was bound in those 1890's to take up public work. He had £2000 a year and was earning another £1000 at the Parliamentary Bar, which had to be given up on becoming M.P.; contested election expenses were usually c. £500.

'I admired Sir Henry Campbell-Bannerman most of all those whom I have known personally; because he was absolutely genuine. Parliament did not modify my views in any way except that my experience has led me to see how difficult it is to effect any reform in time for it to be effective. Parliamentary life interested me continually and when one is interested one is happy. In my view a vigorous election contest is most enjoyable and my contests have generally been free from disagreeable features such as occur at some elections. I do not say that I have liked being rejected; but even an unsuccessful election is pleasant if one feels that one is fighting for a good cause.' 'I never could speak well in the Commons. The mental atmosphere of the House is critical and my mind is very responsive to the occult influence of an audience. The greatest speeches I remember are: a speech by Mr. Bright in the Bingley Hall; a speech by Mr Gladstone at Birmingham; and one or two speeches by M. Briand at Geneva.' 'My most useful piece of work was in relation to the reform of the franchise in 1916–18 and in particular to Women's Suffrage. I did a good deal also in connection with international relations and matters affecting local government.' He was, of course, defeated in the Coupon election.'[441]

DUNCANNON,[442] VISCOUNT (VERE BRABAZON-PONSONBY), of Stansted, Hants.[443] P.C. Governor Gen. of Canada 1931–1935. Contested Carmarthen Boro' 1906; M.P. (Cons.) Cheltenham 1910; Dover 1913–20.[444] Earl of Bessborough 1920.

B. in London[445] 27 Oct. 1880, e.s. of 8th Earl of Bessborough (1851–1920) and Blanche Vere (d. 1919) da. of Sir John Guest, 1st Bart.; m. 1912 Roberte, da. of Baron Jean de Neuflize; 2s., 1 da.

Educ. Harrow and Trinity Camb. (B.A.); called to the Bar, Inner Temple 1903; Lieut., Bucks Yeomanry. He sat on the L.C.C. for Marylebone East 1907–10. He served with his

---

[441] The subject has deleted Wedgwood's last paragraph, which reads: 'Willoughby Dickinson was and is a handsome gentleman, of a nature too gentle and sensitive for the rage of party warfare. Most of us joke best and speak best but with our own sort and therefore in Parliament. On his very first day in Parliament, Willoughby was bludgeoned and trampled on by one of quite a different species. Joe Chamberlain, especially after the ruinous election, enjoyed "dressing down" an Etonian and one who would have embellished and ennobled politics was driven into a shell from which he never really emerged'. In a letter to Wedgwood enclosing the returned draft, Dickinson wrote: '<u>But please</u> omit the last paragraph. Joe Chamberlain's attack was offensive & uncalled for: but it is better left in oblivion. Moreover your inference is not quite correct, that episode had really little effect upon me – my lack of success in the House was due to the fact that I entered it when my party was in an immense majority and the constant waiting to be called upon, with the comitant disappointment at not being called upon, broke my parliamentary spirit and I took up outside interests, such as international questions et cetera'.

[442] Written by JCW; corrected by the subject.

[443] The subject has deleted 'and Bessborough, Kilkenny'.

[444] The subject has deleted 'contested Dover 1910' and changed 'Dover 1913–18, 1918–20' to 'Dover 1913–20'.

[445] 'In London' inserted by the subject.

Yeomanry in Gallipoli 1915,[446] and on the Staff in France 1916–18. Chevalier of the Legion of Honour, and many other foreign orders, C.M.G. 1919; G.C.M.G. 1931.

Chamberlain's tariff reform campaign launched him into politics, and to sit in the Commons was the 'normal career' and fortunately the normal duty of the eldest son of a peer; and he was an active, ever-present partisan, familiar to all on the front bench below the gangway. His church, the Church of England; his newspaper, *The Times*; his policy, the Empire. He liked 'the fact of belonging to the most interesting and perhaps the most influential assembly in the world'; disliked 'having to spend so many hours daily unable to concentrate on other matters owing to having to wait for the Division Bell to ring.' The Guests[447] are his cousins, and for every reason he governed Canada in succession to Lord Willingdon.

DU PRE,[448] Lt. Col. WILLIAM BARING (1875–   ); of Wilton Park, Beaconsfield,[449] Bucks. Contested Loughboro'[450] 1906; M.P. (Cons.) Bucks. (Wycombe) 1914–18, 1918–22, 1922–3.

B. 5 Apr. 1875, eld. s. of James Du Pre (1846–82) by Selina daughter of the late Richard Stokoe M.D.[451] and gt. nephew and h. of George Du Pre, M.P.; m. 1903 Youri, da. and h. of Capt. H. Townley Wright, R.N.; 3 das. Educ. Winchester and Sandhurst. Lieut. K.R.R., Lieut. Imperial Yeomanry in S.A. War (medal and 3 clasps). In Great War (1914–18); Lt. Col. R.H.A. Sheriff, Bucks., 1911–12.

Labouchere was his father's 1st cousin, but his family was Conservative and his political education was *Punch* and *The Times*. He read Spencer's *First Principles* at 23 and since then was probably agnostic – certainly not a 'dogmatic' Christian. He entered Parliament – 'to justify my existence, the desire for public service or family tradition,' and had the income for it – £5000 to £6000 a year. When Sir Alfred Cripps was made Lord Parmoor in Jan.1914, Du Pre as a local landowner and politically known, got the nomination in competition with Coningsby Disraeli. He was elected on Home Rule and as a thorough follower of Joseph Chamberlain. All contests cost about £1500, and probably £1000 a year. Oddly enough Asquith was something of his living ideal statesman, Abraham Lincoln among the dead. 'I liked the *work* of the House, and was not given enough to do, but I disliked constituency work.' The best speech he heard was Grey's on the outbreak of war; his own best on the Slough dump (1920). His best work was in the War. He lost his seat in 1923 to Lady Terrington, and that settled it.

Du Pre was the excellent type of educated soldier who has over and over again combined soldiering, politics and traditional responsibility. Obviously he ought to have been made an Indian or Colonial governor.[452]

---

[446] 'surviving Suvla Bay,' deleted by the subject.

[447] 'and the Churchills' deleted by the subject. Bessborough's letter of 2 Mar. 1937 returning the corrected draft says: 'The Churchills and my family are both cousins of the Guests, but we are not related. This excision I am afraid rather spoils your last sentence'.

[448] Written by JCW; corrected by the subject.

[449] Address corrected by the subject from 'Wilton, Bucks'.

[450] Amended by the subject from 'Leics. (Loughborough)'.

[451] Details of mother inserted by the subject.

[452] Returning the draft, Du Pre wrote: 'It is almost uncanny that you should have named my own private ambition: a Colonial governorship!'

ESSEX,[453] Sir RICHARD WALTER (1857–19); of Bourton-on-the-Water, Glos.[454] Contested Kennington 1900 M.P. (Lib.) Glos. (Cirencester) 1906–10; Stafford 1910–18; Contested Burslem 1918.

B. 13 Jan. 1857, eld. s. of John Essex ( ), of by. m. (1) 1881 Marie (d. 1883) da. of Jas. Chinchen of Swanage, (2) 1885 Lizzie, da. of John Benson of Newcastle-on-Tyne; four children.

His father was a disciple of and a voter for J.S. Mill, and he learnt from him, and read the Daily News. He was educated mostly at home, and entered business early in life, being chiefly concerned with wall paper printing. He became active in municipal affairs in Wandsworth. Being an admirer of Gladstone and Bright, with freedom as his lodestar, he stood for Parliament in 1900. Then, by dint of much speaking, largely in the chapels, he got elected for Cirencester. Kntd. 1913.

Sir Walter Essex was a speaker of the confident, fluent order, admirably adapted for the platform, and a good Liberal of the old John Bright school. Born and bred in the chapel, he was more interested in politics than in his business (which was ultimately absorbed in Wall-paper Manufacturers Ltd.), but the Whips thought of him as more business-man than politician. Sturdy, loyal, and seeing but one side of any question.

FORTESCUE-FLANNERY,[455] Sir JAMES, Kt. and Bart. (1851–19); of Wethers-field, Essex. Consulting Engineer, M.I.C.E. M.P. (Union.) Yorks. (Shipley) 1895–1900, 1900–06; and Essex (Maldon)[456] 1910, 1910–18, 1918–22.

B. at Liverpool 16 Dec. 1851, eld. s. of Capt. John Flannery of Seacombe;[457] m. 1882,   da. of Osborne Jenkyn; issue Harold Fortescue, two das. Educ. L'pool School of Science; apprentice[458] at Britannia Engine Works, Birkenhead; inspecting Engineer under Sir E.J. Reed, M.P., and acquired a large practice as Consulting Engineer.

He was taught by his mother, a devout Scottish Presbyterian, and picked up a liking for politics in his engineering workshops, reading the L'pool Daily Post. He became J.P. of London and Surrey and placed his name for a candidature before the Liberal Unionist Party Organisation. His chief, Sir Edward Reed, had made a success of Parliament, improving his standing in the profession; probably Flannery meant to do the same. The election cost him near £2000 and a yearly £500. Like Reed he pressed for a strong Navy; and like Reed, the seat and work in Parliament helped him in his profession of consulting engineer and naval architect.

'My ideal living British Statesmen were Joseph Chamberlain and Lord Hartington. I enjoyed most in Parliament the fraternal spirit which permeated all ranks and all parties.' Grey's was the greatest speech he heard; his best work getting for the Engineers of the Navy executive rank and powers. He was kntd. 1899; baronet 1904; retired from the House of Commons[459] in 1922, finding the work too heavy at 70.

---

[453] Written by JCW; sent to the subject, but corrected and retyped by his daughter, as Essex was 'too ill to attend to any matters of business'. Her version omits some of the text, especially the last two sentences.

[454] The daughter's version adds 'North Drive, Streatham'.

[455] Written by JCW; corrected by the subject.

[456] 'and Essex (Maldon)' inserted by the subject.

[457] The subject has written 'Elizabeth' in the space left for mother's details, and then deleted it.

[458] 'apprentice' substituted by the subject for 'pupil'.

[459] 'from the House of Commons' inserted by the subject.

As a politician he was[460] conspicuous; chiefly as advocating a strong British Navy[461] and[462] as an engineer entirely successful; and, with those two facts[463] in view, this typical Liverpool citizen certainly made a success of his 24 years in Parliament.

FREEMAN–THOMAS,[464] (RT. HON.) FREEMAN (1866–19   ); of Ratton. Junior Ld. of Treasury 1905–06; Governor of Bombay 1913–19; Governor of Madras 1919–24; Governor Gen. of Canada 1926–31; Viceroy of India 1931–6. Warden of Cinque Ports 1936–. M.P. (Lib.) Hastings 1900–05; Cornwall (Bodmin) 1906–10. Lord Willingdon 1910; Viscount 1924; Earl 1931; Marquess of Willingdon 1936 onwards.

B. 12 Sept. 1866, s. of Frederick Freeman-Thomas (18   –1868) and Mabel, da. of Speaker Brand, 1st Visct. Hampden; m. 1892 Marie Adelaide, da. of 1st Earl Brassey (q.v.); issue one surv. s. Visct. Rattendone. Educ. Eton and Trinity College, Camb.,[465] being captain at cricket of Eton XI & played for 4 years in Cambridge XI.[466] He grew up under the influence of his mother and her father the Speaker, both Liberals; got on to the East Sussex C.C.; then A.D.C. to his father-in-law when Governor of Victoria 1895–8. He won Hastings in 1900 and lost it in 1906, – a reversal of the obvious; but got in again in 1906 for Bodmin.

He was low Church, preferred the Westminster Gazette and rarely spoke 'either from modesty, shyness or the feeling that during a debate others had made the points I wanted to make much better than I could, and therefore I was considered better fitted to help in the organisation of the party and on this I concentrated more than anything else. I was never a good Parliamentarian, for I was always too much inclined to see the other side's point of view.' What he liked in the life were the many advantages gained from constant association with fellow members of all types, classes and conditions.

Few in history rise from squire to marquess; fewer still do it to the complete satisfaction of conscience and of friends. Some governors save money out of their salaries; this he never did, and therefore he is still 'a comparatively poor man which has been and is good for me.' He made a good governor for other reasons. A certain patriotism and loyalty to his training put him outside ambition and career, free also from fear of masters or of ruin. It does not matter that other governors save their salaries. What does matter is that they too often fear. So we differ over his best piece of work. He thinks his Viceroyalty ending in peace; others think it was his governorship of Bombay during the War. England was ill served then in India by all but him, as is set out in the Mesopotamia Commission's Report. Yet Lord Willingdon was not an exceptional member of Parliament. Others might do as well. He has had luck; and above all, there has ever been Lady Willingdon, Tom Brassey's daughter, driving him on.

---

[460] 'not' deleted by the subject.

[461] 'chiefly as advocating a strong British Navy' inserted by the subject.

[462] 'and' substituted for 'but' by the subject.

[463] 'those two facts' substituted for 'that' by the subject.

[464] Written by JCW; corrected by the subject.

[465] 'Trinity College, Camb.,' inserted by the subject.

[466] 'at cricket . . . Cambridge XI' substituted by the subject for 'both cricket elevens'.

GELDER,[467] Sir (WILLIAM) ALFRED; alderman of Hull, architect and surveyor. M.P. (Lib.) Lincs. (Brigg) 1910, 1910–18; contested 1918.

<u>B</u>. 12 May 1855, s. of Wm. Gelder of North Cave, Yorks. and . <u>m</u>. 1877 Elizabeth (<u>d</u>. 1934), da. of Thos. Parker of Hull; two s., one da.

He took politics like religion from his father and mother 'based upon the teaching contained in the New Testament.' He had been on the Hull School Board, becoming Chairman of the Hull Education Committee; on the Hull Corporation, alderman 37 years, mayor 1899–1903 (five years); kntd. 1903; Chairman of the Licensing Bench 25 years. He originated and carried through large schemes of public improvement with profit to the rate-payer for which he received the Honorary Freedom of the City. Hull has always been represented by, and happy in, its aldermen.

Each election cost him over £1000 and about £750 a year during the nine years he represented the Brigg Division in Parliament 'without having assistance from any party or public funds.' Parliamentary life did not appeal to him although he made many friends; he objected to platitudes and time-wasting by faddists and extremists of all parties. His best work was in municipal life. 'The ordinary M.P. has very little chance to make any impression for good when he starts his career at 55. To be of real effective service a man should enter Parliament at an early period of life and also be prepared to devote the whole of his time to the very necessary work in connection with the Nation's affairs.' Of course he did not get the coupon and was defeated in 1918. Alderman Gelder fits well into Miss Holtby's '*South Riding*'. It is a pity that Government and Party machine failed to use him at Westminster; and he is an outstanding case for reform in the direction of Committee rule on French lines.

GILES,[468] (Sir) CHARLES TYRRELL, of Wimbledon. K.C. M.P. (C) Cambs. (Wisbeach) 1895–1900; contested Wisbeach 1900; Southampton Jan. 1910.

<u>B</u>. 2 Feb. 1850, son of Alfred Giles, M.P. Southampton, and . <u>m</u>. 1881 Isa Mary, da. of Jeremiah Colman of Carshalton; 1s. 1da. Educ. Harrow and King's College, Cambridge

My father[469] was elected for Southampton in 1878.[470] I was called to the Bar in 1874. After his defeat in 1880, I took up politics to help him, and acted as his Election[471] Agent (*gratis*) in 1883 at a bye-election. He was elected unopposed. Upon the passing of the Corrupt and Illegal Practices Act of 1883 I edited[472] the third edition of Cunningham on Elections.[473] So I became competent to advise him and his colleague, Admiral

---

[467] Written by JCW; reviewed by the subject, but not corrected.

[468] Written by the subject, with details in heading added by JCW; edited and corrected by the subject (who has written at the end: 'My dear Sir, Is this reduced enough?').

[469] 'My father' substituted by the subject for 'The Crimean War started my interest in national politics and that interest was increased by a love of history and geography, in both of which I was proficient as a boy and at my degree. I was also influenced by my Father. He'.

[470] 'I was always on more intimate terms with him than my elder brothers, especially after' deleted by the subject.

[471] 'Election' substituted for 'Parliamentary' by the subject.

[472] 'I edited' substituted for 'I undertook the serious labour of editing' by the subject.

[473] 'principally to protect him' deleted by the subject.

Commerel, V.C., and did so throughout the General Elections of 1885 and 1886. We were successful at both.[474]

In 1888 I reorganised the Wimbledon Association at the request of[475] Cosmo Bonsor M.P., and assisted it acting as Chairman & President for over fifty years.[476] My father[477] died on the 3rd March 1895, aged 79, I was then free[478] and agreed to contest North Cambridgeshire on 5th April. I was elected on the 17th July, defeating Arthur Brand, a Liberal Whip. I think the contest cost me about £600 and each year about £500. I did not receive anything from Headquarters but the Duke of Bedford and Lord de Ramsey were good supporters to my Conservative Association and personal friends. In Sept. 1900 our local Chief[479] Agent was very ill and I was told his chance would be improved if I could relieve his mind of anxiety about election matters. I did my best at his bedside, but he died, and three weeks after his death the general election of 1900 came on. Chaos resulted;[480] I was defeated.

While in Parliament my chief interest was Agriculture and[481] my best speech was on the Agricultural Rating Bill of 1896. Before entering Parliament I had some practice at the Parliamentary Bar. This I lost when in Parliament and never recovered. I think my best work was in starting[482] a Bill to extend the Workmen's Compensation Act to agricultural labourers. It became the Workmen's Compensation Act of 1900.

Lord Salisbury was my ideal statesman, but the speech that made most impression on me in my long lifetime was Disraeli's in announcing that Queen Victoria's title should be Empress of India!

As a small boy when assisting at chaff cutting my left hand was nearly cut off. This caused Capt. Pretyman and me to introduce a Bill to protect workers from injury.[483] Our Bill became the Chaff-Cutting Machines (Accident) Act, 1897.

GOLDSTONE,[484] (Sir) FRANK WALTER (1870–19   ); school-teacher. M.P. Lab: Sunderland 1910–18. Contested 1918.

B. 7 Dec. 1870; s. of Thos. F. Goldstone (Sunderland)[485] stained glass artist, by Sarah Trigg (née Blott) of Cambridgeshire.[486] m. 1895 Eliz. Alice, da. of Luke Henderson of

---

[474] 'for which I earned sincere expressions of gratitude from Admiral Commerel' deleted by the subject.

[475] 'at the request of' substituted for 'for'.

[476] 'assisted it . . . for over fifty years' substituted for 'acted as Chairman for very many years' by the subject. He has also deleted the following sentence: 'I think my activities had been noted by the Conservative Association so that I had feelers to become a candidate, but I declared that I was not free during my old father's lifetime'.

[477] 'My father' substituted by the subject for 'He'.

[478] 'I was then free' substituted by the subject for 'and I was invited to'.

[479] 'Chief' inserted by the subject.

[480] 'many of my supporters never got to the poll' deleted by the subject.

[481] 'I think' deleted by the subject.

[482] 'and advocating amongst Agriculturist M.P.s the introduction of' deleted by the subject.

[483] 'protect workers from injury' substituted for 'prevent the frequent maimings that took place in the country'.

[484] Written by JCW; corrected by the subject.

[485] '(Sunderland)' inserted by the subject.

[486] Mother's name inserted by the subject.

Whittingham, Nhd.; one s., one da. Educ Sunderland Council School and Borough Rd. College, Isleworth. Schoolmaster at Sheffield.

He was a Congregationalist, and friendship with other young schoolmasters at and after college gave him political views generously based on Gladstone, Blatchford, Henry George, Ruskin, Dickens and the 'Clarion'. The Executive of the National Union of Teachers decided to put up a candidate to succeed Macnamara (*q.v.*)[487] and selected Goldstone, who found for himself the seat at Sunderland. He was getting £360 a year and the N.U.T. paid election expenses £810 (1910), £1012 (1918).[488] Parliament increased his earning capacity, but he was disillusioned as to the date of the millenium[489] and the stupidity of opponents. Only Goldstone would have 'enjoyed most the successful speeches of my political friends' not to mention 'the daily meetings of the Executive of the Party'.

He concentrated on education. Being a Whip, he was somewhat hampered, but his best speech was his second on the Holmes Circular in 1911. Asquith's on the death of Arthur Lyttelton was the best he remembers hearing. He says his best work was as Chairman of the Party's Education Committee, and membership of the Departmental Committee on whose report the 1918 Education Act was based. Not getting the 'coupon' he was defeated in 1918.

Goldstone served[490] on a Royal Comn. (1929) and was made[491] a knight (1931).[492] The idea that 'our lower orders' are dangerous is an illusion.

GOOCH,[493] George Peabody (1873–19   ); historian. M.P. Bath 1906–10. Contested Bath twice (1910); Reading 1913.

B. in London 1873, 3rd s. of Chas. Cubitt Gooch (b.1811–d. 1889)[494] and Mary, da. of Rev. Edmund[495] Blake; m. 1903 Else, da. of Julius[496] Schön of Berlin.[497] 2[498] sons.

Educ. Eton,[499] King's Coll., London, and Trinity, Camb., M.A.; studied in Berlin and Paris. His family was Conservative, and he became a Liberal at Cambridge. 'Strongly influenced as a boy by Burke *Reflections on the French Revolution* and Mill *On Liberty*. Carlyle's gospel of the superman influenced me for a year or two but no more. The Whig presentation of English history by Hallam and Macaulay left a much deeper mark.' He was 'brought up as a Church-going Anglican, with family prayers. About the age of

[487] There is no biography of Macnamara.
[488] 'and £250 to £600 a year for the organisation' deleted by the subject.
[489] *Sic.*
[490] 'Goldstone served' substituted by the subject for 'If Goldstone had been Goldstein, he would now be in a concentration camp. But they put "Sunderland"'. Goldstone wrote in a letter to Wedgwood of 3 Feb. 1937, returning the draft, that 'The "Goldstein" par. did not appeal to me & hence I have ventured to make it less picturesque. Not that I have any objection to "tilts" at Germany'.
[491] 'was made' substituted by the subject for 'they made'.
[492] 'and a pillar of the state' deleted by the subject.
[493] Written by JCW; corrected by the subject.
[494] Father's vital dates inserted by the subject.
[495] 'Rev. Edmund' inserted by the subject.
[496] 'Julius' inserted by the subject.
[497] 'Berlin' inserted by the subject.
[498] '2' inserted by the subject.
[499] 'Eton' inserted by the subject.

17 ceased to be orthodox. A little later greatly impressed by Kant and Hegel and Spinoza.' His politics developed 'owing to my increasing dislike of what was called by its critics imperialism, embodied in Chamberlain, Rhodes, Milner, Kipling. I never thought of Parliament till the South African War, which stirred me to the depths. It was not a career, but only an opportunity of opposing what I disliked.'

His chief[500] interests were in Foreign Affairs and Housing. He had done much social and teaching work in the University settlements in London,[501] and got his candidature at Bath through the Eighty Club. The first election cost £700. Yearly expenses were small. In the House he was P.P.S. to Mr Bryce, the Chief Sec. for Ireland, 1905–7,[502] then specialised in Foreign Affairs. Gladstone and Lincoln in the past, Campbell-Bannerman and Lloyd George in the present attracted him most.[503] 'My belief in democratic institutions was, if possible, strengthened by my Parliamentary[504] experience.'[505] Lloyd George's Budget speech (1909) was the most historic utterance[506] he heard.

His *History of Modern Europe 1878–1919* & his *History & Historians in the Nineteenth Century*[507] are his best-known books; his work as Joint Editor of[508] *British Documents on the Origins of the War 1898–1914* may be his most important contribution to knowledge. But thirteen[509] other histories stand to his name. He was President of the Historical Association, 1922–5; President of the National Peace Council 1933–6;[510] and is President of the English Goethe Society.

Gooch, last of the Liberals of the school of Mill, was an admirable member of Parliament, crammed with knowledge, yet simple and single-minded; an example to us all.[511] But it is not for his short service in the House, nor even for his historical work, that Gooch will be chiefly remembered. His friends have for him the same sort of devotion that they have for Lord Robert Cecil. For, more even than Cecil, he has the courage of a martyr in the cause which he thinks right.

GOOCH,[512] (Sir) HENRY CUBITT (1871–19   ); Ald. Of London C.C. M.P. (Union:) Peckham   1908–10.

[500] 'chief' inserted by the subject.

[501] Wedgwood has a footnote indicator here: the footnote reads: 'Probably he was related to Peabody'. Gooch has deleted both. In his letter returning the draft, dated 4 Feb. 1937, he writes:'I was called after George Peabody (though no relation) because my father was in his business, & later a junior partner in the firm of J.S. Morgan which continued the work under another name'.

[502] '1906' corrected to '1905' by the subject.

[503] 'attracted him most' substituted by the subject for 'were his conception of the best statesmen'.

[504] 'my Parliamentary' inserted by the subject.

[505] 'He liked getting to know the leading actors,' deleted by the subject.

[506] 'most historic utterance' substituted by the subject for 'best'. (In his questionnaire, Gooch had identified this speech as his answer to question 21, but added that 'as it was bad, perhaps it hardly qualifies'.

[507] '& his *History & Historians in the Nineteenth Century* are his' substituted by the subject for 'is his'.

[508] 'as Joint Editor of' substituted by the subject for 'on'.

[509] 'thirteen' substituted by the subject for 'fourteen'.

[510] '1933–6' inserted by the subject.

[511] Wedgwood's note:'Perhaps not in the matter of dress.We see him still in a black frock coat, brown shoes and a bowler hat, with his head up in the air'.

[512] Written by JCW; corrected by the subject.

B. 7 Dec. 1871, 2nd s. of Chas. Cubitt Gooch (   ) by Mary, da. of Rev. E. H.[513] Blake; m. 1897, Maud Mary, da. of Rev. J.H. Hudleston of Cayton Hall,[514] nr. Harrogate; two s., one da.

Educ., Eton and Trinity (B.A., LL.B. Honours);[515] called to Bar; studied abroad 1895–6. London School Board 1897–1904; member of Burnham Education Coms. On the L.C.C. 1907–10 and 1914–34; ald. 1914–19; Chairman L.C.C Education Com.; Vice-Chairman of L.C.C 1922–3; Chairman 1923–4; President of Cambridge House; kntd. 1928. J.P. 1906.[516]

His public life was educational and municipal; Parliament was only a short interlude; and he did not practise at the Bar. He worked entirely in[517] London. 'I took up this sort of work as I desired to do[518] public & social work.[519] At no time did any book influence[520] my political views; which resulted somewhat naturally from my general outlook & were confirmed by experience.[521] By religion I was a moderate Anglican. I was not interested in the political side of any book or[522] newspaper, (finding the best guidance in varied &[523] prolonged actual administration and the advice & example[524] of experienced friends); but the correspondence in the "Times" and the cartoons in "Punch" were helpful. I had done social work for over[525] twenty years in a poor parish in[526] Peckham when I was first elected M.P. I was chiefly interested in Education in Parliament, and elsewhere. I did not enjoy making or hearing speeches; nor electioneering which was merely a means to an end.[527] My short Parliamentary life was only a brief & happy[528] interlude in a long municipal career; and apart from the universal kindness which I received, did not really attract me. So I returned in January 1911 to my municipal life, – with its human contacts & varied personal administration.'[529]

Nevertheless he has been a good supporter of this History and is a fine example of a very practical[530] form of public service. Ever since the L.C.C. started, the close[531]

---

[513] 'Rev. E.H.' inserted by the subject.

[514] 'Cayton Hall' inserted by the subject.

[515] 'Honours' inserted by the subject.

[516] 'J.P. 1906' inserted by the subject.

[517] 'entirely in' substituted by the subject for 'almost entirely for'.

[518] 'do' substituted by the subject for 'enter'.

[519] 'public & social work' substituted by the subject for 'public life'.

[520] 'influence' substituted by the subject for 'form'.

[521] '& were confirmed by experience' inserted by the subject.

[522] 'book or' inserted by the subject.

[523] 'varied &' inserted by the subject.

[524] '& example' inserted by the subject.

[525] 'over' substituted by the subject for 'some'.

[526] 'a poor parish in' inserted by the subject.

[527] 'which was merely a means to an end' inserted by the subject.

[528] '& happy' inserted by the subject.

[529] 'with its human contacts & varied personal administration.'" inserted by the subject.

[530] 'very practical' substituted by the subject for 'less showy'.

[531] 'and overlapping' deleted by the subject.

association between the Council and Parliament has tended to benefit[532] both Chambers.[533]

GREEN,[534] WALFORD DAVIS, of Bishopsteignton, Devon. Barrister. M.P. (C) Wednesbury 1895–1900, 1900–05.

B. 24 Aug. 1869, s. and h. of Rev. Walford Green, D.D., Pres. Wesleyan Conference, ( ) and   ; m. Annie da. Of C.E. Carpenter; two das.

Educ., Leys and King's, Camb. (M.A.); called to the Bar, Inner Temple.

He began by being a Home Ruler at school, reading political history and Disraeli's and Trollope's novels. Seeley's books and Maine's *Ancient Law* directed his politics with Arthur Balfour as the ideal and the *Standard* for news. He wrote books on Chatham and George Canning; was broadly Christian, and ambition had something to do with sending him to Parliament. Each election cost £2,000 and £250 a year; and his income then was only £800 a year. Empire, Education, Housing, these were his interests, but he tended to deal only with Education. Parliament disillusioned him as to all ideals and he hated the interminable letter writing. The last hour of the great debates pleased him best, and he remembers being impressed by Chamberlain's defence of his South African policy. Ill health led to his retirement.

GRIFFITH-BOSCAWEN,[535] RT. HON. Sir ARTHUR SACKVILLE TREVOR (1865–19). Parl. Sec. Ministry of Pensions 1916–19; to the Ministry of Agriculture 1919–21; Minister of Agriculture 1921–2; Minister of Health 1922–3. M.P. Unionist KENT (Tonbridge) 1892–5, 1895–1900, 1900–5; Dudley 1910–18; 1918–21; SOMERSET (Taunton) 1921–2. Contested Taunton 1922; Mitcham 1923.[536]

B. near Wrexham, 18 Oct. 1865; 2nd s. of Capt. Griffith-Boscawen (b. 1835[537]–d.) and Helen Sophia, eld. da. of Admiral[538] Norwich Duff; m. (1) 1892 Edith Sarah (d. 1919) da. of S Williams of Boons Park, Kent; (2) 1921 Phyllis Maud da. of Wm. Dereham of Rawdon Hall, Holyport Berks;[539] one da. Penelope b. 1922.[540]

Educ. Rugby and Queen's Coll., Oxford, (M.A. President of Union 1888). First Class honours in Final Classical School.[541] He was Conservative at debates at Rugby and

[532] 'tended to benefit' substituted by the subject for 'increasingly benefited'.

[533] The last sentence of Wedgwood's version has been deleted by the subject. It read: 'Consequently the L.C.C., unlike other City Councils, is developing a Ministry on Parliamentary lines, though as yet Department Committees have not yet arrived to trouble Ministers in Parliament'. Gooch has written 'no' beside this, and in his letter of 1 Feb. 1937, returning the draft, he wrote: 'The last sentence does not I believe represent actuality, as I have seen it from the chair of L.C.C. Committees. The L.C.C. Chairman of Ctes conducts his Dept. from the chair at weekly – fortnightly etc. meetings; wh. all is discussed by his Committee, with the presence of the L.C.C. staff. The Chairman of a Cte is therefore I believe quite different from a Minister, resembles any other Chairman of any big municipality's Ctes. The Chairman of the whole L.C.C. stands outside politics during his Chairmanship, & took no part in administration'.

[534] Written by JCW; not corrected by the subject (note on file says 'draft not returned').

[535] Written by JCW; corrected by the subject.

[536] 'Taunton' and 'Mitcham' inserted by the subject.

[537] Father's birth date corrected by the subject.

[538] 'Admiral' inserted by the subject.

[539] Father-in-law's address inserted by the subject.

[540] Daughter's details inserted by the subject.

[541] Sentence inserted by the subject.

Oxford, for he was always a strong Anglican, inspired by *Sybil* and the 'Standard'. Chamberlain, living, and Disraeli, dead, were his ideal statesmen. His ambition was to get into the House and his father assisted though doubtful of the wisdom of such a career.[542] In 1890 the Tonbridge division was without a local candidate, being shaky, and a friend got him adopted. He was elected on Church Defence, Protection and Disraelian Imperialism. (His elections cost him £1200 to £1500 and £400 to £500 a year). Once in Parliament, in opposition he enjoyed the life; less so when his party was in power though he was P.P.S. to the Chancellor (Sir M. Hicks-Beach)[543] 1895–1900. 'The House of Commons inevitably broadens one's views. It is the greatest education in the world. Though remaining a strong Tory, Church and State man and Imperialist, I became more and more interested in "social reform" – and I learned to respect my opponents, among whom I had many personal friends.'

The greatest speech he heard was Gladstone introducing Home Rule in 1893, 'after which I was a Home Ruler for 10 minutes until Sir Edward Clarke's wonderful reply.' Sometimes speeches did convince him, as Sir H. Fowler on the Indian Cotton Duties in 1894. So his best work was his Housing bill of 1912[544] 'in which I proposed the principles of State aid for housing and slum clearing, since adopted by all parties.' His own best speech he reckons one, made right at the end as Minister of Agriculture, against the introduction of Canadian Store cattle. And then for that the Daily Express and Dudley[545] rejected him, and Taunton &[546] Mitcham too in 1923, and an intelligent, hard-working Parliamentary career of thirty years came to an untimely end.[547] He has done much since, for the Church and for Transport, but never more surrounded with the friendly atmosphere of his old House of Commons. 'But I have been fortunate in other ways &[548] am happy and contented', which makes a good curtain.

GUEST,[549] (Capt. Rt.Hon.) FREDERICK EDWARD; Treasurer of the Household, 1912–15; Chief Whip 1917–21; Secretary of State for Air 1921–2. Contested King's Swinford 1905; Cockermouth 1906; Brigg 1907; M.P. (L) Dorset (East) 1911–18, 1918–22; contested 1922; M.P. Glos. (Stroud) 1923–4; Bristol North 1924–9; contested 1929; Plymouth (Drake) (C) 1931–5, 1935.

B. 14 June 1875, 3rd s. of 1st Lord Wimborne (q. v.); m. 1905 Amy, da. of Henry Phipps of U.S.A.; two s., one da. Entered 1st Life Guards and served White Nile 1900 (despatches), South Africa 1901–2; Great War (A.D.C. to Gen. French 1914–16); in East Africa 1916–17 (despatches twice, D.S.O.) returning home to become Chief Whip.

The Guest politics came from Lady Wimborne. In 1900 his brother Ivor was elected for Plymouth. His newspaper was the 'Sportsman', and 'after ten years of soldiering, travelling and racing I thought it time to become a serious citizen – all my family had

[542] 'though doubtful . . . such a career' inserted by the subject.
[543] Chancellor's name inserted by the subject.
[544] '1912' substituted by the subject for '1911 (or 1912)'.
[545] '(or Taunton)' deleted by the subject.
[546] 'Taunton &' inserted by the subject.
[547] 'came to an untimely end' substituted by the subject for 'closed in disaster'.
[548] 'But I have been fortunate in other ways &' substituted by the subject for 'I'.
[549] Written by JCW; corrected by the subject.

been politicians. My grandfather had been Free Trade M.P. for Myrthr Tydvil – my uncle Randolf[550] Churchill had been Chancellor of the Exchequer – my Father fought Bristol twice – my Mother was a born politician.' So the Bimbashi of the Egyptian Cavalry, with an hereditary weakness for Free Trade, was pushed into Parliament by Churchill and became his P.P.S. East Dorset cost £1,700 and £600 a year. Asquith was his ideal – or Pitt, in the past. But he enjoyed the good fellowship amongst all parties and deliberately set himself to understand M.P.s and procedure so that he might become a Whip. In that he succeeded and it was his only political ambition.[551]

During the War, in the intervals of Flanders and East Africa, he forced the conscription issue to the front by dining the right people. The Other Club, fashioned by Churchill and F.E. Smith, was run by Freddie Guest; and there soldiers, Newspaper proprietors, dukes and statesmen dined and wined in a harmony all unknown elsewhere. In an East African mess at Moschi, some silly soldier-man ventured on the usual sneer at the Minister of Munitions. 'Mr Lloyd George is a friend of mine' said the guardsman,[552] and the snub resounded through the Army.[553]

GWYNN,[554] STEPHEN LUCIUS (1864–   ); writer. M.P. Galway city (Nat.) 1906–10, 1910, 1910–18.

B. 13 Feb. 1864; s. of Rev. John Gwynn D.D. (b. 1827–d. 1917),[555] by Lucy, eld. da. of Smith O'Brien M.P. for Ennis and later for County Limerick;[556] m. 1889 Mary Gwynn (da: of Rev. James Gwynn). Two sons living Rev. Aubrey Gwynn S.J., lectures in Ancient History [two words illegible][557] Coll. Dublin, & Denis Rolleston Gwynn, writer.[558]

'I grew up normally Unionist, as my father was. Only one da. of Smith O'Brien's was Nationalist. I went to Brasenose, Oxford, (Scholar 1882) and was soon obliged to think about Ireland and resent much I heard. Probably this was some trick of my ancestors. After taking my degree in 1886 I was a teacher[559] in various places till 1896 when I went to London as a free lance writer, having a wife and five children. The Boer War affected me strongly and I wrote accordingly, not helpful to my trade; and perhaps in this way I was brought in contact with Irish Nationalists. But so far back as 1888 I refused an offer to be Ritchie's private secretary because I was a Home Ruler.

In 1904 my income from writing had become appreciable and in that year my wife came into about £1,000 a year. My inclination towards politics had been increased by an observation of Arthur Elliot's that all parties in the House of Commons had been renewed except the Irish. So I offered myself to the party authorities; was nearly chosen

[550] *Sic.*

[551] The subject has deleted the following sentence: 'Principally he thought of polo, of East Africa, and of flying – in all of which he was expert'.

[552] 'with inimitable hauteur' deleted by the subject.

[553] The subject has deleted the following sentence: 'Probably Guest always thought of himself first, but it was not a bad first'.

[554] Written by JCW; corrected by the subject.

[555] Father's vital dates inserted by the subject.

[556] Details of O'Brien's parliamentary career inserted by the subject.

[557] Gwynn's son was professor at University College Dublin.

[558] Details of wife and sons inserted by the subject.

[559] 'a teacher' substituted by the subject for 'tutor'.

for West Clare in 1905[560] and subsequently at a bye–election[561] Nov. 1906[562] came in as Member for Galway city. The conditions for an Irish Member were very special. We had really only one interest, though incidentally one touched much of interest. For instance I was on the Dardanelles Commission.

His work was running the propaganda for the Party. He hated most waiting to be allowed to speak, and puts Grey's speech of Aug 1914[563] or Hugh Cecil's defence of the conscientious objectors as the best he heard. As for his own speeches, which were delivered (sadly):[564] – 'I took no interest in my speeches, but one about Old Age Pensions as affected by Irish vital statistics was all right.'

He says nothing of his War record. In Jan. 1915, at the age of 51, he joined the 7th Leinsters as a private; was gazetted Lieut. in 6th Connaught Rangers, Apr. 1915; Capt. July 1915. He served in France with the 16th Irish Division 1916–17 (Chevalier, Légion d'honneur, 1917). When it was all over, and his constituency had vanished and the Old Party had vanished too, still Gwynn hovers between Dublin and London writing, ever writing, more and more books; *Saints and Scholars, Walter Scott, Horace Walpole, Mary Kingsley*, the *History of Ireland*, much about Ireland, a good deal 'in praise of France', many biographies – mostly eighteenth century, but Mary Kingsley from memory of that great woman[565] – and his *Collected Poems*. But when we mourn over the vanishing of the Old Party, it is of those very gentle and brave men we think – Stephen Gwynn and Willie Redmond, the Protestant and the Catholic, who went to the trenches for the honour of Ireland.

HAMBRO,[566] Capt. ANGUS VALDEMAR; of Wimborne; M.P. (C) South Dorset 1910; 1910–18, 1918–22.

B. 8 July 1883, 3rd s. of Sir Everard Hambro, K.C.V.O. (18   –   )[567] and bro. of Eric Hambro M.P. Wimbledon 1906–08;[568] m. (1) 1907 Rosamund Maud (d. 1914) da. of Major Kearsley of Nantwich, Cheshire.[569] 1 s. 1 da.; (2) 1916 Vanda, da. of John Charlton of Malpas; 4 da. Educ. Eton.

He was Church of England and read the *Times*; his father started him on political thought, and his brother got in for Wimbledon in 1906. Balfour, and before that, Chamberlain were his ideals, and he went in with farming experience and tariff reform views. His father saw him through the expense; – £700 in 1910 and £500 a year; – but he had an unearned income of £1,700. He was not a keen politician, liked meeting his friends in the House, made but one speech, and left in 1922 for a more domestic and profitable life.

---

[560] 'in 1905' inserted by the subject.

[561] 'at a bye-election' substituted by the subject for 'about'.

[562] '1906' substituted by the subject for '1905'.

[563] 'of Aug. 1914' inserted by the subject.

[564] Gwynn puts a note by this word: 'were they? Sadness in the hearers?'

[565] 'much about Ireland . . . that great woman' inserted by the subject.

[566] Written by JCW; corrected by the subject.

[567] Hambro's note returning the biography says: 'Father was b. 1841 d. 1925'.

[568] Details of brother inserted by the subject.

[569] Details of wife's father inserted by the subject.

Asquith's speech on the declaration of war was the best he heard. In Dec.[570] 1914 he was given a commission in the Dorset Yeomanry; served in [blank][571] and was transferred to the Reserve in Jan. 1917. He is a J.P. of Dorset, was sheriff in 1934–5, and is an alderman of the Dorset County Council & Deputy Lieutenant.[572]

HAMILTON,[573] Capt. Lord ERNEST WILLIAM; writer. M.P. (C) N. Tyrone 1885–86, 1886–92.

B. Sept 5th 1858, 6th s. of 1st Duke of Abercorn and m. 1891 Pamela, (d. 1931) da. of F.A. Campbell; issue 2 sons[574] and 2 da.

Educ Harrow and R.M.C., Sandhurst; joined the 11th Hussars, retiring as Capt. In 1885.[575]

'I was forced into the position of an M.P. through the death of my father which incapacitated my eldest brother from holding a family seat. I was pushed into his place. Having got into the House, my one object was to get out again, and I was lucky enough to find a means of escape through the scullery window, which left the Whips much puzzled as to my mysterious disappearances. Those were the days of Irish debates and all-night sittings and the member's lot was not a happy one.' So for forty years he wrote instead of listening, and Ulster thoroughly approved, though peace did not come to Tyrone.

HAMILTON,[576] Major Sir George Clements, of Cransford Hall, Saxmundham; electrical engineer. M.P. (C) Cheshire (Altrincham) 1913–18, 1918–22, 1922–3; Ilford 1928–9, 1929–31, 1931–5, 1935.

B. 1st November 1877, y.s. of Ven. George Hans Hamilton D.D. (b. 1823, d.1905)[577] and Lady Louisa Hamilton (sister of 4th Earl of Leitrim)[578] m. 1906 Eleanor, d. of Henry Simon of Didsbury; 1 s. 1 dau.

Educated Aysgarth and Charterhouse; apprenticed to Messrs. Scott & Mountain, engineers, and served that firm in India, Bulgaria, Greece, Russia and Egypt. He is a Churchman, reads the 'Times' and believed in 'Joe Chamberlain'.[579] He was interested in politics from a boy, and 'enjoys everything in Parliamentary life'.[580] The war never shook him. He took a commission, Lieut, in the Cheshire Territorials, 7 Oct. 1914; transferred as Major to the 16th London Regt., 19 Jan. 1915; to the Territorial Reserve as Command

---

[570] 'Dec.' substituted for 'Oct.' by the subject.

[571] Hambro's note returning the biography adds: 'My war record. Not very much owing to illness. I was put on light duty at the War Office 1916. Returned to the House 1917 as Parl. Private Sec. to Under Sect of State for Air at that time John Baird. [name?] Stonehaven now'.

[572] '& Deputy Lieutenant' inserted by the subject.

[573] Written by JCW; corrected by the subject. The quotation is taken from Hamilton's letter to JCW, in lieu of a completed questionnaire.

[574] '2 sons' inserted by the subject.

[575] 'in 1885' inserted by the subject.

[576] Written by JCW; corrected and retyped by the subject.

[577] Dates supplied by the subject.

[578] Details within brackets supplied by the subject.

[579] Wedgwood's version of the sentence reads: 'He was "Churchman", "Times" and "Joe Chamberlain"'.

[580] The subject has omitted '—and that includes the Lobby, bar, and smoking room'.

Substitution Officer, 31 Oct. 1916 and Controller of Enrollment to Directorate of National Service, 1 April 1917.[581] Attached to Royal Air Force as 2nd in Command at the Engine Repair Shops Pont de l'Arche, France, December 1917.[582] On 13 Feb. 1918 recalled to London and appointed Controller of Contract Claims, Ministry of Munitions.[583]

He was P.P.S. to Sir Lamington Worthington Evans,[584] Minister of Pensions, 1919–20, and acted as Chairman of the Committee which revised the Officers' Pensions Warrants. 1921 appointed Chairman of the War Office Departmental Committee which recommended the amalgamation of the Pay Office and Records Office of the War Department.[585]

Is Chairman of the Expanded Metal Co. Ltd. etc. etc.[586]

HANCOCK,[587] JOHN GEORGE, of Nottingham. M.P. (Lab.) Mid-Derby 1909–10, 1910, 1910–18; (Lab. Nat.) Derbyshire (Belper) 1918–22; 1922–23; contested 1923.

B. 15 Oct. 1857, s. of Joseph who was born on December 29th 1829 and Ruth (maiden name) Alvey who was born August 3rd 1831.[588]

We were married at Pinxton Parish Church on October 9th 1882. My wife was Mary Hoten daughter of Thomas and Emma Hoten and was born on August 29th 1857. Our five children are all living and all married. Our issue Louie was born on March 17th 1887 – Frank on January 13th 1889 – Algie on February 13th 1891 – Harold on November 18th 1893 – John on July 2nd 1896.[589]

Worked in the pit 1870–82; check weighman 1882–92; formed Pinxton branch of Notts. Miners Association; agent and financial secretary to Notts. Miners 1896–1921, and continued as agent to 1927 and still treasurer. He was a local preacher of the United Methodist Church.

His grandfather (d. 1866) had a vote for some property, so that these miners had an interest in politics. 'He used to tell us about attempts to buy it'. 'My parents were very poor and the family was large, so we had very few books and they were all of a religious character.' They read *Reynolds* and the *Christian World*. 'I never wanted to be an M.P. but the

[581] 'and Controller of Enrollment to Directorate of National Service, 1 April 1917' substituted by the subject for 'and ceased military duty and attached to Directorate of National Service, 1 Apr. 1917'.

[582] Sentence inserted by the subject.

[583] Sentence substituted by the subject for 'On 13 Feb. 1918 he became Controller of Contract Claims, Ministry of Munitions, and was transferred to the Royal Air Force while attached to the Ministry'.

[584] Name of the minister supplied by the subject.

[585] 'and acted as . . . War Department' inserted by the subject.

[586] Wedgwood's version ends: 'kntd. 1922. Not a profound politician; but during his five years he was out the House was noticeably less jovial and rubicund'. Hamilton's letter of 9 Mar. 1937 returning his draft says: 'You are a comic! Please do not put references to smoke room and rubicundness in an official document like the history of Parliament, which will probably be read by my great grandchildren many years hence! I do want to *appear* decent, though I know I am not!!!' He added that 'I announced to my Annual Meeting of the Ilford Constitutional Association last night that I was not standing again, owing to Doctors' orders, and I further said that if my successor when appointed wanted to have a Bye Election in Ilford I was prepared to apply for the Chiltern Hundreds. I do not, therefore, know exactly when I resign from the House of commons, but it wont be later than the next General Election'.

[587] Written by JCW; corrected by the subject.

[588] Details of father and mother inserted by the subject.

[589] Hancock has written these details at the foot and in the margin of Wedgwood's draft.

Notts. Miners Association nominated me in 1903. I had £220 a year earned, and £20 unearned, and was chairman of the school board and president of the village Coop.; also eight years on the Nottingham Town Council. Both the miners and the Liberal Party, through Sir Arthur Markham, put him up for Mid-Derby without expense. His wage as agent was reduced to £120 a year, but in common with all miner members of that day the Federation paid him £350 a year. He thinks his first speech, 20 Mar. 1911, was his best. In 1918 he took the coupon and became National Labour, but the rift between Hancock and his fellows was never deep and his Association continued him in office.

HARE,[590] Major Sir THOMAS LEIGH, Bart. of Stow Hall, King's Lynn. M.P. (C) Norfolk S.W. 1892–5, 1895–1900, 1900–5; contested same 1906, 1910.

B. 4 Apr. 1859, s. of Sir Thomas Hare, 2nd Bart. (1808–1880) and Jane Norman d. 1875.[591] m. 1886 Ida (d 1929), da. of 3rd Earl Cathcart; one da.

Educ. Eton; served in Scots Guards and 24th Regt.

'I took no particular interest in politics (*qua* politics) but was pressed by my friends to stand for my Division of this county, so did so from a sense of duty. I was, and am, a landowner, so my "earning capacity" was not affected though my outgoings, what with numberless subscriptions, travelling expenses, an election every third or fourth year, a house in London, and various other things, increased by – on an average – a thousand a year. Lord Salisbury was my idea of a British statesman and I thought highly of (the then) Mr Balfour and Joseph Chamberlain. A speech by Mr Chamberlain on Home Rule was one of the best I ever heard. I myself never made a speech in the House so everyone was satisfied. I am glad that I had some Parliamentary experience. It was, at times, very interesting, but I was not much grieved when I lost my seat. I disliked canvassing, smoking concerts, public dinners, fetes, etc.'

He was made a baronet in 1905, as was fitting in the useful and normal public career of the English country gentleman.

HARRIS,[592] Sir PERCY ALFRED, Bart.; Deputy Chairman of L.C.C. 1915–16. Contested Ashford 1906, Harrow 1910. M.P. (Lib.) Leicestershire (Harborough) 1916–18, contested 1918; M.P. S.W. Bethnal Green 1922–3, 1923–4, 1924–9, 1929–31, 1931–5, 1935.

---

[590] Written by JCW; corrected by the subject.

[591] Father's vital dates and mother's name and death date inserted by the subject.

[592] Written by JCW; sent to the subject who did not correct it, but wrote back to Wedgwood on 5 Mar. 1937: 'I thought the record you were making for the Parliamentary history was to be historical and mere statement of facts. Instead of that, you have thought fit to put in your personal impressions of myself which you are entitled to have, and if you like to sign them and put them in as your personal impressions, I have no right to take any exception, but if this statement is supposed to be historical, I object very strongly.

Firstly, I have no doubt your reference to harrow is meant to be in a humorous vein, but it certainly had nothing to do with my title. Actually, as a matter of fact, I tried to get out of it. Herbert Samuel was then in the Cabinet and it was on his nomination my name was put forward, without consulting me. I pointed out I had no ambition in that particular direction, and it was stated it was too late to put anyone else forward and it would be a pity if this recognition of the Liberal Party should be lost.

Actually, the main reason of my recognition was that I had done 28 years of administrative work on the London County Council and done a tremendous amount of work for London, which though this may not be known in the Potteries, was generally recognised throughout London.

B. 1879, 2nd s. of Wolf Harris of (b.   d.   ) and   . m. 1901 Frieda, da. of John Astley Bloxam, F.R.C.S.; issue, Jack Wolfred Ashford.

Educ. Harrow and Trinity Hall, Cambridge (Hist. Honours 1897). Called to the Bar, Middle Temple, 1899; travelled three times round the world and lived three years in New Zealand. He represented Bethnal Green on the L.C.C. 1907–34. During the War he was appointed by the Army Council on a special comn. to organise volunteer corps; Hon. Assist. Director Volunteer Services, W.O., 1916. He has written on New Zealand and on London government. He became interested in Liberal politics at Harrow under Edward Bowen; Mill, Macauley,[593] and Marshall's *Political Economy* contributed; his religion much that of all of us – 'broadminded Deism'. He was asked to stand by the Liberal Chief Whip in 1904 because of his association with New Zealand. Free Trade, Education and Housing are all that he will call his interests.

Just as the Liberal Party was departing, Percy Harris arrived. Bethnal Green stood by their County Councillor and now he remains the sole survivor, elected again and again as a Liberal without prefix or suffix in perpetual three-cornered fights. Yet he is not a fighter and even the Tory and Labour back benches now tolerate the last of the Liberals. He may speak in peace the un-voiced liberalism of London, and often does so with exaggerated mildness; but he would only have been at home in the 1906–10 Parliament which was composed of his kind. He was made a baronet in 1932 as a tribute to Harrow and his pleasant, perennial liberalism. We even have his permission to say that he is a Jew.[594]

HARVEY,[595] THOMAS EDMUND, of Leeds. M.P. (Lib.) West Leeds 1910, 1910–18; contested Dewsbury 1922; M.P. Dewsbury 1923–4; contested North Leeds 1929 & Combined English Universities, 1937.[596]

B. 4 Jan. 1875, s. of Wm. Harvey of Leeds (1848–1928) and Anne M. Whiting (1851–1934).[597] (His sister m. Arnold Rowntree, M.P.); m. 1911, Irene, y.da. of Prof. Silvanus Thompson, F.R.S.; issue none.[598]

Educ. Bootham, Leeds and Christ Church, M.A., also in Berlin and Paris. *News from Nowhere, Merrie England*, and the writings of T.H. Green influenced him, the *Manchester Guardian* held him, but born in the Society he came increasingly to share the Quaker view of life. He was on the staff of the British Museum Library 1900–4, but his life was devoted to what was then called Social work. He was Warden of a Quaker settlement, and finally, in 1906, Warden of Toynbee Hall (unpaid).

---

[592] *(continued)* Secondly, as for the suggestion I am not a fighter, how do you think I have held Bethnal Green for 30 years? I may not shout quite so loudly, and make so much noise, as some people, and may be you don't like my particular methods, but I don't think you have any right to introduce your own personal predilections in a book that is subscribed for by all Members of Parliament.

I should prefer you to limit your statement to the facts that I gave you and omit comments which no doubt will be indulged in my Obituary Notice'. Wedgwood has written at the top of the letter: 'Ackd. Promised to insert w[ho's] w[ho] only'.

[593] *Sic.*

[594] Wedgwood has written in the margin: 'Have we?'

[595] Written by JCW; corrected by the subject.

[596] Date of North Leeds contest corrected by the subject, who also inserted '& Combined English Universities, 1937'.

[597] Vital dates of father and name and dates of mother inserted by the subject.

[598] 'none' inserted by the subject.

Allen Baker (q.v.) persuaded him to join in a fight for East Finsbury and he sat on the L.C.C. 1904–7 when he lost the seat and was coopted onto the Central Unemployed Body. Then he got onto the Stepney Borough Council 1909; then candidate for Herbert Gladstone's seat in Leeds. Income about[599] £600 a year unearned. His father paid his election expenses *c.*£700; annual cost not more than £140.

Once in the House he did all that a Quaker should, or more than all. He cared for the rights of the Africans and the poor; he stood in war for peace; all social reform was his province. Finally he lost his seat (1918) by supporting a 'peace' candidate at the Stockton bye-election. He was P.P.S. to Ellis Griffiths,   , 1912–13, and to Masterman,[600]   , 1913–14. During all the War, and till 1921, he was engaged on relief work for the Society of Friends in France. Since his defeat in 1925 he has devoted himself increasingly to religious work.

He liked best good debates and the comradeship of a good cause; disliked the lack of touch with the work of administration. His best speech was moving the conscientious objector amendment to the Conscription Bill (1916); Hugh Cecil's (in 1917 against depriving conscientious objectors of their votes)[601] the best he heard. His best work – the defence of obscure persons against oppression by the State.

'Ted' Harvey was the nearest approach to completely unselfish sainthood that we had in the House in this period. He was too gentle.[602]

HAWORTH,[603] Sir ARTHUR ADLINGTON, Bart.; merchant of Manchester. Junior Lord of the Treasury 1912. M.P. (Lib.) South Manchester 1906–10, 1910, 1910–12; contested 1912 and 1918.

B. 22 Aug, 1865, s. and h. of Abraham Haworth (1830–1902), of Altrincham, and Elizabeth Goodier (dau. Elizabeth Adlington, Quaker family, dating back to Geo. Fox, in town of Adlington, Lancs).[604] m. Lily, da. of John Rigby, of Altrincham; issue Arthur Godfrey, one da.

'I was brought up in a Liberal and Nonconformist household and after leaving Rugby, where I formed strong political views, became a worker in my home Liberal Party. I was a keen advocate of the Disestablishment of the Church as the control by the secular arm of Parliament was to me utterly unreconcilable with my idea of a Spiritual Church. I was not seeking to become an M.P. and it was a speech on that subject which brought me an invitation to become the Liberal Candidate for South Manchester. I fought my election for the 1906 Parliament mainly on the Free Trade issue and obtained a large majority though the seat had been held by a Unionist in the previous Parliament. I was

[599] 'about' inserted by the subject. Harvey's letter to Wedgwood of 8 Mar. 1937 says: 'I am sorry to say I cannot accurately remember my income when first elected for Parliament. It was I think about £600 or £700, but I cannot now be sure'.

[600] Space left by Wedgwood for insertion of Griffiths' and Masterman's ministerial posts.

[601] The passage in brackets is substituted by the subject for 'on the same subject'.

[602] The last two sentences have been enclosed in square brackets by the subject, who wrote to Wedgwood on 8 Mar. 1937: 'The penultimate sentence made me ashamed, for I know how ill it is deserved and I hope you will leave it out'. The letter also refers to Harvey's decision to stand as an Independent Progressive for the Combined English Universities.

[603] Written by JCW; not corrected, but reviewed, by the subject.

[604] Wedgwood has inserted Haworth's father's vital dates and details of his mother as supplied by Haworth in a letter of 17 Mar. 1937.

in business in an old firm of cotton yarn agents of which my father was the head, and enjoyed it having an income of several thousands a year. My election expenses were about £700 but a number of friends subscribed, without my asking, a considerable proportion. I had perforce to neglect my business and my earning capacity suffered. I gave the Association £100 a year for registration and had to subscribe to a few clubs, etc., but not to a great extent. My most important speech in Parliament was one moving the rejection of a Bill in favour of the Metric system in which I was successful. I did not much enjoy Parliamentary life and disliked having to vote always for my Party when I disagreed or to vote against the Government which I did on several occasions. I was defeated at a bye-election on being appointed a junior Lord of the Treasury, unpaid, on the nominal ground that it was "an office of profit under the Crown". I did not intend to seek to re-enter Parliament but could not refrain from fighting another Manchester seat as a protest against Mr Lloyd George's abominable "Coupon", "Hang the Kaiser" Election, when I advocated a League of Nations and was of course, in the height of the War fever, badly beaten. I look back on that contest with more satisfaction than anything else in my political career. I am now out of politics, though still a Liberal, and I find my time very fully occupied with Education, Social and Religious work in which I think my former status as an M.P. is not without its influence.'

He was made a baronet in 1911, and is a good example of what public life lost by the proscription of the Liberals.

HEATH,[605] ARTHUR RAYMOND, of Kitlands,[606] Holmwood, Surrey. M.P. (C) Lincs. (Louth) 1886–92.

B. Oct. 18th[607] 1854, e.s. of Admiral Sir Leopold G. Heath, K.C.B. (d. 1907) of Anstee Grange and Kitlands, Holmwood.[608] m. 1881, Flora Jean, da. of Edw. Baxter of Kincaldrum, Forfar. Their elder son was killed in the War, the second son Capt. F.D. Heath[609] survives. Educ. Marlboro'[610] and Trinity College, Cambridge (LL.B. 1877); called to the Bar, Inner Temple, 1879.[611]

In 1884–5 he helped to organise Dorington's campaign in the Cirencester Division, met A. Whitmore (q.v.)[612] and was pushed by him into fighting Louth div. of Lincolnshire.[613] The group of 'Junior Conservatives' which he joined did much speaking round the country.[614] He liked 'the general very pleasant camaraderie amongst the younger members of the party especially amongst the hunting set of whom there were in those days a good

---

[605] Written by JCW; corrected by the subject.

[606] 'Kitlands' inserted by the subject.

[607] Day and month of birth inserted by the subject.

[608] 'of Anstee Grange and Kitlands, Holmwood' substituted by the subject for 'of Holmwood and'.

[609] 'The second son Capt. F.D. Heath' inserted by Heath in the space left by Wedgwood.

[610] 'Marlboro' substituted by the subject for 'Harrow'.

[611] The subject has deleted the first sentence of the biography: 'With £3,500 a year and every sport as pastime, he went into politics with the rest of them'. Wedgwood had inserted a footnote after 'sport': 'He rode in the first House of Commons Point to Point, 6 Apr. 1899. "The race was carried on in 1890 and 1891 when one of the riders was killed and the race was discontinued"'.

[612] There is no biography of Whitmore.

[613] 'div. of Lincolnshire' inserted by the subject.

[614] 'did much speaking round the country' substituted by the subject for 'roamed round the country, speaking'.

proportion and also liked the excitement of speaking at meetings and the general atmosphere of politics and political society. The[615] younger members of those days[616] worked very hard in their[617] political duties and played hard in their different[618] sporting interests.' Chamberlain's rapier play on the Irish question pleased him best; and his own[619] best work was the Free Education Bill which he and other young Tories brought in before it was 'killed by the Whips'. There were 153 villages in his constituency. 'The rural[620] people of those days knew little of politics except the different colours of the two parties. My wife worked very [hard] in helping me.[621] Our constituents were very kind and hospitable. We were both very young and I enjoyed it all quite apart from politics.'

HEMMERDE,[622] EDWARD GEORGE; K.C. Contested Winchester 1900, Shrewsbury 1906; M.P. (Lib.) East Denbigh   1906–10; contested Portsmouth 1910; M.P. N.W. Norfolk   1912–18; M.P. (Lab.) Cheshire (Crewe) 1922–3, 1923–4.

B.   1871, s. of   Hemmerde, manager of Imperial Ottoman Bank, (   ) and

m. 1903 Lucy Elinor (divorced 1922) da. of C.C. Colley; one da. Educ. Winchester (Cricket XI), and University College, Oxford (1st class Mods.); barrister, Inner Temple; K.C. 1908; recorder of Liverpool since 1909.

Father Dolling at Winchester, and 'Truth' weekly, gave him his politics. At Oxford where he was intimate with F.E. Smith, he determined on Parliament as his career, and it is well known that they tossed up which party each should join, feeling that there was not room for both geniuses in any one party. But this is like other 'well-known things'. When he first stood he was earning £750 a year and had just won the Diamond Sculls (1900); by 1904 he was one of the best Liberal platform orators and acting the part to perfection. Taxation of Land Values and Home Rule were his subjects, but the whole Tory past was at his mercy. He got his seat at last 'by publicly announcing that I intended to fight East Denbighshire against all comers and doing so.' It 'cost me about £800. I fought in all ten contested elections and the fights cost me personally roughly £2,000. My election fights at Winchester, Shrewsbury, N.W. Norfolk and Portsmouth cost me nothing. My three fights at Crewe not more than a total of £450, most of the expenses being paid by popular subscriptions. I never subscribed to any clubs, charities, etc. in any constituency which I contested or represented; and except at Crewe, when I was receiving £400 a year salary, I never contributed to the support of the organisation. At Crewe I think I found £150 a year.'

He thinks his politics were detrimental to his practice, but once upon a time he made £15,000 a year. The greatest speech he remembers was Alexander Ure's reply to Balfour

---

[615] 'The' substituted by the subject for 'We'.

[616] 'of those days' inserted by the subject.

[617] 'their' substituted by the subject for 'our'.

[618] 'their different' substituted by the subject for 'our'.

[619] 'own' inserted by the subject.

[620] 'rural' inserted by the subject.

[621] Sentence substituted by the subject for an ellipsis (in a quotation from Heath's letter to Wedgwood of 19 Sept. 1936).

[622] Written by JCW. A note on the file says 'copy not sent out'.

when charged with the 'frigid or calculated lie'. He approved most of his own work and speeches on the Land Question, and in particular his speech criticising the first Labour Budget in 1904.

Conceit and intense ambition inspired Hemmerde. He had all F.E. Smith's brains without his bonhomie. Most M.P.s are conceited and strenuously conceal it; a touch of orientalism and a handsome person betrayed Hemmerde's failing, and he was never 'F.E.' – never known by his Christian name. He got his recordership, got into financial troubles, lost his safe Denbighshire seat, and became a liability to the party he had served so well. They mud-raked his past and present, and all the time Hemmerde remained a child who never grew up – ever optimistic and ever more bitterly resenting lack of appreciation. Nobody loved him, Labour would not give him office, and he never understood. A queer financial kink in the brain destroyed the greatest adventurer in modern politics.

HERBERT,[623] (THOMAS) ARNOLD, of Kensington Park Gardens and[624] Marlow, Bucks. K.C. M.P. (Lib.) Bucks. (South) 1906–10, contested 1910 (Jan.)

B. 1 Sept. 1863, s. of Thos. Martin Herbert, Professor of Philosophy at the Lancashire Independent College, (18 –) and

m. 1896, Elizabeth G. (d. 1917), da. of A. Haworth, J.P. of Bowdon (18 –). Educ. Mill Hill, St John's College, Cambridge (1st Class Classical Tripos, bracketed Senior Law Tripos, Foundation Scholar and McMahon Law Scholar of St. John's). Called to the Bar, Inner Temple, 1889 (Equity Scholar); practised in Chancery divn.; K.C. 1913.

'Always interested in politics because it was the atmosphere of my surroundings. My political views were not formed by any particular books but by my general education and reading which of course included Bentham, Mill, Adam Smith and the like. My religious convictions were of the Nonconformist type, founded on freedom of thought. My favourite newspapers were *Times, Manchester Guardian, Westminster Gazette, Spectator*. The attack upon Free Trade made me wish to become an M.P. I had no previous political experience and it was regarded as and seemed rather a hopeless task to attack a Tory stronghold like S. Bucks. It took years of hard work to nurse and educate the constituency. It cost me £2,000 to win the seat and £150 a year while a member. My ideal statesman at the time was Gladstone. Naturally my chief interest in Parliament was Free Trade and its consequences. Occasionally my views on minor points were altered by speeches in Parliament but when that was so the change was generally wrong. Parliamentary life was a decided obstacle to professional success unless one was physically very strong. I thoroughly enjoyed Parliamentary life, feeling that one was among men conversant with great things, and men, sometimes extremely modest, who could give one information about almost anything.

My best piece of work was getting through the Bill to amend the cost of Distress[625] as a private member's Bill without having won a place in the ballot. It tought[626] me a good deal about Parliamentary procedure.'

---

[623] Text written by the subject and lightly edited and heading supplied by Wedgwood; further corrected by the subject.

[624] 'Kensington Park Gardens and' inserted by the subject.

[625] 'cost of Distress' inserted by the subject into the space left by Wedgwood.

[626] *Sic.*

HOBHOUSE,[627] Rt.Hon. HENRY of Hadspen House, Castle Cary, Som.; barrister; Ecclesiastical Comnr.; P.C. 1902. M.P. (U) Somerset (East) 1885–6, 1886–1892, 1892–5, 1895–1900, 1900–5.

B. 1 Mar. 1854, s. and h. of Henry Hobhouse of same (1811–1862) and Charlotte Etruria Hobhouse.[628] m. (1) 1880, Margaret (d. 1921) 7th da. of R. Potter of Standish, Glos.; issue – Stephen H. Hobhouse,[629] Arthur Lawrence M.P. (Lib.) Wells, 1922–3, John R. Hobhouse[630] and 2 da.; (2) 1923, Anne, da. of William Grant of Forres.

Educ. Eton and Balliol (1st class Lit.Hum. 1875); called to the Bar, Lincoln's Inn 1880, practised as Parliamentary draftsman and counsel; member of Commission on Secondary Education and other Commissions and Committees.[631]

He was a moderate Liberal and firm Free Trader but opposed to Irish Home Rule. He concentrated most on Local Government, Education and Free Trade. His contests cost about £1,300 each, and his seat about[632] £250 a year. He was Chairman of Private Bill Committees from 1895–1905, a position for which his experience was invaluable. He liked the intercourse in Parliament with a variety of men, and disliked long hours and all night sittings. He never spoke at length. Gladstone on the Home Rule Bill in 1886 was the greatest speech he heard. He retired in 1905 because he thought Local Government work more fruitful.[633] He was Chairman of the Somerset C.C., 1904–24, and of the C.C. Assn. 1914–20.[634] He has written treatises on Local Government.

HOLMES,[635] DANIEL[636] TURNER; schoolmaster and lecturer. M.P. (Lib.) Lanarkshire (Govan) Dec. 1911–18; contested 1918.

B. 23 Feb. 1863, s. of James Holmes of Irvine, Ayrshire, dec'd 1921 (–) and Elizabeth Turner, daughter of Daniel, died 1918.[637] m. 1896, Margaret, da. of Peter Eadie, Provost of Paisley; issue Margaret m. Rt. Hon. W. Wedgwood Benn, M.P., and Hermione m. Lawrence Lister of Pietermaritzburg.[638] Educ. London University (1st class honours) and Universities of Paris and Geneva; taught at Greenock Academy, and at Paisley Grammar School until 1900, then lecturing on literature, or walking and reading.

'It was impossible to avoid being touched by political emotion during the 80's and 90's of last century. In all the large towns and most of the smaller, Parliamentary Associations were formed on the model of Westminster and these gave splendid opportunities for practice in public speaking and debate. The overpowering prestige of

---

[627] Written by JCW; corrected by the subject.

[628] Father's dates and mother's name inserted by the subject.

[629] 'Stephen H. Hobhouse' inserted by the subject.

[630] 'John R. Hobhouse' inserted by the subject.

[631] 'and other Commissions and Committees' inserted by the subject. A sentence after this – 'Then he came into the House for his own division and had to give up his profession in consequence.' – has been deleted by the subject.

[632] 'his seat about' inserted by the subject.

[633] 'especially as' deleted by the subject.

[634] 'and of the C.C. Assn. 1914–20' inserted by the subject.

[635] Written by JCW; corrected by the subject.

[636] 'Daniel' substituted by the subject for 'David'.

[637] Details of father and mother inserted by the subject.

[638] Name of Margaret and name and marriage of Hermione inserted by the subject.

Gladstone, especially during his Midlothian campaign, caused such political enthusiasm as has never been since known.' Burns, Ruskin, Carlyle, Mill, Macaulay, formed him. His religious convictions 'found expression in the "Lord's Prayer" the ethical parts of the Decalogue and in the slogan "Thou, God, seeest me".' His chief political interest was the fostering of rational freedom, social, industrial and economic. Grey and Gladstone were his admired statesmen.

Holmes enjoyed most 'the social life of the place: the political and literary discussions with well-equipped members: the composing of epigrammatic couplets on the daily happenings of the House'. Of the speeches he heard he put first Hugh Cecil's conscientious objectors speech, and Lloyd George's in the Maurice Debate (1918) 'For brilliancy, dexterity, art, and artfulness, this was a marvellous effort.' But he bracketed also Clemenceau's speech in Paris to the British Parliamentarians (Feb. 1916). His own best speech was on the Scottish Temperance Bill (1912). His best work – 'in schoolmastering; in aiding the establishment of village libraries in the Highlands and Islands of Scotland and in the propagation of Liberalism in the West of Scotland.' In Dec. 1918 he was refused the 'coupon' and defeated.[639]

HOLT,[640] Sir RICHARD DURNING, Bart. Manager[641] of the Ocean Steam Ship Co[642] of Liverpool. M.P. (L) Northumberland (Hexham) 1907–10, 1910, 1910–18; contested Eccles Division, Lancashire 1910, Rossendale 1922, 1924, 1929, N. Cumb. 1923 1926 (bye).[643]

B. Nov. 13th[644] 1868, s. and h. of Robert D. Holt (–) of Sefton Park, Liverpool, and of High Borrans, Westmorland, and last Mayor & First Lord Mayor of Liverpool.[645] m. 1897 Eliza, da. of John Wells of New Brunswick; issue – Grace Durning, married Hon A.P. Methuen, Anne Durning, M.A., Dorothy Isabel Durning – m. Thomas H. Naylor.[646]

Educ. Winchester and New College, Oxford; entered Alfred Holt & Co. as a partner. From 1896 a member, and from 1927 Chairman of the Mersey Docks and Harbour Board; since 1932 Chairman of Elder, Dempster Lines also: hon. LL.D. of Liverpool 1933; Baronet 1935.

'My father was leader of the Liberal party in Liverpool. We were all Liberals at home and keenly interested in local and Parliamentary elections. Visiting politicians stayed in our house.' Books did not influence him, and he formed his views independently of any newspaper. 'A Protestant Dissenter from Church of England, commonly called Unitarian.' He came to Parliament 'because it is the most interesting career – with the best chance of controlling big events. It seemed the proper thing for an intelligent man to

---

[639] The subject has deleted the sentence at the end: 'It is still doubted and disputed whether his best contributions were his epigrams or his daughters'. A note below this text reads: 'Declines to submit this "unsolved problem" to posterity. W.J.P.'

[640] Written by JCW; corrected by the subject.

[641] 'Manager' substituted by the subject for 'owner'.

[642] 'Ocean Steam Ship Co' substituted by the subject for 'Blue Funnel Line'.

[643] Details of contested elections inserted by the subject.

[644] Day and month of birth inserted by the subject.

[645] 'and last mayor . . . Liverpool' inserted by the subject.

[646] Details of daughters inserted by the subject, except Anne Durning, M.A.

do', and he had then £5,000 a year. He sought in Parliament 'to prevent any avoidable charge upon the taxpayer and consumer and maintain political, religious, and commercial liberty.' Gladstone was his ideal, and Parliament did not modify his views. He liked the chance of getting things better done and disliked nothing in the life.

If the Liberal party had not been liquidated in 1918 'Dick'[647] Holt would long since have been a Peer in comfort. As it is he has made more desperate fights to get back to Parliament than any man, and remains the sort of Liberal who will never give in. Meanwhile his Blue Funnel fleet grows, finds freight in the worst of seasons, and covers the seven seas.

HOPE,[648] Sir HARRY, Bart.; of Kinettles, Forfar. Contested Elgin and Nairn 1906; M.P. (C) Buteshire 1910, 1910–18; Stirling and Clackmannan 1918–22; contested 1922, 1923; M.P. Forfarshire 1924–9, 1929–31.

B. 24 Sept. 1865, s. of James Hope (–) of Eastbarns, Dunbar; m. 1897 Margaret,[649] da. of R.K. Holmes-Kerr of Largs, Ayrshire; 2s., 1da. Knighted 1920, Baronet 1932.

'My father was a staunch Conservative, mother a Liberal and ardent supporter of women's suffrage.'

'After my father's death, and when in Parliament[650] I carried on a large farming business in East Lothian[651] and made a point of never neglecting it, but it was not easy – two nights in the train every week and never a rest either, when in London or at the home end and I did that for twenty years.'[652]

Politics are an expensive luxury.[653] I must have spent, certainly, £10,000 in my 8 contests, and other auxiliary work,[654] but I enjoyed them all, especially Bute and Forfarshire, and in all my contests I never referred to my opponent by name. It is a great mistake to say 'Mr – said – last night', and I was always perfectly friendly with all my opponents. To me, it was an interest and a pleasure to watch the personalities fighting in the House of Commons – some for one object, some for another.[655] I enjoyed meeting the people at our political[656] meetings and[657] in two of the four county constituencies which I contested, I called, personally, on every elector at his home. It was hard work, perhaps thankless, but I liked our Scottish country people and hold that, as the Home[658]

---

[647] The subject appears to have amended 'Dickie' to 'Dick'.

[648] Written by JCW, though almost entirely from the questionnaire; corrected by the subject.

[649] Name inserted by the subject.

[650] 'And when in Parliament' inserted by the subject.

[651] 'in East Lothian' inserted by the subject.

[652] 'and I did that for twenty years.'" inserted by the subject.

[653] There is no quotation mark at the beginning of the sentence, but this and the rest of the paragraph except the last sentence are also directly quoted from the questionnaire, except for the subject's manuscript additions.

[654] 'and other auxiliary work' inserted by the subject.

[655] 'some for one object, some for another' inserted by the subject. Wedgwood had left an ellipsis at this point.

[656] 'political' inserted by the subject.

[657] 'and' inserted by the subject. Wedgwood had originally finished the sentence at 'contested'. Hope's change restores the sense of his original questionnaire.

[658] 'Home' substituted by the subject for 'House'.

is the foundation of the National structure, it is by improving the conditions of the homes of our people that we can, best, be Empire Builders. I have always supported Womens' interests and I think I gained by their advent to the electoral roll.' He was popular with his Labour opponents too, especially when they got rid of him from Stirling and Bannockburn.[659]

HOPE,[660] Rt. Hon. JAMES FITZALAN (cr. Lord Rankeillour of Buxted 1932) of Heron's Ghyll, Uckfield, Sussex. Treasurer of the Household 1915–16; a Lord of the Treasury 1916–19; Financial Secretary, Ministry of Munitions 1919–21; P.C. 1922; Chairman of Committees 1921–Feb. 1924, and Dec. 1924–29. M.P. (C) Sheffield (Brightside) 1900–05, contested 1906; M.P. Sheffield (Central) 1908–10, 1910, 1910–18, 1918–22, 1922–3, 1923–4, 1924–9, contested 1929.

B. 11 Dec. 1870, s. of J.R. Hope-Scott, Q.C., of Abbotsford, and Victoria Alexandrina, da. of 14th Duke of Norfolk; m. 1892, Mabel, da. of Francis Riddell of Cheesburn, Northumberland; issue, Arthur, Henry,[661] Richard,   and 1 da. Joan.[662] Educ. Oratory School and Christ Church, Oxford.

He started politics at 14, moved by the widespread fear of Gladstonian Liberalism. Burke guided his views, and religious convictions which 'were and are those inculcated by the Catholic Church, rightly understood – which they[663] very seldom are by those outside.' Family connection with Sheffield gave him his chance and he came to Parliament 'because I thought the sharing in the government of the country was the best earthly career for a man not obliged to work'. His political interest was 'to keep the right people in and the others out', and after a time he[664] 'developed an aptitude for the uses and abuses of procedure.' His elections cost about £900 and £450 a year. Pitt was always his ideal. 'Parliament did not modify my views at all in essence although I learnt personal toleration – of most people: also how the machine worked. See my '*Politics and Politicians*'. He is the only man to admit the truth that he[665] liked 'the atmosphere of strife', and disliked 'the vain repetitions of the unimaginative'. Hope's best speech was on 'the third reading of the Finance bill 1924, though it was really bringing to date one on the like occasion in 1902.' The best speech he heard: – 'Before I entered Parliament, Lord Salisbury on the Home Rule Bill in 1893. The most thrilling – on account of the occasion – was Sir E. Grey's in 1914 when he said 'If we run away now' and could not finish the sentence.' *Did speeches affect votes?* 'Hardly at the moment but they sometimes set going new trains of thought. Often, however, preconceived notions, not amounting to convictions, were completely dissipated in debate. Except for set party wrangles, nowhere is the truth better elicited (and "stunts" confuted) than in the House of Commons.'

---

[659] 'especially when . . . Bannockburn' has been crossed out in pencil, presumably not by the subject, who corrected the rest of the biography in pen.

[660] Written by JCW; corrected by the subject.

[661] 'Henry' inserted by the subject.

[662] 'Joan' inserted by the subject.

[663] 'they' inserted by the subject.

[664] 'he' inserted by the subject.

[665] 'the truth. He' amended by the subject to 'the truth that he'.

Possibly a better fighter than Chairman, but the House as a whole quite approved his Chairmanship. His views, however, from first to last, were wholly abhorrent to his opponents.[666]

HOPE,[667] JOHN DEANS; of Haddington. Contested West Perth 1895; M.P. (L) West Fife 1900–6, 1906–10. Represented Haddingtonshire   1911–18; Berwick and Haddington 1918–22.

<u>B</u>. 8 May 1860, s. of James Hope of Eastbarns, Dunbar (–) the eminent Agriculturist.[668] <u>m</u>. 1899, Elizabeth[669] da. of R.K. Holmes-Kerr of Glasgow and Ayrshire; 1 da. Educ. Fettes College and Edinburgh University.[670] He served on three school boards, and on his parish and County Council.

He[671] heard Henry George speak in Edinburgh in 1884,[672] and supported his views ever afterwards. *Progress and Poverty* was his inspiration, and he has been a supporter for 50 (fifty) years of the Salvation Army and a personal friend of the late General Wm Booth,[673] reading *Reynolds* newspaper. He came into Parliament to help land Reform and Home Rule for Ireland and Scotland. Opposed the S. African war & voted against the supplies for it.[674] He served on nine Parliamentary Commissions and for seventeen years on the Kitchen Committee. Offered knighthood in 1918 and declined the honor.[675]

For twenty-two years he sat in Parliament and never made a speech. Always wore carnation in button hole.[676] This was the quintessence of the strong silent Scottish radicalism of the pre-Clydeside era. When John Deans Hope left, Maxton arrived. The men of the Covenant are gone.

---

[666] The last paragraph is marked 'see letters'. A letter from Rankeillour to Wedgwood of 5 Mar. 1937, returning the biography, says: 'as you mention the Chairmanship, I think I ought to say something about the Speakership, to which I was offered the Government nomination in 1928 with (I was told) the assent of both Oppositions'. A note at the bottom of the letter marked 'Private' adds: 'you can hardly add that my main reason for refusing was the prospect of having to practice for 10 years the detestable virtues of impartiality and patience'. Wedgwood's reply of 16 Mar. says: 'I will most certainly add your reasons for refusing the Speakership. They are both characteristic and admirable'. Rankeillour responded immediately on 17 Mar.: 'No – you mustn't use those expressions – One must not flout convention too far. You can say that I refused the Speakership "which he doubtless felt unsuited to his active and militant disposition"'.

[667] Written by JCW; corrected by the subject.

[668] 'Dunbar' and 'the eminent Agriculturist' inserted by the subject.

[669] Wife's name inserted by the subject.

[670] Wedgwood had written 'stockbroker and chartered accountant'. The subject has deleted this and written in brackets in the margin '(retired)'.

[671] 'He' substituted by the subject for 'I'. Hope failed to delete the quotation marks at the end of the sentence: they have been left out here.

[672] '1884' substituted by the subject for '1883, I think'.

[673] 'has been a supporter . . . General Wm Booth' substituted by the subject for 'was an Evangelical Christian'.

[674] Sentence inserted by the subject.

[675] Sentence inserted by the subject.

[676] Sentence inserted by the subject.

HOPKINSON,[677] Sir ALFRED; of Lincoln's Inn, K.C. Contested E. Manchester as a Liberal, 1885, against A.J. Balfour,[678] and S.W. Manchester as Liberal-Unionist, 1892, against Jacob Bright;[679] M.P. (U) Wilts. (Cricklade) 1895–8; English Universities 1926–9.

B. in Manchester 28 June 1851, 2nd. S. of John Hopkinson (1824–1902) Mayor of Manchester 1882–3,[680] and Alice, da. of John Dewhurst of Skipton; m. 1873, Esther (d. 1931) da. of Henry Wells of Nottingham. Issue, – Austin Hopkinson, M.P., and 3 others., also Margaret, m. Sir G.B. Hurst, M.P., and 2 other da. Educ. Owens College Manchester, and Lincoln College,[681] Oxford (Scholar, Honours in Lit.Hum. 1872); Howell Fellow, University College, Oxford (International Law); Honorary Fellow of Lincoln College;[682] Barrister, Lincoln's Inn, 1873, Bencher, 1896, Treasurer 1921. Professor of Law at Owens College till 1889; Q.C. 1892; Principal of Owens College 1898–1904; and chairman of several boards and tribunals: knighted 1910.

'I was first interested in politics in 1857 when my father told us all about the Russian War and the Chartists of the forties, and took active part for John Bright when he was defeated for Manchester in 1857.' 'Books which have had special[683] influence: – John Bright's speeches and later Mill on Liberty, Macaulay's History. Later still, Aristotle. His religion might be called[684] "that of all sensible men and sensible men never say" but in political life people circulated reports that I was a Roman Catholic or an Atheistic or Agnostic. Both untrue but I would not contradict.' Christian and undenominational might be a right description.[685] 'You have to consider your personal interest in a profession. In political life I could indulge "altruistic feelings" quite freely without regard to personal consequences or self interest.' He retired in 1898 to become Vice-Chancellor of Manchester University. The statesman of those he knew personally when living whom he most admired & trusted was Lord Hartington;[686] of an earlier time,[687] Burke and Lord Shaftesbury. As a result of being in Parliament he 'thought better of *nearly* everyone of all parties from meeting in smoking and tea rooms.' The best speech he heard was Hicks Beach, on the Soudan or on Bimetallism. 'I would say to an independent member, be *in* the House with the *outs* (in opposition) or *out* when your own side is in. In any event never expect any personal advantage of any kind and never cherish any personal ambition and you will on the whole like and respect the House of Commons in spite of scenes and dull speeches and waste of time.' 'I would take up some special subject get it up thoroughly & speak on it. The Preservation of Commons, for example, was one on which a private member could do really useful work of lasting value.'[688] With this true

---

[677] Written by JCW; corrected by the subject.

[678] 'against A.J. Balfour' inserted by the subject.

[679] 'against Jacob Bright' inserted by the subject.

[680] Father's dates and 'Mayor of Manchester, 1882–32' inserted by the subject.

[681] 'College' inserted by the subject.

[682] 'Howell Fellow . . . Lincoln College' inserted by the subject.

[683] 'special' inserted by the subject.

[684] 'might be called' substituted by the subject for 'is'.

[685] Sentence inserted by the subject; there are ten further words, but they are mostly illegible: 'subject to [playing?] . . . according to the [?]'.

[686] Amended by the subject from 'His living statesman was Lord Hartington;'.

[687] 'Of an earlier time' substituted by the subject for 'dead'.

[688] Two sentences inserted by the subject.

judgment we must leave the keen intellect whose politics span 80 years, who left behind him in the House loving friends and a most gallant son.

HOPKINSON,[689] AUSTIN, of Audenshaw, Lancs. Engineer. M.P. (Ind.) Lancashire (Prestwich) 1918;   Lancashire (Mossley) 1918–22, 1922–3, 1923–4, 1924–9; contested 1929; M.P. Lancashire (Mossley) 1931–35, 1935.

B. 23 June 1879, 3rd s. of Sir Alfred Hopkinson M.P. Unmd.[690]

He served as Lieut. In Imperial Yeomanry in S.A. War 1900 and was permanently disabled; 2nd Lieut. Royal Dragoons[691] Great War 1914–15, again permanently disabled; rejoined in the ranks 1918; no decorations. What he says is – 'During the War I had a vague notion that the problems of peace would require soldiers in their solution.' A bye-election in his home district started the idea of Parliament; 'possibly a sense of duty made me tell my lawyer to put my name down for the bye-election, but it sounds unlikely.' His religious convictions were too mathematical to be suitable for expression by any means except tensor equations;[692] his earned income was, he says,[693] 1s.10d. a day as a private soldier; his works were bringing him in £8,000 a year; he was on the Audenshaw U.D.C.; and his model was Pericles. The 'exposure of socialist quackery' is his chief interest, and his best piece of work was getting X.Y. to resign.[694]

He believes he could still make a large income if he tried 'but I do not try'. In Parliament[695] he enjoys most 'the companionship of a number of the very best fellows in the world', while disliking 'enforced association with a number of the very worst fellows in the world.' His best speech dealt with the 'socialist bishops during the coal strike of 1926'; the best he heard was Baldwin rejecting the Trades Union Bill, early in 1926.

There are few who have not at some time sworn never to forgive his vitriolic tongue, for he is a bundle of nerves. In the closing hours of the 1931–5 Parliament rumour went round that some carpet-bagger[696] had got the Conservative Party coupon and was opposing 'Hoppy' – that in a three-cornered fight 'Hoppy' would infallibly go down. Then the Lobby became an indignation meeting; Whips were told where they 'got off', and the Prime Minister wrote him a permanent blessing, addressed to all whom it might concern, to confound the machine; and so the independent was saved. They would[697] never understand this sort of thing in Germany – nor why Hoppy should give all his shares in his Works to his workmen – nor why he should go on piloting and crashing his own machine. 'Samedi, dix-huit, une heure après dîner, M. de Bèrgerac est mort assassiné.'

[689] Written by JCW; corrected by the subject.

[690] Wedgwood had written 'Educ.'; Hopkinson inserted 'indifferent', and then crossed out both words and inserted 'He' as the beginning to the following sentence.

[691] '2nd Lieut. Royal Dragoons,' inserted by the subject.

[692] Wedgwood had written (on the basis of Hopkinson's answer in the questionnaire): 'His religious convictions were nil'.

[693] Wedgwood had originally written 'pay'; had crossed this out and written 'he says, was', then deleted that and written 'earned income was, he says'. It is unclear how and when these amendments were made.

[694] Wedgwood had written 'If X.Y. is . . . . . . that work must indeed have been difficult as well as salutary'. Hopkinson wrote in the margin: 'omit this, because it would lead to identification'.

[695] 'In Parliament' substituted by the subject for 'Instead'.

[696] 'carpet-bagger' substituted by the subject for 'local butcher'.

[697] 'go down' substituted by the subject for 'foot the poll'.

HORNE,[698] Sir (WILLIAM) EDGAR, 1ˢᵗ Bart.; contested N. Devon 1906; M.P. (U) Surrey (Guildford) 1910, 1910–18, 1918–22.

B. 21 Jan. 1856, s. of Edgar Horne ('The Hill', Witley, Surrey); m. 1886[699] Margery, da. of George Anderson May, of Elford, Staffs.; issue; – Alan Edgar, William Guy; 1da. Educ. Westminster. Cr. Baronet 1929.

Westminster scholars had the privilege of attending the debates, 'and in fact the whole House was open to us. I took advantage of this often. Later on I assisted Sir Henry Harben's election campaign at Norwich. I became a surveyor and was made President of the Surveyors' Institution.[700] I[701] was employed by the Government to prepare the plans and schedules and subsequently to purchase properties under five Acts of Parliament in connection with the new Government offices.' 'I never had any particular ambition to be a member, or to take up politics as a career, as I have no eloquence or power of public speaking. However,[702] in 1904 I was deeply impressed with Mr. Joseph Chamberlain's attitude in respect of the Colonies, and his attitude towards so called Free Trade; so I went to the Liberal Unionist Party and offered to fight. . . .'[703] After Barnstaple, I 'started[704] for a journey round the world, and when in New Zealand received a telegram asking me if I would stand for Guildford where Sir John Brodrick had lost the seat. . . . I had lived at Shackleford near Godalming since 1886 and had built a house there.[705] As soon as I became a Member I was put upon the Local Legislation Committee and served there during the thirteen years that I was in the House. The work interested me very greatly and as during my professional career I had made the acquaintance of nearly all the leading members of the Bar, I was able, I think, to be of some use. In 1922 I decided to retire: the Government did many things I thought unwise: neglected and refused to adopt the attitude towards the Colonies which I was particularly interested in. Besides that[706] I was becoming more and more immersed in the conduct of the business of the Prudential Assurance Company, of which I had become Deputy Chairman, and which took up a great deal of my time. One speech changed my vote. It was Austen Chamberlain objecting to a Local Authority being allowed to rank a loan as a Trustee security. I heard many fine speeches in the House by Hugh Cecil, Asquith, F.E. Smith, Rufus Isaacs, Lloyd George and others. One I particularly remember is Grey's speech on the day before we declared war.

During the War I served on the Public Expenditure Committee of which Herbert Samuel was Chairman, and on a small sub-committee which had the duty of examining

---

[698] Written by JCW; edited by and retyped for the subject. The version given here is Wedgwood's original, with significant changes in the subject's version indicated in the footnotes.

[699] Date of marriage inserted by the subject.

[700] ', "and in fact . . . Surveyors' Institution." omitted from the subject's version.

[701] 'As a surveyor I' in the subject's version.

[702] '"I never had . . . speaking. However,' omitted from the subject's version.

[703] The subject's version adds: ', but did not win the seat (Barnstaple) for which I stood'. The original quotation, which Wedgwood's extract makes nonsensical, says 'and offered to fight any seat they liked to send me to. I was fairly well off and prepared to pay all my expenses; as a result they sent me to the Barnstaple division of N. Devon and I devoted the next two years till 1906, during my spare time, in endeavouring to convert the electors to my way of thinking. However, they would not have me and I was not disappointed'.

[704] 'Two years later I went' in the subject's version.

[705] 'where Sir John . . . built a house there' omitted from the subject's version.

[706] 'the government did many things . . . Besides that' omitted from the subject's version.

into, and reporting upon, the Army, Navy and Air Force expenditure, the subject was of course one utterly beyond our powers, but I think we did a certain amount of good.'

For forty years he has been councillor, mayor and alderman of Westminster. He took over 'the Pru' when Sir Henry Harben died and converted it into the immense institution it is today. In Germany Edgar Horne would have been a great burgomaster; in England he guides permanent officials from within the shelter of Parliament.[707]

HUNT,[708] Major ROWLAND; of Linley Green, Broseley, Salop. M.F.H. M.P. (U) Salop (Ludlow)   1903–6, 1906–10, 1910, 1910–18.

B. 13 Mar. 1858, s. and h. of Rowland Hunt, of Boreatton, and Florence Marian, da. of R. Humfrey of Stoke Albany; m. (1) 1890, Veronica, da. of Duncan Davidson, of Tulloch, Co. Ross; 2 s., 1 da.; (2) 1932, Evelyn, da. of Rev. T.H. Hunt, of Ruyton Park. Educ. Eton and Magdalene, Camb. Master of beagles and of hounds from Eton onwards. Served 10 years in Northants Militia and with Lovat's Scouts in S. African war. Major City of London Rough Riders 1914.

Rowland Hunt was protectionist enragé from 1877 (in America) onwards; compulsory military training was a side line; the humbug of the Radicals and the wobbling of Mr Balfour his aversion; the Conservative whips his bane.[709] Undaunted by a raging House, he would address us after the front bench had wound up debate. He referred to Queen Boadicea, either to her new statue or her old patriotism, and ever after was known as Boadicea Hunt. Periodically he shook off from his shoes the dust of whips and party, and once, returning to the fold, he marched up the floor accompanied by Sir William Bull. 'The prodigal son and the fatted calf', cried out Jerry McVeagh, and the cheers disturbed the pigeons in Trafalgar Square. He took it all so well; there was no more popular figure in Parliament.

'My three contested elections cost about £500 each; the subscriptions in the constituency were very small.' After the War he went back like Cincinnatus to the plough. He was not quite rich enough for Parliament and fox-hounds.

HUNTER,[710] WILLIAM; advocate, K.C., Solicitor General for Scotland 1910–11. M.P. (L) Lanarkshire (Govan) 1910, 1910–Dec. 1911. Lord Hunter (Senator of College of Justice) 1911.

B. at Ayr 9 Oct. 1865, s. of David Hunter, of Ayr.[711] Unmarried.[712]
Educ. Ayr Academy & Edinburgh University.[713]

---

[707] The last paragraph is omitted from the subject's version.

[708] Written by JCW; reviewed, but not corrected by the subject.

[709] Hunt's letter of 22 June 1937 returning the biography commented that 'I was really quite good friends with the whips except perhaps Acland Hood; & Willie Bridgeman was an old Shropshire friend'.

[710] Written by JCW, although all except the career summary is quoted directly from a note sent to Wedgwood by the subject in lieu of a response to the questionnaire; Wedgwood's text was corrected by the subject.

[711] Wedgwood's template for filling in the dates of the subject's father has been deleted.

[712] 'unmarried' inserted by the subject.

[713] Education details filled in by the subject.

He was returned member for Govan in Jan. 1910, and on 23 Apr. 1910 he took Arthur Dewar's[714] place as Solicitor General for Scotland.

In 1911 he[715] had temporary charge of Mines Bill in the absence of Mr Masterman who had lost his seat at a bye-election.[716] He was raised to the Scots Bench under the judicial title of Hon. Lord Hunter, on 5 Dec 1911.[717] Along with Prof. Scott, Glasgow, he was appointed on 18th Oct 1915[718] by the Secretary for Scotland to make immediate inquiry into the circumstances connected with the alleged increase in the rental of small dwelling houses in industrial districts in Scotland. Following their report in Nov., an Act was passed in Dec. to restrict, in connection with the present war, the increase of the rent of small dwelling houses and the increase of the rate of interest and the calling in of securities on such dwelling houses. In 1915 he acted as chairman of a Royal Commission (Northern Division) in dealing with Defence of the Realm (Licensed Trade Claims). In 1917 he acted as Judge for the purpose of hearing appeals from Munition Tribunals. In 1918 presided over a committee appointed by the Minister of Reconstruction to consider the legislation embodied in the increase of Rent and Mortgage Interest (War Restriction) Act 1915 as amended in relation to the housing of the working classes after the war, and to recommend what steps, if any, should be taken to remove any difficulties which may arise therewith.

In 1919 he went to India and presided over a Commission which inquired into serious riots which had occurred in different towns in India.

In 1920 he was appointed President of the War Compensation Court where the claim in respect of interference with property or business was in Scotland.

As President of the Valuation Appeal Court, had to deal with the great number of appeals which arose under the De-rating Acts passed in 1928.

Resigned position as a judge of the Court of Session on 5 Feb. 1936.'[719]

HUNTER-WESTON,[720] Lt.-Gen. Sir AYLMER, of Hunterston, West Kilbride, Ayrshire; M.P. (U) North Ayrshire October 1916–18, and for Buteshire and North Ayrshire 1918–22, 1922–23, 1923–24, 1924–29, 1929–31, 1931–35. In November 1935 he retired to make room for younger men.[721]

B. 23d September 1864; s. and h. of Lt.-Col.
Gould Weston (b. 1823, d. 1904) and Jane Hunter (b. 1837, d. 1911). They took the name of Hunter-Weston in 1880 when Jane Hunter succeeded her Father, Robert Hunter, 25th Laird of Hunterston;
m. 5.12.1905 Grace, D.St.J. only dau. of William Strang Steel of Philiphaugh, Selkirk: no children.[722]

---

[714] 'Arthur Dewar's' substituted by the subject for 'Alexander Ure's'.

[715] Here and throughout the subject has substituted 'he' for 'I'.

[716] 5 Dec. 1911 deleted by the subject.

[717] 'On 5 Dec. 1911' substituted by the subject for '18 Oct. 1915'.

[718] 'on 18th Oct. 1915' inserted by the subject.

[719] The subject has deleted the quotation marks at the beginning of the text of the biography ('In 1911, he had temporary charge'); but has failed to delete them from the end.

[720] Written by JCW; rewritten and retyped by the subject.

[721] Sentence inserted by the subject in his own version of the text.

[722] Father's dates, mother's name and dates, details concerning surname, date of marriage and children inserted by the subject.

Educated Wellington College and R.M.A. Woolwich. Entered Army R.E. 1884. Served in the Miransai and Waziristan Expeditions, 1891 and 1894–5, including Night Action at Wana Nov. 1894. (Wounded, despatches, Bt. Major. Medal with Clasp). Sudan Campaign 1896 on Sir Herbert Kitchener's staff. Despatches. Medjidieh, 4th Class, Khedive's Medal with Clasp, Queen's Medal. At Staff College 1898–1899. The first Sapper to be Master of the Staff College Hounds.

South African War 1899–1901. Commanded the first Troop of Mounted Engineers used in war. During Lord Roberts' advance when the British were held up by the Boers in their battle position south of Bloemfontein, he slipped through the Boer lines by night and blew up a railway bridge and the telegraph communication north of Bloemfontein, and thus prevented the Boer reinforcements arriving; this led to the surrender of Bloemfontein. He commanded five other Cavalry raids. Served on Staff of the Cavalry Division, and followed Douglas Haig, afterwards Earl Haig, as Chief Staff Officer to Sir John French. Finally commanded a Cavalry Column. (Medal with 7 clasps, D.S.O., Brevet Lt.-Col.). After that war he commanded an R.E. Company at Shorncliffe until appointed to the General Staff, Eastern Command, 1904–1908. Left the Corps of R.E. while still a Major on promotion to Substantive Colonel as Chief General Staff officer, Scottish Command, 1908–11. Assistant Director, Military Training, War Office, 1911–14. In Jan. 1914 appointed Brig.-Gen. to command the Troops at Colchester, including the 11th Infantry Brigade, which he took to France and Flanders at the outbreak of War in August 1914. Promoted Major-General for distinguished service in the Field 26th Oct. 1914. Command 29th Division at that 'Accomplishment of the Impossible', the original landing at Cape Helles, 25th April 195. Thereupon promoted temporary Lt.-Gen. to command the VIIIth Army Corps, which comprised all the British Troops, at the south end of the Gallipoli Peninsula. Commanded the VIIIth Army Corps in France and Flanders until the conclusion of hostilities. (Despatches 10 times, K.C.B., promoted Lt.-Gen. for distinguished service in the Field; 1914 Star and Clasp; British and Victory Medals and Clasp; French and Belgian Croix-de-Guerre; Grand Officer, Order of Belgian Crown; Commander Legion d'Honneur. He is Chancellor of the Order of St. John, and a Governor of Wellington College.[723]

In 1906[724] when commanding his Army Corps in France he received a telegram asking him to allow himself to be nominated for Election as M.P. for his own County: North Ayrshire. He replied by telegram: 'No, I am too busy beating the Bosch.' When, however, it was pointed out to him that it was his duty as Laird of Hunterston he said he would do as bidden by his ain folk, to serve whom was both his duty and his privilege. He was elected in absentia by a large majority, and thus became the only Britisher who has ever been simultaneously a Member of the House of Commons and the Commander of an Army Corps in the Field. During the War he came over to Westminster for a few days at a time when there was a lull in the fighting. When he was

---

[723] This paragraph is based closely on material in a paper headed 'Summary of Facts from Who's Who' which Hunter-Weston presumably enclosed with his response to the questionnaire. Wedgwood had severely summarised these facts in the original biography.

[724] *Sic.* 1916 is meant.

at Westminster arrangements were made, by Special Train, Destroyer, and Motor Car, to enable him to get back to the Ypres front in about six hours.[725]

His best speech was on 'Man Power', delivered on 24th January 1918, during one of these short absences from the Front. Of it he once said to me 'that speech was not made by me,[726] but by a figure in uniform, on two days leave, voicing the cry of the men in the trenches.'

On the cessation of hostilities he was re-elected while still in France, and feeling that this was the job that had been put in his hand he retired from the Army and devoted himself to the welfare of his constituents. His home, Hunterston, is in the middle of his large and scattered Constituency, every part of which he constantly visited, so that everyone, whether Elector or non-Elector, and irrespective of sex, religion or political opinion, had in him a helper and a friend.[727]

In Parliament after the War his best work was not in Speeches, nor in Questions, but in finding practical solutions, 'working it out in all its aspects with the Government department concerned, so that, when you put it before the Minister concerned, it was in a form which he could accept and on which he could act.'

'Hunter Bunter', 27th Laird of Hunterston, was as popular with subordinates as with colleagues, and a great gentleman. I served under him in South Africa and Gallipoli and can aver that his conversion to Parliament came late. Before the landing at Helles, he invited several commanders of units to dinner. Presumably I talked more than befitted a Lt.Cdr R.N.A.S. After dinner he took me up to the privacy and darkness of the Boat Deck. 'Are you connected in any way with politics, Wedgwood?' 'Yes Sir' I stammered. 'Not an M.P.?' The answer had to be in the affirmative. 'Then for God's sake keep it dark, man.'

HUTTON,[728] ALFRED EDDISON textile manufacturer. M.P. (L) Yorks. (Morley), 1892–5, 1895–1900, 1900–6, 1906–10, ? 1910.

B.   1865, s. of J   Hutton, of Eccleshill (–) and

m.

Educ. Mill Hill and Trinity College, Cambridge.

A politician from his cradle, and 'freedom' the inspiration. He was a Congregationalist, reading the *Daily News*. Freedom was his chief political interest and he entered Parliament 'to put the world right'. In fact he concentrated on education, the determined opponent of clerical schools and priestly influence. His best speech was on moving the rejection of Runciman's Education Bill which made concessions to clericalism. He disliked the atmosphere of the House, by which he meant the damning spirit of compromise; and he left because he was 'fed up'. Irrationally, his ideal was Gladstone

---

[725] Wedgwood's version says only 'And then he entered Parliament, "to represent his ain folk" as his forebears had done before him, but service in France and Flanders until the conclusion of hostilities. He had then £8,000 a year, and a faith in the teaching of the Bible'. Hunter-Weston has however omitted the following: 'Being in Parliament enabled me to see even more clearly than I did before the difficulties of both Ministers and Members of all political opinions . . . I enjoyed most getting into close contact with many able men in all lines of life. I disliked the bad atmosphere of the House, and especially of the Committee Rooms, and having to attend when I had nothing definite to do. From earliest days I was paired after 11p.m. with Noel Buxton'.

[726] 'during one of those . . . not made by me' substituted by the subject for 'and that was not me'.

[727] Paragraph written by the subject; not in Wedgwood's version.

[728] Written by JCW; not corrected by the subject (a note on the file says 'draft not returned').

when it should have been Cromwell or Knox. The Member for Morley went farther than John Morley; for him there was no compromise with evil or idolatry.

JARDINE,[729] Sir ERNEST, Bart.; manufacturer of Nottingham. M.P. (U) East Somerset 1910, 1910–18.

B. at Nottingham 23 Sept, 1859, s. of John Jardine, lace machine builder (1825–1895).[730]

m. 1883[731] Ada Jane (d. 1926) da. of James Fletcher of Nottingham; issue 1 s. John, 2 da. Educ. St. Omer Lycee, and Tudor House School, Nottingham. He went into his father's lace machine business, and managed or owned many other factories in Nottingham.

In 1886 he became a strong supporter of Joseph Chamberlain in opposition to Gladstonian Home Rule. To please Chamberlain he stood for Somerset and recovered the seat for the Liberal Unionists. He disliked hanging about the House to vote, wasting time which he badly wanted for his business. 'The strain of running businesses, keeping in close touch with my constituency, and Parliamentary work, was too great. The Re-distribution Bill came into force and much of my constituency was taken away and another piece added, forming the Wells division. My doctor said I was overworking and this redistribution gave me the opportunity to retire.'

He is a chevalier of the Legion of Honour, was made a Baronet in 1919, and was High[732] sheriff of Notts. 1928–9.

JARVIS,[733] Col. Sir WESTON; banker of King's Lynn. M.P. (C) King's Lynn Aug. 1886–92.

B. 26th[734] Dec. 1855, s. and h. of Sir Lewis Jarvis (d. 1 Nov.[735] 1888) of Middleton Towers, King's Lynn, and Emma da of Alexander Bowker of King's Lynn.[736]

m. 1912, Diana, da. of Charles G. Fountaine, of Narford Hall, Norfolk, and widow of Lt.-Col. Walpole Follett. Educ. Harrow. His Bank was merged in Barclays.

His father's house was the Conservative headquarters of the ancient borough, and Weston Jarvis was Church of England and read *The Times*.[737] After the 1886 Election, the Honble. Robert Bourke, the sitting Member, being selected as the next Governor of Madras, a post shortly to become vacant,[738] he was sent for by the heads of the Party, Lord Randolph Churchill being Leader in the House of Commons, who told him, confidentially, what was

---

[729] Written by JCW; corrected by the subject.

[730] Father's vital dates inserted by the subject; 'and' (for mother) deleted by the subject.

[731] Date of marriage inserted by the subject.

[732] 'High' inserted by the subject.

[733] Written by JCW; corrected by the subject who suggested some alternative paragraphs.

[734] Altered by the subject from '20th'.

[735] Day and month of death inserted by the subject.

[736] Details of mother inserted by the subject.

[737] The remainder of this paragraph and all of the following paragraph ('After the 1886 election . . . nonsense talked!'") are in the form of Jarvis' 'Alternative paragraph A'. The alternative paragraph is little different to Wedgwood's original except that it is entirely in indirect speech and in the third rather than the first person. Other significant differences are recorded in the notes.

[738] Sentence to this point substituted by the subject for 'After the 1886 election Bourke, the sitting member, was sent as Governor to Madras'.

going to happen, and that the Government majority in the House of Commons being dependent upon the Liberal Unionists, they couldn't afford to lose a seat. That they were given to understand that he was quite certain to be Elected, and that Consequently he <u>must</u> consent to stand. He had previously no idea of becoming an M.P.

His chief political interest was agriculture, for King's Lynn was dependent upon agricultural prosperity. He was well known to all the farmers and labourers and a strong supporter of the views held by Mr Henry Chaplin and Mr James Lowther.

His election cost £350, and about £250 a year. Disraeli and Palmerston were his ideal statesmen. When afterwards asked what he liked and disliked in the House of Commons, he replied 'I liked the good fellowship of my fellow Members, and getting to know everybody worth knowing, and disliked hearing a good deal of nonsense talked.'

He retired in 1892 having[739] succeeded to an estate heavily mortgaged to build the King's Lynn docks, and rents were falling so heavily that[740] he could no longer afford a Parliamentary career. Meanwhile he had made great friends with Cecil Rhodes. He[741] threw himself into the development of Rhodesia and served through the Matabele rebellion of 1896. He then served through the whole of the Boer War, first in command of a Squadron of the Rhodesian Regiment under Colonel, (later Field Marshal Viscount)[742] Plumer, and afterwards in command of the 21st Battalion[743] Imperial Yeomanry. C.M.G. 1901, M.V.O. 1901, Lieut Colonel[744] in the Army 1902.

He served on the staff of the Duke of Connaught during his mission to Egypt & India (Delhi Durbar) 1902–1903.[745]

He served through the whole of the European War, in command of the 3rd County of London Yeomanry from 1914–1916 in Egypt, Gallipoli and the Sinai Peninsula, and on the staff of the XIXth Corps, B.E.F., in France 1917–1919.

He occupied the position of Chairman of the Council of the Royal Empire Society 1930–1932, and is a vice-President of the Society.[746]

JESSEL,[747] Col. Sir Herbert Merton. M.P. (U) South St. Pancras 1896–1900, 1900–05; contested 1906, 1910 (?) M.P. 1910–18; contested St. George's, Westminster, June 1921. Lord Jessel of Westminster 1924.

<u>B</u>. at Brighton 27 Oct. 1866; y.s. of Rt. Hon. Sir George Jessel, M.P., Master of the Rolls (–);

<u>m</u>. 1894, Maud, da. of Sir Julian Goldsmid, Bart., M.P. Issue – Edward Herbert, and I da.

---

[739] 'having' substituted by the subject for 'as he had'.

[740] 'were falling so heavily that' altered by the subject from 'were falling so that'.

[741] The remainder of this paragraph and all of the following paragraph ('He threw himself . . . (Delhi Durbar) 1902–1903') are in the form of Jarvis' 'Alternative paragraph B'. The alternative paragraph is little different to Wedgwood's original except that it is entirely in indirect speech and in the third rather than the first person. Other significant differences are recorded in the notes.

[742] 'Colonel, later Field Marshal Viscount' inserted by the subject.

[743] 'Battalion' inserted by the subject.

[744] Wedgwood had written 'Hon. Lt.-Col'.

[745] Wedgwood had written 'Later he was on the Duke of Connaught's staff'.

[746] Paragraph added by the subject.

[747] Written by JCW; not corrected by the subject (a note on the file says 'draft not returned').

Educ. Rugby and New College, Oxford; joined 17th Lancers; served in India 1887–90; retired as Captain 1896; afterwards Major, Berks. Yeomanry and hon. Col. City of London Regt. 1905–23.

Politics came to him paternally and in debating at Rugby and in the Discussion Society at New College. He got his seat by succeeding his father-in-law, for his elder brother preferred pheasants to politics. So he retired from the Lancers and read The Times. He wanted to talk Army in the House, but had to take up Local Government instead. This too became interesting (he went into St George's vestry) and 'the change from the Army modified my views of civilians.' £550 to £600 election expenses and about the same annual expenditure. 'It must be remembered that the whole cost of looking after the register was incurred by the local organisation, i.e. the M.P. with slight local help.' He idealised Lord Salisbury and Napoleon; disliked smoking concerts and bad tobacco; liked 'acquaintance with the eminent statesmen of all sides in Parliament, conversations and good fellowship in the smoking room and with my Parliamentary colleagues of all parties.' 'Certainly' speeches affected his vote. Grey's in Aug. 1914 and Asquith's 'We will not sheath the sword' were the best he heard. His best piece of work was 'moving substantial amendments in the London Government Act 1900 and killing proportional representation proposed in the Bill for Representation of the People Act in 1918.' In 1918 his seat was split and as he was not demobilised till 1919 he did not stand.

Jessel carried through the Commons the Old Age Pensions Act of 1911 and the Affiliation Orders Act 1914, through the Lords the Driving Licences Act of 1926. He was an alderman of Westminster and Mayor 1902–3, and held many party offices in London. In Aug. 1914 he rejoined the Army, but was too old for service in France. Jessel was a completely assimilated English Jew – one of those whom racial persecution had rallied to his race to the honour of England; and his chief pride is that his father was the first Jew to be Solicitor General and Master of the Rolls.

JONES,[748] Sir EDGAR REES; barrister. M.P. (Lib) Merthyr-Tydvil, 1910, 1910–18; Merthyr 1918–22.

B. at Cwmaman, 27 Aug. 1878, e.s. of Rev. Morgan H. Jones, Baptist minister,[749] m. 1919, May, da. of George Brackley, of Harringay; 1 s., 1 da. Educ. Univ. Coll., Cardiff, (M.A.). Schoolmaster.

Living in a Welsh mining village, politics could not be avoided. From 15 years of age he was speaking, and a strict Baptist. Social conditions and the horrors of intemperance moved him to speak. He was a pupil teacher and won a scholarship to Cardiff University. Earning £200 a year, he suddenly found himself in Parliament in a fortnight.[750] Gladstone and Lloyd George were his ideals. The speeches he puts as best for the occasion – Grey in Aug. 1914; for style and ability, Hugh Cecil on conscientious objectors. His best piece of work was 'carrying an amendment in Committee which compelled the withdrawal of the first Railway Amalgamation Bill in spite of previous agreement between the Government and the Labour interests,' and the securing of a

---

[748] Written by JCW; corrected by the subject.

[749] The subject has deleted the brackets and space supplied by Wedgwood for father's vital dates and details of mother.

[750] 'The election cost someone £900 and about £150 a year' deleted by the subject.

unanimous report as Chairman of the Welsh Consultative Council of Health for the reorganisation of all the health services in Wales.[751]

During the War he made for himself at the Ministry of Munitions the 'Priority Department' and became Controller thereof. With this introduction he became after the War industrial adviser to the Tin-plate and other industries, and founder and chairman of the National Food Canning Council. He was knighted in 1918.

The school teacher whose whirling arms and words aroused and amused the House, made himself at the Munitions Ministry into an industrial magnate.[752]

KINCAID-SMITH,[753] Capt. MALCOLM. M.P. (Lib) Warwickshire (Stratford) 1906–1909, contested 1909.

<u>B</u>. 6 July 1874, y.s. of Major John[754] Kincaid-Smith, of Polmont, Falkirk, and Mrs Kincaid-Smith[755]   of Aldingbourne, Chichester.

Educ. Eton and R.M.C., Sandhurst. 9th Lancers 1894; served S. African War 1899–1902, captain 1901.

His politics started with the S. African War. Lord Denman introduced[756] him to Gladstone, the Chief Whip. He joined Lord Rosebery's Liberal League and was certainly the most conservative of Liberals – though a staunch supporter of Taxation of Land Values as practised in Canada.[757] His election cost £1,200 and about £300 a year. His interests were in Foreign Affairs and specially in National Military Training. He resigned in 1909 and stood for re-election 'because I was foolish enough to think I could push the issue by that method.' He liked actual debate, but disliked 'hearing somebody else say what I wanted to say myself.' As for his own speeches, 'None good, except in the cab going home.'

Such frank and truthful answers are highly to be recommended for the purposes of this History, and stand to the credit of the bull-headed obstinacy of Capt. Kincaid-Smith. He rejoined the Army for the War and rose to Lieut.-Colonel, mentioned in despatches.

KING,[758] JOSEPH; Contested New Forest 1892, Thanet 1904 and 1906. M.P. (Lib) North Somerset 1910, 1910–18.

<u>B</u>. 31 March[759] 1860, s. of Joseph King, M.R.C.S. of Liverpool (B   –1814)[760] and Phoebe, dau of James Powell, B. 1820.

---

[751] 'and the securing . . . health services of Wales' inserted by the subject.

[752] Wedgwood's last sentence has been deleted by the subject: 'The boom lasted but a short time in South Wales, and Sir Edgar lost most of what he had made, but not his happy and lively ebullience of spirit'.

[753] Written by JCW; corrected by the subject.

[754] 'John' inserted by the subject.

[755] 'Mrs Kincaid-Smith' inserted by the subject.

[756] 'Lord Denman introduced' substituted by the subject for 'He had £2,500 a year and R. Denman (M.P.) introduced'.

[757] 'though a staunch supporter . . . in Canada' inserted by the subject.

[758] Written by JCW; corrected by the subject.

[759] Day and month of birth inserted by the subject.

[760] '1814' is inserted by King in the space intended for the father's death date. It is presumably meant to be his father's birth date, rather than a mistake for '1914' as a death date (compare the birth date for his mother).

m̲. (1) 1887, Maude (d̲. 1927), da. of Henry G. Hine; 1 da.; (2) 1928, Nellie Gertrude Martins. Educ Uppingham and Trinity, Oxford. Studied under Dr. Fairbairn at Bradford and at Giessen University; called to the Bar, Inner Temple, 1890, but never practised; and he has written much on Foreign Affairs and Education.

His home was in Liverpool, his father worked for Mr Gladstone in 1868, and he was trained for the Free Church pastorate. He was evangelical Protestant, steadily broadened by Dean Stanley and Maurice; but his ideal and politics were John Bright, pacifism and justice. Macaulay and Wm. Cobbett had a hand in shaping Joseph King. The Eighty Club brought him into Parliament. He had then £100 a year earned and £900 unearned. For six years he was on the Surrey County Council and he had also been on the Hampstead Board of Guardians.

Joe King says he spoke too often. That was not so, for his interests were intellectual and covered the world. He hated cruelty and injustice and loved his friends as they loved him. He was active and undaunted, as a pro-Boer in 1900, as a pacifist in 1914–18. Once when he rose to speak, they 'espied strangers' and cleared the galleries.[761] No one would nominate him as candidate in 1918, and he says rightly that his 'best piece of work was that I remained a Christian Pacifist and not devoid of humanity and common sense and true speaking during the war.' He hated being excluded from Parliament, and writes in Nov. 1936, 'Considering how cruel the Nazis and Fascisti are, how cowardly and hypocritically incompetent the Government is, and how shameful the whole society of present day Europe is, when it leaves Spain to be tortured and mutilated, I am quite myself still. Sound at heart and raging with disgust and indignation, but loyal to my friends and mindful of my faith as a rebel.' There could be no better illustration of the mind, life and example of Joseph King.

LAMBERT,[762] Rt. Hon. GEORGE; of Spreyton, Devon. Civil Lord of the Admiralty 1905–15; P.C. 1912. M.P. (Lib) Devon (South Molton) 1891–2, 1892–5, 1895–1900, 1900–6, 1906–10, 1910, 1910–18, 1918–22, 1922–3, 1923–4; contested 1924; M.P. (Lib.Nat.) 1929–31, 1931–35, 1935.

---

[761] The remainder of Wedgwood's sentence has been deleted by King. It read: 'once they put him in prison for writing a letter to   in Switzerland'. On a separate sheet King wrote: 'This is inaccurate. Two variants, either correct, are offered:-
   (A) prosecuted for writing to a friend in New York a letter containing military information he offered an apology and paid a fine of £100 or
   (B) once they threatened, but feared, to put him in prison for writing a letter to New York, but imposed a £100 fine instead.
I think (B) will do'.
   On a second sheet of paper, marked 'Private and confidential', King provided the following memorandum: 'I was convicted at Bow Street on October 21ˢᵗ 1916 for giving military information and fined £100. I had placed myself in the hands of my counsel, Gordon Hewart, who told me privately in the House, after going through his brief, that I had a good case against conviction. In Court just before the case was called, and after he had had a talk with Bodkin, the Crown Prosecutor, he came to me and asked me to let him trust him unreservedly in whatever course he took. I consented; he addressed the Court, without calling on me or any witness; and offering my apology for a clear indiscretion, he got me off with £100 fine. A very few days after he became Solicitor General, though he was known as a keen critic of the D.O.R.A. proceedings'.

[762] Written by JCW; corrected by the subject. Lambert wrote back to Wedgwood on 15 May 1937 that he had vetted the biography: 'sometimes you hit the target & sometimes miss the blooming thing altogether'.

<u>B</u>. 25 June 1866, s. of   and
<u>m</u>. 1904 Barbara, da. of G. Stavers of Morpeth; 2s., 2 da. Educ. privately.

Parental tradition made him a Liberal, and 'liberal' too was his religion – no books. He was a yeoman farmer with an inherited but moderate income. Agriculture was his interest, Gladstone his model. Gladstone's introduction of the Home Rule Bill in 1893 was the best speech he heard. His elections cost £1,400 in 1891 and £700 in 1935, a good sample of the fall in election expenses. The annual cost has been £400 a year, and he learnt in Parliament and in office 'to be tolerant of stupidity'.

For ten years he vanished into the Admiralty; but George Lambert has long become an institution which no politics can shift from Devonshire. He is about the only old-fashioned Liberal in the House of Commons and has championed agriculture for 45 years but since Parliament deemed right to fix agricultural wages by law he regards free trade as a thing of the past, and is a rigorous opponent of any attempt to further tax agricultural land.[763]

LAMONT,[764] Sir NORMAN, Bart., Knockdow, Toward, Argyll. Contested Buteshire 1900; M.P. (Lib) Buteshire Mar. 1905–6, 1906–10; contested Jan. 1910.

<u>B</u>. 7 Dec.[765] 1869, s. and h. of Sir James[766] Lamont, 1st Bart., (1828–1913)[767] and Adelaide, da. of Sir George Denys, 2nd Bart. Educ. Winchester and College of Agriculture, Downton.

'I had lately given my first vote as a Conservative, for nearly all my friends were of that persuasion, when[768] on 14 Nov. 1895 I was given a platform ticket to hear A.J. Balfour speak at Glasgow. As he proceeded I felt myself more and more strongly in disagreement with him, particularly on the Tirah Expedition; and "where the British soldier has stood, there we shall remain!" '

Lamont's[769] political views were, in fact, more the outcome of antagonism than of persuasion: of dislike of the principles and policy of *The Morning Post* and of *The Times* rather than of any fervour for those enunciated by *The Daily News*.[770] Hatred of the S. African War and of the policy which led up to it, were perhaps his chief political interest, and combined with his father's wish in inducing him to contest Buteshire against the Lord-Advocate in Oct. 1900.

---

[763] The last sentence has been substituted by the subject for 'Probably he has as few Liberal voters now as he has Liberal principles; for agriculture, which he has championed for 45 years, has long since expunged Free Trade from his tenets. Even in 1910 he was an all too rigorous and intolerant opponent of the taxation of land values and of any Lloyd Georgian attack upon the landed interest'.

[764] Written by JCW; corrected by the subject.

[765] Day and date of birth inserted by the subject.

[766] 'James' inserted by the subject.

[767] Father's year of birth inserted by the subject.

[768] 'when' inserted by the subject.

[769] This paragraph and the following two ('Lamont's political views were, in fact, . . . warmly admired by Lamont') were rewritten by the subject, although almost entirely on the basis of the information provided by Wedgwood. Significant differences to Wedgwood's text are noted in the footnotes.

[770] Wedgwood had written: 'In fact his political views were formed by dislike of the news of the *Morning Post*. He read the *Times* and was Presbyterian'.

The Lamonts were West Indian planters, as well as owning 8000 acres in Argyllshire. Lamont's contests cost an average of £800 each,[771] and an annual expenditure of about £100, out of the allowance of £400 a year given him by his father.

Grey (living) and Strafford (dead) were among statesmen most warmly admired by Lamont.

Lamont was P.P.S. to Campbell-Bannerman, the Prime Minister, 1906–8. His best speech was on West Indian Federation, 17 May 1905; the best he heard 'Arthur Balfour on "Defence of the Empire" May 11, 1905, and Alex. Ure, defending himself against Balfour, Nov. 3, 1909.' His best piece of work; – 'Chairmanship of the Departmental Committee of the Board of Trade on "Labour Exchanges" in 1909.' He has written *Problems of the Antilles*, 1912; *Problems of Trinidad*, 1933; *An Inventory of Lamont Papers*, 1914.

From 1915 to 1923 Lamont was a Member of the Legislative Council of Trinidad and Tobago; and a Governor of the Imperial College of Tropical Agriculture from its foundation.

Sir Norman Lamont was the perfect combination of Liberalism and West Indies; and the West Indies, be it noted, was the only part of the British Empire where black men take a pride in being British subjects.

LANE-FOX,[772] Col. Rt. Hon. GEORGE RICHARD (cr. Lord Bingley of Bramham 1933). Secretary for Mines 1922–4, Nov. 1924–Jan. 1928. M.P. (U) Yorks. (Barkston Ash) 1906–10, 1910, 1910–18, 1918–22, 1922–3, 1923–4, 1924–9, 1929–31.

B. 15 Dec. 1870, s. and h. of J.T.R. Lane-Fox of Bramham, Yorks. (1848–1906) and Lucy, daughter of Humphrey Mildmay.[773]

m. 1903, Mary Agnes, sister of Edward Wood, Viscount Halifax, M.P.; 4 da. Educ. Eton and New College, Oxford.

He served in the War, 1914–17, and was wounded at Ypres[774] being then Major in[775] the Yorks. Hussars. County Councillor and Alderman of the West Riding, 1898–1928.

His politics came from his family and, as usual, from the general reading of history – 'always my favourite subject' – so did his religion, Church of England, and his papers, *Yorkshire Post* and *Times*. The influence of his grandfather, a keen politician, first led him to think of Parliament. He was busy on County, Parish and District Council work and helping his father with the Bramham Moor Hounds. He was adopted for his own Division.[776] Balfour and Disraeli were his guides. He liked Parliament 'for the general interest of being close up to interesting men and government;' disliked constant social functions and political meetings in the constituency. His speech, which he enjoyed most, was winding up the debate on the 3rd Reading of the Coal Mines Bill, 1926. The one that thrilled him most was Grey's on the outbreak of war. His best piece of work was

---

[771] Wedgwood had written: 'His contests cost his father £800 apiece, and £100 a year'.

[772] Written by JCW; corrected by the subject.

[773] Father's vital dates and mother's details inserted by the subject.

[774] 'Ypres' inserted by the subject.

[775] 'Major in' substituted by the subject for 'Colonel of'.

[776] 'and had at that time £2,000 a year' deleted by the subject.

saving his constituency from being swallowed by Leeds. The expense of fighting elections[777] was too great and he retired after 25 years.

The little group of related friends who succeeded to the Tory rule of England comprised Baldwin, Wood, Bridgman and George Lane-Fox. They were a cut above the ruling Tories of the past – no greed, no spoils, no partisanship. Perhaps stupider, but much better for England and for Democracy than the quick, clever, bitter brains of the preceding generation. Anthony Eden is probably of the same group. They have no ambition, many doubts, but never whine or pass on the blame, or complain of being misunderstood. Such indifferences may be due in the case of Lane-Fox to absence of imagination. Once in a Coal Mines Debate, Joshua Ritson, the Durham miner, burst into Swinburne's 'Proserpine' – 'Here where the world is quiet . . .' for Lane-Fox was asleep.

LANSBURY,[778] Rt. Hon. GEORGE; saw miller & veneer cutter[779] of Bow. P.C. 1929. First Commissioner of Works 1929–31; Leader of the Labour Party 1931–5. Contested Walworth[780] 1894 & 1895.[781] M.P. (Labour) Bow and Bromley 1910–2, contested same at bye-election[782] 1912; M.P. Bow and Bromley 1922–3, 1923–4, 1924–9, 1929–31, 1931–5, 1935.

B. at Halesworth, Suffolk, 21 Feb. 1859, s. of George Lansbury, of Warwickshire[783] (1834–1875),[784] railway sub-contractor, and Mary Anne Ferris of Radnorshire; m. 1880, Elizabeth Jane (d. 1933) da. of Isaac Brine, of Somerset, a timber merchant of London.[785] 4 s.; 8 da. including Dorothy[786] m. to Ernest Thurtle, M.P.

Educ. In a Church school till 13; went to Australia for freedom 1884; came back into his father-in-law's business at Bow, 1885. 'Like Topsy I just grew into politics after 1870.' The general reading of simple history did it even more than doses of Walker, Henry George, Karl Marx and Hyndman. 'I hope I am a Christian.' 'I really have no favourite paper.' 'I never had more than a passing thought about becoming anything – M.P., Guardian, Councillor – I just fell into it. I have one trait which has never left me. I try to do any job that comes my way, but have never consciously schemed or intrigued to get a position, they have come my way, but I have always liked to try and serve. There is no merit in this. There are two sets of people in the world, Givers and Takers. God had run out of Takers when I was born so I became a Giver. This is sheer egoism but my family to their cost know it is true. Service called me to politics as a child and has kept me there ever since.' 'There is no place in a true Democracy for careerists.' His

---

[777] 'fighting elections' substituted by the subject for 'his seat (£500 a year)'. In a letter to Wedgwood of 5 May 1937 Bingley had written: 'I don't in the least mind being called stupid – but I don't want to seem unduly mean – so I should really prefer that you should make the omissions that I suggest – I had to fight nine elections, costing about £1000 each time'. See also above, pp. 112, 117.

[778] Written by JCW; corrected by the subject.

[779] 'saw miller & veneer cutter' substituted by the subject for 'furniture manufacturer'.

[780] 'Walworth' inserted by the subject.

[781] '& 1895' inserted by the subject.

[782] 'at bye-election' inserted by the subject.

[783] 'Warwickshire' substituted by the subject for 'Oxford'.

[784] Father's year of birth inserted by the subject.

[785] Amended by the subject from 'Isaac Brine, a timber merchant of Somerset'.

[786] 'Dorothy' substituted by the subject for 'Daisy'.

trade: – 'I started as an office boy about ten or eleven years of age, and am now connected in a small way with a timber and veneer business. I have been an editor and newspaper proprietor. Managed successfully and also badly some big business, but I could never be a really good business man, am too soft.' Mazzini, and Gladstone whose speeches[787] in 1875 or 1876, closing with a magnificent peroration about Montenegro, was the greatest he ever heard – were an inspiration, 'but of women politicians Annie Besant was head and shoulders above them all.'

His fundamental views were not affected by Parliament, but 'experience of M.P.s convinces me that the average Member desires to do his best. The party system dragoons us all. If we were all free one would find unity of purpose working for the common good.' He likes in Parliament, 'Friendship and power to help change things'; dislike![788] 'A lot of humbug is talked about our sacrifices. I never feel I have made any. I want to be in the House of Commons.' 'It is difficult to say what has been my best piece of work. I think I have been a good administrator as well as a fairly good Parliament man. My record on Poplar Guardians, Borough Council, County Council, Office of Works, testifies to my ability to do a job of work. I think I am also a fairly good agitator and propagandist; there is no reason why all these should not go together. I think my short term as Leader of the Labour Party was perhaps my best piece of National political work. My years since 1892 on the local bodies at Poplar also gives me a little satisfaction as also does the work as Poor Law Commissioner, on the Unemployment Committees in London, editing and keeping the *Daily Herald* going and work for Womens' Suffrage and public propaganda on behalf of what I thought was religion and socialism.'

This is not egotistical. It is George Lansbury and the truth as he sees it. John Burns said of him that he had a heart of gold and a head of feathers. The feathers are brotherhood, sympathy and love; but he is too loving a pacifist even to hate evil. The complete absence of selfishness in Lansbury and Attlee is remarkable.

LARMOR,[789] Sir JOSEPH; of St John's College, Cambridge. M.P. (U) Cambridge University 1911–18, 1918–22.

B. at Magheragall, Antrim, 11 July 1857; s. and h. of Hugh Larmor and Anna, da. of Joseph Wright, of Stoneyford. Unmd. Educ. Queen's College, Belfast, and St. John's, Cambridge.

In early life he served five years with much acceptance as Professor of Natural Philosophy in Queen's College, Galway, 1880–5, before returning to Cambridge to avoid vacation of his college fellowship. There he lectured in Mathematics, Lucasian Professor 1903–32; Secretary of the Royal Society 1901–12. He had no political ambitions. Accepted under pressure nomination as an independent candidate at a bye-election in Cambridge in 1911: received support of the Conservative Committee on the withdrawal of their candidate. Knighted in 1909. He contested two elections at Cambridge; finally retired in 1922 on grounds of health and pressure of University work. A member of the

---

[787] 'speech' amended by the subject to 'speeches'.

[788] *Sic.*

[789] Written by JCW; not corrected by the subject (note on file says 'draft not sent out').

Speaker's Committee on Electoral Reform. He was an onlooker and took little interest in political debate, being overshadowed by his brilliant colleague, Rawlinson.[790]

LAWSON,[791] Hon. HARRY LAWSON WEBSTER (1862–1933); owner of the Daily Telegraph. MP (Lib.) West St. Pancras 1885–6, 1886–92, contested 1892, contested East Gloucestershire 1892 (a tie, re-contested), MP Glos. (East) Feb. 1893–5, contested 1895, contested N.E. Bethnal Green ?1900, contested Bury as Lib. Unionist 1902, MP Mile End (Unionist) 1905–1906, contested Mile End 1906; MP Mile End 1910, 1910–16. 2nd Lord Burnham 1916 onwards.

b. 18 Dec. 1862, e.s. & h. of Edward Levy Lawson (1st Lord Burnham 1903) of Hall Barn, Bucks, (18 –1916) and Harriet da. of Benjamin Webster; m. 1884 Olive da. of Gen. Sir Henry de Bathe; no issue.

Educ. Eton and Balliol (1st History Mods). The Telegraph had been taken over by his grandfather in 1855 for a bad debt, and started then as the first 1d. daily paper. He sold it to Lord Iliffe (q.v.)[792] in 1928.

As a young man at Balliol he was greatly influenced by Jowett, and became Conservative at the time of the So. African War and some few years later he took over the management of the Daily Telegraph in which he had taken little active part. Probably his greatest work was the Burnham scale which raised and settled the salaries of teachers. But his change over was caused chiefly by a growing interest in Imperial questions.

Few private Members worked harder than Lawson, on the 3rd bench above the gangway. He was on the L.C.C also 1897–1904. Yet it is his work on Commissions that will always be best known. He was on the Royal Comn. on Civil Establishments 1889–94; took a prominent part in the Speaker's Conference on Parliamentary reform; a member of the Bryce committee on House of Lords reform; chairman of the 'Burnham' Committee on teachers salaries; a member of the Empire & Overseas Settlement committee of the Colonial Office. He was on the Simon Commission & the Indian Round Table conferences, but became increasingly dubious of the final constitution.

During the war he trained & commanded the reserve regiment of the Bucks Yeomanry. After the war he was chairman of all these committees: – International Service and Officers resettlement, restoration of ex-service men to civil life, War Office promotion committee, King's Fund for disabled ex-servicemen. Companion of Honour, 1917, GCMG 1927.

Outside his strictly Parliamentary work he was President of the I.L.O. in 1921, 1922, 1926, and built up the Standing Orders of that Geneva institution. He was chairman also of the 1st World Press Conference there 1927, President of the Imperial Press conferences at Ottawa and Melbourne 1920, 1925. President of the Anglo-Swedish Society.

And for many years he was President of the Newspaper Press Fund, and Chairman of the Newspaper Proprietors Assocn. Few men have worked at all things as hard as did Lord Burnham, and none with such constant and universal popularity. He worked to the

---

[790] 'Rawlinson' written in pencil over an ellipsis.
[791] Written by JCW from notes supplied by the subject's brother, but not typed.
[792] Biography not there.

end; and died, without any illness, quietly in his sleep, 20 July 1933. Will, unsettled real and personal estate of £229,558; net personalty £197,481. He was succeeded in the peerage by his brother.

LAWSON,[793] Sir WILFRID, Bart.; of Isel Hall, Cockermouth. Contested Mid-Cumberland 1886, Cockermouth Jan. 1910; M.P. (Lib.) Cumberland (cockermouth) 1910–   1916.

   B. 21 Oct. 1862, s. and h. of Sir Wilfrid Lawson, Bart., M.P. (–1906); m. 1891 Mary Camilla, da. of Turner A. Macan, of Elstow, Beds.,; no issue.

A natural instinct and his father's politics made him political. Fawcett's *Political Economy* and J.R. Lowell's *Poetical Works* taught him. The *Manchester Guardian* was his paper. He had been on the local School Board, and a J.P., and he had an income of £1,200 a year in 1886. His election cost £1,000 and £800 a year. Peace and temperance were, of course, his subjects, but attending Divisions was his fate. He liked in the House 'its general friendliness and tolerance.' His best speech, he says, was against going to war with Germany in 1914, so he did not get the coupon or stand again,

He was just one more Lawson of Isel, without his father's wit, but with all his father's principles. Not a good mixer, perhaps, and with the House against him he folded his tents.

LEES-SMITH,[794] Rt. Hon. HASTINGS BERTRAND; postmaster General 1929–31; P.C. 1931; President of the Board of Education 1931; M.P. (Lib.) Northampton 1910; 1910–18; contested Don Valley 1918, as Ind. Radical; M.P. (Labour) Yorks. (Keighley) 1922–3, contested 1923, M.P. 1924–29, 1929–31; contested 1931; M.P. Yorks (Keighley) 1935.

   B. in India Jan: 26th[795] 1878, 2nd s. of Major H. Lees-Smith, R.A., (died 1882) and Jessie 2nd daughter of Hastings Reid I.C.S. Judge of the High Court of Bombay.[796] m, 1915, Joyce, da. of S.H. Holman; 2 sons born 1919 & 1921. educated Westminster School & abroad.[797]

   Educated Aldenham; took[798] up cadetship at R.M.A. Woolwich but did not like Army life & resigned[799] and went[800] to Queen's College, Oxford (M.A.) D.Sc. London.[801] There he helped to found Ruskin College, becoming Vice-Principal; Professor of Economics at Bristol University, and Reader in Public Administration at London University. Owing to

---

[793] Written by JCW; not corrected by the subject (a note on the file says 'Died 28 Aug. 37').

[794] Written by JCW; corrected by the subject.

[795] Day and month inserted by the subject.

[796] Father's year of death and details of mother inserted by the subject.

[797] Details of sons inserted by the subject, as is 'educated Westminster School & abroad'. These educational details presumably refer to the sons, as Lees-Smith's own educational details are given at the beginning of the biography.

[798] 'took' substituted by the subject for 'did not take'.

[799] 'but did not like Army life & resigned' inserted by the subject.

[800] 'instead' deleted by the subject.

[801] 'D.Sc. London' inserted by the subject.

health, joined R.A.M.C. Sanitary Corps 1915 as a private, obtaining the rank of Corporal[802] and served one year[803] in France in the ranks. Invalided 1917–[804]

Mill – *On Liberty* – and listening to speeches in Hyde Park, started him in politics at 14. He was Church of England, and wanted to be an M.P. 'because I thought it was the finest and most interesting life.' Ruskin College had given him experience of public work and his profession was the exposition of public service. He had no income but what he earned; and even that dwindled to half when he got into the House. He got his seat almost by accident in this manner: – 'by making a speech in a village in Northamptonshire where the Chairman of the Northampton Liberal Association was present. As a result I was asked to go to Northampton.' His chief interests were the standard of living, unemployment insurance, and national finance; his statesmen Cobden, Bright and Gladstone, dead, with Campbell-Bannerman and Haldane, living. His elections cost, Jan.1910, £600; Dec. 1910, £400, Dec. 1918 £1,000, and his last six elections since joining the Labour Party, £150 to £250; while the House cost him £300 a year.

He says 'Parliament made me less republican and gave me an even greater belief in Parliamentary Government. I enjoyed meeting and working with some of the finest of my fellow countrymen.' He thinks his best speech was 'at the end of 1916 when returning from the Front urging for peace by negotiation.' But he is wrong: the best was the other day on Foreign Affairs. His best piece of work, 'the Minority Report of the Savidge Tribunal.' Grey's was the best speech he heard. The books he has written illustrate the value of the man and his work: – *A People's Guide to the Insurance Act*; *Studies in Indian Economics*; *India and the Tariff Problem*, 1909; *Second Chambers in Theory and Practice*, 1923: *A Guide to Parliamentary Papers*, 1924. He also edited *The Encyclopaedia of the Labour Movement*.

This was a very brave and a very quiet man; he never pushed himself as a Liberal, and always faced the storm. Since joining the Labour Party he has devoted himself, rather sadly and fruitlessly, to teaching Parliament to his colleagues. He deceived no man, not even an elector; being always the responsible mentor,[805] humanised by dreams and knowing the limitations of politics and of human nature. So many of the Labour Front Bench suffer from mental agreement with the Government, but Lees-Smith retains criticism and remains a Radical. Really his finest piece of work was done in that small minority during the War. He did not seek the coupon either in 1918 or in 1931.

LEWISHAM,[806] Viscount, WILLIAM LEGGE; of Patshull, Staffs. (Earl of Dartmouth, 1936). Lord Great Chamberlain 1928–36; contested West Bromwich 1906; M.P. (C) West Bromwich 1910, 1910–18.

B. 22 Feb. 1881, s. and h. of the 6th Earl (1851–1936) (q.v.; m. 1905, Lady Ruperta, da. of 1st Marquess of Lincolnshire; issue, b. and 5 da.

---

[802] 'Owing to health . . . rank of corporal' substituted by the subject for 'There is no mention of his war service in *Who's Who*; but he joined up at once'.

[803] 'one year' substituted for 'two years' by the subject.

[804] 'Invalided 1917–' inserted by the subject.

[805] 'mentor' substituted by the subject for 'schoolmaster'.

[806] Written by JCW; not corrected by the subject (a note on the file says 'draft not returned').

Educ. Eton and Christ Church, Oxford. Lt.-Col. Staffs. Yeomanry till 1920; Hon. Col. 7th West Riding Regt. 1910–22; Member of the L.C.C. 1907–10; President of the M.C.C. 1932; G.C.V.O. 1934.

A Protestant, reading the *Times*, he became a politician only when invited to stand as Conservative candidate for West Bromwich 1906. He took his politics from his father's; he had an unearned income of £4,000 a year, and his election cost about £800. Tariffs and Imperial questions were his chief interest, Balfour his ideal. Parliament modified his ideas very little 'apart from lessening the confident certainty of youth.' He seems to have disliked those all night sittings of which he and his party were the cause; but liked 'the opportunity of making many new friends.' His best speech was moving the Address in the House of Lords, Nov. 1936, – Grey's the best he heard. Speeches 'modified my views, though they did not I think affect my vote'.

Lord Lewisham did not seem to enjoy the Commons, especially that War Parliament, as much as his father did; but he did enjoy the office of Lord Great Chamberlain and the control of the House of Lords.

LLOYD GEORGE,[807] Rt. Hon. DAVID. President of the Board of Trade 1905–08; Chancellor of the Exchequer 1908–15; Minister of Munitions 1915–16; Secretary of State for War 1916; Prime Minister 1916–22. M.P. (Lib.) Carnarvon boroughs 1890–2, 1892–5, 1895–1900, 1900–5, 1906–10, 1910, 1910–1918, 1918–22, 1922–3, 1923–4, 1924–9, 1929–31, 1931–5, 1935.

B. at Manchester 17 Jan. 1863, s. of William George (18 –), master of Hope St. Unitarian School, Liverpool, and Elizabeth Lloyd[808] m. 1888 Margaret, da. of Richard Owen of Criccieth. Issue: – Major Richard,[809] Olwen, *m.* Sir T.J. Carey Evans, Megan, M.P. for Anglesey, Major Gwilym M.P.

Educ. Llanystymdwy Church School. Solicitor 1884.

Every Welshman is a politician and Mr Lloyd George[810] remembers the 1868 election. These books formed his political views: – Carlyle, Victor Hugo, Ruskin, Fabian Essays, Kidd's Social Evolution, Macaulay. These were his favourite newspapers in 1890: – *Liverpool Mercury, Daily News*, weekly Welsh papers. The two who led him to think of a Parliamentary career were Michael Davitt, and Michael Jones, Principal of the Bala Congregational College. He was making over £500 a year when first he stood for Parliament and he was already on the County Council. His ideal living British statesman was Gladstone but he had also a great admiration for Joseph Chamberlain. His chief political interest was, and still remains, – fair play for the underdog.

'I am not conscious that Parliament modified my views, except that it gave me a very unpleasant impression of the difficulties of getting things done, and of the tremendous power of vested interests in every direction.' *Did being an M.P. affect your earning capacity?* 'But for the fact that I had a very self-sacrificing brother who kept the practice going, with very occasional assistance, it would have very substantially reduced my income.'

---

[807] Written by JCW; corrected by Frances Stevenson.

[808] Mother's name inserted by Frances Stevenson.

[809] 'Major Richard,' inserted by Frances Stevenson.

[810] 'Mr Lloyd George' substituted by Frances Stevenson for 'he'.

Bilingualism and chapel training make orators of most Welshmen, and 50 years have not moderated[811] George's supremacy as an orator. But it is as master of Parliamentary debate that he obtained power and holds the House. He never knows his case, he refuses to read, his ignorance exasperates both Treasury and colleagues;[812] yet no Phoenix so often rises from its ashes. He trusts entirely to some chance exaggeration of his opponents' and to that rollicking sense of humour which will always bring him the laugh and keep that laugh till every damaging point is forgotten. Possibly Churchill would have won the War quicker and better than Lloyd George, but even Churchill was never such a master in debate, so sure of his House of Commons. And Churchill had not the courage of this Welsh attorney. For six terrific years he ruled England. How he ruled it others can decide; but that he ruled by consent and with acclaim all will agree who ever sat in that Bottomley's Parliament of 1919–22. And then he fell like Lucifer. In one Parliament nine-tenths of the lungs of loud men were shouting for him; in the next the same lungs howled at him. Under such circumstances common men quail and take a peerage; even Churchill takes to a new history; but Lloyd George, despising all men, secure in his family party of four, changes not one jot of the tactics, quips and jibes which suited the Prime Minister, the Welsh agitator, and the man who stood up to Birmingham.

He won the War and destroyed Liberalism; neither was accidental. George had no Liberal foundations, only indignation; – 'fair play for the underdog'. He never understood free trade or the difference between a tax on land values and an increment duty, and his colleagues were so <u>very</u> Liberal and highly educated and respectable in those years 1906 to 1916. None of them except Churchill had anything in common with him, and he reciprocated and expressed himself more poignantly than dull Englishmen could forgive. Runciman, Buxton, Simon, McKenna, Burns, Samuel, even Grey and Asquith, all knew it and him, and writhed. So he slew them and their thousand followers with gusto, and had the amused support of the old guard of Toryism, both for his dealings with the old school and with the Boche. The deed was done by 1922, the party hatchet buried, and Baldwin could arise and disapprove of the party system. Relieved from the vengeance of Lloyd George the old Liberals could climb back into non-party office in a non-party government – could even reverse the tables on the wizard from Wales.

He was never pompous nor vain, but he did not like hearing criticism any more than do other dictators; and there were so many Liberals he disliked that his choice of associates was limited. When the job was done, more and more the great Tories stood aloof; so that he was driven to rely on and joke with the second-rate flies who buzzed round the Downing Street honey-pots. But, in spite of jibes – for his democracy, his geniality, his vision and hatred of snobbery, and above all for his energy and courage, George has more friends today than he had thirty years ago, and a sure and certain place as the greatest Parliamentarian and Prime Minister of this age.

LOWTHER,[813] Major Gen. Sir HENRY CECIL. M.P. (U) Westmorland N. 1915–18; Cumberland N. 1921–22; contested 1922.

---

[811] Wedgwood offered three alternatives here: 'staled'; 'moderated'; 'deflated'.

[812] Frances Stevenson objected to this passage. The correspondence is quoted above, p. 112.

[813] Written by JCW; corrected by the subject.

B. 27 Jan 1869, y.s. of Hon. William Lowther and y. bro. of the Speaker; m. 1920, Dorothy Bois, da. of John Selwyn Harvey.

He joined the Scots Guards, served through the South African War (D.S.O.) and as Military attaché in Paris, Madrid and Lisbon (C.M.G. 1911, C.V.O. 1913). He left with the British Expeditionary Force as Colonel of the 1st Battalion 1st Scots Guards, 1st Division of the 1st Army Corps. He was wounded at the battle of the Aisne[814] (C.B. 1915) and subsequently served on the General Staff at the War Office (K.C.M.G. 1918). He entered the House of Commons in 1915 as M.P. for the Northern Division of Westmorland. In making his maiden speech in 1918, when he moved the Address, he referred to the approaching extinction of the constituency he represented under the provisions of the redistribution scheme of the new Franchise Act, for which he professed to blame his brother, Mr Speaker Lowther. He termed it 'a fratricidal act'. In 1921 when the Speaker retired from Parliament, he succeeded his brother as M.P. for the Penrith and Cockermouth Division of Cumberland, but was defeated there at the General Election of 1922. Retired as Full Colonel with rank of Major General.[815] Since then I have served on the General Council of King Edward's Hospital Fund & on some of its committees.[816]

MADDISON,[817] FRED; composer. M.P. (Lib.) Sheffield (Brightside Div.) 1897–1900; contested 1900; M.P. Burnley 1906–10; contested Darlington 1910 (Dec.)

B. at Boston   1856, s. of   (–) and

m. Jane Ann, da. of Richard Weaherill, farmer of Bewholme, Yorks.; 3 da. Educ. Wesleyan School Hull. He was a compositor and became Chairman of the Hull Branch of the Typographical Association; President of the Hull Trades and Labour Council, and of the Trades Union Congress in 1886. He was the first Labour member of the Hull Corporation. For six years he was on the Tottenham School Board, while he edited the *Railway Review*, the official organ of the Amalgamated Society of Railway Servants. This he resigned on entering Parliament. Then he went into the Co-operative Production movement, and was President of the Labour Association in connection therewith.

His father, and the writings of Mazzini and John Morley in the *Fortnightly Review* started him in politics. He became a broad Unitarian, and his favourite newspaper was the *Daily News*. Ambition and party enthusiasm helped to make him M.P., but H.J. Wilson, M.P. was the prime cause. His income then was £200 a year, and he had been on the Town Council and School Board. His expenses were paid by his nominees of the Liberal Party. He was always non-socialist in his views, Gladstone being his ideal, though Lincoln and Gambetta held high place in his esteem.

Parliament taught him that it was really possible for him to be wrong! 'Parliamentary life was enjoyable to me because of the opportunities it gave of mixing with men of different views and of being at the centre of things. The House of Commons is a good place to keep one young. My greatest dislike was my own election contests with their

---

[814] Wedgwood has written beside this: 'How? details?' Lowther responded in a long note giving a detailed account of the incident (not reproduced here).

[815] Sentence substituted by the subject for 'Subsequently he became a Major General'.

[816] Last sentence added by the subject.

[817] Written by JCW; not amended by the subject (notes on the file say 'draft not sent out' and 'decd. 12 Mar. 1937').

air of unreality and temptation to play to the gallery.' The speech he liked best was Sir Edward Clarke's reply to Chamberlain during the Boer War.

MAJENDIE,[818] JAMES HENRY ALEXANDER, of Hedingham Castle, Essex. Contested Portsmouth May 1900; M.P. (C) Portsmouth, 1900–05; contested 1906.

B. 17 April 1871, s. and h. of Lewis A Majendie, M.P., (–) and Lady Margaret, da. of 25th Earl of Crawford; m. 1893, Beatrice, da. and h. of James Mitchell, of Holbrook, Suffolk; issue and 1 da. Educ. Winchester.

He visited America in 1890 and began an interest in politics, being Church of England and reading the *Times*. Parliament was the ambition and career of his contemporary friends, and he was a country squire with the necessary £4,000 a year. So 'he called at the Conservative Office and said I wished to stand and was promptly offered a hopeless seat. After I was adopted I was offered a practically safe seat in my own county, but refused as I wished to have a sporting shot at Portsmouth as all said the Conservative Association then always sent ambitious men to hopeless seats!' His two elections in 1900 cost £1,350 and £1,100, and the seat about £450 a year. Naturally the Navy was his subject and Chamberlain his leader. Parliament taught him that 'the Back Bencher was a mere article to vote as he was told and was in fact a nonentity as regards opinions of his own!' But he liked 'the real comradeship of us all in 1900, in fact I made heaps of friends with Liberals and the Irish, to say nothing of course of my Conservative friends. I realised that however much we might abuse each other across the floor, in the smoking room, etc, we were friends.' He only disliked 'having to give up the life through ill-health.' His best work was winning a doubtful seat, his best speech was on the Navy, the best speakers were Chamberlain on Tariff Reform and John Redmond in the House.

It pleases him to remember that Jack Pease, then his Radical M.P. came to stay with him and brought his horses to hunt. 'But Squire' they said 'have you gone yellow?' so impossible did it seem in those days for political opponents to be friends.

MALCOLM,[819] (Sir) IAN (ZACHARY); of Poltalloch, Kilmartin, Argyllshire. M.P. (C) Suffolk (Stowmarket) 1895–1900, 1900–5; contested 1906; contested North Salford Jan 1910; M.P. Croydon 1910–18, 1918–1919.

B. in Quebec, 3 Sept. 1868, s. and h. of Col. E.D. Malcolm C.B., (b.1837 d.1931)[820] and his wife née Isabel Wyld Brown.[821] m. 1902, Jeanne Marie, da. of Mrs Langtry (Lady de Bathe); 3s., I da. Educ. Eton and New College, Oxford. In Diplomatic Service at Berlin, Paris and St. Petersburg 1891–96. P.P.S. to Lord Salisbury while Prime Minister 1895–1900; P.P.S. to Chief Secretary for Ireland 1901–3; Secretary Union Defence League 1906–10. During the War he was British Red Cross Officer in France, etc.; went with Mr Balfour to America in 1917, and was private secretary to Mr Balfour at the Paris Peace Conference, 1919. He was rewarded with the post of British Government representative on the Suez Canal Board, and with the K.C.M.G.

---

[818] Written by JCW; not corrected by the subject (a note on the file says 'draft <u>not</u> returned').

[819] Written by JCW; corrected by the subject. Malcolm wrote in response to Wedgwood's letter of 22 Mar. 1937 enclosing the draft that it 'couldn't be better: you could add if you choose that for speaking in the country, especially on Irish & Church matters I was as much in requisition as anyone (after Cabinet Ministers)'.

[820] Father's vital dates inserted by the subject.

[821] Details of mother inserted by the subject.

His politics date from childhood in a politically minded family. The books which influenced him were mainly Disraeli's novels, and he is an Anglo-Catholic, reading the *Morning Post*. He came into Parliament on the suggestion of his uncle, Lord Malcolm, 'because I hoped to take part in the direction of Foreign Affairs.' He had about £700 a year, and Lord Cadogan's influence found him a seat in Suffolk. The contests cost about £1,000 each and he puts the annual expense about the same. Foreign and Church affairs were his chief interests; Salisbury, Beaconsfield and Bismarck were his ideal statesmen. Parliament hardly affected his views; he liked the social side and the study of personalities; disliked Committee work and making speeches in Parliament. What he looks back on with most satisfaction was his work on the Welsh Disestablishment Bill.

Ian Malcolm and George Wyndham were the handsomest and best dressed men of their day. Malcolm was too self-conscious to be a good speaker in the House, nor had he the wit of Harold Nicholson, but he always looked and probably was the perfect diplomatist – rather ignorant, naturally, of the world outside diplomatic circles.[822]

MALLET,[823] Sir CHARLES EDWARD; of Milbrook House, Guildford. Financial Secretary to the War Office 1910–11. Contested W. Salford 1900; M.P. (Lib.) Plymouth 1906–10, 1919; contested Dec. 1910; contested N. Salford 1917; contested S. Aberdeen 1922,1923.

B. Dec. 1862, s. and h. of Charles Mallet (1824–92)[824] and Louisa, d. of George Udny; m. 1895, Margaret, da. of Rt. Hon. Sir H.E. Roscoe, M.P. Educ. Harrow and Balliol (1st class History); called to the Bar, Inner Temple, 1889; Secretary for Indian Students at the India Office, 1912–16. He has written *A History of the University of Oxford*, 1924; *Mr Lloyd George, a Study*, 1930; *Lord Cave, a Memoir*, 1931; *Herbert Gladstone, a Memoir*, 1932; all of which are largely used in this volume; also *Anthony Hope & His Books*, 1935; and other studies.[825]

'My[826] interest in politics began in admiration for Mr Gladstone in the days of the first Midlothian campaign: and that feeling – that no British statesman can compare with him – remains unaltered now. The *Daily News* perhaps was then my favourite organ; now I prefer the *Times*. At Harrow in 1880 I began to learn something of debating: at Oxford between 1881 and 1885 I spent probably far too much time in it. My friends and I – they included at the Union Alfred Spender and Anthony Hope Hawkins – Robert Cecil and Cosmo Lang were on the other side – we, young Liberals, were among the early Home Rulers: and our admiration for Mr Gladstone and our wish to enter Parliament kindled and deepened over that. Studies for the Bar, speaking for the Eighty Club, lecturing, writing, publishing,[827] perhaps gave one a little political experience. I found myself in 1900, with an inadequate income, contesting vainly a Lancashire seat.' 'In Jan. 1906 I was elected for Plymouth, a double member constituency, on the introduction of Herbert Gladstone. I think the election cost £600 or £700 to each candidate, and cost

---

[822] A note in pencil at the bottom of the biography says 'Publications? (10 books given in "Who's Who"'. Malcolm has written in response: '& quite enough too!'

[823] Written by JCW; corrected by the subject.

[824] Father's vital dates inserted by the subject.

[825] 'Also *Anthony Hope* . . . & other studies' inserted by the subject.

[826] 'first' deleted by the subject.

[827] 'publishing' has been substituted by the subject for 'joining in the work of a publishing office'.

us each, as Members, perhaps £200 to £250 a year. With a few exceptions, we took the line that we could not subscribe widely to local charities. Our constituents generally supported us in this.'

'The main issues at the[828] three (Plymouth) elections of 1906 and 1910[829] were Free Trade and Home Rule. The Education question and "Chinese Labour" told in the first, – 1906: the House of Lords and Lloyd George's Budget were issues in Jan. and Dec. 1910. Those questions – with public economy added – were my chief political interests then. I do not think Parliament modified my views . . . It was on the Free Trade question that I did most work in Parliament. I think what I disliked most in the House of Commons was the desultoriness of the life: when I held office for a year as an Under Secretary this feeling was diminished. What I enjoyed most was the friendships made, and the general tone (apart from occasional political bitternesses) of friendliness and good manners. . . . I think my most successful speeches were one in favour of Free Trade and one made in opposing Women Suffrage. The dates may have been 1908 or 1909. . . . Edward Grey, Jack Seely and George Cave – and let me add Harold Cox – seemed to me to have conspicuously the special House of Commons gift. I don't remember any speech affecting my vote except one, from a Minister behind whom I sat, who offered, as I thought, so unsatisfactory an explanation of a certain Ministerial decision, that I could not follow him into the Lobby.'

'I have lately (in 1936)[830] been at Hawarden, singing a paean to W.E.G. – and I think I find him, as the years go by, incomparably greater than any of his successors. But it's a harder world to rule than it was then.'

Charles Mallet was perhaps a greater loss than Harold Baker. We shall never again see the like of the 1906 'varsity' Liberals. They had, alas, no 'apostles' at Oxford so their education never extended to Henry George.[831]

MARKS,[832] Sir GEORGE CROYDON; (cr. Lord Marks of Woolwich 1929); consulting engineer and patent agent. M.P. (Lib.) North Cornwall 1906–10, 1910, 1910–18, 1918–22, 1922–3, 1923–4.

B. at Eltham 9 June 1858, s. and h. of William Marks (born at Wellington, Somerset 1833. died at Eltham 1918)[833] and Amelia, da. of Thomas Croydon of Crediton; m. 1881, Margaret, da. of T. Maynard, of Bath. No issue.

'I was interested in politics as a lad owing to my father being keenly concerned in Liberal associations and hearing his views upon international and domestic problems of the day. My religious convictions followed my home life influences, my parents being Sunday School teachers. . . . The *Daily News* was my original favourite newspaper. My trade was Mechanical Engineering first as an apprentice in Woolwich Arsenal, then as a

---

[828] 'the' substituted by the subject for 'those'.

[829] 'of 1906 and 1910' inserted by the subject.

[830] '(in 1936)' inserted by the subject.

[831] Mallet has written after 'Henry George': 'The Editor's opinion (I never object to it). I don't think I dare try to improve on this scrappiness any more'.

[832] Written by JCW; corrected by the subject (who wrote to Wedgwood on 3 Mar. 1937: 'Many thanks for the "record" notes on my Parliamentary career – the writer is a humorist, if truthful as to my ignorance of politics!').

[833] Dates and places of father's birth and death inserted by the subject.

student Whitworth Exhibitioner at King's College, London, followed by responsible positions with engineering firms in Birmingham, Erith and Dublin; later as a lecturer in London practising as a Patent Agent in London and America and Canada in branch offices of my firm of which I was the head and founder.

My annual income when I stood for Parliament in 1905 as successor to Mr Fletcher Moulton, afterwards Lord Moulton, was about £1,500 to £3,000[834] a year all earned, as I had not investments. I had been a member of Aberystwyth Town Council for some six years.

Mr J. Fletcher Moulton was M.P. for N.E. Cornwall where I had spoken as a personal friend for him and upon his being created a Judge in the Court of Appeal I was adopted by the Launceston Liberal Association as their Candidate and was returned in January 1906.

My chief political interest was popular education, temperance and Free Trade. My first election cost me about £1,100 as the local association never contributed any expenses then or for the nineteen years I was in Parliament. I estimate that my annual expenses for charities, public institutions, Churches and outgoings connected with my residence that I bought in Bude, were about £900 on the average.

My ideal statesman was Mr Gladstone prior to becoming an M.P. and later I supported heartily Campbell Bannerman, Lloyd George and Mr Asquith.

Experience in Parliament led me to feel that there was no monopoly for useful public service in the Liberal Party, and that good men existed in the Conservative and Labour parties whom I could follow and work with provided they were free from party official domination.

My professional fees for consultative opinions were not influenced by being an M.P., but my status was perhaps[835] widened as a public man having knowledge of national affairs. I enjoyed the association with members whose views were not always my own, but a comradeship grew amongst most of those I knew in both sides of the House. I had always the keenest sympathy with the Labour members and later was actively supporting them as a follower and friend of Mr Ramsay MacDonald. I disliked the appeals for money that came from the constituency, although I responded to them,[836] it being assumed that the member must contribute to every cause. I spoke chiefly upon trade and industrial subjects but never unless I knew fully what was needed from my own experience. Speeches seldom affected my votes. I helped to alter the old Patent Laws both by interviews with Ministers and speeches in the House Committees when the amended Patent Acts were going through.'

Croydon Marks was knighted in 1911, C.B.E. 1917. He joined the Labour Party when the Liberal Party seemed dead, was given a peerage, and naturally followed MacDonald into the National Party in 1931.[837] He was a friend of Mr. T. Edison and was associated with him for many years. He was consulting engineer to H.R.H. the late Duke of Edinburgh when Duke of Saxe Coburg Gotha and received the honour of Knight of

---

[834] Altered by the subject from £1,200 to £2,000 (as he had written in the original questionnaire).

[835] 'perhaps' inserted by the subject.

[836] 'although I responded to them' inserted by the subject.

[837] 'Of politics he knew little; of reinforced concrete a great deal. The Gramophone Company was his child.' deleted by the subject, who has placed a question mark in the margin.

Saxe Coburg Gotha.[838] But he was popular in the House among all parties on account of his exceeding good nature and complete absence of conceit or pomposity.

McKENNA,[839] Rt. Hon. REGINALD; barrister. Financial Secretary to the Treasury 1905–7; President of the Board of Education 1907–8; First Lord of the Admiralty 1908–11; Home Secretary, 1911–15; Chancellor of the Exchequer 1915–16. Contested Clapham 1892; M.P. (Lib.) N. Monmouthshire 1895–1900, 1900–06, 1906–10, 1910–18; contested 1918.

B. in London 6 July 1863, y.s. of William Columban McKenna (1819–1887)[840] and Emma Hanby.[841] m. 1908 Pamela, da. of Sir Herbert Jekyll (whose other da. m. Hon Frances McLaren, M.P.) Issue – one son.[842]

Educ. King's College School,[843] London, and Trinity Hall, Cambridge (Scholar and Hons. in Mathematics); practised at the Bar until elected to Parliament.

A politician all his life, for 'my father was always greatly interested in politics'. 'I had many enthusiasms, and in my younger days no little ambition.' Mr Gladstone was his ideal. He was earning £400 a year at the Bar[844] in 1892, with unearned £1,000 a year and his first election cost £750; yearly about £200.[845] McKenna had rowed bow in the Cambridge Eight (1887) and had won the Grand and Steward's Cups at Henley: probably this brought him and Dilke together, but Dilke was always helping young, keen M.P.s. McKenna's chance came in 1905; he was on Campbell-Bannerman's side, and he never looked back. His service at the Admiralty was notable for the great increase in the strength of the Fleet.[846] He says, and he may be right, that his best piece of work at the Exchequer[847] was 'finding the money to meet external liabilities during the War.'[848] He did not get the coupon in 1918. 'I fought to win, but I was not sorry to be defeated. My enthusiasms had waned in the experience of twenty-three years of actual Parliamentary work.' So from 1919 he has been Chairman of the Midland Bank, addressed the country and the shareholders once a year, and was for long the only Banker to urge and welcome going off gold. His economics are still as sound as when he learnt them from Adam Smith and Mr Gladstone. He has written *Post-War Banking Policy*, 1928.

[838] 'He was a friend . . . Knight of Saxe Coburg Gotha' inserted by the subject.

[839] Written by JCW; corrected by the subject.

[840] Father's vital dates inserted by the subject.

[841] Mother's name inserted by the subject.

[842] 'one son' inserted by the subject.

[843] 'School' inserted by the subject.

[844] 'at the Bar' inserted by the subject.

[845] 'Early in his Parliamentary life *Punch* depicted him as man Friday to Sir Charles Dilke's Robinson Crusoe.' deleted by the subject.

[846] Sentence substituted by the subject for 'His Home Office service was the best, for he was the last free Liberal to hold that office. At the Exchequer he was dated and labelled with the McKenna (protective) duties – he who had been ever the leader and expounder of Free Trade'.

[847] 'at the Exchequer' inserted by the subject.

[848] 'That will excuse and explain all.' deleted by the subject.

McMICKING,[849] Major[850] GILBERT; of Miltonise, New Luce,[851] Wigtownshire. M.P. (Lib.) Kirkcudbright 1906–10, 1910–18; Galloway 1918–22.

B. 24 Mar. 1862, 3rd s. of Gilbert McMicking of Miltonise[852] (b. 1824 d. 1890)[853] and Helen da. of Alexander MacFarlane of Thornhill; m. (1) Gertrude (d.1920) da. of Nathaniel Gore; 3 s.;[854] (2) 1921, Ethel, da. of Binny Douglas. Educ. Cheltenham and R.M.A. Woolwich. Joined R.A. 1882. Served in R.H.A 1885–90. Captain 1890 retired 1894.[855] Commanded C.I.V. Battery S. African War (C.M.G., Hon. Major in Army). Rejoined R.A. 1914.

It was not till 1902 that McMicking became political, on Whig traditions and Free Trade. History and a Liberal family made him so. The Westminster Gazette was at its best. Sir[856] Henry Primrose of the Board of Inland Revenue[857] induced him to become an M.P. Cromwell was his ideal statesman, and once in the House, Army questions and Scottish agriculture absorbed him. P.P.S. to Mr Haldane 1908–10 at the War Office. He 'gained some appreciation of the usefulness of compromise;' enjoyed most hearing Asquith wind up debates; and left in 1922 because of the cleavage in the Liberal Party and because dissatisfied with the Coalition Government.

His best piece of work was training[858] R.F.A. in 1914–15. McMicking was a moderate Liberal of the Liberal League[859] type, a little cautious as became a Scot and a soldier.

NEWNES,[860] (Sir) Frank Hillyard (1876–19   ); 2nd Bart. 1910. M.P. (Lib.) Notts. (Bassetlaw) 1906–10.

B. 28 Sept. 1876, s. and h. of Sir George Newnes, Bart., M.P. (d. 1910) and[861] Priscilla, da. of Rev. J. Hillyard; m. 1913 Emmeline A.L., da. of Sir Albert de Rutzen. No issue.

Educ. Clare, Camb., M.A., LL.B.; entered his father's publishing business; called to the Bar 1898 but does not practise. The Newnes were of Liberal Nonconfirmist stock, and Frank began helping his father in politics as well as in business in 1900. Sir George started and[862] owned the *Westminster Gazette*, then edited by J.A. Spender and in all its glory. His father wanted his son to join him[863] in the House, saw Herbert Gladstone, the Chief Whip, and they fixed on Bassetlaw to fight, 1904. His politics were Free Trade and a moderate Liberal policy, but he was not a Liberal Leaguer. The contest cost them

---

[849] Written by JCW; corrected by the subject.

[850] Substituted by the subject for 'Lt. Col.'.

[851] 'Miltonise, New Luce' substituted by the subject for 'Glenluce'.

[852] 'Miltonise' substituted by the subject for 'same'.

[853] Father's vital dates inserted by the subject.

[854] '2 s.' altered by subject to '3 s.'.

[855] 'Joined R.A. 1882 . . . retired 1894' substituted by the subject for 'Capt. R.A., retired 1894'.

[856] The subject has deleted 'Curiously enough' before 'Sir'.

[857] 'Board of Inland Revenue' substituted by the subject for 'Local Government Board'.

[858] 'the' deleted by the subject.

[859] 'Liberal League' is underlined with a question mark placed beside it, presumably by the subject.

[860] Written by JCW; corrected by the subject.

[861] 'and' substituted by the subject for 'by'.

[862] 'Sir George started and' substituted by the subject for 'They'.

[863] Wedgwood had originally written 'wanted him with himself in the House', but amended it himself on the original to 'wanted [his son] [Frank] to join him in the House', and failed to amend the copy sent to Newnes. Newnes has added in 'his son' to make sense of the passage.

£1,750 and £750 a year, almost the whole fell on the Member, but his income was quite adequate. He spoke but once, being P.P.S to Edmund Robertson at the Admiralty; and was defeated by 300 votes in Jan. 1910. Best he liked the friendships he made, and best we liked the care and devotion he showed towards his father. He was[864] without swagger or conceit, and was very popular with all the younger members.

During the War he joined up as a Sub-Lieut. In the R.N.V.R., Apr. 1915; transferred to 12th Bedfordshire Regt., (Capt.), 1916–18, but saw no service in France. He has been director of George Newnes Ltd. Since 1899 (Chairman 1910–29 and again 1935 to date),[865] director of Westminster Gazette Ltd[866] 1908–20; director also of Country Life, of Newnes & Pearson Printing Co Ltd, of C. Arthur Pearson Ltd., of the London Board of the[867] Norwich Union Fire Assurance Co. Ltd., and of other companies. Also he is on the Royal Free Hospital Board of which he was made chairman in 1935,[868] but his recreation is still golf; handicap 8.[869]

O'DONNELL,[870] JOHN. Former M.P. for Mayo South, Ireland 1900–1910.

John O'Donnell was born in Towneyeamon Westport County Mayo in the year 1868. He was the son of Martin O'Donnell a hardworking farmer of that District. He was educated in the Christian Brothers' Schools in Westport. In the Province of Connaught in the West of Ireland where John O'Donnell lived worked and died the congestion of the people on small allotments of land was little short of apalling [sic]. His father's share was some four acres of swamp and heather some three or four miles from the town of Westport. In the Union of Westport alone a population of about 20,000 was trying to live on plots of land upon which existence would be impossible without the annual migration of harvest labourers to Scotland.

It was the foundation of the United Irish League which restored the National Unity broken to fragments by the Parnell split. It may with truth be said that John O'Donnell was one of the two or three men but for whom the United Irish Leage [sic] could not have come into existence. He was it's [sic] first Secretary and with indomitable energy and indifference to hardship he carried the torch of the new movement through mountain and depopulated wilderness and stumped the Country North, South, East and West on it's [sic] behalf. It was while on this campaign that O'Donnell was on one memorable occasion violently dragged from his platform whilst addressing a meeting and imprisoned in Castlebar Jail for daring to utter the word 'grabber' of a local land monopoliser. In Jail his refusal to wear criminal garb or to accept anything less than the status of a political prisoner led to a long course of brutalities which left their lifelong

---

[864] The subject has deleted 'rich', and placed a question mark in the margin. In his letter to Wedgwood of 4 Feb. 1937 Newnes wrote: 'I have queried the word "rich" as it is an exaggeration. My father did not die well off in fact left me nothing except name & opportunity. His losses on the Westminster Gazette were very heavy & greatly contributed to his dying a poor man. So perhaps you could modify this'.

[865] '1910–29 and again 1935 to date' substituted by the subject for 'since 1910'.

[866] 'Ltd' inserted by the subject.

[867] 'London Board of the' inserted by the subject.

[868] 'Royal Free Hospital board . . . chairman in 1935' substituted by the subject for 'various Hospital Boards'.

[869] '8' inserted by the subject.

[870] Written by the subject's son Dec. 1938; corrected probably by *History of Parliament* staff.

mark on his health. It was while O'Donnell was still in prison that Michael Davitt, who was then the member for Mayo South, threw up his seat and departed for the seat of war in the Transvaal. The prisoner in Castlebar Jail was started for the vacant seat being opposed by Major John MacBride.

John O'Donnell's political life was spent in espousing the cause of the oppressed people of his native land in their struggle for relief from the barbarous conditions under which they were compelled to exist. This measure of relief was not attained however without a bitter struggle. He had had fierce encounters both in Parliament and in the Country with the nimblest political wits of the day including one memorable controversy with Mr. T.M. Healy M.P. On another occasion he rushed across the floor of the House of Commons and shook his clenched fist in the face of Mr. A.J. Balfour after one of the latter's mocking insults to Ireland.

He retired from active politics in 1910 and established a prosperous business in Galway City. In 1904 he married Mary Brett a sister of Thomas Brett a well known West of Ireland Merchant. There were six children born of the Marriage two of whom died in early childhood. He died on the 12th day of August 1920.

ORMSBY-GORE,[871] GEORGE RALPH CHARLES, of Brogyntyn, Oswestry. M.P. (C) Salop (Oswestry)   1901–4.

B. 21 Jan 1855, s. and h. of 2nd Lord Harlech (–1904) and Emily, da. of Admiral Sir G.F. Seymour; m. 1881, Margaret Ethel Gordon, da. of 10th Marquess of Huntly; issue Rt. Hon. William Ormsby Gore, M.P. Educ. Eton and Sandhurst; entered Coldstream Guards.

His grandfather, his father and his uncle were all in Parliament, so that when he left the Army he followed in their footsteps. He read *The Times*, supported the agricultural interest; was 'strictly Protestant', and entered Parliament on an allowance from his father. That contest cost £1,000. Beaconsfield and Chamberlain were his ideal statesmen. He liked best debates in the House of Commons; disliked most public meetings. Of all the speeches he heard, he preferred one by Lord Hartington on Home Rule about 1887 at Derby. He is Lord Lieutenant of Co. Leitrim and Merionethshire, and Constable of Harlech Castle since 1927.

RHYS[872] (RICE),[873] Hon.[874] WALTER FITZURYAN, of Dynevor Castle, Llandilo. M.P. (U) Brighton 1910, 1910–11; Lord Dynevor 1911.

B. 17 Aug 1873, s. and h. of 6th Baron and Selina, da. of Hon. Arthur Lascelles; m. 1898 Lady Margaret Villiers, da. of 7th Earl of Jersey; issue Charles, M.P. 2 other s. one da.

Educ. Eton and Christ Church, Oxford. Asst. Private Sec. to Lord George Hamilton M.P. at the India Office, 1899–1903, and to the Earl of Selborne at the Admiralty, 1903–5.

'Many of my ancestors had sat in the Commons since 1585. Disraeli's novels, preaching Tory Democracy, greatly appeal to me. The *Standard* newspaper was my

---

[871] Written by JCW; not corrected by the subject (a note on the file says 'draft not returned').
[872] Footnote by Wedgwood: 'He resumed the old spelling in lieu of Rice in 1917 by Royal Licence'.
[873] Written by JCW; corrected by the subject.
[874] 'Hon.' inserted by the subject.

favourite.' ' I was chiefly interested in Tariff Reform, the maintenance of a strong Navy and hostile to the Taxation of Land Values, which had just been introduced. Each election cost me about £1000. I looked on Benjamin Disraeli as the greatest statesman of modern times. Parliament in no way modified my views and our system of British Democracy had always appealed to me. To speak in the House of Commons was not an easy matter and when I made my maiden speech on the Navy I was very nervous beforehand until I was actually making my speech, when I found that I was able to say what I intended in a clear voice, but I think my best speech was in the House of Lords soon after I went there on the death of my Father (a harsh rule which compelled me to leave the Commons) against the Second Reading of the Bill to Disendow the Church in Wales, when it came up a second time under the Parliament Act. I spoke for thirty five minutes without a note and was much congratulated. No speech ever affected my vote and I had studied the questions before debate too greatly for that to happen.

The best speakers in the House of Commons were to my mind at that time Bonar Law, F.E. Smith, John Redmond and Asquith. This was before the first two had risen to the eminence that they attained later. The great feature was the fact that the Liberal Government had to rely on the Irish Nationalist Members' votes to retain office and this caused the Unionist opposition to shout continually to Mr Asquith (the P.M.) 'On the knee Asquith!'

In 1913 (when in the House of Lords) I carried out an extensive political campaign, addressing in that year nearly one hundred meetings in different parts of the country. I could not keep pace with all the invitations I received to speak, so I assume that my speeches were appreciated, and I spoke chiefly against the three big issues at that time, namely, Welsh Disendowment, Home Rule for Ireland and the new Land Taxes.'

Afterwards he was at the Ministry of Munitions during[875] the War, 1916–18;[876] County Councillor of Carmarthenshire 1919–35, and Lord Lieutenant of the County from 1928.

SANDON,[877] Viscount, JOHN HERBERT DUDLEY RYDER, of Sandon, Staffs. M.P. (C) Gravesend 1898–1900. 5th Earl of Harrowby 1900. J.P. and D.L. for London.

---

[875] 'during' substituted by the subject for 'throughout'.

[876] '1916–18' inserted by the subject.

[877] Written by JCW; corrected, substantially added to and retyped by the subject's wife. Lady Harrowby wrote to Wedgwood on 15 Mar. 1937: 'My husband shewed me your typed sheet about him, and I have amended and altered it as enclosed. It may be that I ought not to have put in other than his Parliamentary activities. Of course, if that is so, do not scruple to alter it.

He entirely refuses – in spite of your threat of blackmail – to add a wise commentary on his views and experience of Parliament [as it only lasted 2 years to his deep regret] but I know how happy he was in it, and one of the first things he did was to take up the cause of the Thames River Pilots. He actually divided the House against the Government on this subject! And I think won his case, thereby earning the eternal gratitude of the Pilots. He has been a bad attendant in the House of Lords the last few years, partly owing to pressure of work in Staffordshire, and partly due to the fact of having sold, on account of death duties, his London homes, first one and then the other.

He says he thinks it is rather fulsome, but I tell him it is just facts! With which I think you will agree'. Lady Harrowby wrote a second note to Wedgwood on the following day: 'There is one thing I entirely forgot yesterday and that was that my husband voted against nearly all his friends and with his Political enemies at the time of the Parliament Bill. He felt sadly but very strongly that it was the best of the two evils, but it cost him, temporarily, the friendship of many men. As you will remember, feeling ran very high during that time, the "Globe" going so far as to say they hoped conservative Clubs would kick out every member who had voted that way, and also that no honest man would ever shake them by the hand again'.

Born in London 1864, son and heir of the 4th Earl, and Susan, daughter of Villiers Dent; married 1887 Hon. Mabel Danvers, daughter of Rt. Hon. W.H. Smith, M.P., and Viscountess Hambleden; issue, Major (Dudley) Ryder, Viscount Sandon M.P., and the Lady Frances Ryder, C.B.E. Educated Trinity College Cambridge, where he had been Secretary of the University Conservative Club. Became a partner in Coutts' Bank. He was the 6th generation of Ryders to sit in the House of Commons, and is descended from three generations of Cabinet Ministers. (His Uncle, Grandfather, and great-Grandfather being all of Cabinet rank.)[878] His Father-in-Law was leader of the Government in the House of Commons. The fight at Gravesend, when he defeated in a bye-Election Mr Walter Runciman, now President of the Board of Trade,[879] cost £1000 and £500 a year, and in 1898 his income was about £2000 a year.[880] The first meeting of Parliament after his accession he was invited by Lord Salisbury to Move the address in the House of lords, and in congratulating him the Prime Minister referred to his name as one 'precious to us on this side of the House.' In this connection it is interesting to note that his great-Grandfather received a letter of four pages, still at Sandon, written in Mr Pitt's own hand asking him to move the address in the House of Commons. Lord Salisbury's letter was one half-sheet typed, though of course personally signed. Autre temps, autre moeurs!

Since he succeeded to the Peerage he was for many years Alderman in the Stafford County Council, and Chairman of the Public Health Committee. His views are strongly Imperialistic; witness his entertainment at Sandon of Dominion Prime Ministers at the time of the Coronation of Edward VII and George V. He always had great faith in Mr. Joseph Chamberlain's campaign for Tariff Reform. He travels and takes great pleasure in putting the Dominion and foreign Chambers of Commerce in touch with those of Staffordshire. Sandon Hall was lent by him during the War for a Convalescent Military Hospital. He is President of the Staffordshire Allotment Association; President of the Pottery & Glass Trades Benevolent institution; President of the North Staffs. British Legion, and President of the Staffordshire Territorial Association, in which he takes a deep personal interest. He has been Lord Lieutenant of the County since 1927. He does his duty better than most, but with regrets for the great days when he was a banker and M.P., and had his hand on the pulse of the city and Parliament.

SASSOON,[881] Rt. Hon. Sir PHILIP, Bart.; Under-Secretary for Air, 1924–29, 1931–7; P.C. 1929. M.P. (C) Kent (Hythe) 1912–18, 1918–22, 1922–3, 1923–4, 1924–9, 1929–31, 1931–35, 1935.

---

[878] Wedgwood does not refer to the three generations of cabinet ministers. His text, after referring to Harrowby's father-in-law, says: 'So the whips found him a seat at Gravesend'.

[879] Wedgwood's version does not refer to Runciman.

[880] Apart from the last sentence, the remainder of the biography is by Harrowby's wife. Wedgwood's version continues: 'Chamberlain was and has remained his ideal statesman. The bank has gone, and since 1900 he has been ruling Staffordshire from Sandon, Lord Lieut. since 1927'.

[881] Written by JCW; rewritten and retyped by the subject. Sassoon's letter of 22 Apr. 1937 to Wedgwood says: 'With reference to the suggested biographical note I have taken the liberty of altering slightly, not only the last paragraph, but the whole page. I have kept very close to your original suggestion, and I hope that what I send you herewith will meet with your requirements'.

B. 4th Dec. 1888, s. of Sir Edward[882] Sassoon, 2nd Bart. and Aline, da. of Baron Gustave de Rothschild. Educ. Eton and Christ Church, Oxford. Private Secretary to Sir Douglas Haig, 1915 to Feb. 1919; P.P.S. to Mr Lloyd George while Prime Minister 1919–22. Trustee of National Gallery (Chairman since 1933), of Tate Gallery, British School at Rome and Wallace Collection.[883]

'Politics were part of my family upbringing'.[884] So, when his father, the sitting member for Hythe, died in 1912, he took his father's place and became the youngest member of the House of Commons.[885] For current information on affairs, he relied on the *Times*. 'Tariff Reform was then my chief political interest and, since the War, Air'. 'Parliament has, I hope, widened my views. I have learnt more of the difficulties of Parliamentary Government, without losing faith in it.' In his political career[886] he has enjoyed most 'the sense that I was taking some part in my country's affairs; next, my association with other members'. The experience he most disliked was 'making my maiden speech'. He puts his first introduction of the Air Estimates as his best speech. But these annual performances are all good and it is a pity he does not speak more often.[887] He ranks Grey's speech of 3rd Aug. 1914 as the greatest he ever heard.

Sassoon's interest in air matters extends beyond his duties in the House of Commons and the Air Ministry. He believes that an Under Secretary of State for Air should know how to fly, the men who fly and the conditions in which flying takes place. He has learnt to fly and commanded an Auxiliary Air Force Squadron, numbers many friends throughout the Service and has visited almost every flying station at home and overseas on more than one occasion.[888]

SYKES,[889] Sir MARK, bart. (1879–1919); of Sledmere, Yorks. Contested Buckrose 1910 Jan & 1910 Dec; M.P. (C) Central Hull July 1911–18, 1918–19 (Feb).

b. 16 Mar. 1879, o.s. of Sir Tatton Sykes 5th bart. of Sledmere (18 –1913) and Jessica da. of Rt. Hon. George Cavendish Bentinck M.P. m. 1903 Edith Violet da. of Sir John Gorst M.P.

He was at Beaumont and at Jesus Coll., Camb., but had no continuous education, travelling with his father in the East. At the age of 21 he was given an allowance of £4,000 a year by his father. His wife's enthusiasm sent him into Parliament; and to prepare for that career he became private secy. to George Wyndham at Dublin.

Being in the Yorkshire Militia (1897–1914), he served in the So. Africa War. In 1901, while he was in South Africa he was approached on the subject. A letter written

---

[882] 'Edward' substituted by the subject for 'Philip'.

[883] Details of trusteeships inserted by the subject.

[884] Sassoon has left out 'and religious convictions "those of my family"'.

[885] Wedgwood had written: 'He relied on the *Times*, and became an M.P. to fill his father's place, when he had only just left Oxford'.

[886] 'In his political career' inserted by the subject.

[887] 'does not speak more often' substituted by the subject for 'makes no others'.

[888] Paragraph written by the subject to replace Wedgwood's original: 'Sasson's failing is a modesty or shyness which excludes both ambition and comfort. He never expects to be anything but Under-Secretary for Air. Between him and all the rank and file of the House there is a great gulf, fixed by him. Across it we only see a sad smile as of apology for not having been killed in the War'.

[889] Written by JCW, but not typed; not corrected by the subject's son (who wrote the response to the questionnaire which is extensively quoted).

to a friend at that time is worth quoting to illustrate his frame of mind: 'I have just written a snorter to some individuals who want to know whether I will stand at the next election for the Buckrose division as a Conservative. I have told them that . . . I have no sympathy with the opposition, but I consider the present government the most hopeless incompetent jelly that has ever quivered in a British Cabinet.' In 1907 he returned from his travels and decided to turn to political work; in a letter he wrote 'I am now home for good and making a political plunge. Tory Democracy is what I am going to try and push for all its worth.' 'He had a great love of English literature, particularly the prose of Swift and his political writings shewed a strong influence of Swift's terse and vigorous style.' He was a rich man who might have lived an idle pleasant country life.

Meanwhile his knowledge of the Near East was becoming of real importance. He had a true insight into the Oriental mind, had travelled in very little known country, and understood the manners customs and political opinions of the various tribes. He always kept in touch with Professor Browne at Cambridge who, himself a great expert, had originally taught Mark the subject on which he was now becoming such an authority.

Mark Sykes's election addresses astonished many of the older Conservatives. He had studied the conditions in the Hull slums, in Middlesborough and of the North East coast fishermen, he knew how bad these conditions were and he spoke with such vigour that his socialistic ideas shocked some of the Tories.' 'His maiden speech was made on Nov. 27th 1911. His subject was his favourite Eastern question and he spoke with great brilliance.' 'He was greatly interested in the Irish question.'

In the War he was to go to France, with the Yorkshire Regt. he had raised, but he was wisely switched off to diplomatic work in the Near East. He was at Petrograd, Aden, Basra & Kut. When France took objection to British action in Syria during 1916 Sykes had to settle the matter single-handed, whence came the Sykes-Picot agreement. It was with difficulty that he ultimately rescued Palestine from the French sphere and Foreign Office ignorance. So he became interested in Zionism, and when Russia fell Sykes felt that the problems of Palestine and the Jewish question could be solved together if Zionism tended to draw the Salonica Jews out of the Ottoman rut. He decided that there was room for a Jewish as well as an Arab nationality. He spoke fluently French, Turkish and Arabic. From 1917 he was engaged at the Foreign and Colonial Offices on the same subjects. In 1918 he was back at Aleppo. From that he went to the Paris Conference and there he died suddenly of pneumonia. He was an able, independent & beloved member of the House.[890]

WILLS,[891] Sir GILBERT ALAN HAMILTON, Bart., of Batsford Park, Moreton-in-Marsh, Glos. M.P. (U) Taunton 1912–18; Weston-super-mare 1918–22. cr. Lord Dulverton 1929. (1st Baron)

---

[890] Wedgwood's footnote: 'From notes by Sir Richard Sykes bart, see also "Life & Letters of Mark Sykes" by Shane Leslie'.

[891] Written by JCW; corrected by the subject.

B. 28 Mar. 1880, 2nd[892] s. of Sir Frederick Wills, Bart., M.P. Lib Unionist[893] (1900–1906)[894] the Bristol tobacco manufactuerer, and Anne, da. of Rev. James Hamilton; m. 1914 Victoria may, da. of Rear Admiral Sir E. Chichester, Bart.; 3 s. . . .

Educ. Privately, and Magdalen, Oxford (M.A.); was a Master of Hounds for 16 seasons;[895] and joined[896] North Devon Yeomanry. Extra A.D.C. to Lord Aberdeen Lord Lieut. of Ireland 1908–12.

The circumstances which led to his entering Parliament are given in a letter to the Editor[897] as follows:-

'Somewhere about the year 1911 the father of our mutual friend, and one-time colleague, Willie Peel, was not expected to live long, and I was approached by the local Powers to accept nomination as a reserve candidate for the old Borough of Taunton in case their gloomy forebodings materialised, on the grounds that I was the 'one and only person', in an area not inconsiderable, who could possibly hold what was then a veritable Conservative stronghold! Being a good deal younger in 1911 than I am now, I gave some credence to these emphatic statements, but before the event in 1912 which automatically translated Peel to 'another place' I had regretted my hasty decision. It was, however, by then too late to withdraw with any decency, and you were probably amongst those who greeted my bashful arrival at the Speaker's table in stony, if dignified silence! So the true answer to Question 6 is 'because I got caught napping'! He prefers to be 'handed down to posterity as one who for ten years was numbered amongst His Majesty's faithful Commons, but who achieved very little beyond making some very good friends.'[898]

We must turn to a war record which included the survival of Suvla Bay, and did not end until the War was over. (Dispatches twice & O.B.E.)[899]

He owns 5,000 acres, inherited a goodly patrimony,[900] has been Chairman of the Imperial Tobacco Co. since 1924,[901] and if his invocations of Mr Speaker have been forgotten, Wills' Gold Flake and Three Castles are probably the best known consolations in the world.

YOUNG,[902] Rt. Hon. Sir (EDWARD) HILTON; (Lord KENNET of the Dene,[903] 1935). Barrister. P.C. 1922; Secretary for Overseas Trade 1921; Financial Secretary to the Treasury 1921–2; Minister for Health 1931–5. Contested East Worcestershire Jan. 1910,

---

[892] '2nd' inserted by the subject.

[893] 'Lib. Unionist' inserted by the subject.

[894] '1900' inserted by the subject and '1909' altered to '1906': Wills seems to have misinterpreted the dates as those of his father's parliamentary service, rather than his birth and death.

[895] 'was a Master of Hounds for 16 seasons' substituted by the subject for 'entered his father's business'.

[896] 'joined' inserted by the subject.

[897] Wedgwood has deleted 'to Col. Wedgwood'; the subject has inserted 'to the Editor' in its place.

[898] 'amongst whom I hope that you will permit me to number yourself", which is not good enough.' deleted, probably by Wedgwood.

[899] '(Dispatches twice & O.B.E.)' inserted by the subject.

[900] 'a goodly patrimony' substituted by the subject for '£5,000,000'. Dulverton has added in the margin: 'I hardly think figures are necessary but in any case it should be one [million], & not five'.

[901] The subject has deleted '(?its foundation)'.

[902] Written by JCW; corrected, partly rewritten and retyped by the subject.

[903] 'of the Dene' inserted by the subject.

Preston Dec. 1910; M.P. (Lib) Norwich 1915–18, (Lib. Nat.)[904] 1918–22, 1922–3; contested 1923; M.P. Norwich 1924–9; (Cons.)[905] Kent (Sevenoaks) 1929–31, 1931–5.

B. 20 Mar. 1879, 3rd s. of Sir George Young, 3rd Bart. (1837–1930) and Alice Eacy da. of Evory Kennedy M.D. of Belgard Castle, Co. Dublin;[906] m. Kathleen, da. of Canon Lloyd Bruce, and widow of Captain Robert Scott, R.N.; issue one s. Wayland Hilton Young b. 1924.[907]

Educ. Eton and Trinity, Cambridge (M.A. 1907). Called to the Bar, Inner Temple, 1904. In the War he was made Lieut. R.N.V.R., Aug. 1914; served in H.M.S. Iron Duke and with naval Mission to Serbia; in H.M.S. Centaur (actions[908] 22 Jan. and 11 May 1916) at Harwich; with R.N. guns on Flemish front 1917 (D.S.C and Croix de Guerre);[909] in Vindictive at Zeebrugge Mole (losing an arm, and promoted Lt. Cmdr.) 1918; commanded armoured train in Archangel campaign 1919 (D.S.O. for services in action). Thereafter he either held office or served on missions, or represented this country at the Hague, almost continuously until he went[910] to the Lords.

He[911] came to the House in 1919 with the training of a barrister and financial journalist, and was received as a constructive worker and attractive speaker, especially on financial affairs. Thereafter he either held office or represented his country on missions, almost continuously, until he went to the House of Lords.[912] He was brought up a whig: joined the liberal party in youth as an instrument of social reform: thought after the war that the times needed robuster individualism: left the liberals because of their cooperation with socialists (the occasion was Mr Lloyd Georges land policy): & after a period of independence joined the Conservatives at the time of the general strike.

In office as Minister of Health his principal task was a recasting of housing policy which was followed by unexampled activity in the increase and improvement of housing accommodation for the working classes. The basis of his policy was the simultaneous stimulation of private enterprise without subsidy, and of subsidised municipal enterprise specifically directed to clearing the slums and remedying overcrowding. His five year

[904] '(Lib. Nat.)' inserted by the subject.

[905] '(Cons.)' inserted by the subject.

[906] Father's vital dates and mother's details inserted by the subject.

[907] Details of son inserted by the subject.

[908] 'served in . . . HMS Centaur (actions' substituted by the subject for 'in Turkey and the Balkans; in actions'.

[909] 'served' deleted by the subject.

[910] 'went' substituted by the subject for 'retired'.

[911] The remainder of the biography is written by the subject. The text is Kennet's typescript as amended by himself. Wedgwood's original paragraph reads: 'Unfortunately Lord Kennet's replies to the questionnaire verge on the ribald [footnote by Wedgwood: 'He answers 21 "Oh, I should say Briand on the entry of Germany into the League, and that's not what you want" – and 15, "You, my dear Jos."'], and he must be reconstructed from outside. In 1909 Charles Trevelyan came back from a meeting in Worcestershire saying that he had heard the finest speech ever made by a candidate, that he had listened to a future Prime Minister. But every day Hilton lived he seemed to school himself to eliminate all emotion and enthusiasm from speech and life. The ghosts of vanished causes and of vanished colleagues stalked beside him. When the Liberal party was liquidated he survived. He had no part in the massacre, but they had been his friends and leaders, and he was accepting hospitality and office in uncongenial and second rate company. And so the man who had stormed over the mole at Zeebrugge, who had faced death in a dozen forms with frank open eyes for five years, never again enjoyed facing the House of Commons and the ghosts. He became hermetically sealed in the shell of his reserve. They pinned up his coat sleeve and his heart'.

[912] This sentence has been incorporated into Kennet's text from the previous paragraph.

slum campaign provided for rehousing over a million slum dwellers: and his Housing Act of 1935 established a national standard of accommodation, and provided for remedying overcrowding by rebuilding obsolete industrial housing areas. Proposals which he made for strengthening the finance of National Health Insurance and extending it to boys on leaving school, for improved maternity services, & for pensions for black coated workers, were adopted during or shortly after his term of office. Out of office his principal public services were, in connection with his missions, to help in the restoration of financial stability after the war. His mission to Poland was the turning point from chaos to order in the Polish budget & currency: his royal commission on Indian currency stabilised the rupee and designed India's new central bank. In Iraq he guided the infant state towards budgetary solvency, and designed and established its currency. In connection with other inquiries, he was responsible for the reform of the constitution of the university of London, and assisted in the development of the financial organs of the League of Nations.

He wrote a standard text book on financial administration and some well known poems: and was at one time President of the Royal Statistical Society and of the Poetry Society. He wrote *A Bird in the Bush* (essays on birds) and *By Sea and Land* (an account of his experiences in the war).

He was a distinguished speaker in the House and after dinner, at times even on the platform. He as a good expositor but no debater; active in construction but uninterested in party politics; clear sighted as to ends, but unskilled in the means of gaining ends. After going to the lords he took no further part in party politics, but devoted himself to business administration and Spinosa.

Index

Index

Trevelyan, Charles
  family influence 30
  parliamentary speech, greatest 107
  personal achievements 71
  personal finances 82
  personal speech, best 96
  political heroes 42
  political influences 30
  political interests 54
  political motivation 30
  religion, influence of 37
Tryon, George 18
Turton, Edmund
  occupation 44

Ullswater, viscount *see* Lowther, James
Ure, Alexander
  as speaker 106

Venables-Llewellyn, Charles
  parliamentary speeches, effect of 103
Verney, Harry
  constituency, expenditure on 92
  family influence 24, 30
  personal achievements 71
  political motivation 30, 31
Verney, (Richard) Greville
  electoral expenses 90
  occupation 44
  personal speech, best 98

Waldegrave Palmer, William *see* Wolmer, lord
Wallace, Robert
  house of commons, departure from 75
  personal speeches 99
  political influences 24
Wardle, George
  electoral expenses 89
  parliamentary speech, greatest 106
  personal finances 84
  personal speech, best 96
  political influences 34
Warner, Courtenay
  personal finances 82
Washington, George
  as political hero 42
Wason, Eugene
  personal achievements 71
Watson, Bertrand
  personal achievements 69
Webb, Henry
  parliamentary experiences, reactions to 61, 62
Wedgwood, Josiah
  biographies, compilation 109–11, 115, 116
  books, influence of 36
  George, Henry, influence of 36
  and *History of Parliament* project 1, 7–10, 115–18

house of commons, views on 5–6, 23, 32
house of lords, membership of 1, 3
Irish nationalism, support for 114
land tax, interest in 4
local government, experience of 47
parliamentary experiences, reactions to 57, 65
parliamentary history, interest in 6–7
parliamentary speeches, reactions to 103
party discipline, reactions to 102, 103
party membership 23
personal achievements 67
personal finances 79, 83, 94
personal history 2–3, 4
personal speech best, 96
political career 3–5, 23, 34
political heroes 42
political interests 56
questionnaire to members of parliament 11–14
religion, influence of 37, 37 n. 5
selection and election 51
Weigall, Archibald 17
  occupation 85
  personal finances 81, 83
  personal speeches 99
  political motivation 31, 34
Welby, Charles
  parliamentary experiences, reactions to 63
  personal achievements 67
Wheler, Granville
  occupation 44
  political interests 55
Whitbread, Samuel
  family influence 23
  house of commons, departure from 72
  occupation 46
  parliamentary speech, greatest 107
Whitehead, Rowland
  constituency, expenditure on 93
  house of commons, departure from 76
  parliamentary experiences, reactions to 63
  personal achievements 67–8
  personal finances 80, 93
  political heroes 41
  political interests 55, 57
Whitehouse, John
  house of commons, departure from 72
  parliamentary experiences, reactions to 58
  personal achievements 71
  religion, influence of 38
Whitelaw, William
  parliamentary experiences, reactions to 65
  parliamentary speeches, greatest 104
Whitley-Thomson, Frederick
  occupation 46
  political interests 56
Whyte, Frederick
  parliamentary speech, greatest 105, 107
  party discipline, reactions to 64
Wiles, Thomas
  occupation 46
  parliamentary speech, greatest 105